Lecture Notes in Computer Science 6349

Commenced Publication in 1973
Founding and Former Series Editors:
Gerhard Goos, Juris Hartmanis, and Jan van Leeuwen

Jaco van de Pol Michael Weber (Eds.)

Model Checking Software

17th International SPIN Workshop
Enschede, The Netherlands, September 27-29, 2010
Proceedings

Volume Editors

Jaco van de Pol
University of Twente
P.O. Box 217
7500 AE, Enschede, The Netherlands
E-mail: j.c.vandepol@ewi.utwente.nl

Michael Weber
University of Twente
P.O. Box 217
7500 AE, Enschede, The Netherlands
E-mail: michaelw@cs.utwente.nl

Library of Congress Control Number: Applied for

CR Subject Classification (1998): F.3, D.2.4, D.3.1, D.2, F.4.1

LNCS Sublibrary: SL 1 – Theoretical Computer Science and General Issues

ISSN 0302-9743
ISBN-10 3-642-16163-4 Springer Berlin Heidelberg New York
ISBN-13 978-3-642-16163-6 Springer Berlin Heidelberg New York

springer.com

Printed in Germany

Typesetting: Camera-ready by author, data conversion by Scientific Publishing Services, Chennai, India
Printed on acid-free paper 06/3180

Preface

This volume contains the proceedings of the *17th International SPIN Workshop on Model Checking Software* (SPIN 2010). The workshop was organized by and held at the University of Twente, The Netherlands, on 27–29 September 2010. The workshop was co-located with the *5th International Conference on Graph Transformation* (ICGT 2010) and several of its satellite workshops, and with the joint PDMC and HiBi workshops, on *Parallel and Distributed Methods for verifiCation* and on *High-performance computational systems Biology*.

The SPIN workshop is a forum for practitioners and researchers interested in state-space analysis of software-intensive systems. This is applicable in particular to concurrent and asynchronous systems, including protocols. The name of the workshop reflects the SPIN model checking tool by Gerard J. Holzmann, which won the ACM System Software Award 2001, and is probably the most widely used industrial-strength model checker around.

The focus of the workshop is on theoretical advances and extensions, algorithmic improvements, and empirical evaluation studies of (mainly) state-based model checking techniques, as implemented in the SPIN model checker and other tools. The workshop encourages interaction and exchange of ideas with all related areas in software engineering. To this end, we co-located SPIN 2010 with the graph transformation, and high-performance analysis communities.

This year, we received 33 submissions, divided between 29 regular and 4 tool papers. Each paper was rigorously reviewed by at least four reviewers, and judged on its quality and its significance and relevance for SPIN. We accepted 13 regular papers, and 2 tool papers for presentation and for publication in this volume. The papers cover the topics of the workshop, as reflected by the following six sessions:

- Satisfiability Modulo Theories for Model Checking,
- Model Checking in Context (Simulation, Testing, UML)
- Implementation and Performance of Model Checking
- LTL and Büchi Automata
- Extensions to Infinite-State Systems
- Concurrent Software

In addition to the submitted papers, the workshop featured three invited speakers, whose extended abstracts can be found in this volume as well. The invited speakers of this year were: Alessandro Cimatti (FBK-IRST, Italy) on *SMT-Based Software Model Checking*, Darren Cofer (Rockwell Collins, USA) on *Model Checking: Cleared for Take Off*, and Javier Esparza (TU Munich, Germany), on *A False History of True Concurrency: from Petri to Tools*. The latter lecture was a joint invited lecture together with the ICGT conference.

We would like to thank all authors of submitted papers, the invited speakers, the Program Committee members, the external reviewers (who are listed elsewhere in this volume), and the Steering Committee, for their help in composing a strong program. Special thanks go to the SC chair Stefan Leue for his guidance throughout the SPIN 2010 organization, to Theo Ruys for his involvement in the initial preparations of this workshop, and to Arend Rensink for the overall coordination of the ICGT+SPIN event. Finally, we thank EasyChair for supporting the electronic submission and reviewing process, Springer for their willingness to publish these proceedings in their Lecture Notes in Computer Science Series, and our sponsors for their financial contribution.

Our special thoughts go to Amir Pnueli (1941–2009), who was one of the founding members of the SPIN Steering and Advisory Committee. We are thankful for Amir's inspiring intellectual contribution to the verification community, and in particular for his involvement in the SPIN workshop series.

July 2010

Jaco van de Pol
Michael Weber

Conference Organization

Program Chairs

Jaco van de Pol	University of Twente, The Netherlands
Michael Weber	University of Twente, The Netherlands

Program Committee

Jiří Barnat	Masaryk University Brno, Czech Republic
Dragan Bošnački	Technical University of Eindhoven, The Netherlands
Stefan Edelkamp	University of Bremen, Germany
Patrice Godefroid	Microsoft Research, Redmond, USA
Ganesh Gopalakrishnan	University of Utah, USA
Jan Friso Groote	Technical University of Eindhoven, The Netherlands
Orna Grumberg	Technion, Israel
Gerard Holzmann	NASA/JPL, USA
Radu Iosif	Verimag Grenoble, France
Stefan Leue	University of Konstanz, Germany
Rupak Majumdar	University of California at Berkeley, USA
Eric G. Mercer	Brigham Young University, USA
Albert Nymeyer	University of New South Wales, Australia
Dave Parker	Oxford University, UK
Corina S. Păsăreanu	CMU/NASA Ames, USA
Doron Peled	Bar-Ilan University, Israel
Paul Pettersson	Mälardalen University, Sweden
Scott Stoller	Stony Brook University, USA
Willem Visser	Stellenbosch University, South Africa
Tomohiro Yoneda	National Institute of Informatics, Japan

Steering Committee

Susanne Graf	VERIMAG, France
Gerard Holzmann	NASA/JPL, USA
Stefan Leue (Chair)	University of Konstanz, Germany
Pierre Wolper	University of Liège, Belgium

External Reviewers

Sriram Aananthakrishnan
Mohamed Faouzi Atig
Nikola Beneš
Stefan Blom
Aida Čaušević
Jakub Chaloupka
Yu-Fang Chen
Sjoerd Cranen
Michael Emmi
Christopher Fischer
Shaked Flur
Michael Franssen
Jaco Geldenhuys
Sonja Georgievska
Andreas Gustavsson
Leo Hatvani
Andreas Johnsen
Eun-Young Kang
Jeroen Keiren
Filip Konečný
Matthias Kuntz
Guodong Li
Jay McCarthy
Everett Morse
Kairong Qian
Petr Ročkai
Kristin Y. Rozier
Neha Rungta
Andrey Rybalchenko
Arnaud Sangnier
Christoph Scheben
Sarai Sheinvald
Jiří Šimáček
Damian Sulewski
Jagadish Suryadevara
Nikhil Swamy
Jana Tůmová
Yakir Vizel
Anh Vo
Aneta Vulgarakis
Tim Willemse

Table of Contents

Satisfiability Modulo Theories for Model Checking

Model Checking in Context

Implementation and Performance of Model Checking

LTL and Büchi Automata

Infinite State Models

Concurrent Software

SMT-Based Software Model Checking

Alessandro Cimatti

FBK-irst, Trento, Italy
cimatti@fbk.eu

Formal verification is paramount in the development of high-assurance software. Model checking techniques for *sequential* software combine a high degree of automation and the ability to provide conclusive answers, even for infinite state systems. A key paradigm for scalable software model checking is counter-example guided abstraction refinement (CEGAR) [1]. In this paradigm, an abstraction (or over-approximation) of the program is searched for an abstract path leading to an assertion violation. If such a path does not exist, then the program is safe. When such a path exists, and is feasible in the concrete program, then the path is a counter-example witnessing the assertion violation. If the path is infeasible in the concrete program, it is then analyzed to extract information needed to refine the abstraction.

Lazy abstraction [2] is an approach based on the construction and analysis of an abstract reachability tree (ART) using predicate abstraction. The ART represents an approximation of reachable states obtained by unwinding the control flow automaton (CFA) of the program. An ART node typically consists of a location in a CFA, a call stack, and a formula representing a region or a set of data states. The formula in an ART node is obtained by means of predicate abstraction. An ART node is expanded by applying the strongest post operator followed by predicate abstraction to the region and to the outgoing CFA edge of the location labelling the node.

One source of inefficiency in the lazy abstraction is that unwinding of CFA can induce a huge number of paths (and nodes) in ART that are explored independently. Large block encoding (LBE) has been proposed in [3] to tackle the problem. Essentialy, in LBE each edge in the CFA corresponds to a rooted directed acyclic graph (DAG) in the original CFA. Such an edge can be thought of as a summary of the DAG. The LBE approach is based on the recent advances of Satisfiability Modulo Theory (SMT). SMT solvers, such as MathSAT [4], can efficiently decide important fragments of first order logic, by combining SAT-based boolean reasoning and specialized constraint solvers. SMT techniques allow to effectively reason about multiple paths without explicitly enumerating them, and provide effective algorithms for abstraction computation [5,6], and interpolation techniques for predicate extraction [7].

The verification of *concurrent* software poses additional challenges, due to the interleavings induced by program executions. In many practical cases, a concurrent program consists of several threads (or processes) whose executions follow some (domain-dependent) scheduling policy. For instance, in SystemC (a de-facto standard language for writing executable models of system-on-chips),

J. van de Pol and M. Weber (Eds.): SPIN 2010, LNCS 6349, pp. 1–3, 2010.

the scheduling policy is cooperative (or non-preemptive), and there is at most one running thread at a time.

Several approaches to the verification of such concurrent programs are possible. One approach is to encode the concurrent programs into a set of communicating processes, one explicitly modeling the scheduler, and the others model the threads. Such an encoding is appealing because we can benefit from the optimization (or reduction) performed by highly optimized explicit-state model checkers such as SPIN [8]. The key issue is to devise a suitable finite state model.

Another approach is to translate the concurrent program into a sequential program, by introducing additional code modeling the scheduler, and then use an "off-the-shelf" model checker for sequential software. Although the backend provides abstraction capabilities, treating the threads and the scheduler in the same way is problematic. In fact, the abstraction is often too aggressive on the scheduler, and many refinements are needed to re-introduce the useful details that have been abstracted away.

In [9], an improved approach to the verification of concurrent programs is proposed, that combines explicit-state model checking techniques and lazy abstraction. In this approach, the scheduler is no longer modeled as part of the program, but is embedded in the model checking algorithm. The algorithm keeps track of scheduler states explicitly. The threads, on the other hand, are analyzed as in lazy abstraction, and explored by expanding ARTs. The above approach has been implemented into a tool chain for SystemC verification. The tool chain includes a SystemC front-end derived from Pinapa [10] and a new software model checker, called SyCMC, that uses extensions built on top of NuSMV [11] and MathSAT [4]. The experiments show promising performance of the algorithm on benchmarks taken from the SystemC distribution.

Directions for future research include direct support for domain-specific communication primitives, the evaluation of partial-order reduction techniques, and a more aggressive use of SMT-based techniques for the integration between the explicitly represented scheduler and symbolically abstracted threads.

References

1. Clarke, E.M., Grumberg, O., Jha, S., Lu, Y., Veith, H.: Counterexample-guided abstraction refinement for symbolic model checking. J. ACM 50(5), 752–794 (2003)
2. Beyer, D., Henzinger, T.A., Jhala, R., Majumdar, R.: The software model checker BLAST. STTT 9(5-6), 505–525 (2007)
3. Beyer, D., Cimatti, A., Griggio, A., Keremoglu, M.E., Sebastiani, R.: Software model checking via large-block encoding. In: FMCAD, pp. 25–32. IEEE, Los Alamitos (2009)
4. Bruttomesso, R., Cimatti, A., Franzén, A., Griggio, A., Sebastiani, R.: The MathSAT 4SMT Solver. In: Gupta, A., Malik, S. (eds.) CAV 2008. LNCS, vol. 5123, pp. 299–303. Springer, Heidelberg (2008)
5. Cavada, R., Cimatti, A., Franzén, A., Kalyanasundaram, K., Roveri, M., Shyamasundar, R.K.: Computing Predicate Abstractions by Integrating BDDs and SMT Solvers. In: FMCAD, pp. 69–76. IEEE, Los Alamitos (2007)

6. Cimatti, A., Dubrovin, J., Junttila, T., Roveri, M.: Structure-aware computation of predicate abstraction. In: FMCAD, pp. 9–16. IEEE, Los Alamitos (2009)
7. Henzinger, T.A., Jhala, R., Majumdar, R., McMillan, K.L.: Abstractions from proofs. In: POPL, pp. 232–244. ACM, New York (2004)
8. Holzmann, G.J., Peled, D.: An improvement in formal verification. In: Proceedings of the 7th IFIP WG6.1 International Conference on Formal Description Techniques VII, London, UK, pp. 197–211. Chapman & Hall, Ltd., Boca Raton (1995)
9. Cimatti, A., Micheli, A., Narasamdya, I., Roveri, M.: Verifying SystemC: a software model checking approach. In: FMCAD (to appear, 2010)
10. Moy, M.: Techniques and tools for the verification of systems-on-a-chip at the transaction level. Technical report, INPG, Grenoble, Fr. (December 2005)
11. Cimatti, A., Clarke, E.M., Giunchiglia, F., Roveri, M.: NuSMV: A New Symbolic Model Checker. STTT 2(4), 410–425 (2000)

Symbolic Object Code Analysis

Jan Tobias Mühlberg and Gerald Lüttgen

Software Technologies Research Group
University of Bamberg, 96045 Bamberg, Germany
{jan-tobias.muehlberg,gerald.luettgen}@swt-bamberg.de

Abstract. Current software model checkers quickly reach their limits when being applied to verifying pointer safety properties in source code that includes function pointers and inlined assembly. This paper introduces an alternative technique for checking pointer safety violations, called *Symbolic Object Code Analysis* (SOCA), which is based on bounded symbolic execution, incorporates path-sensitive slicing, and employs the SMT solver Yices as its execution and verification engine. Experimental results of a prototypic SOCA Verifier, using the Verisec suite and almost 10,000 Linux device driver functions as benchmarks, show that SOCA performs competitively to source-code model checkers and scales well when applied to real operating systems code and pointer safety issues.

1 Introduction

One challenge when verifying complex software is the proper analysis of pointer operations. A recent study shows that most errors found in device drivers involve *memory safety* [6]. Writing software that is free of memory safety concerns, e.g., free of errors caused by pointers to invalid memory cells, is difficult since many such issues result in program crashes at later points in execution. Hence, a statement causing a memory corruption may not be easily identifiable using conventional validation and testing tools, e.g., *Purify* [31] and *Valgrind* [27].

Today's static verification tools, including *software model checkers* such as [4,7,8,13], are also not of much help: they either assume that programs do "not have wild pointers" [3], perform poorly in the presence of pointers [25], or simply cannot handle certain software. A particular challenging kind of software are operating system (OS) components such as device drivers, which are usually written in C code involving function pointers, pointer arithmetic and inlined assembly. Further issues arise because of platform-specific and compiler-specific details concerning memory layout, padding and offsets [2]. In addition, several approaches to model checking *compiled programs* given in assembly or bytecode [5,23,33,35] and also to integrating *symbolic execution* [17] with model checking [12,11,16,29,34] have recently been presented. However, these are tailored to exploit specific characteristics of certain programming paradigms such as object-oriented programming, or lack support for data structures, function pointers and computed jumps, or require substantial manual modelling effort (cf. Sec. 5).

This paper introduces and evaluates a novel, automated technique to identifying memory safety violations, called *Symbolic Object Code Analysis* (SOCA).

J. van de Pol and M. Weber (Eds.): SPIN 2010, LNCS 6349, pp. 4–21, 2010.

This technique is based on the *symbolic execution* [17] of compiled and linked programs (cf. Sec. 2). In contrast to other verification techniques, SOCA requires only a minimum of manual modelling effort, namely the abstract, symbolic specification of a program's execution context in terms of function inputs and initial heap content. Our extensive evaluation of a prototypic SOCA implementation, also reported in this paper, shows that SOCA performs competitively to state-of-the-art model checkers such as [4,8,13] on programs with "well-behaved" pointers, and that it scales well when applied to "dirty" programs such as device drivers which cannot be properly analysed with source-code model checkers.

Technically, the SOCA technique traverses a program's *object code* in a systematic fashion up to a certain depth and width, and calculates at each assembly instruction a *slice* [36] required for checking the relevant pointer safety properties. It translates such a slice and properties into a bit-vector constraint problem and executes the property checks by invoking the *Yices* SMT solver [10] (cf. Sec. 3). To the best of our knowledge, SOCA is the only program verification technique reported in the literature, that features full support for pointer arithmetics, function pointers and computed jumps. While SOCA is based on existing and well-known techniques, combining and implementing these for object code analysis is challenging. Much engineering effort went into our SOCA implementation, so that it scales to complex real-world OS code.

The particular combination of techniques in SOCA is well suited for checking memory safety. Analysing object code is beneficial in that it inherently considers compiler specifics such as code optimisations, makes memory layout obvious, and does away with the challenge of handling mixed input languages involving assembly code. Symbolic execution, rather than the concrete execution adopted in testing, can handle software functions with many input parameters, whose values are typically not known at compile time. It is the existence of efficient SMT solvers that makes the symbolic approach feasible. Symbolic execution also implies a path-wise exploration, thus reducing the aliasing problem and allowing us to handle even complex pointer operations and computed jumps. In addition, slicing can now be conducted at path-level instead of at program-level, resulting in drastically smaller slices to the extent that abstraction is not necessary for achieving scalability. However, the price of symbolic execution is that it must be bounded and can thus only analyse code up to a finite depth and width.

To evaluate our technique, we have implemented a prototypic SOCA tool, the *SOCA Verifier*, for programs compiled for the 32-bit Intel Architecture (IA32) and performed extensive experiments (cf. Sec. 4). Using the *Verisec* benchmark [21] we show that the SOCA Verifier performs on par with the model checkers *LoopFrog* [19] and *SatAbs* [8] with regards to performance, error detection and false-positive rates. We have also applied the SOCA Verifier to 9296 functions taken from 250 Linux device drivers. Our tool is able to successfully analyse 95% of these functions and, despite the fact that SOCA performs a bounded analysis, 28% of the functions are analysed exhaustively. Therefore, SOCA proves itself to be a capable technique when being confronted with checking pointer-complex software such as OS components.

2 Pointers, Aliasing and Intermediate Representation

The verification technique developed in this paper aims at ensuring that every pointer in a given program is valid in the sense that it *(i)* never references a memory location outside the address space allocated by or for that program, and *(ii)* respects the usage rules of the Application Programming Interfaces (APIs) employed by the program. There exist several categories of memory safety properties — *(1) dereferencing invalid pointers*: a pointer may not be NULL, shall be initialised, and shall not point to a memory location outside the address space allocated by or for the program; *(2) uninitialised reads*: memory cells shall be initialised before they are read; *(3) violation of memory permissions*: when the program is loaded into memory, its segments are assigned with permissions that determine whether a segment can be read, written or executed; *(4) buffer overflows*: out-of-bounds read and write operations to objects on the heap and stack, which may lead to memory corruption and give way to various security problems; *(5) memory leaks*: when a program dynamically allocates memory but loses the handle to it, the memory cannot be deallocated anymore; *(6) proper handling of allocation and deallocation*: OSs usually provide several APIs for the dynamic (de)allocation of memory, whose documentation specifies precisely what pairs of functions are to be employed, and how.

Aliasing in source & object code. A major issue for analysing pointer programs is aliasing. Aliasing means that a data location in memory may be accessed through different symbolic names. Since aliasing relations between symbolic names and data locations often arise unexpectedly during program execution, they may result in erroneous program behaviours that are particularly hard to trace and debug. To illustrate this, the following C program shows a complicated way of implementing an infinite loop:

```
#include <stdio.h>
#include <sys/types.h>

int main (void) {
 int32_t  i, *p2=&i;
 int16_t *p1=&((int16_t*) &i)[0];

for (*p1=0; *p1<10; (*p1)++)
 { *p2=0; }

printf ("%08x: %d\n", p1, *p1);
printf ("%08x: %d\n", p2, *p2);
printf ("%08x: %d\n", &i, i);
return (0); }
```

At least three different outcomes of the program's execution can occur as a result of varying assumptions made about pointer aliasing by the developer and the compiler, as well as compiler optimisations applied to the code. In the following listing we give the output of the program when compiled with gcc version 4.1.2 (left) and gcc version 4.3.1 (middle and right).

```
$ gcc -O2 e_loop.c
$ ./a.out
bfc76f2c: 10
bfc76f2c: 0
bfc76f2c: 0
```

```
$ gcc -O2 e_loop.c
$ ./a.out
bfc7428c: 10
bfc7428c: 10
bfc7428c: 10
```

```
$ gcc -O1 e_loop.c
$ ./a.out
-> does not terminate
```

More surprises are revealed when disassembling the program that produced the output shown in the middle of the above listing:

```
80483ba: xor    %eax,%eax          ;; eax := 0;
80483c4: lea    -0xc(%ebp),%ebx    ;; ebx := ebp - 0xc
80483c8: add    $0x1,%eax          ;; eax := eax + 0x1
80483cb: cmp    $0x9,%ax           ;; (ax = 9)?
80483cf: movl   $0x0,-0xc(%ebp)    ;; *p2 (= ebp - 0xc)          := 0
80483d6: mov    %ax,(%ebx)         ;; *p1 (= ebx = ebp - 0xc) := ax
80483d9: jle    80483c8            ;; if (ax <= 9) goto 80483c8
```

One can see at instructions 80483cf and 80483d6 that *p1* and *p2* are pointing to the same location in memory, and that **p2* is actually written before **p1*. This is unexpected when looking at the program's source code but valid from the compiler's point of view since it assumes that the two pointers are pointing to different data objects. As another consequence of this assumption, register *eax* is never reloaded from the memory location to which *p1* and *p2* point.

This example shows that source-code-based analysis has to decide for a particular semantics of the source language, which may not be the one that is used by a compiler. Hence, results obtained by analysing the source code may not meet a program's runtime behaviour. While this motivates the analysis of compiled programs, doing so does not provide a generic solution for dealing with pointer aliasing, as aliasing relationships may depend on runtime conditions.

Intermediate representation. A program is stored by us in an intermediate representation (IR) borrowed from *Valgrind* [27], a framework for dynamic binary instrumentation. The IR consists of a set of *basic blocks* containing a group of statements such that all transfers of control to the block are to the first statement in the group. Once the block is entered, its statements are executed sequentially until an *exit* statement is reached. An exit is always denoted as `goto <t>`, where `<t>` is either a constant or a temporary register that determines the next program location to be executed. Guarded jumps are written as `if (<b>) goto <t>`, where `<b>` is a temporary register of type boolean, which has previously been assigned within the block.

The listing below depicts an example for assembly statements and their corresponding IR statements. It shows how, e.g., the `xor` statement is decomposed into explicitly loading (`GET`) the source register `0` into the temporary registers `t8` and `t9`, performing the `xor` operation into the temporary register `t7`, followed by storing (`PUT`) the result back. All operands used in the first block of the example are 4 bytes, or 32 bits, in size.

IA32 Assembly	**IR Instructions**	
`xor %eax,%eax`	`t9 = GET:I32(0)`	`;; t9 := eax`
	`t8 = GET:I32(0)`	`;; t8 := eax`
	`t7 = Xor32(t9,t8)`	`;; t7 := t9 xor t8`
	`PUT(0) = t7`	`;; eax := t7`
`lea -0xc(%ebp),%ebx`	`t42 = GET:I32(20)`	
	`t41 = Add32(t42,0xFFFFFFF4:I32)`	
	`PUT(12) = t41`	

As can be seen, the IR is essentially a typed assembly language in static-single-assignment form [22], and employs *temporary registers*, which are denoted as *t<n>*, and the *guest state*. The guest state consists of the contents of the registers that are available in the architecture for which the program under analysis is compiled. While machine registers are always 8 bits long, temporary registers may be 1, 8, 16, 32 or 64 bits in length. As a result of this, statement `t9 = GET:I32(0)` means that *t9* is generated by concatenating machine registers 0 to 3. Since each IR block is in static-single-assignment form with respect to the temporary registers, *t9* is assigned only once within a single IR block. As a valuable feature for analysing pointer safety, Valgrind's IR makes all load and store operations to memory cells explicit.

3 SOCA – Symbolic Object Code Analysis

This section introduces our new approach to verifying memory safety in compiled and linked programs, to which we refer as *Symbolic Object Code Analysis* (SOCA). The basic idea behind our approach employs well-known techniques including *symbolic execution* [17], *SMT solving* [20] and *program slicing* [36]. However, combining these ideas and implementing them in a way that scales to real applications, such as Linux device drivers, is challenging and the main contribution of this paper.

Starting from a program's given entry point, we automatically translate each instruction of the program's *object code* into Valgrind's IR language. This is done lazily, i.e., as needed, by iteratively following each program path in a depth-first fashion and resolving target addresses of computed jumps and return statements. We then generate systems of bit-vector constraints for the path under analysis, which reflect the path-relevant register content and heap content of the program. In this process we employ a form of program slicing, called *path-sensitive and heap-aware program slicing*, which is key to SOCA's scalability and makes program abstraction unnecessary. Finally, we invoke the SMT solver *Yices* [10] to check the satisfiability of the resulting constraint systems and thus the validity of the path. This approach allows us to instrument the constraint systems on-the-fly as necessary, by adding constraints that express, e.g., whether a pointer points to an allocated address.

SOCA leaves most of a program's input and initial heap content unspecified in order to allow the SMT solver to search for inputs that may reveal pointer errors. Obviously, our analysis by symbolic execution cannot be complete: the search space has to be bounded since the total number of execution paths and the number of instructions per path may be infinite. Our experimental results (cf. Sec 4) show that this boundedness is not a restriction in practice: many interesting programs, such as Linux device driver functions, are relatively "shallow" and may still be analysed either exhaustively or to an acceptable extent.

Translating IR into Yices constraints. To translate IR statements into bit-vector constraint systems for Yices, we have defined a simple operational semantics for Valgrind's IR language. Due to space constraints we cannot present this semantics here and refer the reader to [24] instead. Instead, we focus directly on examples illustrating this translation.

As a first example we consider the `PUT(0) = t7` statement from the example above. Intuitively, the semantics of *PUT* is to store the value held by *t7* to the guest state, in registers 0 to 3 (i.e., *r0* to *r3* below):

IR Instruction	Constraint Representation

`PUT(0) = t7`	`(define r0::(bitvector 8)(bv-extract 31 24 t7))`
	`(define r1::(bitvector 8)(bv-extract 23 16 t7))`
	`(define r2::(bitvector 8)(bv-extract 15  8 t7))`
	`(define r3::(bitvector 8)(bv-extract  7  0 t7))`

Here, the `bv-extract` operation denotes bit-vector extraction. Note that the IA32 CPU registers are assigned in reverse byte order, while arithmetic expressions in Yices are implemented for bit-vectors that have their most significant bit at position 0. Since access operations to the guest state may be 8, 16, 32 or 64 bit aligned, we have to translate the content of temporary registers when accessing the guest state.

Similar to the *PUT* instruction, we can express *GET*, i.e., loading a value from the guest state, as the concatenation of bit-vectors, and the *Xor* and *Add* instructions in terms of bit-vector arithmetic:

IR Instruction	Constraint Representation
`t9 = GET:I32(0)`	`(define t9::(bitvector 32) (bv-concat` ` (bv-concat r3 r2) (bv-concat r1 r0))`
`t7 = Xor32(t9,t8)`	`(define t7::(bitvector 32) (bv-xor t9 t8))`
`t41 = Add32(t42,` ` 0xFFFFFFF4:I32)`	`(define t88::(bitvector 32)` ` (bv-add t87 (mk-bv 32 4294967284)`

More challenging to implement are the IR instructions *ST* (*store*) and *LD* (*load*) which facilitate memory access. The main difference of these instructions to *PUT* and *GET* is that the target of *ST* and the source of *LD* are variable and may only be computed at runtime. To include these statements in our framework we have to express them in a flexible way, so that the SMT solver can identify cases in which safety properties are violated. In Yices we declare a function *heap* as our representation of the program's memory. An exemplary *ST* statement `ST(t5) = t32` can be expressed in terms of updates of that function:

IR Instruction	Constraint Representation

`ST(t5) = t32`	`(define heap.0::(-> (bitvector 32) (bitvector 8))`
	` (update heap   ((bv-add t5 (mk-bv 32 3)))`
	` (bv-extract  7  0 t32)))`
	`(define heap.1::(-> (bitvector 32) (bitvector 8))`
	` (update heap.0 ((bv-add t5 (mk-bv 32 2)))`
	` (bv-extract 15  8 t32)))`
	`(define heap.2::(-> (bitvector 32) (bitvector 8))`
	` (update heap.1 ((bv-add t5 (mk-bv 32 1)))`
	` (bv-extract 23 16 t32)))`
	`(define heap.3::(-> (bitvector 32) (bitvector 8))`
	` (update heap.2 ((bv-add t5 (mk-bv 32 0)))`
	` (bv-extract 31 24 t32)))`

Since the above *ST* instruction stores the content of a 32-bit variable in four separate 8-bit memory cells, we have to perform four updates of *heap*. Byte-ordering conventions apply in the same way as explained for *PUT*. Constraints for the *LD* instruction are generated analogous to *GET*.

Encoding pointer safety assertions. Being able to translate each object code instruction into constraints allows us to express the safety pointer properties given in Sec. 2 in terms of assertions within the constraint systems. The simplest case of such an assertion is a null-pointer check. For the *ST* instruction in the above example, we state this assertion as `(assert (= t5 (mk-bv 32 0)))`. If the resulting constraint system is satisfiable, Yices will return a possible assignment to the constraint system variables representing the program's input. This input is constructed such that it will drive the program into a state in which *t*5 holds the value `NULL` at the above program point.

However, many memory safety properties demand additional information to be collected about a program's current execution context. In particular, answering the question whether a pointer may point to an "invalid" memory area requires knowledge which cells are currently allocated. We retain this information by adding a function named *heaploc* to our memory representation:

```
(define heaploc::(-> (bitvector 32) (record alloc::bool init::bool
 start::(bitvector 32) size::(bitvector 32))))
```

This allows us to express assertions stating that, e.g., pointer *t*5 has to point to an allocated address at the program location where it is dereferenced, as:

```
(assert (= (select (heaploc t5) alloc) false))
```

All other pointer safety properties mentioned in Sec. 2 may be encoded along the lines of those two examples. Most of them require further additional information to be added to the *heaploc* function. To reduce the size and search space of the resulting constraint systems we check assertions one-by-one with a specialised *heaploc* function for each property. The full details of our generation of constraint systems can be found in [24].

Path-sensitive slicing. To ensure scalability of our SOCA technique, we do not run Yices on an entire path's constraint system. Instead we compute a slice [36] of the constraint system containing only those constraints that are relevant to the property to be checked at a particular program location.

The approach to path-sensitive program slicing in SOCA employs an algorithm based on system dependence graphs as introduced in [14]. Our slices are extracted using conventional slicing criteria (L, var) denoting a variable var that is used at program location L but, in contrast to [14], over the single path currently being analysed instead of the program's entire control flow. The slice is then computed by collecting all statements on which var is data dependent by tracing the path backwards, starting from L up to the program's entry point. While collecting flow dependencies is relatively easy for programs that do only use CPU registers and temporary registers, it becomes difficult when dependencies to the heap and stack are involved.

Handling memory access in slicing. Consider the following two IR statements: `01 ST(t5) = t32; 02 t31 = LD:I32(t7)`. To compute a slice for the slicing criterion $(02, t31)$ we have to know whether the store statement ST may affect the value of $t31$, i.e., whether $t5$ and $t7$ may alias. We obtain this information by using Yices to iteratively explore the potential address range that can be accessed via $t5$. This is done by making Yices find a satisfying model e for $t5$, as described below. When reading a model, which is represented by Yices as a bit-vector, we compute its integer representation and further satisfying models e' such that $e > e'$ or $e < e'$ holds, until the range is explored.

To use Yices as efficiently as possible when searching for satisfying models, we employ stepwise adding or retracting of constraints. Since we remember only the maximal and minimal satisfying models for a given pointer, this is an over-approximation because not the entire address range may be addressable by that pointer. However, using this abstraction presents a trade-off concerning only the size of the computed slices and not their correctness, and helps us to keep the number of Yices runs and the amount of data to be stored small.

By computing the potential address range accessed by a pointer used in a load statement, $t7$ in our example, and looking for memory intervals overlapping with the range of $t7$, we can now determine which store operations may affect the result of the load operation above. Despite being conservative when computing address ranges, our experience shows that most memory access operations end up having few dependencies; this is because most pointers evaluate to a concrete value, i.e., the constraint system has exactly one satisfying model, rather than a symbolic value which represents potentially many concrete values.

Handling computed jumps. A major challenge when analysing compiled programs arises from the extensive use of function pointers, jump tables and jump target computations. While most source-code-based approaches simply ignore function pointers [4,8,13], this cannot be done when analysing object code since jump computations are too widely deployed here. The most common example for a computed jump is the *return* statement in a subroutine. To perform a return, the bottom element of the stack is loaded into a temporary register, e.g., $t1$, followed by a `goto t1` statement, which effectively sets the value of the program counter to $t1$. In our approach, jump target addresses are determined in the same way as addresses for load and store operations, i.e., by computing a slice for each jump target and then using Yices to determine satisfying models for the target register.

Optimising GET & PUT statements. A potential problem with respect to the scalability of our approach arises from the vast number of *GET* and *PUT* statements in IR code. In particular, the frequent de-/re-composing of word-aligned temporary registers into guest registers and back into temporary registers introduces lots of additional variables in the SMT solver. These *GET* and *PUT* statements are introduced into our IR in order to make the IR block generated for a single CPU instruction reentrant with respect to the guest state. Thereby the need to repeat the translation from object code to IR whenever an instruction is used in a different execution context is avoided, at the expense of having to deal with larger constraint systems.

An efficient way around this issue is to optimise unnecessary *GET* and *PUT* operations away, based on a *reaching definition* analysis for a given register and path. Practical results show that this simple optimisation greatly reduces the memory consumption of Yices for large constraint systems. We can apply the same optimisations to memory accesses in cases where the address arguments to *LD* and *ST* evaluate to constant values. From our experience, dealing with unnecessary *GET*, *PUT*, *LD* and *ST* statements, by performing the above optimisations on IR level for an entire execution path, results in more efficient constraint systems and shorter runtimes of SOCA and Yices than when allowing Valgrind to perform similar optimisations at basic-block level.

Determining a valid initial memory state. Another challenge when implementing symbolic execution as an SMT problem is given by the enormous search space that may result from leaving the program's initial memory state undefined. OS components, including functions taken from device drivers, make regular use of an external data environment consisting of heap objects allocated and initialised by other OS modules. Hence, this data environment cannot be inferred from the information available in the program binary. In practice, data environments can often be embedded into our analysis without much effort, by adding a few lines of C code as a preamble, as is shown in [26].

4 Experimental Results

To evaluate our SOCA technique regarding its ability to identify pointer safety issues and to judge its performance when analysing OS components, we have implemented SOCA in a prototypic tool, the *SOCA Verifier*. The tool comprises 15,000 lines of C code and took about one person-year to build; details of its architecture can be found in [24]. This section reports on extensive experiments we conducted in applying the SOCA Verifier to a benchmark suite for software model checkers and to a large set of Linux device drivers. All experiments were carried out on a 16-core PC with 2.3 GHz clock speed and 256 GB of RAM, running 16 instances of the SOCA Verifier in parallel. However, an off-the-shelf PC with 4 GB of RAM is sufficient for everyday use, when one must not verify thousands of programs concurrently to meet a paper submission deadline.

4.1 Experiments I: The Verisec Benchmark

To enable a qualitative comparison of the SOCA Verifier to other tools, we applied it to the Verisec benchmark [21]. Verisec consists of 298 test programs (149 faulty programs – *positive* test programs – and 149 corresponding fixed programs – *negative* test programs) for buffer overflow vulnerabilities, taken from various open source programs. These test cases are given in terms of C source code which we compiled into object code using *gcc*, and are provided with a configurable buffer size which we set to 4. The bounds for the SOCA Verifier were set to a maximum of 100 paths to be analysed, where a single instruction may appear at most 500 times per path. Yices was configured to a

Table 1. Comparison of SatAbs, LoopFrog and SOCA

	$R(d)$	$R(f)$	$R(\neg f\|d)$
SatAbs (from [21])	0.36	0.08	n/a
LoopFrog (from [19])	1.0	0.26	0.74
SOCA	0.66	0.23	0.81

timeout of 300 seconds per invocation. Of these bounds, only the timeout for Yices was ever reached.

In previous work [19,21], Verisec was used to evaluate the C-code model checkers *SatAbs* [8] and *LoopFrog* [19]. To enable a transparent comparison, we adopted the metrics proposed in [38]: in Table 1 we report the *detection rate* $R(d)$, the *false-positive rate* $R(f)$, and the *discrimination rate* $R(\neg f|d)$. The latter is defined as the ratio of positive test cases for which an error is correctly reported, plus the negative test case for which the error is correctly not reported, to all test cases; hence, tools are penalised for not finding bugs and for not reporting a sound program as safe.

As Table 1 testifies, the SOCA Verifier reliably detects the majority of buffer overflow errors in the benchmark, and has a competitive false-positive rate and a better discrimination rate than the other tools. Remarkable is also that the SOCA Verifier failed for only four cases of the Verisec suite: once due to memory exhaustion and three times due to missing support for certain IR instructions in our tool. Only our detection rate is lower than the one reported for LoopFrog. An explanation for this is the nature of Verisec's test cases where static arrays are declared globally. This program setup renders Verisec easily comprehensible for source-code verification tools since the bounds of data objects are clearly identifiable in source code. In object code, however, the boundaries of data objects are not visible anymore. This makes the SOCA Verifier less effective when analysing programs with small, statically declared buffers.

Hence, despite having used a benchmark providing examples that are in favour of source code analysis, our results show that object code analysis, as implemented in the SOCA Verifier, can compete with state-of-the-art source-code model checkers. However, as our tool analyses object code, it can be employed in a much wider application domain. Unfortunately, benchmarks that include dynamic allocation and provide examples of pointer safety errors other than buffer overflows are, to the best of our knowledge, not publicly available.

Fig. 1*(a)* displays the CPU times consumed for analysing each test case in the Verisec benchmark. The vast majority of test cases is analysed by the SOCA Verifier within less than three mins per case. As shown in Table 2, the average computation time consumed per test case is 18.5 mins. In total, about 92 CPU hours were used. The memory consumption of both, the SOCA Verifier and Yices together, amounts to an average of only 140 MBytes and a maximum of about 3 GBytes, which is a memory capacity that is typically available in today's PCs. Notably, Ku reported in [21] that the SatAbs tool crashed in 73 cases and timed out in another 87 cases with a timeout of 30 mins. The runtime of the SOCA Verifier exceeds this time in only 7 cases.

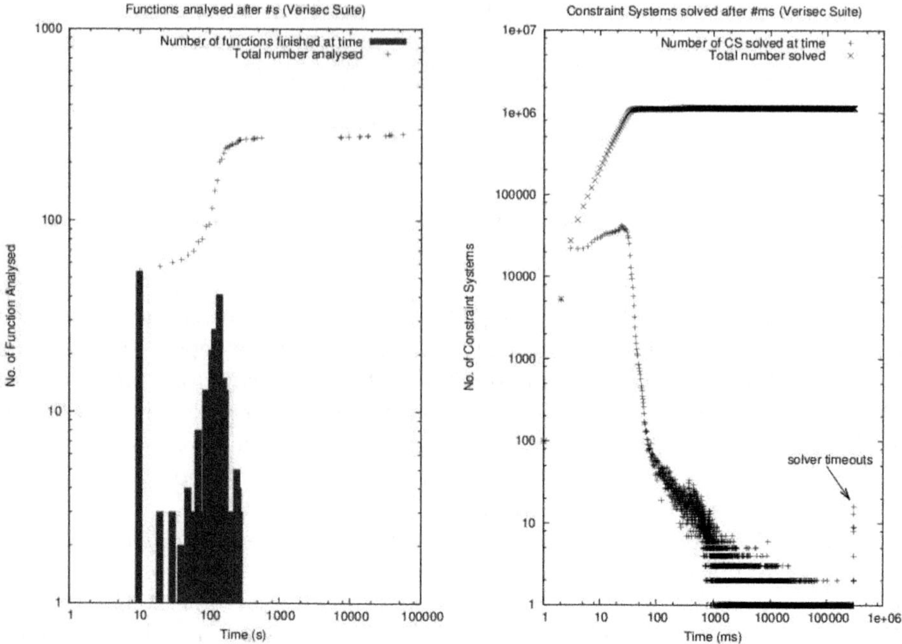

Fig. 1. Performance results for the Verisec benchmark. *(a)* Numbers of test cases verified by time (left). *(b)* Numbers of constraint systems solved by time (right).

Table 2. Performance statistics for the Verisec suite

	average	standard deviation	min	max	total
per test case					
total runtime	18m30s	1h33m	162ms	15h21m	91h54m
slicing time	28s150ms	41s808ms	28ms	5m15s	2h19m
Yices time	17m59s	1h33m	110ms	15h20m	89h19m
no. of CS	4025.11	173.76	11	8609	11994834
pointer operations	8.73	37.74	4	242	2603
per Yices invocation					
runtime	267ms	4s986ms	1ms	5m	88h59m
CS size	891.64	7707.95	0	368087	
memory usage	6.82MB	46.54MB	3.81MB	2504.36MB	

In Fig. 1*(b)* we show the behaviour of Yices for solving the constraint systems generated by the SOCA Verifier. For the Verisec suite, a total of 11,994,834 constraint systems were solved in 89 hours. 2,250,878 (19%) of these systems express verification properties, while the others were required for computing control flow, e.g., for deciding branching conditions and resolving computed jumps. With the timeout for Yices set to 5 mins, the solver timed out on 34 constraint systems, and 96% of the constraint systems were solved in less than one second. Thus, the SOCA Verifier's qualitative performance is competitive with state-of-the-art software model checkers. In addition, it is sufficiently efficient to be used as an automated debugging tool by software developers, both regarding time efficiency and space efficiency.

4.2 Experiments II: Linux Device Drivers

To evaluate the scalability of the SOCA Verifier, a large set of 9296 functions originating from 250 Linux device drivers of version 2.6.26 of the Linux kernel compiled for IA32 was analysed by us. Our experiments employed the Linux utility `nm` to obtain a list of function symbols present in a device driver. By statically linking the driver to the Linux kernel we resolved undefined symbols in the driver, i.e., functions provided by the OS kernel that are called by the driver's functions. The SOCA technique was then applied on the resulting binary file to analyse each of the driver's functions separately. The bounds for the SOCA Verifier were set to a maximum of 1000 paths to be analysed, where a single instruction may appear at most 1000 times per path, thereby effectively bounding the number of loop iterations or recursions to that depth. Moreover, Yices was configured to a timeout of 300 seconds per invocation.

Table 3. Performance statistics for the Linux device drivers

	average	standard deviation	min	max	total
per test case					
total runtime	58m28s	7h56m	21ms	280h48m	9058h32m
slicing time	8m35s	2h13m	0	95h39m	1329h46m
Yices time	48m36s	7h28m	0	280h30m	7531h51m
no. of CS	3591.14	9253.73	0	53449	33383239
pointer operations	99.53	312.64	0	4436	925277
no. of paths	67.50	221.17	1	1000	627524
max path lengths	727.22	1819.28	1	22577	
per Yices invocation					
runtime	845ms	8s765ms	1ms	5m2s	8295h56m
CS size	4860.20	20256.77	0	7583410	
Memory usage	5.75MB	14.76MB	3.81MB	3690.00MB	

Our results in Table 3 show that 94.4% of the functions in our sample could be analysed by the SOCA Verifier. In 67.5% of the functions the exhaustion of execution bounds led to an early termination of the analysis. However, the analysis reached a considerable depth even in those cases, analysing paths of lengths of up to 22,577 CPU instructions. Interestingly, 27.8% of the functions could be analysed exhaustively, where none of the bounds regarding the number

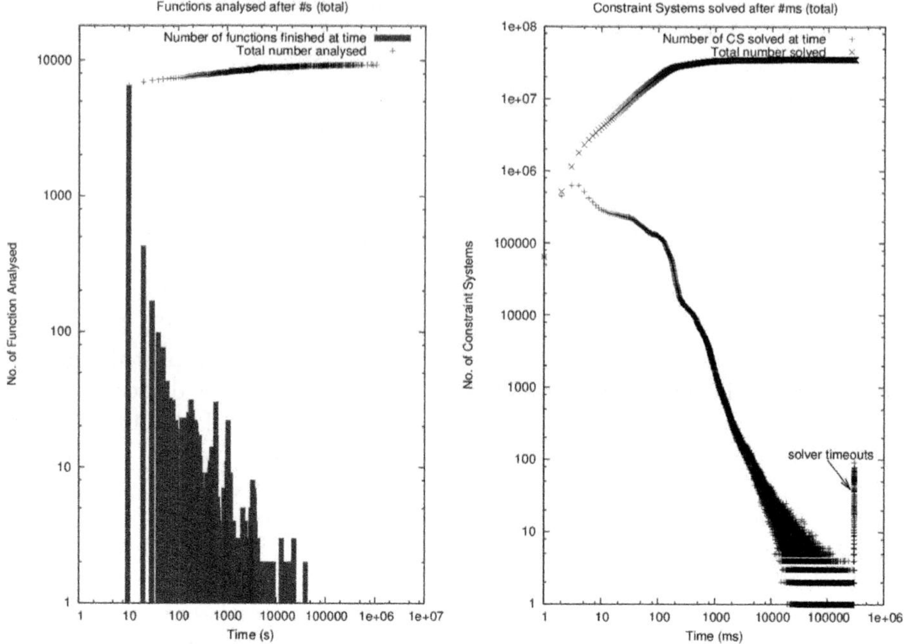

Fig. 2. Performance results for the Linux device drivers. *(a)* Numbers of test cases verified by time (left). *(b)* Numbers of constraint systems solved by time (right).

of paths, the path lengths, or the SMT solver's timeout were reached. As depicted in Fig. 2*(a)*, the SOCA Verifier returned a result in less than 10 mins in the majority of cases, while the generated constraint systems were usually solved in less than 500 ms. The timeout for Yices was hardly ever reached (cf. Fig. 2*(b)*).

As an aside, it should be mentioned that in 0.98% (91 functions) of the sample Linux driver functions, the SOCA Verifier may have produced unsound results due to non-linear arithmetic within the generated constraint systems, which is not decidable by Yices. In addition, our verifier failed in 5.6% of the cases (522 functions) due to either memory exhaustion, missing support for particular assembly instructions in our tool or Valgrind, or crashes of Yices.

Our evaluation shows that the SOCA Verifier scales up to real-world OS software while delivering very good performance. Being automatic and not restricted to analysing programs available in source code only, the SOCA Verifier is an efficient tool that is capable of aiding a practitioner in debugging pointer-complex software such as OS components. The application of the SOCA Verifier is, however, not restricted to verifying memory safety. In [26] we presented a case study on retrospective verification of the Linux Virtual File System (VFS) using the SOCA Verifier for checking violations of API usage rules such as deadlocks caused by misuse of the Linux kernel's `spinlock` API.

5 Related Work

There exists a wealth of related work on automated techniques for formal software verification, a survey of which can be found in [9]. We focus here on more closely related work, namely on *(i)* model checking bytecode and assembly languages, *(ii)* approaches combining model checking with symbolic execution, and *(iii)* program slicing.

Model checking bytecode & assembly languages. In recent years, several approaches to model checking *compiled programs* by analysing bytecode and assembly code have been presented. In [32,35], *Java PathFinder* (*JPF*) for model checking Java bytecode was introduced. *JPF* generates the state space of a program by monitoring a virtual machine. Model checking is then conducted on the states explored by the virtual machine, employing collapsing techniques and symmetry reduction for efficiently storing states and reducing the size of the state space. These techniques are effective because of the high complexity of *JPF* states and the specific characteristics of the Java memory model. In contrast, the SOCA technique to verifying object code involves relatively simple states and, in difference to Java, the order of data within memory is important in IA32 object code. Similar to *JPF*, *StEAM* [23] model checks compiled C++ programs by using a modified Internet Virtual Machine to generate a program's state space. In addition, *StEAM* implements heuristics to accelerate error detection.

BTOR [5] and *[mc]square* [28,33] are tools for model checking assembly code for micro-controllers. They accept assembly code as their input, which may either be obtained during compilation or, as suggested in [33], by disassembling a binary program. Since the problem of disassembling a binary program is undecidable in general, the SOCA technique focuses on the verification of binary programs without the requirement of disassembling a program at once.

All the above tools are explicit model checkers that require a program's entire control flow to be known in advance of the analysis. As we have explained in Sec. 3, this is not feasible in the presence of computed jumps. The SOCA technique has been especially designed to deal with OS components that make extensive use of jump computations.

Combining model checking with symbolic execution. *Symbolic execution* was introduced by King [17] as a means of improving program testing by covering a large class of normal executions with a single execution, in which symbols representing arbitrary values are used as input to the program. This is exactly what our SOCA technique does, albeit not for testing but for systematic, powerful memory safety analysis. A survey on recent trends in symbolic execution with an emphasis on program analysis and test generation is given in [30].

Several frameworks for integrating symbolic execution with model checking have been developed, including *Symbolic JPF* [29] and *DART* [11]. *Symbolic JPF* is a successor of the previously mentioned *JPF*. *DART* implements directed and automated random testing to generate test drivers and harness code to simulate a program's environment. The tool accepts C programs and automatically extracts function interfaces from source code. Such an interface is used to seed the analysis with a well-formed random input, which is then mutated by collecting and negating path constraints while symbolically executing the program under analysis. Unlike the SOCA Verifier, *DART* handles constraints on integer types only and does not support pointers and data structures.

A language agnostic tool in the spirit of *DART* is *SAGE* [12], which is used internally at Microsoft. *SAGE* works at IA32 instruction level, tracks integer constraints as bit-vectors, and employs machine-code instrumentation in a similar fashion as we do in [26]. *SAGE* is seeded with a well-formed program input and explores the program space with respect to that input. Branches in the control flow are explored by negating path constraints collected during the initial execution. This differs from our approach since SOCA does not require seeding but explores the program space automatically from a given starting point. The SOCA technique effectively computes program inputs for all paths explored during symbolic execution.

DART-like techniques, also known as *concolic testing*, are described in [16,34]. These techniques rely on performing concrete executions on random inputs while collecting path constraints along executed paths. These constraints are then used to compute new inputs that drive the program along alternative paths. In difference to this approach, SOCA uses symbolic execution to explore all paths and concretises only for resolving computed jumps.

Another bounded model checker for C source code based on symbolic execution and SAT solving is SATURN [37]. This tool is specialised on checking locking properties and null-pointer de-references and is thus not as general as SOCA. The authors of [37] show that their tool scales to analysing the entire Linux kernel. Unlike the SOCA Verifier, their approach computes function summaries instead of adding the respective code to the control flow, unwinds loops a fixed number of times and does not handle recursion.

Program slicing. An important SOCA ingredient other than symbolic execution is *path-sensitive* slicing. *Program slicing* was introduced by Weiser [36] as a technique for automatically selecting only those parts of a program that may affect the values of interest computed at some point of interest. Different to conventional slicing, our slices are computed over a single path instead of an entire program, similar to what has been introduced as *dynamic slicing* in [18] and *path slicing* in [15]. In contrast to those approaches, we use conventional slicing criteria and leave a program's input initially unspecified. In addition, while collecting program dependencies is relatively easy at source code level, it becomes difficult at object code level when dependencies to the heap and stack are involved. The technique employed by SOCA for dealing with the program's heap and stack is a variation of the *recency abstraction* described in [1].

6 Conclusions and Future Work

This paper presented the novel SOCA technique for automatically checking memory safety of pointer-complex software. Analysing object code allows us to handle software, e.g., OS software, which is written in a mix of C and inlined assembly.

Together with SOCA's symbolic execution, this simplifies pointer analysis when being confronted with function pointers, computed jumps and pointer aliasing. SOCA achieves scalability by adopting path-sensitive slicing and the efficient SMT solver Yices. While the SOCA ingredients are well-known, the way in which we integrated these for automated object code analysis is novel. Much effort went into engineering our SOCA Verifier, and extensive benchmarking showed that it performs on par with state-of-the-art software model checkers and scales well when applied to Linux device driver functions. Our verifier explores semantic niches of software, especially OS software, which currently available model checkers and testing tools do not reach. Obviously, the lack of abstraction makes SOCA less useful for programs manipulating unbounded data structures.

Future work shall be pursued along several orthogonal lines. Firstly, since device driver functions may be invoked concurrently, we plan to extend SOCA to handle concurrency. To the best of our knowledge, the verification of concurrent programs with full pointer arithmetic and computed jumps is currently not supported by any automated verification tool. Secondly, we intend to evaluate different search strategies for exploring the paths of a program, employing heuristics based on, e.g., *coverage criteria*. Thirdly, as some inputs of device drivers functions involve pointered data structures, we wish to explore whether *shape analysis* can inform SOCA in a way that reduces the number of false positives raised. Fourthly, the SOCA Verifier shall be interfaced to the *gnu debugger* so that error traces can be played back in a user-friendly form, at source code level.

Acknowledgements. We thank the anonymous reviewers for their valuable comments, especially for pointing out some recent related work.

References

1. Balakrishnan, G., Reps, T.: Recency-abstraction for heap-allocated storage. In: Yi, K. (ed.) SAS 2006. LNCS, vol. 4134, pp. 221–239. Springer, Heidelberg (2006)
2. Balakrishnan, G., Reps, T., Melski, D., Teitelbaum, T.: WYSINWYX: What You See Is Not What You eXecute. In: Meyer, B., Woodcock, J. (eds.) VSTTE 2005. LNCS, vol. 4171, pp. 202–213. Springer, Heidelberg (2008)
3. Ball, T., Bounimova, E., Cook, B., Levin, V., Lichtenberg, J., McGarvey, C., Ondrusek, B., Rajamani, S.K., Ustuner, A.: Thorough static analysis of device drivers. SIGOPS Oper. Syst. Rev. 40, 73–85 (2006)
4. Ball, T., Rajamani, S.: Automatically validating temporal safety properties of interfaces. In: Dwyer, M.B. (ed.) SPIN 2001. LNCS, vol. 2057, pp. 103–122. Springer, Heidelberg (2001)
5. Brummayer, R., Biere, A., Lonsing, F.: BTOR: Bit-precise modelling of word-level problems for model checking. In: SMT 2008, pp. 33–38. ACM, New York (2008)
6. Chou, A., Yang, J., Chelf, B., Hallem, S., Engler, D.: An empirical study of operating system errors. In: SOSP 2001, pp. 73–88. ACM, New York (2001)
7. Clarke, E., Kroening, D., Lerda, F.: A tool for checking ANSI-C programs. In: Jensen, K., Podelski, A. (eds.) TACAS 2004. LNCS, vol. 2988, pp. 168–176. Springer, Heidelberg (2004)

8. Clarke, E., Kroening, D., Sharygina, N., Yorav, K.: SATABS: SAT-based predicate abstraction for ANSI-C. In: Halbwachs, N., Zuck, L.D. (eds.) TACAS 2005. LNCS, vol. 3440, pp. 570–574. Springer, Heidelberg (2005)
9. D'Silva, V., Kroening, D., Weissenbacher, G.: A survey of automated techniques for formal software verification. IEEE Transactions on Computer-Aided Design of Integrated Circuits and Systems 27(7), 1165–1178 (2008)
10. Dutertre, B., de Moura, L.: The Yices SMT solver. Technical Report 01/2006, SRI (2006), `http://yices.csl.sri.com/tool-paper.pdf`
11. Godefroid, P., Klarlund, N., Sen, K.: DART: Directed automated random testing. In: PLDI 2005, pp. 213–223. ACM, New York (2005)
12. Godefroid, P., Levin, M.Y., Molnar, D.: Automated whitebox fuzz testing. In: NDSS 2008, Internet Society (2008)
13. Henzinger, T., Jhala, R., Majumdar, R., Necula, G., Sutre, G., Weimer, W.: Temporal-safety proofs for systems code. In: Brinksma, E., Larsen, K.G. (eds.) CAV 2002. LNCS, vol. 2404, pp. 526–538. Springer, Heidelberg (2002)
14. Horwitz, S., Reps, T., Binkley, D.: Interprocedural slicing using dependence graphs. ACM TOPLAS 12(1), 26–60 (1990)
15. Jhala, R., Majumdar, R.: Path slicing. SIGPLAN Not. 40, 38–47 (2005)
16. Kim, M., Kim, Y.: Concolic testing of the multi-sector read operation for flash memory file system. In: Oliveira, M.V.M., Woodcock, J. (eds.) SBMF 2009. LNCS, vol. 5902, pp. 251–265. Springer, Heidelberg (2009)
17. King, J.: Symbolic execution and program testing. ACM Commun. 19(7), 385–394 (1976)
18. Korel, B., Laski, J.: Dynamic slicing of computer programs. J. Syst. Softw. 13(3), 187–195 (1990)
19. Kroening, D., Sharygina, N., Tonetta, S., Tsitovich, A., Wintersteiger, C.: Loop summarization using abstract transformers. In: Cha, S(S.), Choi, J.-Y., Kim, M., Lee, I., Viswanathan, M. (eds.) ATVA 2008. LNCS, vol. 5311, pp. 111–125. Springer, Heidelberg (2008)
20. Kroening, D., Strichman, O.: Decision Procedures. Springer, Heidelberg (2008)
21. Ku, K.: Software model-checking: Benchmarking and techniques for buffer overflow analysis. Master's thesis, University of Toronto (2008)
22. Leung, A., George, L.: Static single assignment form for machine code. In: PLDI 1999, pp. 204–214. ACM, New York (1999)
23. Leven, P., Mehler, T., Edelkamp, S.: Directed error detection in C++ with the assembly-level model checker StEAM. In: Graf, S., Mounier, L. (eds.) SPIN 2004. LNCS, vol. 2989, pp. 39–56. Springer, Heidelberg (2004)
24. Mühlberg, J.T.: Model Checking Pointer Safety in Compiled Programs. PhD thesis, Department of Computer Science, University of York (2009)
25. Mühlberg, J.T., Lüttgen, G.: BLASTing Linux code. In: Brim, L., Haverkort, B.R., Leucker, M., van de Pol, J. (eds.) FMICS 2006 and PDMC 2006. LNCS, vol. 4346, pp. 211–226. Springer, Heidelberg (2007)
26. Mühlberg, J.T., Lüttgen, G.: Verifying compiled file system code. In: Oliveira, M.V.M., Woodcock, J. (eds.) SBMF 2009. LNCS, vol. 5902, pp. 306–320. Springer, Heidelberg (2009)
27. Nethercote, N., Seward, J.: Valgrind: A framework for heavyweight dynamic binary instrumentation. SIGPLAN Not. 42(6), 89–100 (2007)
28. Noll, T., Schlich, B.: Delayed nondeterminism in model checking embedded systems assembly code. In: Yorav, K. (ed.) HVC 2007. LNCS, vol. 4899, pp. 185–201. Springer, Heidelberg (2008)

29. Păsăreanu, C., Mehlitz, P., Bushnell, D., Gundy-Burlet, K., Lowry, M., Person, S., Pape, M.: Combining unit-level symbolic execution and system-level concrete execution for testing NASA software. In: ISSTA 2008, pp. 15–26. ACM, New York (2008)
30. Păsăreanu, C., Visser, W.: A survey of new trends in symbolic execution for software testing and analysis. Software Tools for Technology Transfer 11(4), 339–353 (2009)
31. Rational Purify IBM Corp., http://www.ibm.com/software/awdtools/purify/
32. Rungta, N., Mercer, E., Visser, W.: Efficient testing of concurrent programs with abstraction-guided symbolic execution. In: Păsăreanu, C.S. (ed.) SPIN 2009. LNCS, vol. 5578, pp. 174–191. Springer, Heidelberg (2009)
33. Schlich, B., Kowalewski, S.: [mc]square: A model checker for microcontroller code. In: ISOLA 2006, pp. 466–473. IEEE, Los Alamitos (2006)
34. Sen, K., Marinov, D., Agha, G.: CUTE: A concolic unit testing engine for C. In: ESEC/FSE-13, pp. 263–272. ACM, New York (2005)
35. Visser, W., Havelund, K., Brat, G., Joon, S., Lerda, F.: Model checking programs. Formal Methods in System Design 10(2), 203–232 (2003)
36. Weiser, M.: Program slicing. In: ICSE 1981, pp. 439–449. IEEE, Los Alamitos (1981)
37. Xie, Y., Aiken, A.: SATURN: A scalable framework for error detection using boolean satisfiability. ACM TOPLAS 29(3), 16 (2007)
38. Zitser, M., Lippmann, R., Leek, T.: Testing static analysis tools using exploitable buffer overflows from open source code. SIGSOFT Softw. Eng. Notes 29(6), 97–106 (2004)

Experimental Comparison of Concolic and Random Testing for Java Card Applets*

Kari Kähkönen, Roland Kindermann, Keijo Heljanko, and Ilkka Niemelä

Aalto University, Department of Information and Computer Science
P.O. Box 15400, FI-00076 AALTO, Finland
{Kari.Kahkonen,Roland.Kindermann,Keijo.Heljanko,
Ilkka.Niemela}@tkk.fi

Abstract. Concolic testing is a method for test input generation where a given program is executed both concretely and symbolically at the same time. This paper introduces the LIME Concolic Tester (LCT), an open source concolic testing tool for sequential Java programs. It discusses the design choices behind LCT as well as its use in automated unit test generation for the JUnit testing framework. As the main experimental contribution we report on an empirical evaluation of LCT for testing smart card Java applets. In particular, we focus on the problem of differential testing, where a Java class implementation is tested against a reference implementation. Two different concolic unit test generation approaches are presented and their effectiveness is compared with random testing. The experiments show that concolic testing is able to find significantly more bugs than random testing in the testing domain at hand.

1 Introduction

This paper discusses the use of concolic testing [1,2,3,4,5,6] to generate tests for Java applets written for the Sun Java Card platform [7,8]. In particular, we consider a new open source concolic testing tool we have developed called the LIME Concolic Tester (LCT) which is included in the LIME test bench toolset (`http://www.tcs.hut.fi/Research/Logic/LIME2/`). The tool can automatically generate unit test data and also stub code needed for unit testing in the JUnit testing framework. The main improvements in LCT over existing Java concolic testing systems such as jCUTE [2] are the following: (i) the use of state-of-the art bitvector SMT solvers such as Boolector [9] make the symbolic execution of Java more precise, (ii) the twin class hierarchy instrumentation approach of LCT allows the Java base classes to be instrumented unlike in previous approaches such as jCUTE, (iii) the tool architecture supports distributed testing where the constraint solving is done for several tests in parallel in a distributed manner, (iv) the tool is integrated with runtime monitoring of interface specifications [10] and the runtime monitors are used to guide the test generation order; and (v) the tool is freely available as open source. Distributed constraint solving has been previously

* Work financially supported by Tekes - Finnish Funding Agency for Technology and Innovation, Conformiq Software, Elektrobit, Nokia, Space Systems Finland, and Academy of Finland (projects 126860 and 128050).

J. van de Pol and M. Weber (Eds.): SPIN 2010, LNCS 6349, pp. 22–39, 2010.

employed by the Microsoft Whitebox fuzzing tool SAGE [11,12] that uses a distributed constraint solver Disolver while LCT uses a non-distributed constraint solver but can work on several branches of the symbolic execution tree in parallel.

We are interested in testing embedded software and, in particular, Java Card applets. In this paper we focus on the following *differential testing* scenario. An applet is being developed and a set of modifications has been made to it that should not change its class behavior, i.e., method calls to classes should behave as in the original version. Such modifications could be optimizations, changes in the internal data structures, refactoring of the code, clean ups removing redundant code etc. Hence, we have two versions of the same class which we call the *reference implementation* (the original version) and the implementation under test IUT (the modified version). Now the problem is to test whether the reference implementation and IUT have the same class behavior. In practice, the testing process starts by identifying modified classes and then it boils down to treating each modified class as an IUT and testing it against the corresponding original class taken as the reference implementation. Random testing techniques are often quite successful in such unit testing settings. In this paper we study how concolic testing and, in particular, the LCT tool can be used for this testing scenario. We develop two approaches to using concolic testing for checking whether an IUT of a class has the same class behavior as its reference implementation. Then we study experimentally how well the test sets generated by LCT using concolic testing techniques are able to detect differences in class behavior when compared to random testing.

The main contribution of this paper is the experimental work comparing the concolic testing approach to random automated testing. The context is Java Card applets designed for the Java Card smart card platform. In the experiments we compare the bug detection capabilities of both concolic and random testing by using a smart card application called the Logical Channel Demo [8] as the reference implementation. In order to provide a sufficient number of buggy implementations to serve as IUTs in the experiments, a Java source code mutant generator tool is used to provide mutated versions of the reference implementation. The experimental setup consists of a large number of experiments where a buggy mutated implementation is tested against the reference implementation. The results clearly show that the concolic testing approach is more effective in finding bugs than random testing.

There has been significant earlier work in experimentally evaluating concolic testing [1,2,3,4,5,6]. Hybrid concolic testing [13] interleaves random testing with concolic execution, and the experiments in [13] report on four times higher branch coverage with hybrid concolic testing compared to random testing on red-black trees and on the text editor vim. Experimental research on Whitebox fuzz testing efficiency [14,11,12] have used quite a different experimental test setup than we have in this paper and, thus, the results are hard to directly compare. However, also in the Whitebox fuzz testing context techniques based on symbolic execution techniques seem to be able to find many bugs missed by fully randomized testing.

The structure of the rest of this paper is as follows. Section 2 introduces concolic testing while the design choices done in the design of the LCT concolic testing tool are discussed in Sect. 3. Section 4 introduces differential testing, a method for comparing the behavior of two implementations of a class, and describes how LCT can be used for differential testing. Section 5 discusses our experimental setup for applying differential testing to Java Card applets. Finally, Sect. 6 sums up the paper.

2 Concolic Testing

Concolic testing [1,2,3,4,5,6] (also known as dynamic symbolic execution) is a method for test input generation where a given program is executed both concretely and symbolically at the same time. In other words, the test inputs are generated from a real executable program instead of a model of it. The main idea behind this approach is to at runtime collect symbolic constraints on inputs to the system that specify the possible input values that force the program to follow a specific execution path. Symbolic execution of programs is made possible by instrumenting the system under test with additional code that collects the constraints without disrupting the concrete execution.

In concolic testing, each variable that has a value depending on inputs to the program has also a symbolic value associated to it. When a sequential program is executed, the same execution path is followed regardless of the input values until a branching statement is encountered that selects the true or false branch based on some variable that has a symbolic value. Given the symbolic value of this variable, it is possible to reason about the outcome of the statement symbolically by constructing a symbolic constraint. This constraint describes what the possible input values are that cause the program to take the true or false branch at the statement in question. A *path constraint* is a conjunction of symbolic constraints that describes the input values that cause the concrete execution to follow a specific execution path.

In concolic testing the program under test is first executed with concrete random input values. During this test run, symbolic execution is used to collect the path constraints expressed in theory T for each of the branching statements along the execution. These collected constraints are used to compute new test inputs to the program by using off-the-shelf constraint solvers. Typical solvers used in concolic testing are SMT (Satisfiability-Modulo-Theories) solvers such as Yices [15], Boolector [9] and Z3 [16] and typical theories include linear integer arithmetic and bit-vectors. The new test inputs will steer the future test runs to explore previously untested execution paths. This means that concolic testing can be seen as a method that systematically tests all the distinct execution paths of a program. These execution paths can be expressed as a *symbolic execution tree* which is a structure where each path from root to a leaf node represents an execution path and each leaf node has a path constraint describing the input values that force the program to follow that specific path.

The concrete execution in concolic testing brings the benefit that it makes available accurate information about the program state which might not be easily accessible when using only static analysis. It is possible to under-approximate the set of possible execution paths by using concrete values instead of symbolic values in cases where symbolic execution is not possible (e.g., with calls to libraries to which no source code is available). Furthermore, as each test is run concretely, concolic testing does not report spurious defects.

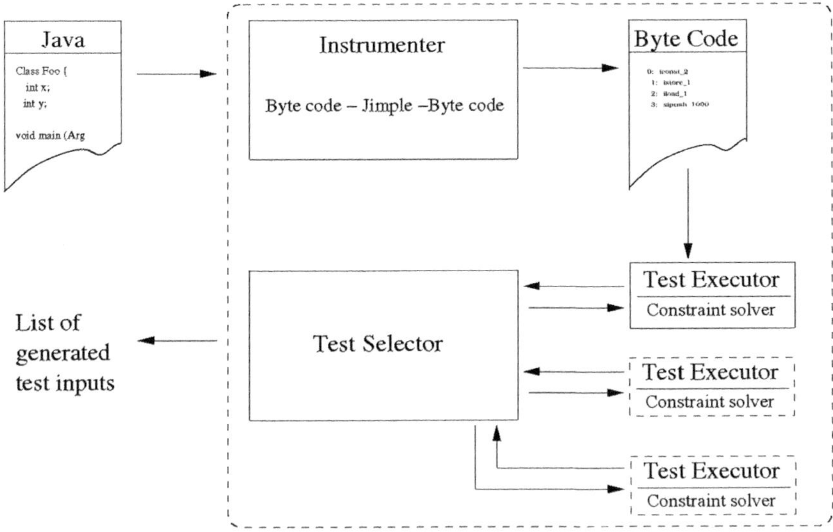

Fig. 1. The architecture of LCT

3 LIME Concolic Tester

The LIME Concolic Tester (LCT) is an open source test input generator for Java programs that is based on concolic testing. It takes a sequential Java program that has been compiled into bytecode as input and generates tests that attempt to cover all the execution paths of the program. LCT supports multiple search strategies which affect the order in which the execution paths are explored. During the testing process uncaught exceptions are reported as defects.

LCT is a part of the LIME Interface Test Bench developed in the LIME project (`http://www.tcs.hut.fi/Research/Logic/LIME2`). In the LIME project an interface specification language and the supporting LIME Interface Monitoring Tool (LIMT) [17] have also been developed and LCT allows the monitoring tool to guide the testing process in order to cover the specifications quickly. More details of this is given in Sect. 3.4.

As different test runs do not depend on each other, the problem of generating test inputs is easily parallelized. LCT takes advantage of this fact by having a separate test server that receives the symbolic constraints from the instrumented programs and selects which unexplored execution paths are tested next. This allows the tool to take advantage of multi-core processors and networks of computers.

The rest of this section discusses the implementation of LCT in more detail.

3.1 Architectural Overview

The architecture of LCT is shown in Figure 1 and it can be seen as consisting of three main parts: the instrumenter, the test selector and the test executors which are also used to run the constraint solvers in a distributed fashion. The instrumenter is based on a tool called Soot [18] which can be used to analyze and transform Java byte code. Before a program is given to the instrumenter, the input locations in the source code are marked so that the instrumenter knows how to transform the code. LCT provides a static class that is used for this in the following fashion:

- `int x = LCT.getInteger()` gets an int type input value for `x`, and
- `List l = LCT.getObject("List")` indicates that `l` is an input object.

After the input variables have been marked in the source code, the program is given to the instrumenter that transforms the code into an intermediate representation called Jimple and adds the statements necessary for symbolic execution into it. When the instrumentation is finished, the code is transformed into byte code that can be run over a standard Java Virtual Machine. This modified version of the program is called test executor. To guarantee that every test execution terminates, the length of the concrete execution is limited by a user configurable depth limit.

The test selector is responsible for constructing a symbolic execution tree based on the constraints collected by the test executors and selecting which path in the symbolic execution tree is explored next. The communication between the test selector and test executors has been implemented using TCP sockets. This way the test selector and test executors can run on different computers, and it is easy to run new test executors concurrently with others. The test selector can use various search strategies for selecting the next execution path to be explored. It is also possible to use LCT in a random mode, where no symbolic execution tree is constructed and the input values are generated completely randomly.

LCT provides the option to use Yices [15] or Boolector [9] as its constraint solver. In case of Yices, LCT uses linear integer arithmetic to encode the constraints and in the case of Boolector, bit-vectors are used. LCT has support for all primitive data types in Java as symbolic inputs with the exception of float and double data types as there is no native support for floating point variables in the used constraint solvers. We are currently targeting embedded software with limited data type support and better handling of complex data is part of future research. At the moment LCT can generate input objects that have their fields initialized as new input values in a similar fashion to [2].

3.2 Instrumentation

After the input locations have been marked in the source code, adding the code for symbolic execution to a given program can be made in a fully automatic fashion. To unit test a method, the user can, for example, write a test driver that calls the method to be tested with symbolic input values. LCT also supports generating such test drivers automatically not only for unit testing of methods but also for testing interfaces of classes through sequences of method calls.

To execute a program symbolically every statement that can read or update a variable with its value depending on the inputs must be instrumented. The approach taken in LCT is to instrument all statements that could operate on symbolic inputs regardless of whether a statement operates only with concrete values during test runs or not. This means that a majority of the lines in the code will be instrumented. LCT uses the Soot framework [18] to first translate the program under test to an intermediate language which is then modified and transformed back into bytecode. A similar approach is taken in jCUTE [3].

To make symbolic execution possible, it is necessary to know for each variable the associated symbolic expression during execution. For this reason we use a symbolic memory S that maps primitive type variables and object references to symbolic expressions. We also need to construct the path constraints for unexplored execution paths. The approach taken in LCT to construct the memory map and path constraints follows closely that described in [1,2]. To update the symbolic memory map, every assignment statement in the program is instrumented. At assignment of type $m = e$, where e is an expression, the symbolic value $S(e)$ is constructed and the mapping $S(m)$ is updated with this value. In case of new input values, $m =$ `INPUT`, a new symbolic value is assigned to $S(m)$. Every branching statement, e.g., `if`(p), must also be instrumented. Symbolic evaluation of p and its negation are the symbolic constraints that are used to construct the necessary path constraints. A more detailed description of the instrumentation process can be found in [19].

3.3 Search Strategies

The LCT tool contains a number of search strategies to control the exploration order of the different branches of the symbolic execution tree. The techniques are traditional depth-first and breadth-first search, priority based search using heuristic values obtained from the runtime monitors written in the LIME interface specification language, as well as randomized search. As this paper focuses on test generation methods that explore the full symbolic execution tree, the order in which branches are explored makes little difference; hence, we do not discuss these strategies here. Further details can be found in [19].

3.4 Test Generation for Programs with Specifications

The described concolic testing method reports uncaught exceptions as errors (i.e., it generates tests to see if the program can crash). This testing approach can be greatly enhanced if it is combined with runtime monitoring to check if given specifications hold during the test runs. In the LIME project a specification language has been developed together with a runtime monitoring tool [10] that allows the user to use propositional linear temporal logic (PLTL) and regular expressions to specify both external usage and internal behavior of a software component [10,17].

The LIME interface specification language allows the user to write specifications that are not complete models of the system and to target the specifications to those parts of the systems that are seen as important to be tested. Also, the specifications provide additional information about the system that could be used to indicate when the program is close to a state that violates the specifications. We have extended the concolic testing method to take the LIME interface specifications into account so that the testing can be guided towards those execution paths that cause specifications to be monitored and especially towards those paths that can potentially cause the specifications to be violated.

To guide the concolic testing, the LIME Interface Monitoring Tool (LIMT) [10,17] has been extended to compute a heuristic value to indicate how close the current execution is to violating the monitored specifications. In LCT the instrumentation described earlier has been augmented with a call to LIMT to obtain the heuristic value at every branching statement where a symbolic constraint is constructed. The test input selector is then notified about the heuristic value and it can use the value to assign a priority to the unvisited node resulting from executing the branching statement. Further details can be found in [19].

3.5 Generating JUnit Tests

LCT also provides the possibility to generate JUnit tests based on the input values generated during concolic testing. The support for JUnit tests is limited to unit testing methods that take argument values that can be generated by LCT. To generate JUnit tests for a selected method, LCT first creates automatically a test driver that calls the method with input values computed by LCT. The generated input values are then stored and used to generate JUnit tests that can be executed even without LCT. It is also possible to generate a test driver for an interface. In this case LCT generates a test driver that calls nondeterministically methods of that interface with symbolic input arguments. The number of calls is limited by an user specified call sequence bound.

3.6 Limitations

The current version of LCT has been designed for sequential Java programs and multi-threading support is currently under development. Sometimes LCT can not obtain full path coverage for supported Java programs. This can happen in the following situations: (i) *Non-instrumented code*: LCT is not able to do any symbolic reasoning if the control flow of the program goes to a library that has not been instrumented. This is possible, for example, when libraries implemented in a different programming language are called. To be able to instrument Java core classes, we have implemented custom versions of some of the most often required core classes to alleviate this problem. The program under test is then automatically modified to use the custom versions of these classes instead of the original counterpart. This approach can be seen as an instance of the twin class hierarchy approach presented in [20]. (ii) *Imprecise Symbolic reasoning*: Symbolic execution is limited by the ability of constraint solvers to compute new input values. LCT does not currently collect constraints over floating point numbers. LCT also does an identical non-aliasing assumption which the jCUTE tool does as well. The code "`a[i] = 0; a[j] = 1; if (a[i] == 0) ERROR;`" is an example of this. LCT assumes that the two writes do not alias and, thus, does not generate constraint $i = j$ required to reach the `ERROR` label; (iii) *Nondeterminism*: LCT assumes that the program under test and the libraries it uses are deterministic.

4 Differential Testing

Often, a software developer modifies source code in situations where the behavior of the code should not change, e.g., when cleaning up or refactoring code or when implementing a more optimized version of a given piece of code. Differential testing (terminology strongly influenced by [21]) is a technique that searches for differences in the behavior between the original code and the code after such modifications.

The basic idea behind differential testing is to compare the externally visible behavior of two implementations of the same class. Usually one of the implementations, called the reference implementation, is trusted to be correct. The task is then to test, whether the other implementation, called implementation under test (*IUT*), is correct as well by searching for differences in the behaviors of the two implementations.

For comparing the behaviors of two implementations, a black-box notion of class equivalence is used. Only the externally observable behavior of method calls is considered. Thus, two method calls are defined to have equivalent behavior if the following conditions are fulfilled:

1. Either both calls throw an exception or neither of them throws an exception.
2. If neither call throws an exception, they return equivalent values.
3. If both methods throw an exception, they throw equivalent exceptions.

The exact definition of equivalence of return values and exceptions may depend on the context in which differential testing is used. For example, return values in Java could be compared using the `equals` method. Sometimes, however, this notion of equivalence might be insufficient. Floating point values, for instance, could be considered equivalent even if they are not exactly the same as long as their difference is small enough. The definition of equivalent behavior used in this work only takes return values and thrown exceptions into account. In a more general setting, also other effects of methods calls that can be observed from the outside, like modified static variables, fields of the class that are declared public or method arguments that are modified, could be compared as well for a more refined notion of behavioral equivalence.

Two sequences of method calls to a class are considered to show equivalent class behavior if the behavior of the nth call in one sequence is equivalent to the behavior of the nth call in the other sequence. Two implementations of a class are considered to be *class behavior equivalent* if every sequence of method calls on a fresh instance of one of the implementations shows equivalent class behavior as the same sequence of method calls on a fresh instance of the other implementation. Determining whether two classes are class behavior equivalent is quite challenging as very long sequences of method calls might be needed to show non-equivalent behavior of the classes. In order to circumvent this difficulty, the notion of *k-bounded class behavior equivalence* is introduced. Two implementations of a class are considered to be k-boundedly class behavior equivalent if every sequence of at most k calls on a fresh instance of one of the implementations shows equivalent class behavior as the same sequence of calls on a fresh instance of the other implementation.

In the following, two concolic-testing-based and one random-testing-based technique for checking for bounded class behavior equivalence are introduced. All three approaches are symmetric in the sense that they treat the IUT and the reference implementation in the same way.

Decoupled differential testing. The basic idea behind using LCT for checking a pair of an IUT and an reference implementation for k-bounded class behavior equivalence is to let LCT generate sequences of method calls of length k and compare the behavior of the IUT and the reference implementation based on those sequences of method calls. The most obvious way to do this is to let LCT generate a test set for the IUT and another one for the reference implementation independently. Each test in the test sets consists of a sequence of method calls that can then be used for comparing the behavior of the IUT and the reference implementation. As LCT in this approach generates test sets for the IUT and the reference implementation individually, this approach is referred to as *decoupled differential testing*.

LCT is in the first step of the decoupled differential testing approach used to generate two test sets with call sequence bound k – one for the IUT and one for the reference implementation. Each test generated in this way consists of a sequence of methods calls to one of the implementations. The tests, however, do not evaluate the behavior of the method calls in any way. In the second step, the tests are therefore modified. Each test in the test set for the IUT is modified in a way such that each method that is executed on the IUT is executed on the reference implementation as well and an exception is thrown if and only if the behaviors of such a pair of method calls are non-equivalent. Calls to methods of the IUT are added to the test set of the reference implementation in the same way. In the last step of the decoupled differential testing approach, these modified tests are executed and an error is reported if any test signals non-equivalent behaviors.

In the decoupled differential testing approach, test sets for both the IUT and the reference implementation are generated. It would also be possible to only generate and use tests for either the IUT or the reference implementation. This approach, however, would make it quite likely that some classes of errors are missed. The developer of the IUT might, for instance, have forgotten that some input values need special treatment. In such a case, the `if` condition testing for these special values would be missing in the IUT and the LCT could achieve full path coverage without ever using any of the special input values, which would result in the described bug not being found by the generated test set. Therefore, a bug can easily be missed when only the test set for the IUT is used while it is found if the test set for the reference implementation is included, assuming the LCT reaches full path coverage when generating the test set for the reference implementation. A bug introduced by a developer who adds optimizations specific to a limited range of special input values could for similar reasons be missed if only the test set for the reference implementation but not the one for the IUT is used.

The main disadvantage of decoupled differential testing is that there may be situations in which non-equivalent behavior remains undetected even if full path coverage is reached on both the IUT and the reference implementation. A simple example of such a situation is a method that takes one integer argument and returns that argument in the reference implementation but returns the negation of the argument in the IUT. This difference in class behavior does not show if the method is called with zero as argument. Still, LCT can reach full path coverage on both implementations without using any other argument than zero. Thus, the non-equivalent behavior may remain undetected even if LCT reaches full path coverage on both implementations. This motivates coupled differential testing, which circumvents the described issue by checking for non-equivalent behaviors in the code that is instrumented and run by LCT.

Coupled differential testing. In the coupled differential testing approach, LCT is directly run on a class that compares the behavior of the IUT and the reference implementation. This comparison class has one instance each of the IUT and the reference implementation and has one method for every externally visible method of the IUT and the reference implementation. Each method in the comparison class calls the corresponding methods in the IUT, and the reference implementation, compares their behaviors and throws an exception if and only if they are not equivalent. Therefore, a sequence of method calls on the comparison class can be executed without an exception being thrown if and only if the IUT and the reference implementation show equivalent class behavior for this sequence of calls.

The comparison class is generated in the first step of the coupled differential testing approach. LCT is then used in the second step to generate a test set for the comparison class. Finally, the tests are executed and non-equivalent behavior is reported if any of the tests in the test set throws an exception. Thus, the main difference between coupled and decoupled differential testing is, that the behavior comparison code is added before LCT is run in the coupled differential testing approach while it is added after LCT is run in the decoupled differential testing approach.

An advantage of coupled differential testing is that non-equivalent behavior of the IUT and the reference implementation is reflected in the control flow of the code instrumented and run by LCT. If the reference implementation and the IUT show non-equivalent behavior, then the control flow eventually reaches the location in the comparison class at which the "non-equivalent behavior"-exception is thrown. If there is any sequence of method calls of length k that leads to this location, then LCT generates a test that reaches the location if full path coverage is reached and the call sequence bound used in the test generation is at least k. This implies that, any sequence of calls leading to non-equivalent behavior is guaranteed to be found by coupled differential testing as long as LCT reaches full path coverage and the call sequence bound is sufficiently large. As said before, such a guarantee can not be given for decoupled differential testing.

Random differential testing. LCT can be used in random mode to explore random execution paths. In the random differential testing approach LCT is used to generate a set of random tests, i.e., JUnit tests that execute random sequences of methods with random arguments, for the reference implementation. These random tests are then modified to compare behaviors of calls in the same way as the tests in decoupled differential testing. Alternatively, random tests could be generated for the IUT or even for the comparison class used in coupled differential testing. As both of theses approaches, however, compare the IUT and the reference implementation based on random call sequences, they lead to comparable results.

5 Experiments

LCT was experimentally evaluated by running LCT-based differential testing on Java Card example code called Logical Channels Demo [8] and a number of slightly mutated versions of that code. A short introduction to the Java Card technology and a description of the Logical Channels Demo is given in Sect. 5.1. LCT was used to check different implementations of the Logical Channels Demo for bounded class equivalence using the methods described in Sect. 4. The original version of the Logical Channels

Demo was used as the reference implementation and mutated versions of the Logical Channels Demo that show different class behavior were used as IUTs. A mutation generator called μJava [22] was used to generate the mutated versions. μJava and its use are described in Sect. 5.2. The numbers of IUTs for which the non-equivalent class behavior was detected by the individual testing approaches were used to compare effectiveness of concolic-testing-based differential testing to that of random differential testing. Section 5.3 describes the exact test set up while Sect. 5.4 discusses the results of the experiments.

5.1 Java Card and the Logical Channels Demo

The Java Card Technology [7,8] enables Java programs to execute on smart cards. Java smart card programs, called applets, are an interesting class of Java programs. As they tend to be smaller than "real" Java programs, they are well suited for being used as test data in controlled experiments. For the experimental evaluation of LCT, smart card example code called Logical Channels Demo was used. The idea behind the Logical Channels Demo is to use a smart card to charge a user for connecting to a data communication network. Although the Logical Channels Demo is designed for demonstration purposes and lacks some features like proper user authentication, it is a non-trivial application that is similar to other Java Card applications. The Logical Channels Demo has previously been used for two LIME related case studies [23,24].

Java Card applets. Java Card applets are Java programs that can be run on smart cards. When executed, Java Card applets communicate with an off-card application. There are some differences between Java Card applets and normal Java applications. Most notably, Java Card applets can only use a very limited subset of the Java features due to the limitations of the hardware they run on. For example, the basic data types `long`, `float`, `double`, `char` and `String` are not supported and the support of `int` is optional. Also, multidimensional arrays and most standard Java classes are not supported. In addition, Java Card applets use special methods for throwing exceptions that are intended to be caught by the off-card application.

The Logical Channels Demo. The Logical Channels Demo is one of several demos that are part of the Java Card Development Kit [8]. The Logical Channels Demo allows to use a smart card in a device that provides access to a network for a certain fee. The network is divided into several areas and the user has a home area, in which the fee is lower than in the rest of the network. The smart card on which the Logical Channels Demo is installed keeps track of the user's account's balance.

The Logical Channels Demo consists of two applets: one manages the user's account, and the other receives the state of the network connection from the off-card application and debits the account accordingly. The main purpose of the Logical Channels Demo is to illustrate how these two applets can be active and communicate with the off-card application simultaneously.

The Logical Channels Demo has been used in a previous case study to illustrate the use of the LIME interface specification language [23]. In course of that case study, the Java Card specific packet based argument passing and value returning mechanisms were replaced with standard Java arguments and return values in the Logical Channels Demo. The resulting modified version of the Logical Channels Demo was used for the evaluation of LCT as well.

Usually, Java Card applets need a Java Card simulator in order to be executed on a normal PC. As it would be challenging to use the LCT test generation in conjunction with a Java Card simulator, the Logical Channels Demo was modified in a way that allows the applets to run without a simulator. This was achieved by replacing Java Card API methods with stub code. The stub code behaves in the same way the Java Card API does in all respects that were of importance in the used testing setup.

The different testing approaches described in Sect. 4 compare the behavior of two implementations of one class. The Logical Channels Demo, however, consists of two applets, i.e., the behavior of two classes has to be compared simultaneously if one wants to compared two implementations of the Logical Channels Demo. In order to make it still possible to use the behavior comparison methods, a simple wrapper class that has one instance of each applet and provides methods that call the methods of the applets was added. Then, two implementations of the Logical Channels Demo could be compared by comparing the behavior of their wrapper classes.

The modified version of the Logical Channels Demo contains 328 lines of code. The comparison class used in coupled testing adds additional code that stores and compares return values and exceptions. The Logical Channels Demo does not contain any loops and therefore has only a finite number of execution paths.

5.2 The Mutations

In order to evaluate LCT experimentally, the differential testing methods described in Sect. 4 were used to compare pairs of implementations of the Logical Channels Demo. Mutated versions of the Logical Channels Demo, i.e., versions that contain small errors, were used to simulate faulty IUTs, and the bug-free version of the Logical Channels Demo was used as the reference implementation.

For the generation of the mutated classes, μJava [22] version 3 was employed. μJava generates mutations of Java programs by introducing small changes, e.g., by replacing an operator with another operator. While μJava ensures that the mutated programs can be compiled without errors, it does not guarantee that they really affect the program behavior. μJava may, for instance, generate a mutation that alters the value of a variable that is never used again.

μJava can generate two types of mutations: method-level and class-level mutations. A method-level mutation makes a small modification to the code inside one method, e.g., changes the sign of an operand in an expression. A class-level mutation modifies properties of and access to the class's fields and methods, e.g., turns a non-static field into a static field. Class-level mutations often only change the behavior of programs that use at least two instances of the mutated class. A static field, for instance, behaves just like a non-static field as long as only one instance of the class it belongs to is created. Therefore, a test setup that creates multiple instances of each class would be required to find class mutations. The used test setup, however, only creates one instance of each tested class and therefore would be unable to detect class methods. Hence, only method-level mutations were generated.

μJava generated 287 mutations of the Logical Channels Demo. For the experiments, only mutations that alter the behavior of the applets in a way that can theoretically be detected using the described class comparison methodology, i.e., ones that change the behavior of the applets w.r.t. the notion of equivalent behavior introduced in Sect. 4, were of interest. All mutations that do not change the behavior in such a way were classified and removed. Random differential testing was used to determine which mutations obviously changed the class behavior. The mutations for which no non-equivalences of behavior were discovered in this way were evaluated manually in order to determine whether or not they change the class behavior. Out of the 287 mutations, 65 did not affect the class behavior and were removed. The remaining 222 mutations were used for the experimental evaluation of LCT.

5.3 Test Setup

For experimental evaluation of LCT, the three differential testing approaches described in Sect. 4 were applied. The mutated classes were used as IUTs and the original Logical Channels Demo as the reference implementation. Bounds from one to three were used, i.e., the behaviors of pairs the original Logical Channels Demo and a mutant were checked for 1-bounded, 2-bounded and 3-bounded class equivalence.

The definition of equivalent method behavior introduced in Sect. 4 does not give an exact definition of when values returned or exceptions thrown by methods are equivalent. All methods in the Logical Channels Demo either return nothing or values of primitive types. Therefore, whether or not return values are equivalent was determined using the Java "==" operator. Java Card applets throw a special type of exception which contains a two-byte error code that indicates the exceptions cause. Such exceptions were considered equivalent if they contain the same error code. All other (native Java) exceptions were considered equivalent, if they were of the same class.

During experimentation, LCT was configured to use the SMT-solver Boolector [9]. LCT's depth limit was set high enough to allow LCT to always explore the full symbolic execution tree. The number of generated tests for random differential testing was set to 10000. All other LCT options were set to their default values.

5.4 Results and Discussion

The differential testing approaches introduced in Sect. 4 were run on every pair of the original Logical Channels Demo and one of the mutants described in Sect. 5.2 with bounds ranging from one to three. Then, the number of pairs for which non-equivalent class behavior was reported was used to compare the effectiveness of the different testing approaches. Also, the number of tests generated and the times needed for test generation and execution by the two concolic-testing-based approaches were compared.

Table 1 shows for each approach and each bound the number of mutations caught, i.e., the number of mutants for which behavior that differs from the original was correctly reported. At bound one, random differential testing was able to catch 95 out of the 222 mutations. Decoupled differential testing caught 121 and coupled differential testing caught 123 mutations. At bound two, these numbers increased to 151 for random, 185 for decoupled and 187 for coupled differential testing. At bound three, decoupled

Table 1. The number of correctly detected mutations for the different approaches and depths

Approach	1-bounded	2-bounded	3-bounded
Decoupled	121 (54.50%)	185 (83.33%)	221 (99.95%)
Coupled	123 (55.41%)	187 (84.23%)	221 (99.95%)
Random	95 (42.79%)	151 (68.02%)	184 (82.88%)

Table 2. A more detailed listing of the numbers of mutations caught. The numbers for combinations not listed (e.g., only caught by random differential testing) are zero.

Caught by approach(es)	1-bounded	2-bounded	3-bounded
All	95	150	184
Coupled and decoupled	26	35	37
Coupled and random	0	1	0
Only coupled	2	1	0
None	99	35	1

and coupled differential testing both caught all but one mutation while random differential testing caught only 184 mutations. These results illustrate that random differential testing is suited to catch many of the μJava mutations. Using the concolic-testing-based approaches, however, pays off in a significantly higher mutation detection rate.

While Table 1 shows the individual detection rates for the approaches, it does not provide more detailed information about the results, e.g., whether there were mutations caught by random differential testing that were not caught by the concolic-testing-based approaches. This more detailed information can be found in Table 2.

Independently of the bound, coupled differential testing caught every mutation that was caught by random or decoupled differential testing. At bounds one and two, coupled differential testing caught two mutations that were not caught by decoupled differential testing. The reason is that some mutations alter the class behavior only for very few input values. If a mutation, for instance, replaces the condition `if(a < 42)` where `a` is a method argument with `if(a <= 42)`, then the mutation is only caught if the corresponding method is called with argument 42. Decoupled differential testing can, however, reach full path coverage without using 42 as argument. Therefore, there is a chance that decoupled differential testing misses the described mutation. For coupled differential testing in contrast using 42 as argument is the only way to reach the location in the code where the "different behavior" exception is thrown. Therefore, coupled differential testing can not reach full path coverage without catching the mutation. The mutations that were caught by coupled but not by decoupled differential testing during the experiments were similar to the described mutation. It was, however, observed that many similar mutations were caught by decoupled differential testing even though they alter the behavior only for a very limited number of values. The reason is that the used SMT-solver tended to assign values that occur as constants in the given constraints to variables during the experiments, e.g., `42` in the given example.

Table 3. The average numbers of tests generated per mutant and the average times spent per mutant for generating tests, executing tests and in total

	1-bounded		2-bounded		3-bounded	
	Decoupled	Coupled	Decoupled	Coupled	Decoupled	Coupled
Tests generated	22.1	11.3	169.6	147.4	1306.2	1398.2
Generation time	81.90 s	48.21 s	109.23 s	67.30 s	288.05 s	293.18 s
Execution time	3.12 s	1.56 s	4.68 s	1.92 s	13.08 s	4.63 s
Total time	85.02 s	49.77 s	113.91 s	69.22 s	301.13 s	297.81 s

At bound three, coupled and decoupled differential testing both caught all but one mutation. Manual inspection of the one mutant that was never caught revealed that a sequence of at least four method calls is needed to make the mutant show behavior that differs from the behavior of the original Logical Channels Demo. Decoupled, coupled and random differential testing were executed with bound four for the mutation and all three methods were able to then catch the mutation. Generating the tests, however, took almost 33 minutes for decoupled and almost one hour for coupled differential testing. Therefore, no bound four tests were generated for the other mutations.

Table 3 shows the average numbers of tests generated per mutant and the average time required for generating and executing the tests for decoupled and coupled differential testing. Like the tests generated by decoupled and coupled differential testing, the random tests were generated using LCT. As random tests generation is not part of the LCT's core functionality, LCT generates random tests not as efficiently as dedicated random test generation tools. Thus, no times for random test generation are listed.

Generally, the number of tests generated by decoupled and coupled differential testing can be expected to grow exponentially in the bound used. At bound one, decoupled differential testing generated 22.13 tests on average and coupled differential testing generated 11.32 tests on average. At bound two, the average numbers of tests generated increased to 169.56 for decoupled and 147.36 for coupled differential testing and at bound three to 1306.22 and 1398.18, respectively. In order to give random differential testing a fair chance, the number of tests generated by random differential testing was chosen to be significantly higher than the average number of tests for the concolic-testing based approaches, namely 10000.

In coupled differential testing, every method call in the comparison class executes the same method once in each implementation. Thus, every method call in the comparison class executes exactly the same method twice if the IUT and the reference implementation are exactly identically. Therefore, there is exactly the same number of paths in the comparison class as in one of the implementations alone. In such a situation, LCT generates every test twice in decoupled differential testing, once for the IUT and once for the reference implementation. In coupled differential testing in contrast, LCT generates every test only once for the comparison class. Therefore, the number of tests generated in decoupled differential testing is twice the number of tests generated in coupled differential testing if the IUT and the reference implementation are identical. This observation suggests that the average number of tests generated should be larger in decoupled differential testing. Indeed, the number of tests generated by decoupled differential testing was almost twice as high compared to coupled differential testing at bound one. At bound two, however, decoupled differential testing generated only about 15% more tests and at bound three decoupled differential testing even generated less tests than coupled differential testing.

The reason why the number of tests generated by coupled differential testing increased faster than the number generated by decoupled differential testing is that the mutants used as IUTs and reference implementation in the experiments are not exactly the same. Every method that is implemented differently in the IUT and the reference implementation contributes to an increase of the number of paths in the comparison class. Consider, e.g., a method that is implemented in a way that there are three paths through the method in the IUT and two paths in the reference implementation. Assume that the implementations differ in a way such that there are combinations of input values that allow to execute every combination of a path in the IUT and a path in the reference implementation. Then, there are six possible paths through the corresponding method in the comparison class. Thus, coupled differential testing will try six paths through the corresponding method in the comparison class, while decoupled differential testing will only try five paths, three for the IUT and two for the reference implementation. This effect increases the number of tests generated in coupled differential testing. The effect is even stronger for paths on which the method is called more than once. In the example, there are $6^2 = 36$ paths that consist of calling the described method twice in the comparison class. In the IUT in contrast there are only 3^2 paths that consist of two calls of the method and in the reference implementation there are only 2^2. Assuming that there are no other methods in the tested class this means that coupled differential testing will generate 36 tests at bound two while decoupled differential testing will only generate $3^2 + 2^2 = 13$ tests. This illustrates that the effect is stronger at higher depths which explains that the number of tests generated by coupled differential increased faster than the number of tests generated by decoupled differential testing. Also, the effect can be expected to be stronger if the differences between the IUT and the reference implementation are more extensive than those caused by the mutations used for the experiments.

Table 3 also shows the time spent generating and executing tests by decoupled and coupled differential testing. The test were executed on a Linux computer with 4 GB memory and an Intel Core 2 Duo E6550 processor running at 2.33 GHz. The times for test generation and execution grow less quickly than the number of tests generated due to the fact that some steps like the instrumentation during test generation and starting the Java virtual machine and the JUnit test runner during test execution take roughly the same amount of time independently of the bound.

6 Conclusions

This paper introduces the LIME concolic tester (LCT), a new open source concolic testing tool for Java programs, and discusses the main design choices behind LCT. The paper focuses, in particular, on differential testing of Java Card applets using LCT. A setting for differential testing of applets is defined and two alternative approaches to generating test sets for differential testing using concolic testing and LCT are devised.

The two approaches are compared experimentally to random testing in the Java Card application domain. The experiments show that the proposed concolic testing approaches compare favorably to random testing and the test sets generated by LCT can find more bugs than considerably bigger sets of randomly generated tests.

Acknowledgements. The authors would like to warmly thank the anonymous referees for very detailed feedback to improve on this paper and also on interesting suggestions for further research.

References

1. Godefroid, P., Klarlund, N., Sen, K.: DART: Directed automated random testing. In: Proceedings of the ACM SIGPLAN 2005 Conference on Programming Language Design and Implementation (PLDI 2005), pp. 213–223. ACM, New York (2005)
2. Sen, K.: Scalable automated methods for dynamic program analysis. Doctoral thesis, University of Illinois (2006)
3. Sen, K., Agha, G.: CUTE and jCUTE: Concolic unit testing and explicit path model-checking tools. In: Ball, T., Jones, R.B. (eds.) CAV 2006. LNCS, vol. 4144, pp. 419–423. Springer, Heidelberg (2006)
4. Cadar, C., Ganesh, V., Pawlowski, P.M., Dill, D.L., Engler, D.R.: EXE: automatically generating inputs of death. In: Proceedings of the 13th ACM Conference on Computer and Communications Security (CCS 2006), pp. 322–335. ACM, New York (2006)
5. Tillmann, N., de Halleux, J.: Pex – White box test generation for .NET. In: Beckert, B., Hähnle, R. (eds.) TAP 2008. LNCS, vol. 4966, pp. 134–153. Springer, Heidelberg (2008)
6. Cadar, C., Dunbar, D., Engler, D.R.: KLEE: Unassisted and automatic generation of high-coverage tests for complex systems programs. In: Proceedings of the 8th USENIX Symposium on Operating Systems Design and Implementation (OSDI 2008), pp. 209–224. USENIX Association (2008)
7. Chen, Z.: Java Card Technology for Smart Cards: Architecture and Programmer's Guide. Prentice-Hall, Englewood Cliffs (2000)
8. Sun Microsystems: Java Card Development Kit 2.2.2 (2009), `http://java.sun.com/javacard/devkit`
9. Brummayer, R., Biere, A.: Boolector: An efficient SMT solver for bit-vectors and arrays. In: Kowalewski, S., Philippou, A. (eds.) TACAS 2009. LNCS, vol. 5505, pp. 174–177. Springer, Heidelberg (2009)
10. Kähkönen, K., Lampinen, J., Heljanko, K., Niemelä, I.: The LIME Interface Specification Language and Runtime Monitoring Tool. In: Peled, D. (ed.) RV 2009. LNCS, vol. 5779, pp. 93–100. Springer, Heidelberg (2009)
11. Godefroid, P., Levin, M.Y., Molnar, D.A.: Automated whitebox fuzz testing. In: Proceedings of the Network and Distributed System Security Symposium, NDSS 2008, pp. 151–166. The Internet Society (2008)
12. Godefroid, P., Levin, M.Y., Molnar, D.A.: Active property checking. In: Proceedings of the 8th ACM & IEEE International Conference on Embedded Software, EMSOFT 2008, pp. 207–216. ACM, New York (2008)
13. Majumdar, R., Sen, K.: Hybrid concolic testing. In: Proceedings of the 29th International Conference on Software Engineering (ICSE 2007), pp. 416–426. IEEE Computer Society, Los Alamitos (2007)

14. Molnar, D., Li, X.C., Wagner, D.A.: Dynamic test generation to find integer bugs in x86 binary Linux programs. In: Proceedings of the 18th USENIX Security Symposium (USENIX Security 2009), pp. 67–81. USENIX Association (2009)
15. Dutertre, B., de Moura, L.: A Fast Linear-Arithmetic Solver for DPLL(T). In: Ball, T., Jones, R.B. (eds.) CAV 2006. LNCS, vol. 4144, pp. 81–94. Springer, Heidelberg (2006)
16. de Moura, L.M., Bjørner, N.: Z3: An efficient SMT solver. In: Ramakrishnan, C.R., Rehof, J. (eds.) TACAS 2008. LNCS, vol. 4963, pp. 337–340. Springer, Heidelberg (2008)
17. Lampinen, J., Liedes, S., Kähkönen, K., Kauttio, J., Heljanko, K.: Interface specification methods for software components. Technical Report TKK-ICS-R25, Helsinki University of Technology, Department of Information and Computer Science, Espoo, Finland (December 2009)
18. Vallée-Rai, R., Co, P., Gagnon, E., Hendren, L.J., Lam, P., Sundaresan, V.: Soot - a Java bytecode optimization framework. In: Proceedings of the 1999 Conference of the Centre for Advanced Studies on Collaborative Research (CASCON 1999), p. 13. IBM (1999)
19. Kähkönen, K.: Automated test generation for software components. Technical Report TKK-ICS-R26, Helsinki University of Technology, Department of Information and Computer Science, Espoo, Finland (December 2009)
20. Factor, M., Schuster, A., Shagin, K.: Instrumentation of standard libraries in object-oriented languages: The twin class hierarchy approach. In: Proceedings of the 19th Annual ACM SIGPLAN Conference on Object-Oriented Programming, Systems, Languages, and Applications (OOPSLA 2004), pp. 288–300. ACM, New York (2004)
21. Person, S., Dwyer, M.B., Elbaum, S.G., Pasareanu, C.S.: Differential symbolic execution. In: Proceedings of the 16th ACM SIGSOFT International Symposium on Foundations of Software Engineering (SIGSOFT FSE 2008), pp. 226–237. ACM, New York (2008)
22. Ma, Y.S., Offutt, J., Kwon, Y.R.: MuJava: An automated class mutation system. Software Testing, Verification and Reliability 15(2), 97–133 (2005)
23. Kindermann, R.: Testing a Java Card applet using the LIME Interface Test Bench: A case study. Technical Report TKK-ICS-R18, Helsinki University of Technology, Department of Information and Computer Science, Espoo, Finland (September 2009)
24. Holmström, P., Höglund, S., Sirén, L., Porres, I.: Evaluation of Specification-based Testing Approaches. Technical report, Åbo Akademi University, Department of Information Technologies (September 2009), `https://poseidon.cs.abo.fi/trac/gaudi/lime/raw-attachment/wiki/MainResults/t34-report.pdf`

Combining SPIN with ns-2 for Protocol Optimization*

Pedro Merino and Alberto Salmerón

University of Málaga, Campus de Teatinos, 29071, Málaga, Spain
{pedro,salmeron}@lcc.uma.es

Abstract. This paper presents an approach to integrate the analysis capabilities of the SPIN model checker and the ns-2 network simulator into a single framework. The traffic-oriented model of the protocols is managed by ns-2, while SPIN automatically generates the most suitable configurations of each ns-2 run in order to meet some designer requirements. These requirements are specified with assertions and with an annotated temporal logic that can be translated into SPIN's Büchi automata. SPIN verification algorithms help us to automatically discard those ns-2 configurations that do not satisfy the expected requirements. With this approach we can automatically obtain the suitable values of parameters like buffer size, timeout to retransmit and window size, to optimize the performance of a protocol implementation in a given scenario. The paper presents the architecture for this integration, the modified temporal logic and its successful application to obtain optimized versions of protocols for videostreaming in wireless networks.

1 Introduction

The successful deployment of new networking systems, like those involving mobile phones, depends on the use of the proper techniques to produce robust and efficient implementation of communication protocols. In the design phase it is necessary to check that the protocol is free of negative behaviors like deadlock, its ability to handle situations such as connection loss or traffic congestion or its capacity to meet an expected throughput. Analysis of these concerns can be done by computer-aided simulations based on models of the protocols or by gathering data from real implementations. Aspects like correctness and reliability can be effectively checked with model checkers like SPIN [1] (actually, this was the original focus of the tool). Performance analysis can be done by monitoring the network; however, large scale analysis is mostly performed with network simulators, like ns-2 [2].

A major problem in performing a full model based analysis is that the formal methods community and the communication protocols community usually

* This work has been partially funded by the Government of Andalusia under grant P07-TIC3131, the Spanish Ministry of Innovation and Science (MICINN) under grant TIN2008-05932 and FEDER from the European Comission.

J. van de Pol and M. Weber (Eds.): SPIN 2010, LNCS 6349, pp. 40–57, 2010.

employ different bases to describe the protocols and the desired properties or behavior and to perform the analysis. Model checking based analysis normally considers extended communicated finite state machines as models, temporal logic to represent properties and reachability analysis to check correctness and reliability. The critical part usually is the correct abstraction level to make the specification verifiable with standard computer resources. Network simulators usually consider probability distributions to model the source of data or the behavior of transmission media, algorithms to describe the processing of the messages and scripts to describe the simulation scenarios. The key issue to obtain good results is the choice of the initial configuration to start simulation, defining values for packet size, buffer size, window size, timeouts, etc. Some works geared to the integration of both types of analysis consist in extending model checker languages with performance oriented features, like time and probability [3] [4] [5]. Other approaches consider metamorphosing and model transformation to use the right tool from the same initial description [6].

In this paper, we propose a new method to combine model checkers and networks simulators to take advantages of both tools without the need to use separated modelling languages. The combination works as follows. The model of the protocol is the one oriented to performance analysis with the network simulator, which produces a run for a given scenario and an initial configuration. The model checker makes the network simulator generate all the simulations by generating all possible initial configurations to be analysed. However, we do not execute all the simulations completely; that would take days or weeks for realistic protocols. We allow the protocol designer to specify temporal logic formulas that describe desired evolutions, considering performance as the key objective. The satisfaction of these formulas produces the desired initial configurations and acts as a powerful mechanism to discard unproductive simulations of the networks simulator. The resulting framework can be used to automatically tune a protocol to give the desirable performance in a specific scenario.

We have implemented the proposal combining the model checker SPIN and the network simulator ns-2 and demonstrated its utility in the tuning of parameters to optimize video download in wireless environments.

This paper presents novelties compared with related works, such as the workflow automation tool ANSWER [7]. Its main objective is to ease the burden of performing exhaustive simulations with several configurable variables and its posterior analysis. An XML configuration file is used to specify the variables that must be combined to generate the set of different scenarios, the metrics to check and other options. Configuration variables can be nested, which is useful to maintain the coherence of variables that have dependences between them. The *launcher* module of ANSWER generates the set of scenarios declared on the XML file, performs the corresponding simulations, and stores the output metrics in an organized way, to help correlate the scenario with its metrics. All these scenarios are completely simulated, while our approach uses properties to prune the space state, saving simulation time.

ANSWER uses a framework for data collection and statistical analysis [8], while we rely on the model designer to provide the relevant metrics. This framework also provides support for gathering statistics by performing a series of independent runs of the same scenario, e.g. until a confidence interval is reached. Our tool does not support this kind of statistical analysis, as each generated simulation scenario is only run once for checking properties.

The idea of using temporal formulas for pruning a state space has also been used in the area of planning. TLPlan [9] uses LTL formulas to declare objectives that must be met by a plan along a path, instead of just an objective state. This inspired the trajectory constraints of PDDL3 [10], which also uses temporal operators.

The rest of the paper is organized as follows: network simulators and protocols for video downloads are introduced in Sect. 2. The ideas behind our integrated approach are discussed in Sect. 3. The specification of properties for controlling the simulations is covered in Sect. 4. A study regarding video download over TCP is shown in Sect. 5. Section 6 discusses some implementation details of our prototype tool. Finally, Sect. 7 summarizes our conclusions and points to future work.

2 Background

2.1 Network Simulators

One of the most used tools when evaluating network protocols and scenarios are network simulators. Network simulators can help profile the performance of a protocol during the design phase, or evaluate several alternatives in a given scenario when deploying a networked system. These tools are built to be able to cope with large scenarios comprising real-world network elements such as routers, nodes with their own TCP/IP stacks and applications making use of these resources.

ns-2 [2] is an extensible network simulator, used by a large community as their tool of choice to test new protocols or analyze network scenarios. ns-2 is an event-oriented simulator, i.e., time advances according to the scheduled events. It provides a number of protocols (such as TCP and UDPP) and network elements that can be used to simulate both wired and wireless networks.

ns-2 has been developed using C++ and OTcl (an object-oriented variant of Tcl). This makes the simulator easy to use and adapt through dynamic scripts, while also being efficient for large simulations. OTcl is mostly used for declaring network topologies and simulation scenarios, and for attaching actions to certain hooks, e.g. logging the reception of a packet, while protocols and other network elements are developed in C++. Both sides are not independent and can communicate to send commands, invoke hook procedures, etc.

ns-3 [11] is being developed as an eventual replacement for ns-2, written from scratch in C++ and Python. However, ns-3 has not yet matched all the features offered by the previous version, and many scientific papers still use ns-2 to implement and analyze new protocols.

2.2 Video Download over TCP

Multimedia is one of the key services of the Internet. Improvements on the bandwidth and quality of the connections has increased the demand of audio & video content, either streamed or downloaded. Many efforts have been directed towards defining appropriate protocols for multimedia streaming in real time. One such protocol is the RTP (Real-time Transport Protocol), usually over UDP. The datagram-oriented nature of UDP allows frames to be sent separately without confirmation from the receiver. Lost frames may produce errors in the playback, but the real-time nature of multimedia streaming discourages retransmissions.

However, one of the most successful Internet video services of recent years, YouTube[1], is built around downloading the content over a simple TCP connection, using HTTP as with any other web content. Since the video content is not broadcast in real-time, there is less pressure on the transport protocol, which does not have to deal with the mentioned challenges. However, a key point of these video services is that playing can start before downloading the whole video. After a small portion of the video has been downloaded and buffered, playing starts while the video is still being downloaded in the background. This means that the video can stall if the buffer runs out while playing, e.g. if the data rate demanded for the video playback is significantly larger than the download rate. One solution is to use an adaptive initial buffer size instead of a fixed one, so that if the data connection is slow more video will be buffered before starting the playback.

Figure 1 shows a high level model of video playback over TCP, which we will use as a running example through the rest of the paper. The client and server are regular web clients which use the HTTP protocol over TCP to download web content, like the video being played. The client has a playout buffer where the video being downloaded is stored. The playback process will retrieve the video frames from this buffer. To simplify the model a constant frame size and rate is assumed. We also assume the server outputs the video at a constant bit rate, which is smaller than the bandwidth capacity of the link between the client and the server.

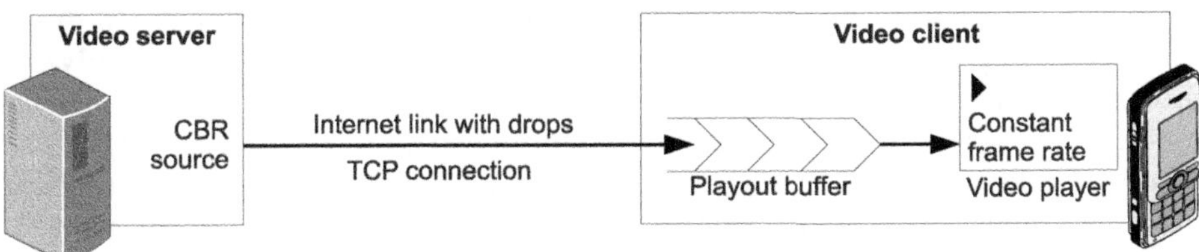

Fig. 1. Overview of video download over TCP

Figure 2 shows a simple state diagram for the client. The key element in the client is the playout buffer. When the buffer is empty, e.g. right at the start,

[1] http://www.youtube.com

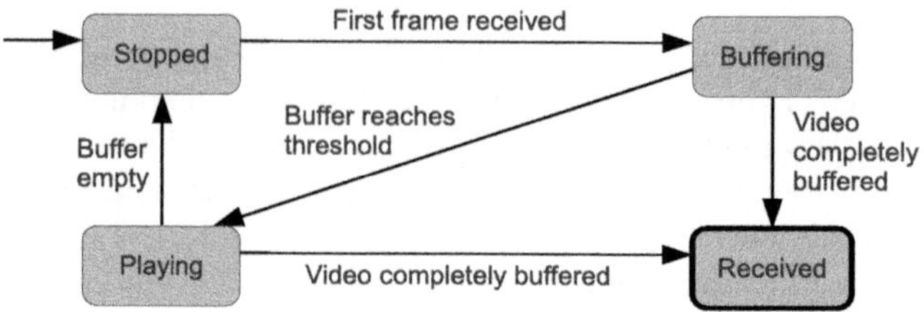

Fig. 2. State diagram of the client

the playing is stopped. As soon as the first video frame is received the client is said to be buffering. However, playing cannot start until the playout buffer reaches a certain threshold. If during playback the buffer empties, e.g. because the playing rate is significantly higher than the receiving rate, the playing stops and buffering must happen again. When the video is completely received from the server it is guaranteed that it will not stop playing again, so we consider this the final state.

There has also been an increment in the demand of Internet services, including multimedia, from mobile devices such as mobile phones or laptops connected through mobile telephony networks. These devices have their own set of challenges which stem from the fact that the network link has less bandwidth and is more prone to network errors or disconnections, e.g. when moving from one cell to another, or when entering a zone with bad coverage. Although the lower layers of the mobile protocol stack are prepared to deal with these kind of issues, some of these still affect the upper transport layers, e.g. IP and TCP. For instance, a short disconnection time may be interpreted by TCP as a sign of congestion and thus activate the congestion control mechanism. This is because TCP was conceived for wired computer networks, where the impact of errors in the channel is considered negligible and congestions are much more frequent.

This has led to the appearance of some TCP variants that try to address some of the key challenges that mobility poses. One of these variants is Freeze-TCP [12], which improves the response against predictable disconnection drops. In the event of an impending disconnection the client warns the server in advance in order to "freeze" the connection. When connection is reestablished the client notifies the server and the connection is "unfrozen", i.e., it returns to the same state as before the disconnection. In standard TCP the client sends probes to poll the connection, slowing down with each failed attempt. In addition, after the reconnection is detected, there is a slow start phase during which the connection is underutilized. One of the advantages of Freeze-TCP over other TCP variants is that it uses existing TCP mechanisms and only requires modifying the client. Still, some information must be shared between layers so TCP can detect an impending disconnection. However, while Freeze-TCP can cope with long or frequent disconnections, it is not suitable for managing connections with a high error rate. We will use a mobile scenario for our case studies, thus Fig. 1 shows

```
1  set node0 [$ns node]
2  set node1 [$ns node]
3
4  set tcpserver [new Agent/TCP]
5  set tcpsink [new Agent/TCPSink]
6  $ns attach-agent $node0 $tcpserver
7  $ns attach-agent $node1 $tcpsink
8  $ns connect $tcpserver $tcpsink
9
10 set tcpvideoserver [new Application/Traffic/CBR]
11 set tcpvideoclient [new Application/TCPVideo/Client]
12 $tcpvideoserver attach-agent $tcpserver
13 $tcpvideoclient attach-agent $tcpsink
```

Fig. 3. Excerpt of a ns-2 scenario definition for video downloading over TCP

a mobile phone as the video client connected to the server through a link that may drop every few seconds.

This scenario can be described as a ns-2 model such as the excerpt on Fig. 3. The two networked nodes in the scenario are created in the first two lines, while their TCP layers are instantiated and connected in lines 4 to 8. Lines 10 to 13 create the video client and server applications.

3 Integration Approach

In this section we describe the ideas and architecture behind our integration approach. The starting point is the specification of the protocol in a dual way, one view for ns-2 and a second view for SPIN. Both views depend on the requirements of the actual scenario where the protocol should run and the additional constraints given by the designer. From these views, the main tasks are generating a series of simulation scenarios according to a specification, launching these simulations and searching for the ones that satisfy the given properties. The SPIN model checker is used to drive the whole process, while ns-2 is used to run each generated scenario and provide information back to SPIN in the form of measured variables. A high level workflow of this approach can be seen in Fig. 4.

The protocols and other network elements can be configured to create a particular instance of a scenario. For instance, in keeping with the running example outlined in the previous section, we can set some scenario parameters, as shown on Fig. 5. The link between the nodes is set up in the first line with parameters such as bandwidth or delay, while the TCP segment and window size are set on the server on lines 3 and 4. The rest of the code set the configuration of the video application. SPIN can generate combinations of these variables automatically to run and compare different configurations of the protocols in a given scenario.

However, SPIN is not directly aware of the implications of the selection of a particular configuration, it only knows about these values. The behavior of the protocols, the dynamics of the network, etc., is managed by ns-2, which uses this information to simulate the evolution of the system. To allow SPIN to check the satisfiability of certain properties of interest to the simulation, ns-2 exposes some

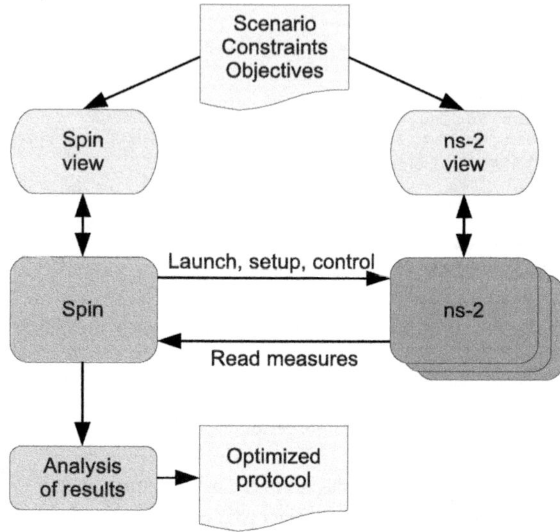

Fig. 4. Overview of our integrated approach

```
$ns duplex-link $node0 $node1 $link_bw $link_delay DropTail

$tcp_ set packetSize_ $segment_size
$tcp_ set window_ $max_tcp_window

$server_ set packetSize_ $segment_size
$server_ set rate_ $cbr_rate
$client_ set frame_rate_ $frame_rate
$client_ set frame_size_ $frame_size
$client_ set buffer_size_ $buffer_size
```

Fig. 5. Configuring the elements of a ns-2 scenario

of its internal state so that SPIN can reason about it. Thus, each tool holds a different view of the system derived from the initial specification and constraints set by the designer.

Regarding the state space exploration, the resulting structure resembles a tree at the beginning and after a certain depth is made of linear branches, as can be seen on Fig. 6. The generation of the possible initial configurations for the simulations creates a tree-like space state. At each step a configuration variable is given a value, and there are as many branches from a step as possible values. On the other hand, we consider each simulation run to be linear, i.e., given an initial configuration, the ns-2 simulator will keep running forward without creating any alternative that may be backtracked to. Thus, each simulation run produced by ns-2 is represented in SPIN as a single branch with several states, one for each valuation of the measurement variables that is shared from ns-2 to SPIN. In the following section, we give a more rigorous description of the state space.

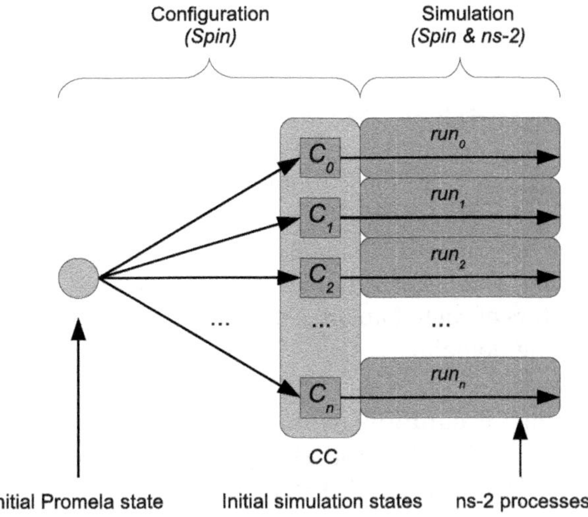

Fig. 6. Overview of the space state generated by SPIN from the ns-2 simulations

4 Temporal Properties for Controlling Simulations

Given a series of variables that can be set in a simulation scenario, running all possible scenarios that can be generated from those variables may be too time consuming to be of any use. However, most of the time these simulations are performed in order to check certain properties, e.g. if the protocol under study meets certain performance objectives. This information can be used to guide the simulation generation and execution process, instead of performing a brute-force approach by running every possible scenario completely.

There are several kinds of properties that may be useful in order to control the simulations in this sense, usually setting an objective that they have to meet or a constraint to discard a set of unwanted simulations. In addition to guiding the selection of initial configurations to simulate, setting objectives may help in stopping simulations early and thus reducing the time and number of states needed. These properties may be expressed over the configuration variables or over the evolution of the measured variables during a simulation. In this section these properties are described and examples are given based on the running example of Sect. 2.2.

4.1 Extending LTL

State space. We define CC as the finite ordered sequence of initial simulation configurations $C_i : 0 \leq i \leq n$. Each initial configuration C_i is a valuation of the configuration variables $cvar$, $C_i : cvar \rightarrow domain(cvar)$, with $C_i \neq C_j$ for every $i, j \in [0, n], i \neq j$, being n the cardinality of CC. The sequence of states traversed during a simulation with initial configuration C_i is $run(C_i) = s_{i0}, s_{i1}, s_{i2} \ldots$, with $run(C_i)_0 = s_{i0}$[2].

Propositions and variables. As variables we may use both the configuration variables *cvar* that determine the initial configuration of a simulation and the variables *mvar* measured during a simulation run. Let $var = cvar \cup mvar$ be the set of variables, and $domain(v)$ the domain of variable $v \in var$. We assume that variables are in standard domains such as boolean, integer and real. A proposition is either a boolean variable, or is constructed using the equality or comparison operators of each domain, e.g $=$ and $<$, between variables and values of the corresponding domain.

Formulas over initial configurations. We define the satisfiability of a standard LTL formula ltl using the propositions defined above over the members of CC as $C_i \models ltl$ iff $run(C_i)_0 \models ltl$, where $run(C_i)_0 \models ltl$ follows the standard LTL semantics.

Scope and evaluation of formulas. The objective of evaluating LTL formulas over the set of initial configurations CC is to obtain one or more initial configurations whose runs satisfy the given formula. We define two formula scope operators to specify how many of these initial configurations have to be returned, $\textit{scoped\_ltl} ::= \textit{FIRST}(ltl) \mid \textit{ALL}(ltl)$.

FIRST restricts the evaluation of the LTL formula to return the first initial configuration which satisfies the formula, while the evaluation of a formula scoped with *ALL* returns all the initial configurations which satisfy the formula.

We now define the evaluation of scoped LTL formulas over CC. Let $EVAL : CC \times \textit{scoped\_ltl} \rightarrow 2^{CC}$ be the evaluation function which, given a finite ordered set CC of initial configurations and a scoped LTL formula *scoped_ltl*, returns the set of initial configurations in CC which satisfy *scoped_ltl*. We define $EVAL$ by induction over the elements of CC

$$EVAL(CC, \textit{scoped\_ltl}) = EVAL(C_0, \textit{scoped\_ltl})$$

We separate the rest of the definition depending on the kind of scope operator used:

$$EVAL(C_i, \textit{FIRST}(ltl)) = \begin{cases} C_i & \text{if } C_i \models ltl \\ EVAL(C_{i+1}, \textit{FIRST}(ltl)) & \text{if } C_i \not\models ltl \text{ and } i < n \\ \emptyset & \text{if } C_i \not\models ltl \text{ and } i = n \end{cases}$$

$$EVAL(C_i, \textit{ALL}(ltl)) = \begin{cases} C_i \cup EVAL(C_{i+1}, \textit{ALL}(ltl)) & \text{if } C_i \models ltl \\ EVAL(C_{i+1}, \textit{ALL}(ltl)) & \text{if } C_i \not\models ltl \text{ and } i < n \\ \emptyset & \text{if } C_i \not\models ltl \text{ and } i = n \end{cases}$$

[2] From a theoretical point of view these sequences may be infinite, but the ones generated by ns-2 are finite.

4.2 Example Properties

The examples in this section follow the model described in Sect. 2.2. The property language above may be used to specify the objective of a series of simulations in order to obtain the initial configuration or configurations that meet that objective. For instance, we may be interested in obtaining the configurations in which the video is completely downloaded. This event is registered in the status of the video client (see Fig. 2), which we assume is available as a measured variable during the simulation. This objective can be declared with the following extended LTL formula:

$$f_1 = ALL(\Diamond \mathit{status} = \textsc{Downloaded})$$

This formula will be evaluated for each initial configuration C_i, and only those runs that satisfy it will be returned. We can also express the initial configurations that we do not want using extended LTL formulas. During the playback the video may stop for rebuffering, e.g. because of an inadequate selection of transmission parameters to deal with the status of the transmission medium. We have to specify that current status is STOPPED, but also that the video was playing before stopping: We may use the following formula to ignore these initial configurations:

$$f_2 = ALL(!\Diamond(\mathit{status} = \textsc{Playing} \wedge \Diamond(\mathit{status} = \textsc{Stopped})))$$

We may also specify formulas that discard simulations just by their initial configurations. All possible configurations given the configuration variables and their possible values are going to be generated and checked. However, some of these may not be interesting, e.g. because their configurations are unrealistic. For instance, we may want to discard the simulations that configure the network link between the client and the server with an extremely low bandwidth and high delay, as they represent border cases that we are not targeting:

$$f_3 = ALL(!\Box(\mathit{bandwidth} < 64\mathit{Kbps} \wedge \mathit{delay} > 250\mathit{ms}))$$

We can combine these properties to express more complex objectives. For instance, if we are looking for the first simulation in which the video is completely downloaded but we do not want extreme corner cases, we can combine f_1 and f_3:

$$\begin{aligned} f_4 = FIRST(\ & \Diamond(\mathit{status} = \textsc{Downloaded}) \\ & \wedge!\Box(\mathit{bandwidth} < 64\mathit{Kbps} \wedge \mathit{delay} > 250\mathit{ms})) \end{aligned}$$

4.3 Further Optimizations

The SPIN view of the protocol could also provide support for a specific kind of state space exploration optimization, which takes advantage of the knowledge a designer may have over the behavior of the scenario. The designer has to provide a relationship $\mathcal{R}$ between simulation configurations, objectives and outcomes, which is used as follows. If a certain configuration meets (or fails to meet) an objective, it can be deduced that certain similar configurations (according to $\mathcal{R}$) will have the same outcome, and thus do not have to be run. The results would be the same with respect to the objectives set, while saving simulation time. $\mathcal{R}$ can either relate configurations that met an objective (and thus would be written as $\mathcal{R}^{\models}$) or do not met it ($\mathcal{R}^{\not\models}$), but not both at the same time.

This can be defined more rigorously as follows. Let $\mathcal{R}^{\models} \subseteq C_i \times C_j \times ltl$ ($\mathcal{R}^{\not\models}$ is defined similarly) be a relationship defined using propositions over the variables of C_i and C_j. Let $v \in cvar$ and $v_i = C_i(v)$. $\mathcal{R}^{\models}$ and $\mathcal{R}^{\not\models}$ are defined as boolean formulas using propositions of the form defined in Sect. 4.1 between the variables of C_i and C_j and the values of their domains, e.g. $v_i > v_j$ or $v_i = 10$. Additional knowledge derived from a relationship $\mathcal{R}^{\models}$ or $\mathcal{R}^{\not\models}$ is defined as:

$$C_i \models ltl \Rightarrow C_j \models ltl \qquad \text{iff } i < j \text{ and } (C_i, C_j, ltl) \in \mathcal{R}^{\models}$$

$$C_i \not\models ltl \Rightarrow C_j \not\models ltl \qquad \text{iff } i < j \text{ and } (C_i, C_j, ltl) \in \mathcal{R}^{\not\models}$$

We extend the satisfiability operator $\models$ to support the additional knowledge expressed in a relationship $\mathcal{R}^{\models}$ or $\mathcal{R}^{\not\models}$:

$$C_i \models_{\mathcal{R}^{\models}} ltl = \begin{cases} true & \text{if } \exists j : j < i, (C_j, C_i, ltl) \in \mathcal{R}^{\models} \\ C_i \models ltl & \text{if } \nexists j : j < i, (C_j, C_i, ltl) \in \mathcal{R}^{\models} \end{cases}$$

$$C_i \models_{\mathcal{R}^{\not\models}} ltl = \begin{cases} false & \text{if } \exists j : j < i, (C_j, C_i, ltl) \in \mathcal{R}^{\not\models} \\ C_i \models ltl & \text{if } \nexists j : j < i, (C_j, C_i, ltl) \in \mathcal{R}^{\not\models} \end{cases}$$

For instance, we can use this to reduce the state space that needs to be explored while evaluating the formula f_1 in Sect. 4.2 thanks to the additional knowledge the designer has on the system. One of the configuration parameters is the playout buffer size, called ***buffer***. We know for sure that if an initial configuration meets the objective declared on f_1, increasing the size of the playout buffer in the client will not affect the rest of the system, and thus the objective will be met as well. We can express this additional knowledge with the following relationship:

$$(C_i, C_j, f_1) \in \mathcal{R}^{\models}_{\text{buffer}} \text{ if } \textit{buffer}_i < \textit{buffer}_j \text{ and } v_i = v_j \text{ for every } v \in cvar, v \neq \textit{buffer}$$

The pairs of initial configurations in this relationship are those which have the same initial configuration but only differ on their ***buffer*** variable, which is greater on C_j. By enriching the evaluation of formula f_1 with the additional knowledge provided by this relationship we guarantee the same results, while reducing the space state at the same time.

5 Case Study: Downloading YouTube Videos

To test our integrated approach we choose as our case study an application that downloads and streams a video over TCP to a mobile TCP client, e.g a mobile

Table 1. Configuration variables and their possible values for the case study

Variable	Values
Link uptime	20 s
Link downtime	100 ms – 1 s
Link delay	100 ms
Link bandwidth	384 Kb
Max. TCP window	5 KB – 10 KB
TCP segment size	0.1 KB – 0.3 KB
Playout buffer length	1 s – 10 s
Freeze warning	0.2 – 2.0 RTTs in advance

phone, as described in Sect. 2.2. This is the same schema that a YouTube video follows when it is transmitted over HTTP. However, for the sake of simplicity we ignore the impact of the HTTP header overload, which is about a kilobyte compared with the several megabytes of video content. This scenario is similar to the one studied in [13], which also uses ns-2 to simulate a set of configurations.

The scenario comprises two nodes connected through a link with drops, which drops periodically for a given amount of time. Each node has a TCP agent with an application on top: one node has an `Application/TCPVideo/Client` instance while the other has an `Application/Traffic/CBR` instance. The first application was developed in C++ to simulate both the reception of video using TCP and the playback engine at the client. The client has a playout buffer (a simple counter) in which all TCP segments are placed upon arrival. This buffer is read 30 times per second to simulate the fetching of each video frame by the playback engine at 30 fps. The client also makes its state (see state diagram on Fig. 2) available through an instance variable. The scenario itself is defined using regular ns-2 commands such as the excerpts seen in Figs. 3 and 5.

The configuration variables and their possible values are defined in Table 1. These variables are related to both the environment, e.g. the duration of uptime and downtime periods of the link, and the elements of the protocol stack, e.g. segment size and maximum window size for TCP. The combination of the different valuations of each variable constitutes the set of initial configurations that we want to analyze.

We are interested in those initial configurations in which the video can be downloaded fully without stopping for rebuffering once playing has started. This objective is a combination of the ones in formulas f_1 and f_2 in Sect. 4.2. The first part of the formula states that we want the initial configurations to reach the DOWNLOADED state, e.g. the video has been completely downloaded. At the same time, the second part of the formula prevents any simulation where the video stops during playback from being returned. This objective is expressed with the following formula:

Table 2. Results for the experiments using regular TCP, depending on the properties used

Properties	**None**	*objective*	*objective* and $\mathcal{R}^{\models}_{\text{buffer}}$
Number of SPIN states	85367	17468	15860
Simulations run	1100	1100	966
Simulations not run	–	–	134
Objective met	–	169	169
Rejected by objective	–	931	931
Total time	351 s	146 s	122 s

$$\begin{aligned} \textit{objective} = ALL(\ &\Diamond(\textit{status} = \text{DOWNLOADED}) \\ &\wedge!\Diamond(\textit{status} = \text{PLAYING} \wedge \Diamond(\textit{status} = \text{STOPPED}))) \end{aligned}$$

We can optimize our search further and add a relationship that declares that increasing the playout buffer size of an initial configuration that already satisfied the formula above guarantees that the new initial configuration will satisfy the formula as well:

$$(C_i, C_j, \textit{objective}) \in \mathcal{R}^{\models}_{\text{buffer}} \quad \text{if } \textit{buffer}_i < \textit{buffer}_j \\ \text{and } v_i = v_j \text{ for every } v \in \textit{cvar}, v \neq \textit{buffer}$$

The experiments were performed on an Intel Core i7 920 2.6GHz with 4GB of RAM running Ubuntu Linux. We used SPIN version 5.2.4 (running on a single core) and ns-2 version 2.33. Table 2 shows some measures taken from the experiments. The columns shows the results of the experiments when neither objectives nor optimization are used, when the objective formula is set, and when additional knowledge is also used, respectively. The first row contains the number of states analyzed by SPIN. The second and third rows give the number of simulations that had to be run to find out if they satisfied the given objective, and the number of simulations that did not have to be run because their outcome could be deduced from the additional knowledge expressed in $\mathcal{R}^{\models}_{\text{buffer}}$, respectively. The fourth row shows how many simulation runs meet the objective. The fifth row gives the number of simulations that were stopped early thanks to the second part of the objective formula. Finally, the sixth row shows the total time spent on each experiment, including both simulation and model checking.

These results show that there is a notable improvement in the experiment running time when properties are used. In addition to only returning the desired initial configurations, setting objectives helps stopping simulations early and thus reduces the space state that needs to be explored. In this case, the state space was about 5 times smaller when properties were used. Using additional knowledge also reduces the number of simulations that must be run because their outcomes can be inferred. This can be seen on the third row of the third column, where 134 simulations (of the 1100 total) did not have to be run to check the satisfiability of the objective.

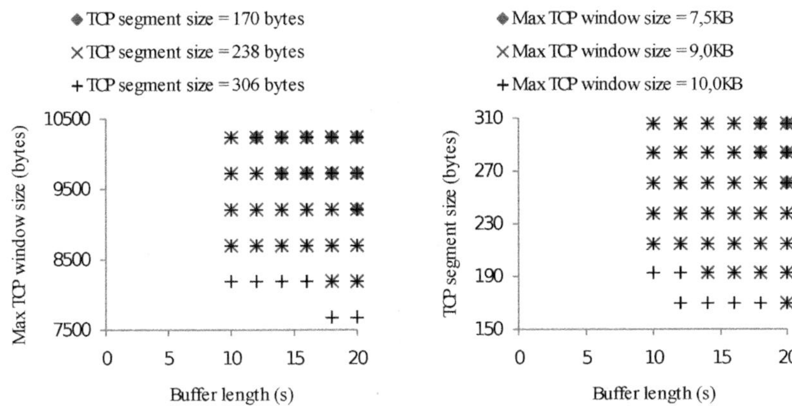

Fig. 7. Influence of maximum TCP window size and TCP segment size in the first experiment

Figure 7 shows the influence of the configuration variables on the evaluation of the objective. The graph on the left plots the maximum TCP window size against the playout buffer length, for several values of TCP segment size. As the window size increases video playback can start sooner, as the playout buffer fills more quickly. The graph on the right shows the converse relationship, plotting the TCP segment size against the playout buffer length. From that graph it can be deduced that using bigger segments means less video must be buffered before playback can start. From both graphs it can be seen that no simulation with a playout buffer of less than 10 seconds satisfies the objective. This is caused by a combination of the video length and the disconnections during the transmission, i.e., the sum of the duration of the disconnections suffered during the video transmission is long enough so that, combined with the slow start phase of TCP, it is almost impossible to overcome this gap with less than 10 seconds of margin.

As we mentioned in Sect. 2.2, applications in mobile environments have to face new challenges such as fluctuating network conditions. One solution to improve the performance in these environments is to use a transport protocol designed for mobility such as Freeze-TCP [12]. In our analysis we will use an existing ns-2 model of the protocol available from [14]. Freeze-TCP depends on the ability of the mobile device to predict impending network disconnections. This notification should come from the physical layer, as it can monitorize the quality of the received signal. We simulate these notifications and issue them automatically a given amount of time before the disconnection happens. The time of when the freeze warning must be sent is also a sensible parameter of Freeze-TCP, and as such we have added it to the configuration variables to optimize it.

Figure 8 shows the influence of the freeze warning on the performance of this experiment. Freeze warnings are measured in RTTs (round-trip times) and, according to [12], ideally they should be sent 1 RTT before the disconnection. However, as can be seen on the figure, this also depends on the duration of the

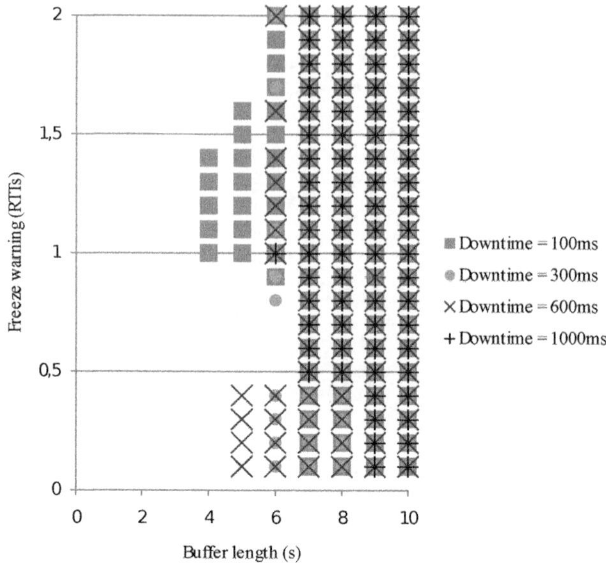

Fig. 8. Influence of freeze warning in the second experiment

link downtime periods. A smaller downtime means that the warning can be sent some time before the disconnection really happens, putting less pressure on the prediction algorithm. The bigger the downtime, the less important is to predict it precisely, as the duration of the disconnection is considerably larger than the idle time wasted freezing the connection earlier. Comparing this graph with the ones in Fig. 7 it can be seen that the freeze mechanism allows a smaller playout buffer to be used, as the effect of the disconnections is partially mitigated.

6 Implementation Details

Our prototype implementation[3] follows the architecture described in Sect. 3, integrating SPIN with an external network simulator like ns-2, which is possible thanks to the ability to use embedded C code in Promela. We have defined a Promela template that must be instantiated for a given scenario and constraints to control the whole process. Figure 9 shows an excerpt of an instance of the template.

To instantiate the template, a script reads a configuration section in the ns-2 model file that declares which configuration variables will be used, which measured variables will be read during the simulation and the properties. The model variables will be declared in Promela as embedded C variables. No more information from the ns-2 model (e.g., network topology or protocol behavior) is needed

[3] The prototype tool and the case study will be made available at http://www.gisum.uma.es/tools/spinns2

```
1  c_state "double link_delay" "Global"     // Configuration variables
2  c_state "int max_tcp_window" "Global"
3  c_state "double time" "Global" "-1.0"    // Measured variables
4  c_state "short status" "Global"
5
6  inline generateConfig() {
7      generate_link_delay();
8      generate_max_tcp_window();
9  }
10 inline runSimulation() {
11     c_code {
12         if (wasRunning == 1) {
13             terminatePreviousBranch();
14             wasRunning = 0;
15             now.running = 0;
16         }
17         startSimulation();
18         wasRunning = 1;
19         now.running = 1;
20     };
21     do
22     :: (running) -> c_code {
23             ss_getMeasureTime("time", &now.time) == -1);
24             if (now.time < 0)
25                 now.running = 0;
26             else
27                 ss_getMeasureShort("status", &now.status);
28         };
29     :: (!running) -> break
30     od;
31     c_code {
32         finishSimulation();
33         wasRunning = 0;
34     }
35 }
36 init {
37     c_code { ss_launchServerSocket(); };
38     generateConfig();
39     runSimulation();
40 }
```

Fig. 9. Extract of an instance of the Promela template for generating and controlling simulations

for the template. We use SPIN to obtain the never claim from the extended LTL formula.

SPIN is responsible for generating all the possible initial configurations and for running the corresponding simulations on ns-2. A new ns-2 process is spawned for each simulation, and communication is handled through input redirection and sockets, using standard C functions embedded in Promela. During the simulation, the ns-2 process reports back to SPIN the measured values of the variables of interest through a socket. Lines 23 and 27 on Fig. 9 show the time (which is always included by default) and status variables being read from the simulator. These values can be communicated either periodically, e.g., throughput, or whenever a significant change occurs, e.g., a state change. These values will create new states in SPIN while the simulation is still running. If a simulation run is pruned in SPIN because a property is violated, the ns-2 process is killed (line 13) and the next simulation is configured and started, which saves simulation time. We check this using the `wasRunning` variable (line 12), which is outside of the state vector. The prototype also maintains a database with the initial configurations and their corresponding results, which is used to check properties regarding additional knowledge over the initial configurations as defined in Sect. 4.3.

On the ns-2 side we have implemented two classes in C++ to prepare the simulation environment and handle the communication with SPIN, respectively, which are instantiated when ns-2 is launched. The network model under analysis must make use of the environment provided by these classes to expose the measure variables of interest to SPIN. Once a simulation has started, the only communication between the ns-2 process and SPIN occurs when the former notifies the latter of a new set of variable values.

7 Conclusions and Future Work

We have presented an approach to integrate on-the-fly model checking with network simulators. This proposal has implemented in a prototype tool that takes advantage of the SPIN model checker and the ns-2 network simulator to perform large scale property-driven simulation of network scenarios. This tool has been proven useful for generating scenarios that verify a certain performance property of interest, while also terminating unpromising simulations early to avoid wasting simulation time. This is especially useful when the number of different possible scenarios is quite large and the simulation time of each run makes it impractical to perform each one of them in its entirety. We are looking into new and more complex scenarios to further validate and improve our approach.

The work can be extended in several ways. The first one is to increase the information directly managed by SPIN. Apart from the temporal formulas, we plan to also describe in Promela part of the behavior of the protocol to increase efficiency and the ability to check more properties.

Regarding the tool, we are also looking into improving its usability by developing a GUI front-end. Another direction in which the tool can be improved in both usability and expressiveness is allowing the use of different property specification languages. For instance, currently only one LTL formula at the same time is supported, which may reduce the combinations of objectives that can be expressed. New property specification languages may be supported for different purposes, e.g. a quality-of-service oriented language or even graphical notations like SDL's message sequence charts or UML's sequence diagrams.

Finally, the core of the tool can also be extended in a number of ways. The multi-core capabilities of SPIN may be used to launch several simulations at once, thus taking advantage of modern multi-core CPUs. Other network simulators could also be supported by the tool, such as ns-3, or OMNeT++, although the core algorithm is generic and reusable for any simulator. Furthermore, the same architecture could be used with real instrumented protocol implementations, as long as SPIN can be fed the relevant metrics.

Acknowledgments

The authors would like to thank the reviewers for their useful comments.

References

1. Holzmann, G.J.: The SPIN Model Checker: Primer and Reference Manual. Addison-Wesley Professional, Reading (September 2003)
2. The Network Simulator - ns-2 (February 2010), `http://www.isi.edu/nsnam/ns/`
3. Yovine, S.: KRONOS: A Verification Tool for Real-Time Systems. STTT 1(1-2) (1997)
4. Larsen, K., Pettersson, P., Yi, W.: UPPAAL in a Nutshell. International Journal on Software Tools for Technology Transfer 1(1-2) (1997)
5. Kwiatkowska, M., Norman, G., Parker, D.: Prism: Probabilistic model checking for performance and reliability analysis. ACM SIGMETRICS Performance Evaluation Review 36(4), 40–45 (2009)
6. Gallardo, M.M., Martínez, J., Merino, P., Rodriguez, G.: Integration of reliability and performance analyses for active network services. Electronic Notes in Theoretical Computer Science 133, 217–236 (2005)
7. Andreozzi, M.M., Stea, G., Vallati, C.: A framework for large-scale simulations and output result analysis with ns-2. In: Simutools 2009: Proceedings of the 2nd International Conference on Simulation Tools and Techniques, ICST (Institute for Computer Sciences, Social-Informatics and Telecommunications Engineering),Brussels, Belgium, pp. 1–7 (2009)
8. Cicconetti, C., Mingozzi, E., Stea, G.: An integrated framework for enabling effective data collection and statistical analysis with ns-2. In: WNS2 2006: Proceeding from the 2006 Workshop on ns-2: the IP Network Simulator, p. 11. ACM, New York (2006)
9. Bacchus, F., Kabanza, F.: Using temporal logics to express search control knowledge for planning. Artificial Intelligence 116(1-2), 123–191 (2000)
10. Gerevini, A., Long, D.: Preferences and soft constraints in PDDL3. In: Proceedings of the ICAPS-2006 Workshop on Preferences and Soft Constraints in Planning, pp. 46–53 (2006)
11. The ns-3 network simulator (April 2010), `http://www.nsnam.org/`
12. Goff, T., Moronski, J., Phatak, D., Gupta, V.: Freeze-TCP: a true end-to-end TCP enhancement mechanism for mobile environments. In: Proceedings of Nineteenth Annual Joint Conference of the IEEE Computer and Communications Societies INFOCOM 2000, vol. 3, pp. 1537–1545 (March 2000)
13. Shen, X., Wonfor, A., Penty, R., White, I.: Receiver playout buffer requirement for TCP video streaming in the presence of burst packet drops. In: London Communications Symposium 2009 (2009)
14. NICTA: Freeze-TCP (ns-2 and linux implementations) (July 2009), `http://www.nicta.com.au/people/mehanio/freezetcp`

Automatic Generation of Model Checking Scripts Based on Environment Modeling

Kenro Yatake and Toshiaki Aoki

Japan Advanced Institute of Science and Technology,
1-1 Asahidai Nomi Ishikawa 923-1292, Japan
{k-yatake,toshiaki}@jaist.ac.jp

Abstract. When applying model checking to the design models of the embedded systems, it is necessary to model not only the behavior of the target system but also that of the environment interacting with the system. In this paper, we present a method to model the environment and to automatically generate all possible environments from the model. In our method, we can flexibly model the structural variation of the environment and the sequences of the function calls using a class model and statechart models. We also present a tool to generate Promela scripts of SPIN from the environment model. As a practical experiment, we applied our tool to the verification of an OSEK/VDX RTOS design model.

1 Introduction

Recently, model checking is drawing attention as a technique to improve the reliability of software systems [18]. Especially, they are widely applied to a verification of embedded systems. The major characteristics of embedded systems is reactiveness. i.e., they operate by the stimulus from the environment. For example, Real-Time Operating Systems (RTOS), which are embedded in most of the complex embedded systems, operate by the service calls from the tasks running on them. In order to apply model checking to such systems, it is necessary to model not only the behavior of the target system but also that of the environment.

The most typical approach to model an environment is to construct a process which calls all the functions provided by the system non-deterministically. Although it realizes an exhaustive check for all the possible execution sequences, description of properties tends to become complicated because it needs extra assumptions to filter out uninterested sequences from all the sequences. Furthermore, it is prone to suffer state explosion because all the sequences are checked at a time. Another approach is to call specific sequences of functions depending on the properties to check. For example, we limit the range of the function calls to the normal execution sequences and check that certain properties hold in that range. The advantage of this approach is that the property description becomes simple and precise because the assumptions of the properties are implied by the sequences themselves. This enables us to reflect our intention of verification more

J. van de Pol and M. Weber (Eds.): SPIN 2010, LNCS 6349, pp. 58–75, 2010.

clearly on the model. Furthermore, as the range is limited, we are more likely to be able to avoid state explosion.

We consider the latter approach is more realistic because state explosion is a critical problem in model checking. However, we must further consider the structural variation of the environment. For example, the environment of an RTOS consists of a multiple number of tasks and resources. There are also various patterns in their priority values and function call relationships. Although we need to check the system for all the environment variations, the number of the variations is so large that we cannot construct them by hand.

To cope with this problem, we propose an environment modeling method where we model the environment variations in a model called *environment model* and automatically generate all possible environments from the model. To allow the use in practice, we defined the environment model based on UML [10]. In a class model, we can model the structural variation of the environment. In statechart models, we can define the sequences of the function calls. Our method is implemented as a tool called *environment generator* which inputs an environment model and outputs environments as Promela scripts of SPIN. As a practical experiment, we applied the tool to the verification of an RTOS design model which is based on OSEK/VDX RTOS specification [11]. In this paper, we explain the details of our method and the verification experiment of the RTOS model.

This paper is organized as follows. In section 2, we explain the approach of our method. In section 3, we explain the environment model. In section 4, we explain the environment generation and the tool. In section 5, we show the verification experiment. In section 6, we discuss the coverage and parallelization of our method. In section 7, we give a conclusion and future work.

2 Approach

Let us explain how reactive systems are verified using an environment. Fig.1 shows an RTOS and its environment. The RTOS implements data structures such as a task control blocks and a ready queue and provides functions such as `ActivateTask()` and `TerminateTask()`. If these functions are called, the RTOS schedules the tasks based on their priorities. To verify this behavior, we prepare an environment, for example, consisting of two tasks T1 and T2 (T2's priority is higher than T1's). This environment describes a sequence of function calls and state transitions of the tasks expected by the calls. For example, if the function `ActivateTask()` is called to T2, T2 is expected to become running. Then, if the same function is called to T1, T1 is expected to become ready. To verify that the RTOS satisfies this expectation, we apply model checking to the RTOS in combination with the environment. Specifically, in each state of the environment, we check the consistency between the environment state and the internal values of the RTOS. For example, if T1 and T2 are ready and running, the ready queue in the RTOS must contain the identifier of T1, and the variable `turn` (representing the running task) must contain the identifier of T2. By checking this consistency, we verify the behavior of the RTOS.

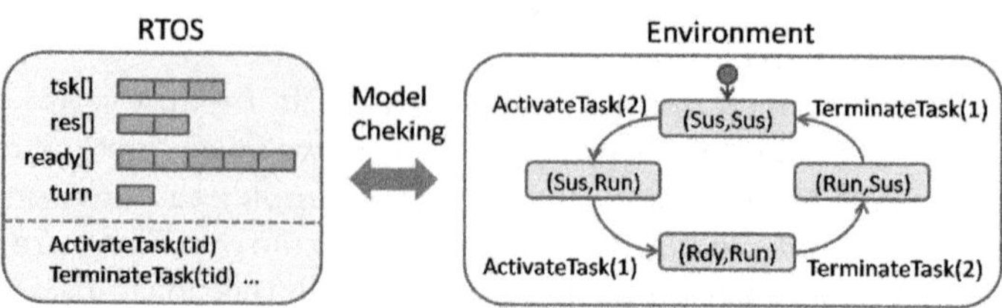

Fig. 1. Model checking with an environment

The problem of this approach is that this environment is only one of the cases of the large number of environment variations. We need to verify the RTOS for all the variations with respect to the structures such as the number of tasks and resources, the patterns of the priority values and function call relationships. But it is unrealistic to construct all of them by hand. One could think of constructing a general environment with m tasks and n resources, but this is prone to suffer state explosion.

To cope with this problem, we introduce a model to describe the environment variations and automatically generate all the environments from the model. Fig. 2 summarizes this idea. To verify the target system (RTOS design model), we first construct an environment model. This model is based on UML in which all possible environment structures are defined using parameters with ranges. Then, we generate all the environment instances from the model using the environment generator. All the generated instances, which are structurally different from each other, cover all the variations of the environment. The environment generator inputs an environment model as a text file and outputs the environments as Promela scripts. Finally, we combine the target system with each environment instance and conduct model checking using SPIN.

Our approach has the following advantages:

1. **Easy syntax:** The syntax of the environment model is based on UML which is familiar to most of the software engineers. This lowers the hurdle for introducing our method to the software development in practice.
2. **Alleviation of state explosion problem:** It alleviates the state explosion problem by structurally dividing the whole environment into individual environment. As each environment can be checked in a relatively small state space, we are likely to be able to check the whole environment without causing state explosion.
3. **Structural difference analysis:** When a bug is detected in model checking, our method allows us to structurally analyze its source, i.e., we can identify the structural boundary of the source of a bug by comparing the check results. For example, when the two results "The case of 2 tasks and no resources is correct" and "The case of 2 tasks and 1 resource is not correct" are obtained, we can presume that the resource handling function contains a bug.

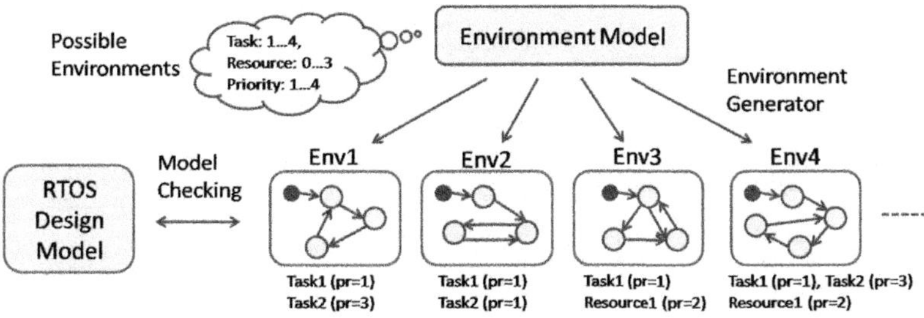

Fig. 2. Environment modeling method

4. **Generality:** It can be generally applied to the verification of reactive systems. Our method is especially effective for the systems whose environment has a lot of structural variations. Examples of such systems are operating systems and middleware systems.

3 Environment Models

In this section, we explain environment models with an example of RTOS. We also present formal definitions in A.1.

3.1 Class Model

Fig. 3 shows the class model of the environment for an RTOS. The class model consists of a class representing a target system and classes representing its environment. In the figure, the class `RTOS` is the target system and the two classes `Task` and `Resource` are the environment classes.

The target class defines two kinds of functions as the interface with the environment. The functions labeled with `fun` are *trigger functions*. They trigger the state transition of the target system. For example, `ActivateTask(tid,dtid)` is the function to activate the task of ID `dtid` (`tid` is the ID of the caller task). The argument of a function is defined with a range like `tid:1..M`. representing the variation of the arguments. The functions labeled with `ref` are *reference functions*. They refer the internal values of the target system. They are used to define assertions (explained later in this section).

The environment classes are defined with attributes, associations, and variables. They are labelled with `attr`, `assoc`, and `var`, respectively. An attribute is defined with a range like `pr:1..P` representing the variation of the attribute values. (`pr` is a priority of a task.) An association is also defined with a range like `res:0..N`. representing the variation of the multiplicity, i.e., the number of objects linked with an object. The associations from the target class to an environment class defines the number of objects which instantiate from the environment class. A variable is a data of an object which can be dynamically changed along with state transitions. It is defined with a default value.

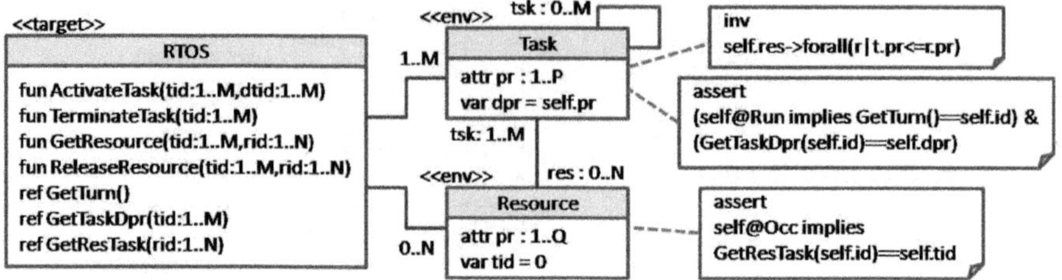

Fig. 3. The class model of an RTOS environment

Invariants can be defined for environment classes. They are written in OCL [22]. An invariant defines a constraint on the structure of objects. For example, `Task` defines an invariant constraining the pattern of links from a task to resources. This invariant reflects the description of the specification that a task can only acquire the resources whose priorities are equal to or higher than that of the task. The OCL expressions in our model is a subset of OCL containing the set operations and the state reference operations.

Assertions are defined for environment classes. An assertion defines a predicate which is checked in each state of objects. In an assertion, the internal values of the target system can be accessed by reference functions to define the consistency between the target system and the environment. For example, `Task` defines an assertion to check if the variable `turn` in the RTOS is equal to the identifier of the running task in the environment. It also checks that the runtime priority of a task is the same in the RTOS and the environment. The reference functions `GetTurn()` and `GetTaskDpr()` are used to obtain the value of `turn` and the runtime priority of the task in the RTOS.

3.2 Statechart Models

In statechart models, we define the state transitions of environment objects expected for the function calls of the target system. Fig. 4 shows the statechart models of `Task` and `Resource`. They describe the normal execution sequences of RTOS. A transition occurs by the call of a trigger function. For example, the transition (1) is caused by `ActivateTask()`. The expression in `[]` is a guard condition described in OCL. In the model, typical expressions are defined as functions like `ExRun()=Task->exists(t|t@Run)`.

A set of *synchronous transitions* can be attached to a transition. By synchronous transitions, we can define the transitions of other objects which occur synchronously with the transition of the self object. For example, the transition (2) defines the synchronous transition `Run->Rdy : GetRun()`. This means: "Along with the transition of the self object, the `Task` object obtained by the OCL function `GetRun()` (the task which is in the state `Run`) transits from the state `Run` to `Rdy`. Currently, asynchronous transitions are not supported.

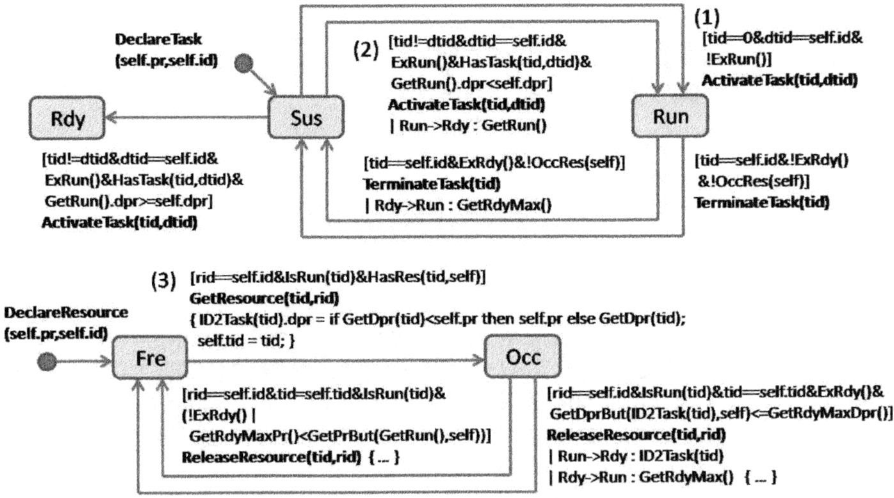

Fig. 4. The statechart model of Task (top) and Resource (bottom)

An action can be attached to a transition. It is a sequence of statements described in {} which are executed along with the transition. In an action, variables of objects are updated. For example, the transition (3) defines an action with two statements which update the variables dpr of a task (the runtime priority), and tid of a resource (the task ID occupying the resource), respectively.

4 Generation of Environments

In this section, we explain the environment generation with the example. As shown in Fig. 5, it is done in three steps: (1) Generation of object graphs, (2) composition of statechart models, and (3) translation into Promela scripts. We also present formal algorithms for (1) and (2) in A.2 and A.3.

4.1 Generation of Object Graphs

Firstly, we generate all the possible object graphs from the class model. An object graph is represented by a set of objects which instantiate from all the classes. Each object holds the values of attributes and associations. The value of an association is a set of objects with which the object links.

We generate object graphs based on a data structure called *graph counter* which represents an object graph by a vector of natural numbers. By counting up the counter, we enumerate all the variation of object graphs. Let us consider the example in Fig. 3 with M=2, N=1, P=2, and Q=2. The graph counter for this model consists of 8 numbers. Each of them corresponds to T1.pr (the task T1's attribute pr), T1.tsk, T1.res, T2.pr, T2.tsk, T2.res, R1.pr and

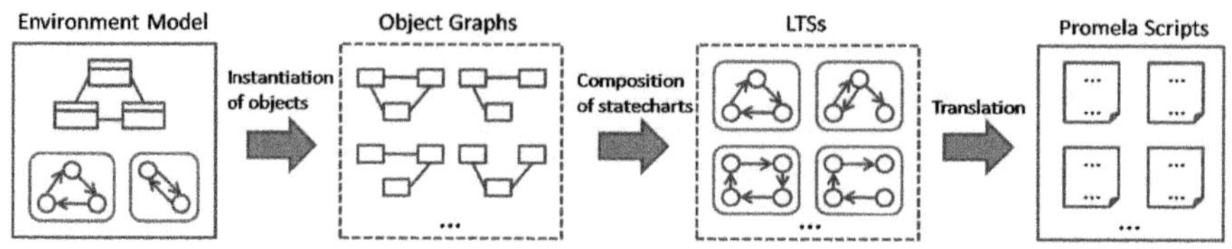

Fig. 5. Environment generation

R1.tsk, respectively. For example, the graph counter L=<2,3,1,1,4,2,2,3> represents an object graph with T1.pr=2, T1.tsk=[T2], T1.res=[], T2.pr=1, T2.tsk=[T1,T2], T2.res=[R1], R1.pr=2, and R1.tsk=[T1,T2]. L[1]=2 means that the T1.pr's value is the 2nd value of the pr's domain {1,2}. Likewise, L[2]=3 means that the T1.tsk's value is the 3rd value of the tsk's domain {[],[T1],[T2],[T1,T2]}.

To enumerate all the graphs, we start with the initial counter <1,...,1> and count it up repeatedly to <1,...,1,2>, and then, <1,...,1,3>. If L[8] reached the maximum number 3 (R1.tsk's domain is {[1],[2],[1,2]}), the next count causes carry over. So, the next counter is {1,...,2,1}. We repeat counting until the counter reaches the maximum value <2,4,2,2,4,2,2,3>. Along with the counting, we translate the graph counter into an object graph and output it if it satisfies invariants.

The computation time of this algorithm increases exponentially as the multiplicities of associations increase. However, the computation space is limited to $O((A+B)\times C)$. (A,B,C is the number of attributes, associations, and objects.)

4.2 Composition of Statechart Models

Next, we compose the statechart models of all objects in each object graph. The result of the composition is an LTS (Labelled Transition System) [6]. Fig. 6 shows an example of an object graph and its LTS. In the LTS, each state contains the states and variables of all the objects. For example, in the initial state (A), the tasks T1 and T2 are in the state Sus and the resource R1 is in the state Fre. The variables dpr of T1 and T2 are 1 and 3, respectively. The variable tid of R1 is 0.

Transitions in statechart models are added to the LTS if their guard conditions are evaluated to true in the LTS state and the object graph. For example, the transition from (A) to (B) by the function ActivateTask(0,1) (AT(0,1)) is added because the guard condition of the transition (1) in Fig. 4 becomes true for the object T1 and the action argument (0,1) in the state (A). If a transition has synchronous transitions, synchronized objects are obtained by evaluating the OCL expression. The synchronized objects transit along with the transition of the self object. For example, in the transition from (C) to (D) by the function ReleaseResource(1,1) (RR(1,1)), along with the self object R1 transits from Occ to Fre, the synchronized objects T1 and T2 transit from Run and Rdy to

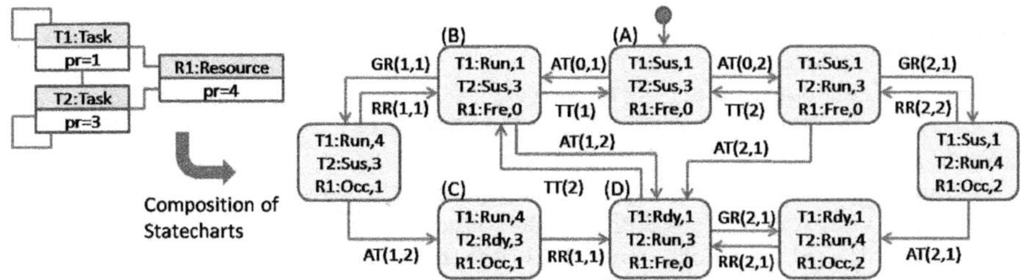

Fig. 6. An object graph and its LTS

Rdy and Run, respectively. This transition also updates the variables of T1 and R1 by executing the corresponding action.

It could be possible to translate all the statechart models directly into Promela and leave the composition to SPIN. However, we do not do so because the OCL expressions attached with the transitions are hard to express directly in Promela. So, we evaluate the OCL expressions and compose the statechart models at this point.

4.3 Translation into Promela Scripts

Finally, we translate each LTS into Promera script. A state of LTS contains the states and variables of all objects. In Promela, the states of objects are represented by a label and the variables of objects are represented by the variables of Promela. For example, Fig. 7 shows the Promela script corresponding to the state (D) of the LTS in Fig. 6. In the script, the three states `Rdy`, `Run`, and `Fre` of the three objects `T1`, `T2`, and `R1` are represented by the label `Rdy_Run_Fre`. The variables of the three objects are represented by the variables `Task1.dpr`, `Task2.dpr`, and `Resource1.tid`. These variables are checked in the guard conditions of the if-statement and updated appropriately after calling the functions `TerminateTask(2)` and `GetResource(2,1)`.

The assertion is checked at the beginning of the state. It is a conjunction of the assertions of all the objects. (In this case, only the assertion of two tasks are conjuncted as the assertion of the resource is true.) The three variables `ret_GetTurn`, `ret_GetTaskDpr_1`, and `ret_GetTaskDpr_2` represent the internal values of the RTOS which are obtained by the reference functions `GetTurn()`, `GetTaskState(1)`, `GetTaskState(2)`, respectively. These variables are set to the return values of the corresponding functions in the inline function `set_ref()` before the assertion check. Expressions in the assertions except for these variables are evaluated during the composition of statechart models.

4.4 Environment Generator

We implemented the environment generator as a command line tool which inputs an environment model as a text file and outputs all the environments as Promela

```
Rdy_Run_Fre:
  set_ref();
  assert ((ret_GetTaskDpr_1==1) &&                    /* Task1 */
          (ret_GetTurn==2 && ret_GetTaskDpr_2==3)); /* Task2 */
  if
  :: Task1.dpr==1 && Task2.dpr==3 && Resource1.tid==0 -> TerminateTask(2);
     Task1_var.dpr=1; Task2.dpr=3; Resource1.tid=0; goto Run_Sus_Fre;
  :: Task1.dpr==1 && Task2.dpr==3 && Resource1.tid==0 -> GetResource(2,1);
     Task1.dpr=1; Task2.dpr=4; Resource1.tid=2; goto Rdy_Run_Occ;
  fi;
```

Fig. 7. Promela script corresponding the state (D) in Fig. 6

files. This tool can be applied generally to any systems as long as we observe the interface between the environment model and the target system. (The Promela script of the target system must contain the inline functions corresponding to the trigger functions and reference functions in the environment model.) Fig. 8 shows the architecture of the tool. It mainly consists of three components realizing the three steps of the environment generation: the graph generator, the state composer, and the Promela translator. It also has the invariant filter for checking invariants for object graphs, and the OCL evaluator for evaluating OCL expressions.

5 Experiment

As an application of our method to a practical system, we conducted an experiment to verify that an RTOS design model conforms to the OSEK/VDX RTOS specification. The design model is implemented in Promela (about 1800 lines) following the approach in [1]. It is implemented as a set of inline functions for the functions `ActivateTask`, `TerminateTask`, and so on. For the verification, we constructed the environment model based on the specification. We have presented this model partially in Fig. 3 and Fig. 4. We generated the environments by the environment generator and conducted model checking for some of them in SPIN.

5.1 Environment Generation

Table. 1 shows the number of generated environments from the model in Fig. 3 with the constants `M`, `N`, `P`, and `Q` set to 4, i.e., tasks and resources are created up to 4 and both of them can take priorities up to 4. We generated environments by moving the number of tasks and resources from 1 to 4. In the Table. 1, T is the number of tasks and R is the number of resources. Actually, the specification does not limit the number of tasks and resources and it allows the number of priorities up to 16. In our model, however, we limited the maximum number of objects

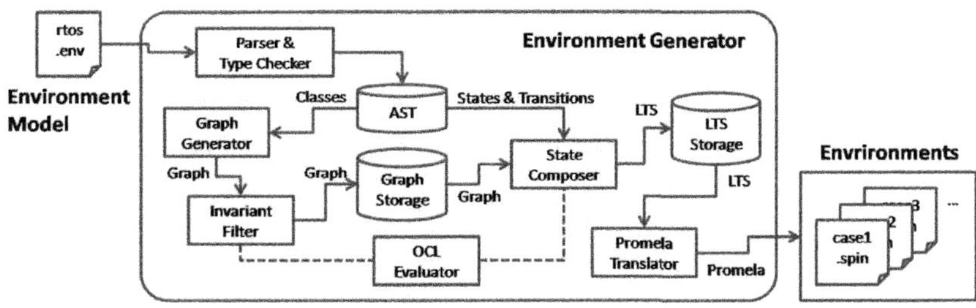

Fig. 8. Architecture of the environment generator

and priorities to 4 so that the environment generation can be completed within a reasonable time. Even in this limited range, we can capture the important behavior of the RTOS. (See Section 6.)

An important problem when constructing an environment model is to prevent generation of isomorphic environments. An example of a pair of isomorphic environments is: (1) an environment of tasks T1 and T2 with priorities 1 and 2, and (2) an environment of tasks T1 and T2 with priorities 2 and 1. Since the identifiers of tasks do not affect the behavior of the RTOS, this pair of environments brings the same result in model checking. In our method, we can reduce such isomorphic environments by making use of invariants. In the example, the following invariant can be added to the class `Task`:

```
Task->forall(t|self.id<t.id implies self.pr<t.pr)
```

It specifies that the priorities of tasks increases monotonically with the increase of identifiers. By this invariant, we can remove the environment (2). The same kind of invariant can be added to the class `Resource`. By removing isomorphic environments, we can drastically reduce the number of generated environments. In the cases of two tasks and two resources, we can reduce the number from 850 to 95 (88.8% reduction). In our method, it is the responsibility of users to add appropriate invariants to reduce isomorphic environments.

Currently, the computation time of the generation algorithm grows exponentially with the number of associations. To make it more scalable, we need to compute the set of object graphs, which satisfy invariants, directly from the class model. To realize this, we are currently considering the use of SAT and SMT solvers [16,4].

5.2 Model Checking

We conducted model checking on some of the generated environments. We selected a representative environment from each case in Table. 1. For example, for the 95 cases in T=2 and R=2, we selected the case No. 95/2=47. Table. 2 shows the results of model checking. As well as the check results ("◯" for no errors and "×" for at least one error), it shows the structures of object graphs,

Table 1. The number of generated environments (CPU:2.4GHz, Memory:4.0GB)

R/T	1	2	3	4
0	4 (0.0s)	6 (0.0s)	4 (0.1s)	1 (0.2s)
1	10 (0.1s)	40 (0.3s)	55 (1.5s)	26 (3.5s)
2	10 (0.2s)	95 (1.5s)	245 (15.7s)	196 (99.5s)
3	5 (0.2s)	100 (6.8s)	425 (169.2s)	N/A
4	1 (1.0s)	39 (66.3s)	N/A	N/A

consumed time and memories. (Times include the compilation time and the verification time.) As the memory consumption indicates, we were able to check all the cases without causing state explosion. This is thanks to the structural decomposition of the environment. If we naively conduct model checking with a non-deterministic environment, we cannot even check the environment of up to 2 tasks and 2 resources causing state explosion with 4.0 Gbyte of memory.

Among 17 cases, 6 cases were unsuccessful. All the failures were caused by assertion violations. Specifically, the runtime priority of a task was inconsistent between the environment and the RTOS. In our method, we can make use of the table to conduct difference analysis to find the source of a bug. By overlooking the table, we can see that the check fails only if there are at least two tasks. With a closer look, we can notice that the check fails only if there is at least one task which is linked with more than one resources. Based on this information, we can presume that the resource handling of the RTOS is incorrect, especially when a task tries to acquire more than one resources.

By examining the counter example traces output by SPIN, we found that the bug was contained in the function `GetResource()`. It is a function called from a task when the task acquires a resource. Correctly, the function must raise the runtime priority of the task to the resource priority only when the runtime priority is lower than the resource priority. (This mechanism is called ceiling priority protocol.) But the function changed the runtime priority every time the task acquires a resource regardless of the resource priority. This bug caused the inconsistency of the runtime priority between the environment and the RTOS. (For example, if T1 first acquires R1 of priority 4 and then acquires R2 of priority 3, the environment expect the runtime priority of T1 to be 4. In the RTOS, however, it was incorrectly changed to 3.) This inconsistency occurs only when a task tries to acquire more than one resources. This result coincides with our presumption based on the difference analysis.

When model checking in SPIN, it is not always easy to pinpoint the source of the bug only from the information of the counter example traces. Our method, however, can provide additional information as a form of a table by which we can conduct difference analysis based on graph structures. This is one of the advantages of our method to structurally decompose the whole environment into individuals.

Table 2. Results of model checking

T,R	No.	Task.pr				Task.res				Resource.pr				Result	Time (sec)	Memory (Mbyte)
		T1	T2	T3	T4	T1	T2	T3	T4	R1	R2	R3	R4			
1,0	2	2				[]								○	3.3	2.70
1,1	5	2				[1]				3				○	3.4	2.70
1,2	5	1				[1,2]				1	4			×	3.6	2.79
1,3	2	1				[1,2,3]				1	2	4		×	4.0	2.89
1,4	1	1				[1,2,3,4]				1	2	3	4	×	5.2	3.09
2,0	3	2	3			[]	[]							○	3.6	2.89
2,1	20	3	4			[1]	[]			4				○	3.7	2.89
2,2	47	2	3			[1]	[2]			2	4			○	4.0	3.09
2,3	50	1	3			[1,2,3]	[3]			1	3	4		×	5.8	3.38
2,4	19	1	2			[1,2,3,4]	[2,3]			1	2	3	4	×	10.4	3.77
3,0	2	1	2	4		[]	[]							○	4.2	3.09
3,1	27	1	2	4		[1]	[1]	[]		2				○	4.9	3.58
3,2	122	1	2	3		[1]	[]	[2]		1	3			○	5.3	3.87
3,3	212	1	2	3		[2]	[1]	[3]		2	3	4		○	6.3	4.36
4,0	1	1	2	3	4	[]	[]	[]	[]					○	5.6	4.06
4,1	13	1	2	3	4	[1]	[]	[1]	[]	3				○	7.8	5.53
4,2	98	1	2	3	4	[1]	[1]	[1,2]	[]	3	4			×	11.1	4.26

6 Discussion

Our method, where a limited range of environment is constructed, stands in contrast to the usual method where a non-deterministic environment is filtered by LTL formula. As we stated in introduction, there is a trade-off between the two methods, i.e., the usual method has an advantage in the coverage of verification, while our method has an advantage in the simplicity and precision of property description and avoidance of state explosion problem. Our method becomes more advantageous for the verification of the systems whose environment has a lot of structural variations. RTOS is a good example of such systems. If the environment has wider structural variations, it can be separated more finely into individuals. As a result, we are more likely to avoid state explosion and more benefit from the structural difference analysis.

To improve the coverage, we need to extend the variation of the environment model as much as possible depending on the computation time of environment generation and model checking. But as it is hard to cover all the cases, we need some criteria as to how far we should extend the variation of the environment model. In our experience, crucial errors concerning the behavioral logic of the system can be discovered even with a small number of objects, and the errors newly discovered by increasing the number of objects are only those concerning system boundaries (such as generating objects which exceeds the limit of an array). So, one of the criteria should be to clarify the important properties of the system and cover at least the variations which can observe the satisfaction of the properties. For example, the important properties about the behavioral logic of RTOS are: (1) Without resources, the task of higher priority must be executed before that of lower priority, (2) If a task occupies multiple resources, its runtime priority is set to the maximum priority of the resources, (3) With resources, the task of higher runtime priority must be executed before that of lower runtime priority. To check these properties, we need at least 2 tasks and 2 resources, i.e., (1) requires 2 tasks, (2) requires 1 tasks and 2 resources, and (3) requires 2 tasks and 2 resources. In this way, we need to clarify the necessary minimum of the variations depending on the properties to check and define the parameter ranges sufficiently wide to cover the variations.

For behavioral coverage, we further need to conduct verification of abnormal execution and interrupt handling. To verify interrupt handling, we need to extend the environment model so that it can deal with multiple processes since interleavings occur between the executions of tasks and the interrupt handler.

Another advantage of our method is that it has a potential for parallelizing model checking. Since all the environments are structurally different from each other, they can be checked independently of others. So, it is effective to check all the cases parallelly by distributing them on a PC cluster. To realize this, we need to address two problems. The first one is load-balancing, i.e., how to distribute all the environments equally to each PC. For this problem, we consider it effective to distribute them based on the length of Promela files. This is because most of the time for checking an environment is occupied by the compilation of the Promela file of the environment. The second one is data-mining, i.e., how to retrieve useful information from the large amounts of check results. For this, we consider it effective to make use of a relational database. By storing the results in the database, we can retrieve necessary information by issuing query on environment structures.

7 Related Work

Many work propose methods to verify UML models in SPIN by translating statechart models into Promela [19,9,14].Our method also applies model checking to statechart models, but our motivation is totally different from these works in that we are using statechart models for describing environments, not the target system itself.

O. Tkachuk, et al. [20] proposes Bandera Environment Generator (BEG) which automatically generates the environment for the verification of Java programs in Bandera. It has been applied to commercial software [21] and has also used as the core tool for the environment generator for web application domain [17]. In BEG, the environment is generated from the specifications of the environment written by the user, called environment assumptions, or by analyzing the programs which implements the environment. The environment assumptions are described as the sequences of the method calls in the form of regular expressions. This approach corresponds to describing a single instance of the environment model in our method. In our method, we can describe a set of the instances as a class model and automatically generate all the possible instances based on the variations in the model.

P. Parizek, et al. [12] proposes a method to verify Java components by Java PathFinder (JPF) and a protocol checker. The protocols of the components are defined by ADL (Architecture Description Language) from which the environment for the components is constructed. This method allows to describe the environment structure by ADL. Compared to this work, our method further describe the variation of the structure using the parameters in the class model.

J. Penix, et al. [15,13] verifies the time partitioning of DEOS RTOS by SPIN. M. Dwyer et al. [5] verifies partial systems described in Ada by translating them into SPIN. In these works, environments are obtained by filtering a universal environment with assumptions described in LTL. This approach is effective when the assumptions can be described simply, but shows weakness when describing precise behavior of environments due to the accumulation of complex LTL assumptions. Compared to these works, we describe the specific behavior of an environment from the beginning using statechart models instead of incrementally refining the universal environment by assumptions. The use of statechart models facilitates the description of environments because the abstraction level is lifted to the familiar level for users.

C. Boyapati et al. [3] developed the Korat tool to automatically generate test cases for unit-testing Java methods. To test a method, it automatically generates all the structural variations of the input object based on the pre-condition. Then the method is tested against the post-condition for all the generated inputs. Our work is close to this work in that the test environment (input) is automatically generated. But our work is more suited for the integration or system-wide testing where the correctness of a system is checked against a sequence of function calls described in statechart models.

Concerning parallel model checking, there are many techniques based on multi-cores [7,8] and clusters [2]. Compared to these techniques where the search algorithm is parallelized, our method can be parallelized based on separation of data, i.e., we can divide the whole environment into individuals by changing its data settings.

8 Conclusion

In this paper, we presented a method for modeling and generating environments for model checking embedded systems. We presented a tool to automatically generate Promela/SPIN scripts from the environment model. As an application to a practical system, we conducted a verification of an OSEK/VDX RTOS design model. In the experiment, we were able to generate sufficient variations of environments efficiently for checking important properties of RTOS. We also confirmed the effectiveness of difference analysis based on the environment structures. Future work is to develop a distributed parallel model checking framework based on our method.

References

1. Aoki, T.: Model Checking Multi-Task Software on Real-Time Operating Systems. In: ISORC, pp. 551–555. IEEE Computer Society, Los Alamitos (2008)
2. Barnat, J., Brim, L., Ročkai, P.: DiVinE 2.0: High-Performance Model Checking. In: 2009 International Workshop on High Performance Computational Systems Biology (HiBi 2009), pp. 31–32. IEEE Computer Society Press, Los Alamitos (2009)
3. Boyapati, C., Khurshid, S., Marinov, D.: Korat: automated testing based on Java predicates. In: ISSTA, pp. 123–133 (2002)
4. de Moura, L.M., Dutertre, B., Shankar, N.: A Tutorial on Satisfiability Modulo Theories. In: Damm, W., Hermanns, H. (eds.) CAV 2007. LNCS, vol. 4590, pp. 20–36. Springer, Heidelberg (2007)
5. Dwyer, M.B., Pasareanu, C.S.: Filter-Based Model Checking of Partial Systems. In: SIGSOFT FSE, pp. 189–202 (1998)
6. Magee, J., et al.: Concurrency: State models & Java programs. Wiley, Chichester (1999)
7. Holzmann, G.J., Bosnacki, D.: The Design of a Multicore Extension of the SPIN Model Checker. IEEE Trans. Software Eng. 33(10), 659–674 (2007)
8. Holzmann, G.J., Joshi, R., Groce, A.: Swarm Verification. In: ASE, pp. 1–6. IEEE, Los Alamitos (2008)
9. Lilius, J., Paltor, I.: vUML: A tool for verifying UML models. In: ASE, pp. 255–258 (1999)
10. OMG. Unified Modeling Language (1989), `http://www.uml.org/`
11. OSEK/VDX. OSEK/VDX Operating System Specification 2.2.3 (2005), `http://portal.osek-vdx.org/`
12. Parizek, P., Plasil, F.: Partial Verification of Software Components: Heuristics for Environment Construction. In: EUROMICRO-SEAA, pp. 75–82. IEEE Computer Society, Los Alamitos (2007)
13. Pasareanu, C.S.: DEOS Kernel: Environment Modeling using LTL Assumptions. Nasa ames technical report nasa-arc-ic-2000-196, NASA Ames Research Center (2000)
14. Pelliccione, P., Inverardi, P., Muccini, H.: CHARMY: A Framework for Designing and Verifying Architectural Specifications. IEEE Trans. Software Eng. 35(3), 325–346 (2009)
15. Penix, J., Visser, W., Park, S., Pasareanu, C.S., Engstrom, E., Larson, A., Weininger, N.: Verifying Time Partitioning in the DEOS Scheduling Kernel. Formal Methods in System Design 26(2), 103–135 (2005)
16. Prasad, M.R., Biere, A., Gupta, A.: A survey of recent advances in SAT-based formal verification. STTT 7(2), 156–173 (2005)
17. Rajan, S.P., Tkachuk, O., Prasad, M.R., Ghosh, I., Goel, N., Uehara, T.: WEAVE: WEb Applications Validation Environment. In: ICSE Companion, pp. 101–111. IEEE, Los Alamitos (2009)
18. Jhala, R., Majumdar, R.: Software model checking. ACM Comput. Surv. 41(4) (2009)
19. Schäfer, T., Knapp, A., Merz, S.: Model checking UML state machines and collaborations. Electr. Notes Theor. Comput. Sci. 55(3) (2001)
20. Tkachuk, O., Dwyer, M.B., Pasareanu, C.S.: Automated Environment Generation for Software Model Checking. In: ASE, pp. 116–129. IEEE Computer Society, Los Alamitos (2003)

21. Tkachuk, O., Rajan, S.P.: Application of automated environment generation to commercial software. In: Pollock, L.L., Pezzè, M. (eds.) ISSTA, pp. 203–214. ACM, New York (2006)
22. Warmer, J., Kleppe, A.: The Object Constraint Language: Precise Modeling with UML. Addison-Wesley, Reading (1999)

A Formal Definitions and Algorithms

A.1 Environment Model

Definition 1 (Environment model). *An environment model EM is defined as:*

$$EM = (I, \mathcal{C}, \mathcal{S})$$

I is a target system. $\mathcal{C} = \{C_1, C_2, ...\}$ is the set of classes. $\mathcal{S} = \{SC_1, SC_2, ...\}$ is the set of statechart models.

Definition 2 (Target system). *The target system I is defined as:*

$$I = (Fun, Ref, Arg)$$

The sets Fun and Ref are the set of trigger functions and reference functions, respectively. The mapping $Arg : F \times 2^{Val}$ relates a function to the domain (variation) of its argument. (For simplicity, we present the definition where a function has only one argument.) The set Val is the set of values.

Definition 3 (Classes). *The class $C_i \in \mathcal{C}$ is defined as:*

$$C_i = (X_i, Y_i, V_i, Size_i, Dom_i, Def_i, Inv_i, Assr_i)$$

The sets X_i and Y_i are the sets of attributes and associations, respectively. We define the union $X_i \cup Y_i$ as $U_i = \{u_{i1}, u_{i2}, ...\}$, and call them members of the class C_i. The set $V_i = \{v_{i1}, v_{i2}, ...\}$ is the set of variables. $Size_i \in N$ is the number of objects which instantiate from the class. The mapping $Dom_i : U_i \rightarrow 2^{Val}$ relates a member to the set of values which represents the domain (variation) of the member. We represent each element in $Dom_i(u_{ij})$ as $d_{ijk}(k = 1, ...)$. The mapping $Def_i : V_i \rightarrow Val$ relates a variable to its default value. We represent each element in $Def_i(v_{ij})$ as e_{ij}. The expression $Inv_i, Assr_i \in Exp$ are an invariant and an assertion. Exp is the set of expressions ($Val \subset Exp$).

In this definition, we omit the definition of multiplicities of associations. The variation of links for an association is directly defined by Dom_i.

Definition 4 (Statechart models). *Let S be the set of states. For the class C_i, the statechart model SC_i is defined as:*

$$SC_i = (S_i, s_{0i}, A_i, T_i)$$

The set $S_i \subset S$ is the set of states. The state $s_{0i} \in S_i$ is the initial state. The set A_i is a set of actions. The set T_i is the set of transitions. For a transition

$(s_1, s_2, g, f, a, st) \in T_i$, $s_1, s_2 \in S_i$ are the source and destination states, respectively. $g \in Exp$ is a guard condition. $f \in Fun$ is a trigger function. $a \in A_i$ is an action. st is the set of synchronous transitions. For a synchronous transition $(t_1, t_2, x) \in st$, $t_1, t_2 \in S$ are the source and destination states, respectively. $x \in Exp$ is the expression representing the synchronized objects.

A.2 Generation of Object Graphs

Definition 5 (Object graphs). *Let $O_i = \{o_{i1}, o_{i2}, ...\}$ be the set of objects which instantiate from the class c_i ($|O_i| = Size(c_i)$). Let $\mathcal{G}$ be the set of object graphs. An object graph $G \in \mathcal{G}$ is defined as:*

$$G = \{g_{ijk} | i = 1..|C|, j = 1..|O_i|, k = 1..|U_{ij}|\}$$

The value g_{ijk} represents the value of the member u_{ik} of the object o_{ij}.

The set of object graphs $\mathcal{G}$ is computed as follows. Firstly, we define the graph counter $Z = \langle z_1, z_2, ...\rangle$ as a vector of length $M = \sum_{i=1}^{|C|}(|O_i| \times |U_i|)$. The correspondence between object members and graph counter elements are defined by the function $Pos(i, j, k) = (\sum_{n=1}^{i-1} |O_n| \times |U_n|) + |U_i| \times (j - 1) + k$. If $Pos(i, j, k) = p$, z_p corresponds to the member u_{ijk}. For each z_i, we define its maximum value as Max_i. If $Pos(i, j, k) = p$, Max_p is equal to $|Dom(u_{ik})|$.

Then, we define a function *GetGraph* which generates an object graph from the graph counter.

$$GetGraph(Z) = (G, Z')$$

where

$$G_{ijk} = d_{ijm} \quad (m = L[Pos(i, j, k)], i = 1..|C|, j = 1..|O_i|, k = 1..|U_i|)$$

$$Z' = \begin{cases} \langle z_1, ..., z_M + 1\rangle & \text{if } z_M < Max_M \\ \langle z_1, ..., z_i + 1, 1, ..., 1\rangle & \text{if } z_i < Max_i,\ z_j = Max_j\ (j = i + 1..M) \\ \langle 1, ..., 1\rangle & \text{if } z_i = Max_i\ (i = 1..M) \end{cases}$$

G and Z' are the generated object graph and the next graph counter, respectively. The last case of Z' means that the counter returns to $\langle 1, ..., 1\rangle$ when it reaches maximum. By this, we know the end of counting.

Finally, the set $\mathcal{G}$ is obtained the following algorithm. In the algorithm, the mapping $Eval_G[o] : Exp \rightarrow Val$ relates an expression to a value which is obtained by evaluating the expression in the context of a graph G and an object o.

1. Let $\mathcal{G} = \{\}$ and $Z = \langle 1, ..., 1\rangle$.
2. Let $(G, Z) = GetGraph(Z)$
3. If G satisfies invariants, i.e., $Eval_G[o_{ij}](Inv_i)$ is a value representing true for all i and j, let $\mathcal{G} = \{G\} \cup \mathcal{G}$.
4. If $Z \neq \langle 1, ..., 1\rangle$, goto 2.

A.3 Composition of Statecharts

Definition 6 (Labelled transition systems). *An LTS L is defined as:*

$$L = (P, p_0, Q, R, B)$$

The set $P = \{p_0, p_1 ...\}$ is a set of composite states. In a composite state p, the state of the object o_{ij} and the value of the variable v_{ijk} are defined as $p[i, j, 0]$ and $p[i, j, k]$, respectively. (Note that $k = 1...$) The state p_0 is the initial state. The set Q is the set of labels. For a label $(f, w) \in Q$, f and w are a trigger function and its argument, respectively. The set R is the set of transitions. For a transition $r = (t_1, t_2, q) \in R$, t_1, t_2, and q are a source state, a destination states, and a label, respectively. The set $B = \{b_0, b_1, ...\}$ is the set of assertions. Each b_i is the assertion defined for the state p_i.

For an object graph G, an LTS L is computed by the following algorithm. In the algorithm, the mapping $Eval_G[o][p][w] : Exp \to Val$ relates an expression to a value which is obtained by evaluating the expression in the context of a graph G, a state p, an object o, and an argument w. The mapping $AEval_G[o][p] : Exp \to Exp$ relates an assertion to an expression which is obtained by evaluating the assertion in the context of a graph G, a state p, and an object o. (The result expression may contain reference functions.) The mapping $Exec_G[o][p][w] : A \times V \to Val$ relates an action and a variable to the value of the variable which is obtained by evaluating the action in the context of a graph G, a state p, and an argument w. For simplicity, we present the algorithm for the case where the expression of a synchronous transition always evaluates to a single object.

1. Let $P = Q = B = \{\}$.
2. Define the initial state p_0 such that $p_0[i, j, 0] = s_{0i}$ and $p_0[i, j, k] = Def_i(y_{ik})$.
3. Let $p = p_0$ and $P_i = \{p_0\}$ (p is a temporal variable).
4. For each object o_{ij}, for each transition $(p_{ij0}, s, g, f, a, st) \in T_i$, and for each argument $w \in Arg(f)$, do the following steps.
   (a) If the guard condition g is true, i.e., the expression $Eval_G[o_{ij}][p][w](g)$ is a value representing true, create a new state q with $q[m, n, 0]$ defined as follows:
      - If $m = i$ and $n = j$, then s.
      - If there exists a synchronous transition $(x, t_1, t_2) \in st$ such that the target object x is o_{mn}, i.e., the expression $Eval_G[o_{ij}][p][w](x)$ is a value representing o_{mn} and $p[m, n, 0] = t_1$, then t_2.
      - Otherwise, $p[m, n, 0]$.

      For all cases, $q[m, n, l]$ is defined as the value $Exec_G(o_{mn}, a, v_{ml})$.
   (b) Let $Q = \{(f, w)\} \cup Q$ and $R = \{(p, q, (f, w))\} \cup R$.
   (c) If $q \notin P$, let $P = \{q\} \cup P$ and $p = q$, and go to 4.
5. For each $p_i \in P$, let $b_i = \bigwedge_{j,k} AEval_G[o_{jk}][p_i](Assr_j)$ and $B = \{b_i\} \cup B$.

Model Checking: Cleared for Take Off

Darren Cofer

Rockwell Collins, Advanced Technology Center
400 Collins Rd. NE
Cedar Rapids, IA 52498
ddcofer@rockwellcollins.com

Abstract. The increasing popularity of model-based development tools and the growing power of model checkers are making it practical to use formal methods for verification of avionics software. This paper describes a translator framework that enables model checking tools to be easily integrated into a model-based development environment to increase assurance, reduce cost, and satisfy certification objectives. In particular, we describe how formal methods can be used to satisfy certification objectives of DO-178C/ED-12C, the soon-to-be-published guidance document for software aspects of certification for commercial aircraft.

Keywords: model checking, verification, certification, avionics.

1 Introduction

Modern commercial aircraft contain millions of lines of complex software, much of it performing functions that are critical to safe flight. This software must be verified to function correctly with the highest levels of assurance, and aircraft manufacturers must demonstrate evidence of correctness through a rigorous certification process. Furthermore, the size and complexity of the on-board software are rising exponentially. Current test-based verification methods are becoming more expensive and account for a large fraction of the software development cost. New approaches to verification are needed to cope effectively with the software being developed for next-generation aircraft.

Formal analysis methods such as model checking permit software design models to be evaluated much more completely than is possible through simulation or test. This permits design defects to be identified and eliminated early in the development process, when they have much lower impact on cost and schedule. Advances in model checking technology, the adoption of model-based software development processes, and new certification guidance are enabling formal methods to be used by the aerospace industry for verification of software.

This paper provides an overview of our work applying model checking to the development of software for commercial and military aircraft. Model checking is being used to provide increased assurance of correctness, reduce development cost, and satisfy certification objectives. We also discuss the new certification guidance supporting the use of formal methods that will be included in DO-178C, the industry standard governing software aspects of aircraft certification.

J. van de Pol and M. Weber (Eds.): SPIN 2010, LNCS 6349, pp.76–87, 2010.

2 Model Checking and Model-Based Development

Model-based development (MBD) refers to the use of domain-specific modeling notations such as Simulink or SCADE to create detailed software designs that can be evaluated for desired behavior before a system is built. MBD environments allow the engineer to create a model of the system early in the lifecycle that can be executed on the desktop, analyzed for desired behaviors, and then used to automatically generate code and test cases. The emphasis in model-based development is to focus the engineering effort on the early lifecycle activities of modeling, simulation, and analysis, and to automate the later lifecycle activities of coding and testing.

Formal methods may be applied in a MBD process to eliminate requirements, design, and coding errors, and should be viewed as complementary to testing. While testing shows that functional requirements are satisfied for specific input sequences and detects some errors, formal methods can be used to increase confidence that a system will always comply with particular requirements when specific conditions hold. Informally we can say that testing shows that the software does work for certain test cases while formal methods show that it should work for all cases. It follows that some verification objectives may be better met by formal, analytical means and others might be better met by testing.

Although formal methods have significant technical advantages over testing for software verification, they are only just beginning to be used in the aerospace industry. The additional cost and effort of creating and reasoning about formal models in a traditional development process has been a significant barrier. Manually creating models solely for the purpose of formal analysis is labor intensive, requires significant knowledge of formal methods notations, and requires that models and code be kept tightly synchronized to justify the results of the analysis.

The value proposition for formal methods changes dramatically with the introduction of MBD and the use of automated analysis tools. Many of the notations in MBD have straightforward formal semantics. This means that it is possible to use models written in these languages as the basis for formal analysis, removing the incremental cost for constructing and updating separate verification models.

In collaboration with the University of Minnesota under NASA's Aviation Safety Program, Rockwell Collins has developed a translation framework that bridges the gap between some of the most popular industrial MBD languages and several model checkers (Fig. 1). These automated tools allow us to quickly and easily generate models for verification directly from the design models produced by the MBD process [1]. The counterexamples generated by model checking tools can be translated back to the MBD environment for simulation. This tool infrastructure provides the means for integration of formal methods directly and efficiently into the MBD process. Software engineers can continue to develop design models using the tools that they are already familiar with.

The translators use the Lustre formal specification language, developed by the synchronous language research group at Verimag, as an intermediate representation for the models [2]. Models developed in Simulink, StateFlow, or SCADE are transformed into Lustre. Once in Lustre, the specification is loaded into an abstract syntax tree (AST) and a number of transformation passes are applied to it. Each

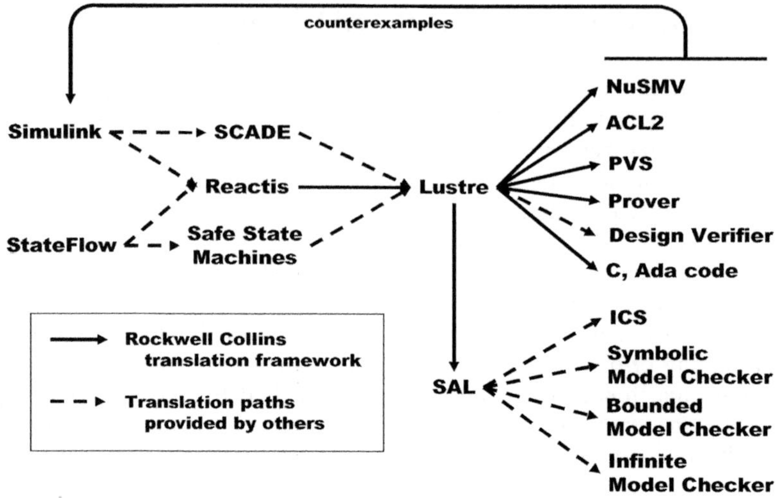

Fig. 1. Rockwell Collins translation framework

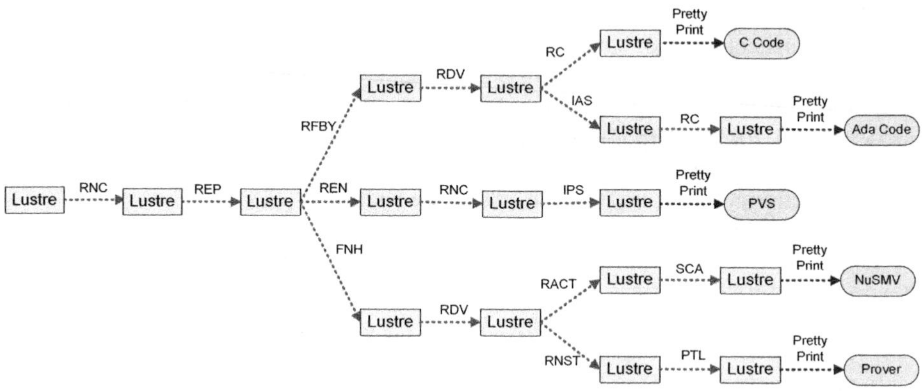

Fig. 2. Illustration of automated transformation steps used to translate Lustre models

transformation pass produces a new Lustre AST that is syntactically closer to the target specification language and preserves the semantics of the original Lustre specification (Fig. 2). This allows all Lustre type checking and analysis tools to be used after each transformation pass. When the AST is sufficiently close to the target language, a pretty printer is used to output the target specification. This customized translation approach allows us to select the model checker whose capabilities are best suited to the model being analyzed, and to generate an analysis model that has been optimized to maximize the performance of the selected model checker.

Since Lustre is the underlying language for SCADE models, the initial translation step is immediate. For Simulink and StateFlow models, we use the Reactis test case generator tool to support the initial translation step. We also use the Reactis simulator as the primary means for playback of the counterexample test cases. To ensure that each Simulink or Stateflow construct has a well-defined semantics, the translator restricts the models that it will accept to those that can be translated unambiguously into Lustre.

Our translation framework is currently able to target eight different formal analysis tools. Most of our work has focused on the NuSMV model checker and the Prover model checker. We can also use the same translation framework to generate C or Ada source code.

3 Benefits of Model Checking

The potential benefits of using formal methods, including model checking, are well-known. In this section we focus on three benefits and how they relate to the aerospace industry.

The traditional justification for the use of formal methods has been to provide increased assurance of correctness, especially for systems or components that implement safety-critical functions. Model checking excels in this area, providing comprehensive exploration of system behavior and exposure of design errors.

However, the strongest motivation for adoption of model checking in the industry seems much more likely to be cost reduction. The ability to detect and eliminate defects early in the development process has a clear impact on downstream costs. Errors are much easier and cheaper to correct in the requirements and design phases than during subsequent implementation and integration phases.

An additional benefit which may become increasingly important is the ability to satisfy certification objectives through the use of formal methods, including model checking. As the first two benefits have been described in detail elsewhere, we will touch on these briefly and devote most of the remainder of the paper to the use of formal methods as part of the certification process.

3.1 Increased Assurance

Model checking performs a comprehensive evaluation of system behavior over all reachable states and allowable inputs. This provides much more effective error discovery capability compared with testing.

As an illustration, in the Certification Technologies for Flight Critical Systems (CerTA FCS) project funded by the U.S. Air Force, we analyzed several software components of an adaptive flight control system for unmanned aircraft [3]. In this project we analyzed the redundancy manager software which implements a triplex voting scheme for fault-tolerant sensor inputs. We performed a head-to-head comparison of verification technologies with two separate teams, one using testing and one using model checking. Neither team communicated directly with the other, and both teams started with identical software models and requirements to be verified.

Both teams developed extensions to their base verification technologies. The model checking team extended their existing tools to add support for several new block types found in the software. Likewise, the testing team also made comparable investments in enhancing their testing environment. These one time, non-recurring costs were not included in the final comparison of the effectiveness of testing and model checking.

The model checking team developed a total of 62 properties for analysis from the original software requirements. Analysis of these properties with the model checker uncovered 12 errors in the redundancy management logic. In similar fashion, the testing team developed a series of tests cases from the same set of software requirements. However, testing failed to find any errors in the software.

The conclusion of both teams was that in this case study, model checking was more effective than testing in finding design errors. Some of the errors found by the model checking team would be difficult, if not impossible, to discover through testing. For example one such error involved a complex timing interaction between the inputs to the voter which resulted in a good sensor being declared faulty.

3.2 Reduced Cost

A key benefit of using model checking in an industrial context turns out to be cost savings. Savings can be achieved through early detection and elimination of errors as well as through automation.

Our first application of model checking to an actual product was the mode logic of the Rockwell Collins FCS 5000 Flight Control System used in business and regional jet aircraft [4]. The mode logic determines which lateral and vertical flight modes are armed and active at any time. Analysis of an early specification of the mode logic found 26 errors. Seventeen of these were found by the model checker. Of these 17 errors, 13 were classified by the FCS 5000 engineers as being possible to be missed by traditional verification techniques such as testing and inspections. One was classified as being unlikely to be found by traditional techniques. The ability to eliminate these errors during modeling, as opposed to during testing in the lab (or worse, during aircraft integration testing) results in significant savings.

In a more recent example, we used our translation and model checking tools to analyze the leader selection software for a multi-node redundant flight control system. The selection logic was implemented using Simulink/Stateflow and its basic functionality validated through simulation. The design was then analyzed using model checking and improved to eliminate the counterexamples identified. The verified design was then autocoded and tested on prototype hardware. The implementation achieved 100% successful test case passage on the first attempt. Eliminating the need for rework cycles to correct errors found during lab testing may have reduced development time by half.

In the CerTA FCS project discussed above, we discovered that not only was model checking more thorough, it was actually less costly than verification through testing. The testing team required 50% more time to develop and execute the required test cases compared to the time needed to formalize properties and analyze them with the model checker. Certainly this may not always be the case, but this experiment demonstrates that the degree of automation possible in an MBD environment makes it possible to perform model checking very efficiently.

3.3 Certification Credit

A third benefit of using formal methods is the evidence that can be provided in satisfaction of certification objectives. Certification can be defined as legal recognition by a certification authority (usually governmental) that a product, service, organization, or person complies with specified requirements. In the context of commercial aircraft, certification consists primarily of convincing the relevant certification authority (the FAA in the U.S. or EASA in Europe) that all required steps have been taken to ensure the safety, reliability, and integrity of the aircraft. Software itself is not certified in isolation, but only as part of an aircraft. Certification differs from verification in that it focuses on evidence provided to a third party to demonstrate that the required activities were performed completely and correctly, rather on performance of the activities themselves.

For software in commercial aircraft, the relevant certification guidance is found in DO-178B, "Software Considerations in Airborne Systems and Equipment Certification" (known in Europe as ED-12B) [5]. Certification authorities in North American and Europe have agreed that an applicant (aircraft manufacturer) can use this guidance as a means of compliance with the regulations governing aircraft certification.

The original version of the document, DO-178, was approved in 1982 and consisted largely of a description of "best practices" for software development. It was revised in 1985 as DO-178A, adding definitions of three levels of software criticality, with development and verification processes described in more detail. The current version, DO-178B, was approved in 1992. It defines five levels of software criticality (A – E) with specific objectives, activities, and evidence required for each level.

DO-178B allows for the use of formal methods to satisfy certification objectives, but it does so as an "Alternative Method." The processes and objectives in the document assume a traditional development process with test-based verification.

In 2005, RTCA and EUROCAE (the publishers of the DO-178/ED-12 standards) initiated work on a revision to be known as DO-178C/ED-12C. A committee (SC-205) was chartered to draft the new document, with the objectives of minimizing changes to the core document, yet updating it to accommodate approximately 15 years of progress in software engineering. Guidance specific to new software technologies was to be contained in "supplements" which could add, modify, or replace objectives in the core document. New supplements are being developed in the areas of tool qualification, object oriented design, model-based development, and formal methods. The current schedule calls for DO-178C to be approved by the end of 2010.

The inclusion of formal methods as a means of compliance with its own technology supplement (rather than an "alternative method") will open the door to aircraft manufacturers obtaining certification credit through the use of formal verification techniques including model checking. In the next section we describe the new certification guidance related to the use of formal methods.

4 DO-178C: New Certification Guidance

DO-178B does not prescribe a specific development process, but instead identifies important activities and design considerations throughout a development process and defines objectives for each of these activities. It assumes a traditional development process producing a collection of lifecycle data items that can be decomposed as follows:

- Software Requirements Process. Develops High Level Requirements (HLR) from the output of the system design process.
- Software Design Process. Develops Low Level Requirements (LLR) and Software Architecture from the HLR.
- Software Coding Process. Develops source code from the software architecture and the LLR.
- Software Integration Process. Combines executable object code modules with the target hardware for hardware/software integration.

The lifecycle data items and the processes that accomplish these transformations are shown in Fig. 3. The results of these processes are verified through the verification process. The verification process consists of review, analysis, and test activities that must provide evidence of the correctness of the development activities. The arcs in Fig. 3 correspond to verification activities and the labels identify the objectives for each activity. In addition, there are "verification of verification" objectives (not shown in the figure) to demonstrate the sufficiency of the verification activities themselves.

In general, verification has two complementary objectives. One objective is to demonstrate that the software satisfies its requirements. The second objective is to demonstrate with a high degree of confidence that errors which could lead to unacceptable failure conditions, as determined by the system safety assessment process, have been removed. As discussed in Section 3, formal methods can be used to meet these objectives – sometimes better than reviews or testing.

In drafting the Formal Methods Technology Supplement (FMTS) for DO-178C the committee had the following goals:

- Identify scope of applicability formal methods. Formal methods should no longer be treated as an "alternative method." Guidance should be provided regarding which objectives can be satisfied through formal methods and how that might be done. The focus of FMTS is the verification process and associated activities and objectives. Partial use of formal methods is acceptable (applied to only some software, some requirements, or some objectives).
- Facilitate communication between applicants and certification authorities. FMTS should specify what evidence should be expected for satisfying objectives, what new process documentation is needed, and what additional or different activities are needed when using formal methods.
- Identify areas deserving of particular scrutiny when formal methods are used. FMTS should help to avoid common errors, and identify important questions that must be addressed during certification.
- Facilitate use of formal methods in the aerospace community. FMTS should not impose higher burdens than a traditional verification process, but it should also not do anything that would reduce the level of assurance provided by DO-178B.

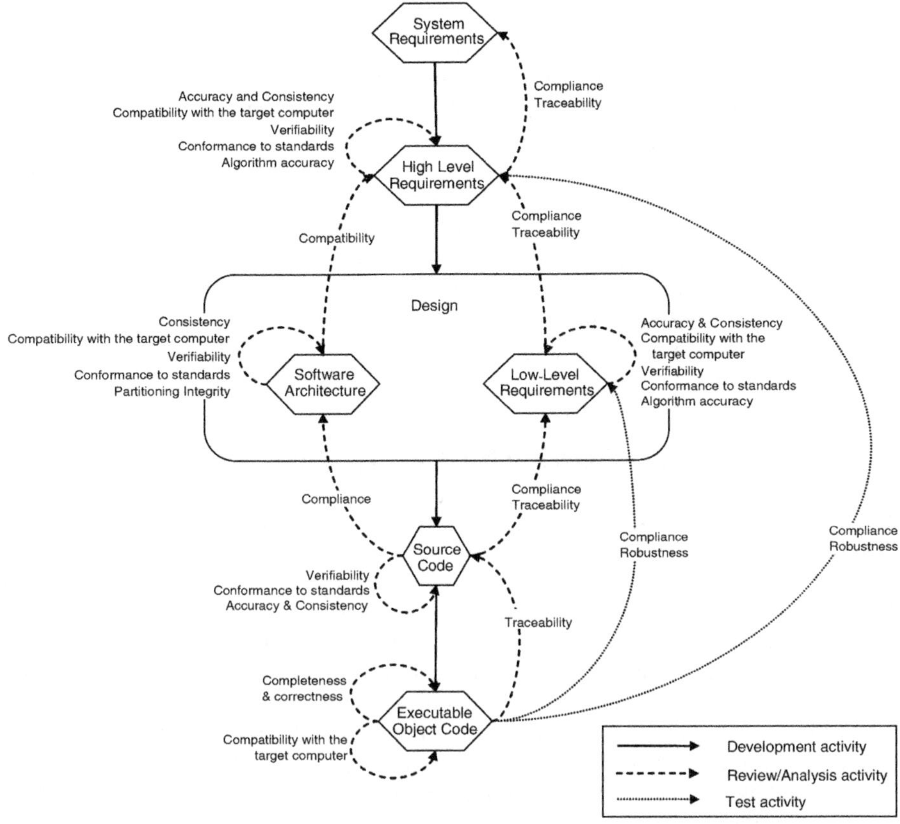

Fig. 3. DO-178 software development and verification activities

General guidance is provided in FMTS that is applicable to the overall verification process when formal methods are used. This includes the following requirements:

- All formal notations used must have unambiguous, mathematically defined syntax and semantics.
- The soundness of each formal analysis method should be documented. A sound method never asserts that a property is true when it may not be true.
- All assumptions related to the formal analysis should be described and justified (e.g. assumptions about execution semantics on the target computer, or assumptions about data range limits).

Specific guidance is provided to describe how formal methods can be used to satisfy each of the common objectives for HLR and LLR shown in Fig. 3. These include compliance with requirements, accuracy and consistency of requirements, compatibility with the target computer, verifiability of requirements, conformance to standards, traceability between lifecycle data items, and algorithmic correctness.

A new objective to demonstrate requirements formalization correctness is defined. If a requirement has been translated to a formal notation as the basis for using a formal analysis, then review or analysis should be performed to demonstrate that the formal statement is a conservative representation of the informal requirement.

In addition, there is provision for some software testing to be replaced by formal analysis. DO-178B requires that test cases corresponding to the software requirements be produced and executed, and that adequacy (completeness) of these test cases be determined via structural coverage metrics. When using formal methods, verification is exhaustive so a requirement that has been verified formally has been completely covered. However, there is no guarantee that some requirement has not been omitted from the design. Four new objectives have been defined in the DO-178C FMTS to provide an equivalent level of assurance with regard to the adequacy of the formal verification activity.

5 Example: Model Checking for Certification Credit

In this section we show by means of an example how model checking could be used to satisfy some of the certification objectives in DO-178C with the FMTS.

In a modern aircraft, the primary way that aircraft status information is displayed to pilots is through computerized display panels. These display panels are designed to replace the dozens of mechanical switches and dials found in earlier aircraft and to present a unified and straightforward interface to critical flight information. The display panels are configurable to allow pilots to select different information for display, including navigational maps, aircraft system status, and flight checklists. However, some information is considered critically important and must always be displayed.

The Window Manager (WM) determines which applications should be displayed on which display area as well as the location of the cursor on the displays. It has several responsibilities related to routing information to the displays. First, the WM must update which applications are being displayed in response to user selections of display applications. Second, the WM must handle hardware or application failures. If a display fails, the WM decides which information is most critical and moves this information to the remaining display. Another responsibility has to do with cursor management: some display applications support the cursor while others do not. It is the responsibility of the WM to ensure that the cursor does not appear on a display that contains an application that does not support the cursor. In the event of a failure, the WM must ensure that the cursor is not tasked to a dead display. A top-level model of a simplified Window Manager is shown in Fig. 4.

The WM is essential to the safe flight of an airplane. If the WM contains logic errors, it is possible that critical flight information will be unavailable to the flight crew. Hence it is required to meet the Level A objectives of DO-178B.

The WM verification effort [6] was conducted several years ago, before any consideration of incorporation of formal methods guidance in DO-178C. At that time, the primary objective was to identify and remove design errors early in the development process. The comprehensive analysis provided by model checking resulted in a higher assurance of correct behavior than test-based verification. Detection and correction of errors earlier in the development process (during design rather than test and integration) reduced the overall development cost.

The WM software was developed using a MBD process consisting of the following major activities:

- HLRs were initially expressed as English "shall" statements that were subsequently formalized as CTL for analysis.
- Software models were developed using model-based design tools (Simulink and Stateflow), and correspond to LLRs.
- The LLR models were analyzed using a model checker to verify whether or not they satisfy the HLRs.
- Source code was automatically generated from the LLRs and tested in conformance with a conventional test-based process.

Approximately 90% of the functional behavior of the WM application (in terms of the number of Simulink blocks) was verified using model checking. The remaining 10% of the model is in one subsystem that contains a significant number of floating point variables. This subsystem does not contain much mode-specific behavior and was verified using conventional methods.

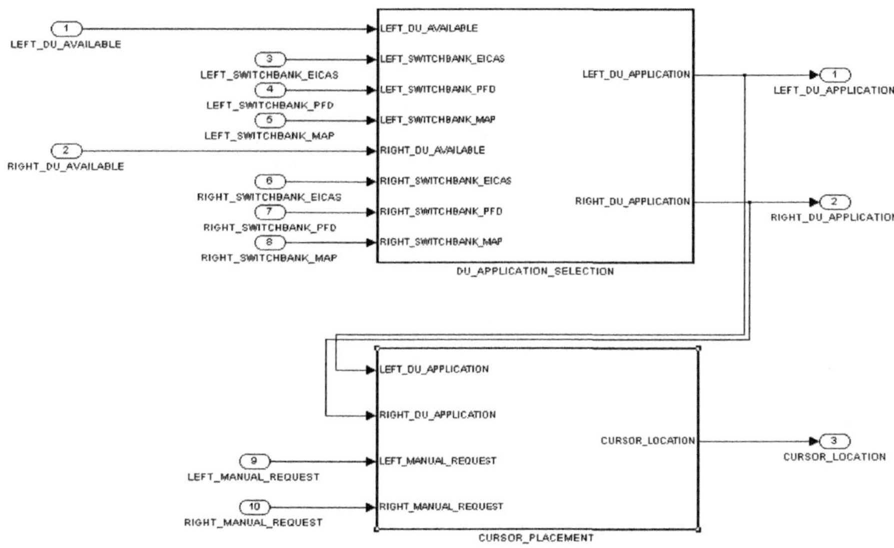

Fig. 4. Top-level Simulink model of a simplified Window Manager

The WM was divided into five subsystem models that were used for analyzing its behavior. Table 1 provides an overview of these subsystems and the analysis results.

The above results show that formal analysis can be applied to large commercial software systems. The 98 errors found resulted in changes to the LLR models or changes to the HLRs. The corrected HLRs and LLRs were re-analyzed and found to be compliant.

Table 1. Window Manager analysis results

Subsystem	Simulink Diagrams	Simulink Blocks	State Space	Properties	Errors found
GG	2,831	10,669	9.8×10^{9}	43	56
PS	144	398	4.6×10^{23}	152	10
CM	139	1,009	1.2×10^{17}	169	10
DUF	879	2941	1.5×10^{37}	115	8
MFD	302	1,100	6.8×10^{31}	84	14
Totals	**4295**	**16,117**	**n/a**	**563**	**98**

The formal methods technology developed in the project was successfully transitioned to the product development organization. By the end of the project, all analysis work was being performed by Rockwell Collins software engineers, with minimal assistance from researchers.

With the new guidance provided in the Formal Methods Technology Supplement to DO-178C, many certification objectives could have been satisfied. Some examples follow.

FM6.2 Software Verification Process Activities

a. Formal notations: Properties to be verified were specified in CTL. Formal definition of CTL may be found in [7]. The models analyzed were specified in Simulink and Stateflow. These models were given formal definition through the translation process, which includes a formal syntax and translation rules for each model element.

b. Soundness: The BDD and SAT algorithms used in the model checker are known to be sound. Details of the BDD algorithm used for model checking and its soundness can be found in [8]. Application of satisfiability solving to the model checking problem and its soundness are described in [9].

c. Assumptions: Any assumptions on the subsystem inputs necessary for the analysis were documented and justified.

FM6.3 Software Reviews and Analysis

i. Requirement formalization correctness: In this project, all requirements were captured and managed using the DOORS tool. For each requirement, the corresponding formalization was captured in DOORS with one or more CTL statements. Multiple independent reviews were conducted to ensure that the CTL statements accurately described the original English-language requirement.

FM6.3.1 Reviews and Analyses of the High-Level Requirements

d. Verifiability of HLR: The ability to express the high-level requirements for the system in CTL is a sufficient demonstration of verifiability in this example.

e. Conformance to standards: Requirements that do not conform to the standard for CTL syntax will be identified and rejected by the analysis tools. This feature of the tool would need to be qualified. Alternatively, conformance to CTL syntax can be easily checked by a manual review.

FM6.3.2 Reviews and Analyses of the Low-Level Requirements

a. Compliance with HLR: Analysis by model checking demonstrated that low-level requirements (the system model) complied with high-level requirements. This feature of the model checking tool would need to be qualified.

6 Conclusion

Adoption of model-based development methods is facilitating the use of model checking for verification of software in commercial aircraft. Model checking can provide increased assurance of correctness, reduced development costs, and (in the near future) satisfaction of certification objectives. Further research is needed to expand the range of models where model checking can be effectively applied. New analysis methods are needed to handle larger data types, floating point numbers, and non-linear functions.

Acknowledgments

The model checking and translation work described in this paper was accomplished with Steven Miller and Lucas Wagner from the Rockwell Collins ATC Automated Analysis group, and Michael Whalen and Mats Heimdahl from the University of Minnesota. The work was supported in part by the NASA Langley Re-search Center under contract NCC-01001 of the Aviation Safety Program (AvSP) and by the Air Force Research Lab under contract FA8650-05-C-3564 of the CerTA FCS program. The Formal Methods Technology Supplement for DO-178C has been developed by the Formal Methods Subgroup (SG6) of RTCA committee SC-205. Thanks to all.

References

1. Miller, S., Whalen, M., Cofer, D.: Software Model Checking Takes Off. Communications of the ACM 53(2), 58–64 (2010)
2. Halbwachs, N., Caspi, P., Raymond, P., Pilaud, D.: The synchronous dataflow programming language LUSTRE. Proceedings of the IEEE, 1305–1320 (1991)
3. Whalen, M., Cofer, D., Miller, S., Krogh, B., Storm, W.: Integration of Formal Analysis into a Model-Based Software Development Process. In: Leue, S., Merino, P. (eds.) FMICS 2007. LNCS, vol. 4916, pp. 68–84. Springer, Heidelberg (2008)
4. Miller, S., Anderson, E., Wagner, L., Whalen, M., Heimdahl, M.: Formal Verification of Flight Critical Software. In: AIAA Guidance, Navigation and Control Conference and Exhibit, San Francisco (2005)
5. DO-178B/ED-12B: Software Considerations in Airborne Systems and Equipment Certification. RTCA/EUROCAE (1992)
6. Whalen, M., Innis, J., Miller, S., Wagner, L.: ADGS-2100 Adaptive Display & Guidance System Window Manager Analysis. NASA Contractor Report CR-2006-213952 (2006)
7. Huth, M., Ryan, M.: Logic in Computer Science: Modelling and Reasoning about Systems, 2nd edn. Cambridge University Press, Cambridge (2004)
8. McMillan, K.L.: Symbolic Model Checking. Kluwer Academic Publishers, Dordrecht (1993)
9. Clarke, E.M., Biere, A., Raimi, R., Zhu, Y.: Bounded model checking using satisfiability solving. Formal Methods in System Design 19(1), 7–34 (2001)

Context-Enhanced Directed Model Checking

Martin Wehrle and Sebastian Kupferschmid

University of Freiburg
Department of Computer Science
Freiburg, Germany
{mwehrle, kupfersc}@informatik.uni-freiburg.de

Abstract. Directed model checking is a well-established technique to efficiently tackle the state explosion problem when the aim is to find error states in concurrent systems. Although directed model checking has proved to be very successful in the past, additional search techniques provide much potential to efficiently handle larger and larger systems. In this work, we propose a novel technique for traversing the state space based on *interference contexts*. The basic idea is to preferably explore transitions that interfere with previously applied transitions, whereas other transitions are deferred accordingly. Our approach is orthogonal to the model checking process and can be applied to a wide range of search methods. We have implemented our method and empirically evaluated its potential on a range of non-trivial case studies. Compared to standard model checking techniques, we are able to detect subtle bugs with shorter error traces, consuming less memory and time.

1 Introduction

When model checking safety properties of large systems, the ultimate goal is to prove the system correct. However, for practically relevant systems this is often not possible because of the state explosion problem. Complementary to verify a system correct, finding reachable *error states* is a potentially easier task in practice. An error state can be found by only exploring a small fraction of the entire reachable state space. Especially for this purpose, directed model checking has found much attention in recent years [1,2,3,4,5,6,7,8,9]. Directed model checking is tailored to the fast detection of reachable error states. This is achieved by focusing the state space traversal on those parts of the state space that show promise to contain reachable error states. A heuristic function is used to assign each state that is encountered during the traversal of the state space a heuristic value. Typically, a heuristic function approximates a state's distance to a nearest error state. These values are used to determine which state to explore next. An advantage of directed model checking is that the heuristic functions are usually abstraction based and computed fully automatically based on the declarative description of the system. Usually, distance heuristics are computed by solving a simplified problem, and then using the length of the abstract error trace as an estimation for the actual error distance in the concrete. They differ in the way of how the given problem is simplified. Overall, the performance of directed model checking has proved to be often much better than the performance of uninformed search methods like breadth-first or depth-first search. However, for large systems, even error detection is very challenging.

J. van de Pol and M. Weber (Eds.): SPIN 2010, LNCS 6349, pp. 88–105, 2010.

To cope with larger and larger systems, additional techniques to tackle the state explosion problem are needed. Among these, approaches that additionally evaluate the relevance of *transitions*, rather than just states, are very promising. Such methods have proved to further alleviate the state explosion problem as the additional information improves the search guidance. As a consequence, the number of states that have to be explored before an error state is encountered can be significantly reduced in practice. Techniques following this approach have first been proposed in the areas of AI planning and directed model checking. For instance, *helpful actions* [10], *preferred operators* [11], and *useless transitions* [12,13] are powerful instantiations of this paradigm. All these techniques have in common that they label applicable transitions with a Boolean flag. This flag indicates whether a transition is relevant or not. States that are reached by a relevant transition are preferred during the traversal of the state space. Another technique that exploits certain properties of transitions is *iterative context-bounding* [14]. This algorithm was proposed in software model checking for error detection in multithreaded programs. The algorithm searches for error traces that exhibit a minimal number of *context switches*, i. e., execution points where the scheduler forces the active thread to change. Transitions that do not induce a context switch are preferred. We will detail these approaches in the section on related work.

In this paper, we introduce context-enhanced directed model checking. Roughly speaking, the main idea of this approach is the following: If there is a transition t that is part of a shortest error trace π, then there often is a subsequent transition in π that *profits* from t. Therefore, we propose to preferably explore states that have been reached by a transition that profits from the effect of the previously applied transition. As a consequence, the search process avoids "jumping" while traversing the state space, i. e., it prefers transitions that belong to the same part of the system. We use the notion of *interference context* to determine how much a transition profits from the execution of another transition. With the above mentioned approaches, our technique shares the property that it labels transitions and defers the expansion of states reached by less relevant transitions. In contrast to these approaches, our method does not assign a Boolean flag to a transition, but an integer value. Our approach is embedded in a multi-queue search algorithm that is well-suited to respect the different levels of relevance. Another distinguishing property is that our approach can also be successfully applied to uninformed search, which is not possible with the other approaches, except for iterative context bounding. We have implemented our approach and applied it to uninformed search as well as directed model checking with several distance heuristics from the literature. We also compare our technique with the useless transitions approach as well as iterative context bounding as outlined above. The experiments reveal that our approach scales much better than the previous approaches in many challenging problems coming from real-world case studies.

The remainder of this paper is organized as follows. Section 2 introduces the preliminaries for this work. In the subsequent section, we introduce context-enhanced directed model checking. Afterwards, in Sec. 4, we discuss related work. In the following section, we empirically evaluate our approach on a number of benchmarks and compare it with plain directed model checking as well as previously proposed techniques for prioritizing transitions. Section 6 concludes the paper and discusses future work.

2 Preliminaries

In this section, we give the preliminaries needed for this work. In Sec. 2.1, we introduce our notation and computational model. This is followed by an introduction to directed model checking in Sec. 2.2.

2.1 Notation

Our approach is applicable to a broad class of transition systems, including parallel systems with interleaving, synchronization and linear arithmetic. We only require that the transitions resemble *guarded commands*, i. e., a transition consists of a *precondition* and an *effect*. Therefore, we define our computational model in a general way, consisting of a finite set of bounded integer variables V and a finite set of *transitions* T. For the sake of presentation, we restrict the form of transitions as stated in the next definition.

Definition 1 (System). *A system $\mathcal{M}$ is a tuple $\langle V, T\rangle$, where V is a finite set of bounded integer variables and T is a finite set of transitions. A transition t is a tuple $\langle pre, eff\rangle$, where*

- *pre is the precondition of t. It is a conjunction over constraints of the form $v \bowtie c$, where $v \in V$, $c \in \mathbb{Z}$ and $\bowtie \in \{<, \leq, =, \geq, >\}$.*
- *eff is the effect of t. It is a set of assignments of the form $v := c$, where $v \in V$ and $c \in \mathbb{Z}$.*

For a transition $t = \langle pre, eff\rangle$, we denote its precondition and effect with $\mathrm{pre}(t)$ and $\mathrm{eff}(t)$, respectively. A *system state* is a function that assigns each variable $v \in V$ a value of v's domain. A transition t is *applicable* in a state s if t's precondition is satisfied by s, i. e., if $s \models \mathrm{pre}(t)$. The successor state $s' = t(s)$ reached by applying t in s is obtained by updating all variables according to the effect of t. Formally, the state space of a system is defined as follows.

Definition 2 (State space of a system). *Let $\mathcal{M} = \langle V, T\rangle$ be a system. The state space of $\mathcal{M}$ is defined as a transition system $\mathcal{T}(\mathcal{M}) = (S, \Delta)$, where S is a set of states and $\Delta \subseteq S \times T \times S$ is a transition relation. There is a transition $(s, t, s') \in \Delta$ iff $s \models \mathrm{pre}(t)$ and $s' = t(s)$.*

For transitions $(s, t, s') \in \Delta$, we will also write $s \xrightarrow{t} s'$. We define a model checking task as a system together with an initial state and a target formula describing the set of error states.

Definition 3 (Model checking task). *Let $\mathcal{M}$ be a system and $\mathcal{T}(\mathcal{M}) = (S, \Delta)$ be its state space. A model checking task is a tuple $\langle \mathcal{M}, s_0, \varphi\rangle$, consisting of a system $\mathcal{M}$, an initial state $s_0 \in S$ and a target formula φ. Target formulas have the same form as preconditions of transitions. The task is to find a sequence $\pi = t_1, \ldots, t_n$ of transitions, with $s_{i-1} \xrightarrow{t_i} s_i \in \Delta$ for $1 \leq i \leq n$ and $s_n \models \varphi$.*

Informally speaking, the target formula describes a set of states with an undesirable property, the so called *error states*. Therefore, we call a sequence π as defined in the last definition an *error trace*.

2.2 Directed Model Checking

In a nutshell, directed model checking is the application of heuristic search [15] to model checking. The main idea of directed model checking is to explore those parts of the state space first that show promise to contain reachable error states. As a consequence, it is possible to detect error states in systems whose entire state space is too huge for brute force methods. In directed model checking, the state space traversal is guided ("directed") towards error states based on specific criteria. Ideally, these guidance criteria are *automatically* extracted from the declarative description of the system under consideration by taking an abstraction thereof. Based on such an abstraction, a heuristic function h is computed that typically approximates a state's distance to a nearest error state. During the search process, h is used to assign each encountered state s a heuristic value $h(s)$. These values are used to influence the *order* in which states are explored, hereby completeness is *not* affected. Figure 1 shows a basic directed model checking algorithm.

```
function dmc(M, s0, φ, h):
    open = empty priority queue
    closed = ∅
    priority = evaluate(s0, h)
    open.insert(s0, priority)
    while open ≠ ∅ do:
        s = open.getMinimum()
        if s ⊨ φ then:
            return False
        closed = closed ∪ {s}
        for each transition t applicable in s do:
            s' = t(s)
            if s' ∉ closed ∪ open then:
                priority = evaluate(s', h)
                open.insert(s', priority)
    return True
```

Fig. 1. A basic directed model checking algorithm

The algorithm takes a model checking task $\langle \mathcal{M}, s_0, \varphi \rangle$ and a heuristic function h as input. It returns *False* if there is a reachable error state, i. e., a state that satisfies φ, otherwise it returns *True*. The state s_0 is the initial state of $\mathcal{M}$. The algorithm maintains a priority queue *open* which contains visited but not yet explored states. When *open.getMinimum* is called, *open* returns a minimum element, i. e., one of its elements with minimal priority value. States that have been expanded are stored in *closed*. Every state encountered during search is first checked if it satisfies φ. If this is not the case, its successors are computed. Every successor that has not been visited before is inserted into *open* according to its priority value. The *evaluate* function depends on the applied version of directed model checking, i. e., if applied with A* or greedy search (cf. [15,16]). For A*, *evaluate*(s, h) returns $h(s) + c(s)$, where $c(s)$ is the length of the path on which s was reached for the first time. For greedy search, it simply evaluates to

$h(s)$. When every successor has been computed and prioritized, the process continues with the next state from *open* with lowest priority value.

To be able to report found error traces, every state stores a pointer to its immediate predecessor state and transition. We finally remark that, depending on the implementation details of the used priority queue, depth-first search and breadth-first search are instances of the algorithm from Fig. 1 when h is the constant zero function.

3 Context-Enhanced Directed Model Checking

In this section, we introduce context-enhanced directed model checking which is based on *interference contexts*. To compactly describe the main idea of our approach, we need the notion of *innocence*. A transition t is innocent if for each state s where t is applicable, there is no constraint of the target formula φ that is satisfied by $\text{eff}(t)$. This means, if there is a conjunct c of φ so that $t(s) \models c$, then c was already satisfied by s. Note that, if the initial state of a system is not an error state, then only applying innocent transitions will never lead to error states.

The main idea of context-enhanced directed model checking is the following. Let s be a state and let t be an innocent transition enabled at s. If t is the first transition of a shortest error trace starting from s, then there must be applicable transitions at $s' = t(s)$ that *profit* from the effect of t. Otherwise t cannot be part of a shortest error trace. Hence, our algorithm focuses on transitions that belong to the same part of the system. In this work, we use *interference contexts* to determine whether a transition profits from a preceding transition.

3.1 Interference Contexts

Our notion of interference contexts is based on the well-known concept of interference. Similar to other work (for example, in the area of partial order reduction [17]), we use a definition that can be statically checked. Roughly speaking, two transitions interfere if they work on a common set of system variables. For a transition t, we will use the notation $\text{var}(\text{pre}(t))$ and $\text{var}(\text{eff}(t))$ to denote the set of variables occurring in the precondition and the effect of t, respectively.

Definition 4 (Interference). *Two transitions t_1 and t_2 interfere, iff at least one of the following conditions holds:*

1. $\text{var}(\text{eff}(t_1)) \cap \text{var}(\text{pre}(t_2)) \neq \emptyset$,
2. $\text{var}(\text{eff}(t_2)) \cap \text{var}(\text{pre}(t_1)) \neq \emptyset$,
3. $\text{var}(\text{eff}(t_1)) \cap \text{var}(\text{eff}(t_2)) \neq \emptyset$.

Informally, this means that two transitions interfere if one writes a variable that the other is reading, or both transitions write to a common variable. We next give a pruning criterion based on interference. To formulate this, we first define the notion of *interference contexts*. Roughly speaking, for a transition t and $n \in \mathbb{N}_0$, the interference context $C_n(t)$ contains all transitions for which there is a sequence of at most n transitions where successive transitions interfere.

Definition 5 (Interference Context). *Let $\langle V, T\rangle$ be a system, $t \in T$ be a transition and $n \in \mathbb{N}_0$. The interference context $C_n(t)$ is inductively defined as follows:*

$$C_0(t) = \{t\}$$
$$C_n(t) = C_{n-1}(t) \cup \{t' \in T \mid \exists t'' \in C_{n-1}(t) : t'' \textit{interferes with } t'\}$$

As we are dealing with finite transition systems, there exists a smallest $N \leq |T|$, so that $C_N(t) = C_{N+1}(t)$ for all transitions $t \in T$. We will denote this context with $C(t)$. Note that this context induces an equivalence relation on the set of system transitions T. It partitions T into subsets of transitions which operate on pairwise disjoint variables. Based on this notion, we now give a pruning criterion which is guaranteed to preserve completeness. Informally speaking, if a state is part of a shortest error trace and has been reached via an innocent transition t, then it suffices to only apply transitions from $C(t)$ at s.

Proposition 1. *Let $\langle \mathcal{M}, s_0, \varphi\rangle$ be a model checking task for a system $\mathcal{M} = \langle V, T\rangle$ and a target formula $\varphi = \bigwedge(v_i \bowtie c_i)$, where $\bowtie \in \{<, \leq, =, \geq, >\}$, $v_i \in V$ and $c_i \in \mathbb{Z}$. Let s be a state in $\mathcal{M}$ that is part of a shortest error trace from s_0 and has been reached by a transition sequence with last transition t. Further assume that t is innocent. Then there is a shortest error trace from s that starts with a transition from $C(t)$.*

Proof. As s is part of a shortest path from the initial state, and t is innocent, there is a shortest error trace π that starts in s which contains a transition t'_π that needs the effects of t, i. e., $\text{var}(\text{eff}(t)) \cap \text{var}(\text{pre}(t'_\pi)) \neq \emptyset$. Otherwise, t would not have been needed and s would not be part of a shortest error trace. We transform π into a shortest error trace π' so that the first transition in π' is contained in $C(t)$. Let $t_1, \ldots, t_n$ be the prefix of π so that t_n is the first transition in π that interferes with t, i. e., $t_1, \ldots, t_{n-1}$ do not interfere with t. Then π' is constructed by an inductive argument. If $n = 1$, i. e., t_1 interferes with t, then $\pi' = \pi$ as $t_1 \in C(t)$. For the induction step, let t_{n+1} be the first interfering transition with t. If t_{n+1} and t_n do not interfere, then they can be exchanged in π' as non-interfering transitions can be applied in any order, leading to the same state. If they do interfere, then by definition $t_n \in C(t)$, which proves the claim.

From Prop. 1, we can derive the following pruning criterion: If there is a shortest error trace from s that starts with a transition from $C(t)$, then all transitions that are not contained in $C(t)$ can be pruned, without losing completeness. Note that the condition for s to be on a shortest error trace can be assumed without loss of generality: If s is *not* part of a shortest error trace, *every* successor can be pruned.

In practice, this pruning criterion does not seem to fire very often: Benefits are only obtained if the system's transitions can be partitioned into at least two sets of transitions that operate on disjoint variables. In such cases, also compositional model checking is applicable. These concepts are known and by no means new. In fact, the pruning criterion can be seen as a version of compositional model checking, where completely independent parts of the system are handled individually. However, the formulation of Prop. 1 lends itself to a way of how to approximate the pruning criterion. This leads to the heuristic approach to prioritize transitions that we are introducing next.

3.2 The Context-Enhanced Search Algorithm

In this section, we describe how we approximate the pruning criterion. The basic idea is actually quite simple: Instead of considering the exact closure $C(t)$ of a transition t, we substitute it with the interference context $C_n(t)$ for some bound $n < N$, where N is the smallest number such that $C_N(t) = C(t)$ for all transitions $t \in T$. Suppose for a moment that we know how to choose a good value for n. Obviously, Prop. 1 does not hold anymore if we replace $C(t)$ with $C_n(t)$. As a consequence thereof, states that are reached via transitions that are not contained in $C_n(t)$ cannot be pruned without loosing completeness. The approximation therefore becomes a heuristic criterion for the *relevance* of transitions. Instead of pruning these states, we suggest to defer their expansion. This can be done by extending the search algorithm from Fig. 1 with a second open queue. States whose expansions we want to defer are inserted in this queue. All other states are inserted in the standard open queue. States from the second queue are only expanded if the standard open queue is empty. The question remains which value we should use for the parameter n. From Def. 5, we know that $C_i(t) \subseteq C_j(t)$ for all transitions t iff $i \leq j$. On the one hand, the higher the parameter, the better $C(t)$ is approximated. However, as we already argued (and also describe in the experimental section), the exact pruning criterion does not fire very often in practice. On the other hand, the lower the parameter the more missclassifications may occur, which hampers the overall performance of the model checking process.

Instead of choosing a constant parameter, we propose to use a multi-queue search algorithm that maintains $N + 1$ different open queues, where $N \in \mathbb{N}$ is defined as above. Overall, we obtain a family of open queues $q_0, \ldots, q_N$, where q_i is accessed (according to the given distance heuristic) iff $q_0, \ldots, q_{i-1}$ are empty, and q_i is not. The basic directed model checking algorithm from Fig. 1 can be converted into our multi-queue search method by replacing the standard open queue with a multi-queue and the corresponding accessing functions as given in Fig. 2. In these queues, states are maintained as follows.

```
function insert(s', priority):
    if t is innocent then:
        if t' ∉ C(t) then:
            prune s'
        else:
            determine smallest n ∈ ℕ such that t' ∈ C_n(t)
            q_n.insert(s', priority)
    else:
        q_0.insert(s', priority)

function getMinimum():
    determine smallest n such that q_n ≠ ∅
    return q_n.getMinimum()
```

Fig. 2. Multi-queue accessing functions for context-enhanced directed model checking

Let s be a state that was reached with transition t, and let $s' = t'(s)$ be the successor state of s under the application of the transition t'. If t is innocent and $t' \notin C(t)$, then we can safely prune s'. If t is innocent and $t' \in C(t)$, then the successor state s' is maintained in queue q_1 if $t' \in C_1(t)$, and maintained in q_i if $t' \in C_i(t)$ and $t' \notin C_{i-1}(t)$. If t is not innocent, then s' is stored in q_0.

According to the given distance heuristic, *getMinimum* returns a state with best priority from the queue q_i with minimal index i that is not empty. The multi-queue is empty iff all queues are empty. Obviously, our approach remains complete, as only the order in which the states are explored is influenced. The advantage of this multi-queue approach is that we do not have to find a good value for n, which strongly depends on the system. By always expanding states from the lowest non-empty queue, the algorithm also respects the quality of the estimated relevance.

4 Related Work

Directed model checking has recently found much attention, and various distance heuristics to estimate a state's distance to a nearest error state have been proposed in this context [1,2,3,4,5,6,7,8,9]. Given a declarative description of the system under consideration, these distance heuristics are usually computed fully automatically based on abstractions. Overall, directed model checking has been demonstrated to significantly outperform uninformed search methods like breadth-first or depth-first search.

To efficiently handle larger and larger systems, additional search enhancements have recently been proposed for directed model checking as well as for AI planning. In particular, techniques to additionally prioritize transitions (rather than only states) are very promising. In the area of AI planning, *helpful actions* [10] and *preferred operators* [11] have been proposed. Both approaches heuristically select transitions that should be preferred during search. However, these concepts are specifically designed for certain distance heuristics.

In the context of directed model checking, a similar approach called *useless transitions* has been proposed [13]. A transition is considered as useless in a state s if it does not start a shortest error trace from s. This criterion is approximated to identify such transitions, which are less preferred during the search. In this approach, the distance heuristic itself is used to estimate whether a transition is useless or not. Hence, the quality of this approach strongly depends on the informedness of the distance heuristic. Furthermore, combining this approach with uninformed search methods is not possible as no distance heuristic is applied there. Complementary to this, context-enhanced directed model checking is independent of the distance heuristic. As we shall see in the experimental section, our approach is successfully applicable to uninformed search.

Musuvathi and Qadeer work in the area of software model checking. They propose a technique for bug detection based on *context bounding* [14]. For multithreaded programs, they propose an algorithm that limits the number of *context switches*, i. e., the number of execution points on a trace where the scheduler forces the active thread to change. Their algorithm is actually a kind of iterative deepening search, where the number of context switches that may occur in each trace is increased in each iteration. They define a context essentially as a thread. In our work, a context switch in the sense of Musuvathi and Qadeer corresponds to two consecutive states s_i and s_{i+1}, where s_i is taken from q_n and s_{i+1} from q_m with $n < m$. We remark that our criterion is stricter than the one proposed by Musuvathi and Qadeer: Exploring a state from a queue with greater index corresponds to a context switch in the sense of Musuvathi and Qadeer, but not vice versa. Moreover, we handle the different levels of interference with a fine-grained multi-queue search algorithm. Musuvathi and Qadeer propose an algorithm that is guaranteed to minimize the number of context switches. Contrarily, our search algorithm does not necessarily minimize them, but performs better in systems with tight interaction of the processes.

Finally, partial order reduction techniques can also be considered as a technique for prioritizing transitions to overcome the state explosion problem [17,18,19]. Partial order reduction exploits the fact that independent transitions need not be considered in every ordering. It reduces the branching factor of the system by computing a subset of the applicable transitions that suffices to preserve completeness. Partial order reduction is orthogonal to our approach of interference contexts, and it will be interesting to investigate the combination of these techniques in the future.

5 Evaluation

We have implemented our algorithm based on interference contexts and empirically evaluate its potential on a range of problems, including academic benchmarks as well as large and practical relevant systems from industrial case studies. We evaluate our algorithm on a number of different search methods, including uninformed search as well as various heuristic search methods as proposed in the literature and implemented in our model checker MCTA [20].

5.1 Benchmark Set

All our benchmarks, including real-world problems from industrial case studies, stem from the AVACS[1] benchmark suite. Our benchmark systems consist of parallel automata with bounded integer variables, interleavings and binary synchronization. Some of them also feature clock variables and actually represent timed automata [21]. Currently, clock variables are ignored by our implementation. Note that all these formalisms are instantiations of our system definition.

The M and N examples come from a case study called "Mutual Exclusion". It models a real-time protocol to ensure mutual exclusion of a state in a distributed system via asynchronous communication. The protocol is described in full detail by Dierks [22]. The S examples ("Single-tracked Line Segment") stem from a case study from an industrial project partner of the UniForM-project [23] where the problem is to design a distributed real-time controller for a segment of tracks where trams share a piece of track. For the evaluation of our approach, we chose the property that both directions are never given simultaneous permission to enter the shared segment. In both case studies, a subtle error has been inserted by manipulating a delay so that the asynchronous communication between these automata is faulty. The F_i examples are versions of the Fischer protocol for mutual exclusion (cf. [24]). The index i gives the number of parallel automata. An error state is reached if two predefined automata are simultaneously

[1] Automatic Verification and Analysis of Complex Systems, `http://www.avacs.org/`

in a certain location. We made error states reachable by weakening one of the temporal conditions in the automata. As a final set of benchmarks, the H examples model the well-known Towers of Hanoi for a varying number of disks. The index of the examples gives the number of involved disks. Initially, all n disks are on the first peg; the goal is to move them all to the second peg, moving only one disk at a time and such that never a larger disk is on top of a smaller one.

5.2 Experimental Setting

We implemented our context-enhanced search algorithm (denoted with *CE* in the following) into our model checker MCTA [20]. All experiments have been performed on an AMD Opteron 2.3 GHz system with 4 GByte of memory. We set a timeout to 30 minutes. We apply *CE* to uninformed search as well as to directed model checking with various distance heuristics.

We compare to the (rather coarse) distance heuristics d^L and d^U [6] as well as to the (more informed) distance heuristics h^L and h^U [2]. All of them are implemented in MCTA. The d^L and d^U heuristics are based on the *graph distance* of automata; synchronization behavior and integer variables are ignored completely. The h^L and h^U heuristics are based on the *monotonicity abstraction*. Under this abstraction, variables can have multiple values simultaneously. The h^L heuristic performs a fixpoint iteration under this abstraction starting in the current state until an error state is reached, and returns the number of iterations as heuristic value. Based on this fixpoint iteration, h^U additionally extracts an abstract error trace starting from the abstract error state, and returns the number of abstract transitions as the estimate. Furthermore, we compare *CE* to various related search algorithms, including iterative context bounding (*ICB*) and the useless transitions approach (*UT*). As threads correspond to processes in our setting, we have implemented *ICB* with process contexts as proposed by Musuvathi and Qadeer [14], denoted with ICB_P. This means that a context switch occurs if two consecutive transitions belong to different processes. Moreover, we implemented *ICB* with our definition of interference contexts, denoted with ICB_I. Here, a context switch occurs if a transition t' does not belong to $C_n(t)$, where t is the preceding transition. After some limited experiments, we set the bound n to 2 because we achieved the best results in terms of explored states for this value. For larger values, no context switches occurred, and hence ICB_I behaves like greedy search. Finally, we also compare *CE* with a multi-queue version of the useless transitions approach [12]. In the tables, we denote this approach with *UT*.

5.3 Experimental Results

We give detailed results for a coarse distance heuristic based on the graph distance (d^U), for a more informed heuristic based on the monotonicity abstraction (h^L), as well as for breadth-first search as uninformed search method. Moreover, we additionally provide average performance results for depth-first search as well as for the distance heuristics d^L and h^U.

Let us start to discuss the results for *CE* with the d^U heuristic from Table 1. First, we observe that for the hard problems, the number of explored states with *CE* is

Table 1. Experimental results for greedy search with the d^U heuristic. Abbreviations: plain: greedy search, *CE*: greedy search + interference contexts, ICB_P: iterative context bound algorithm with process contexts, ICB_I: iterative context bound algorithm with interference contexts, *UT*: useless transitions. Dashes indicate out of memory (> 4 GByte) or out of time (> 30 min). Uniquely best results are given in bold fonts.

	explored states					runtime in s					trace length				
Exp.	plain	*CE*	ICB_P	ICB_I	*UT*	plain	*CE*	ICB_P	ICB_I	*UT*	plain	*CE*	ICB_P	ICB_I	*UT*
F_5	9	21	112	**8**	9	0.0	0.0	0.0	0.0	0.0	6	6	6	6	6
F_{10}	9	36	447	**8**	9	0.0	0.0	0.0	0.0	0.0	6	6	6	6	6
F_{15}	9	51	1007	**8**	9	0.0	0.0	0.0	0.0	0.0	6	6	6	6	6
S_1	11449	10854	44208	14587	**9796**	**0.0**	0.1	0.2	0.2	0.1	823	192	**59**	1022	842
S_2	33859	31986	163020	93047	**31807**	**0.1**	0.3	0.8	0.5	0.5	1229	223	**59**	134	1105
S_3	51526	**43846**	199234	80730	52107	**0.2**	0.3	1.1	0.5	0.8	1032	184	**59**	1584	1144
S_4	465542	**402048**	3.0e+6	1.8e+6	504749	**2.0**	2.1	18.0	8.6	7.5	3132	1508	**60**	783	5364
S_5	4.6e+6	**2.8e+6**	3.8e+7	2.4e+7	4.6e+6	22.6	**18.8**	256.9	136.8	70.6	14034	886	**65**	1014	14000
S_6	–	–	–	–	–	–	–	–	–	–	–	–	–	–	–
M_1	185416	**5360**	100300	56712	7557	156.4	0.1	2.5	1.1	0.1	106224	246	**65**	94	923
M_2	56240	**15593**	608115	82318	294877	1.1	**0.2**	22.5	1.7	67.1	13952	520	**63**	3378	51541
M_3	869159	**15519**	623655	281213	26308	1729.5	**0.2**	23.8	7.2	0.5	337857	562	**82**	3863	1280
M_4	726691	**21970**	3.4e+6	–	100073	428.0	**0.4**	221.3	–	1.8	290937	486	**80**	–	4436
N_1	10215	**5688**	92416	68582	19698	0.3	**0.1**	5.6	3.3	0.7	2669	162	**79**	109	1855
N_2	–	**11939**	645665	161800	96307	–	**0.3**	71.7	8.2	5.1	–	182	**75**	277	8986
N_3	–	**14496**	616306	417181	29254	–	**0.4**	62.4	25.8	1.2	–	623	**84**	1586	784
N_4	330753	**25476**	3.7e+6	889438	239877	23.0	**0.8**	760.8	91.6	17.8	51642	949	**89**	361	1969
H_3	**222**	279	1000	479	244	0.0	0.0	0.0	0.0	0.1	44	**32**	52	82	60
H_4	2276	2133	11726	7631	**545**	0.0	0.1	0.0	0.1	0.5	184	132	116	190	**92**
H_5	20858	**5056**	142359	116200	15435	**0.1**	0.2	0.3	0.4	13.9	708	**238**	266	422	400
H_6	184707	**122473**	1.5e+6	1.1e+6	130213	**0.6**	0.8	4.1	3.2	128.8	2734	1670	**522**	918	1242
H_7	1.6e+6	**876847**	1.5e+7	1.4e+7	1.2e+6	5.7	**5.4**	52.0	42.0	1267.7	11202	4456	**1136**	2100	3922
H_8	1.4e+7	**2.3e+6**	–	–	–	53.8	**17.1**	–	–	–	45280	**5666**	–	–	–
H_9	–	–	–	–	–	–	–	–	–	–	–	–	–	–	–

significantly better than with plain directed model checking as well as the other, related approaches. In the smaller instances (e. g., the F examples and the small S examples), the performance is comparable. Compared to plain directed model checking, we could also solve more problems when *CE* is applied. This mostly also pays off in better search time. Finally, the length of the found error trace is comparable in the F and the small H instances, but mostly much shorter than with plain directed model checking and the *UT* approach. Overall, when using d^U, we could significantly improve directed model checking with *CE*, and also outperformed related approaches in terms of scalability and error trace length.

The results for *CE* and the h^L heuristic are given in Table 2. First, we observe that *UT* performs much better with h^L than with d^U and often leads to the best configuration. As already outlined, *UT* uses the distance heuristic itself to estimate the quality of a transition. Hence, the performance of *UT* strongly depends on the quality of the applied distance heuristic. This also shows up in our experiments: *UT* performs best in the F and S examples. On the other hand, *CE* performs best in M, N and H, and only marginally worse than *UT* in most of the F and S problems. Moreover, *CE* scales

Table 2. Experimental results for greedy search with the h^L heuristic. Abbreviations as in Table 1.

	explored states					runtime in s					trace length				
Exp.	plain	*CE*	*ICB_P*	*ICB_I*	*UT*	plain	*CE*	*ICB_P*	*ICB_I*	*UT*	plain	*CE*	*ICB_P*	*ICB_I*	*UT*
F_5	179	21	112	216	**7**	0.0	0.0	0.0	0.0	0.0	12	6	6	12	6
F_{10}	86378	36	447	95972	**7**	3.3	0.0	0.0	3.8	0.0	22	6	6	22	6
F_{15}	–	51	1007	–	**7**	–	0.0	0.0	–	0.0	–	6	6	–	6
S_1	1704	4903	24590	1971	**1537**	0.0	0.2	0.4	0.1	0.1	84	68	**62**	77	76
S_2	3526	11594	81562	4646	**1229**	0.1	0.4	1.2	0.2	0.1	172	70	**62**	166	76
S_3	4182	5508	89879	6118	**1061**	0.1	0.3	1.4	0.2	0.1	162	73	**62**	109	76
S_4	29167	7728	1.2e+6	108394	**879**	0.7	0.5	14.1	1.2	**0.2**	378	198	**60**	653	77
S_5	215525	2715	1.4e+7	870603	**1116**	5.2	0.4	142.7	7.4	**0.3**	1424	85	**65**	2815	78
S_6	1.7e+6	9812	–	1.3e+7	**1116**	37.4	1.1	–	85.5	**0.4**	5041	130	–	8778	**78**
S_7	1.6e+7	15464	–	–	**1114**	332.5	2.0	–	–	**0.6**	15085	130	–	–	**78**
S_8	7.1e+6	2695	–	–	**595**	129.3	0.5	–	–	**0.3**	5435	81	–	–	**76**
S_9	9.6e+6	4.0e+6	–	–	**2771**	201.1	192.9	–	–	**1.3**	5187	1818	–	–	**94**
M_1	4581	**1098**	102739	3230	4256	0.1	**0.0**	3.1	0.1	0.2	457	89	**66**	433	97
M_2	15832	**1904**	605001	53206	7497	0.3	**0.0**	27.8	1.2	0.5	1124	123	**61**	113	104
M_3	**7655**	8257	622426	141247	10733	**0.1**	0.2	26.1	2.8	0.7	748	180	**86**	100	91
M_4	71033	18282	3.3e+6	525160	**16287**	1.6	**0.7**	239.8	14.5	1.7	3381	334	**81**	118	98
N_1	50869	**1512**	93750	74307	5689	39.0	**0.0**	7.2	59.9	0.3	26053	93	**79**	26029	108
N_2	30476	**2604**	634003	82158	22763	1.2	**0.1**	77.3	3.8	1.5	1679	127	**75**	97	259
N_3	11576	**10009**	607137	177899	35468	0.4	**0.4**	77.1	9.6	2.7	799	224	**86**	106	204
N_4	100336	**20248**	3.7e+6	971927	142946	5.3	**1.1**	755.6	103.2	14.9	2455	396	**85**	134	792
H_3	**127**	256	1017	164	190	0.0	0.0	0.0	0.0	0.0	48	48	48	86	62
H_4	2302	764	11830	7488	**620**	0.0	0.1	0.0	0.1	0.0	300	**94**	124	438	114
H_5	20186	**15999**	144668	121027	31553	**0.2**	0.4	0.5	0.6	1.2	1458	478	**252**	878	890
H_6	230878	**85947**	1.5e+6	1.5e+6	281014	2.2	**2.0**	5.8	5.8	13.4	7284	1350	**558**	2070	2766
H_7	2.0e+6	**622425**	1.5e+7	1.6e+7	2.7e+6	21.4	**17.9**	69.0	67.1	155.3	18500	14314	**1086**	5164	7176
H_8	1.8e+7	**2.1e+6**	–	–	–	206.8	**78.3**	–	–	–	**70334**	74594	–	–	–
H_9	–	–	–	–	–	–	–	–	–	–	–	–	–	–	–

significantly better than the iterative context bounding algorithm for both context definitions. Overall, we observe that *CE* performs similarly to directed model checking with h^L and useless transitions (also in terms of error trace length), and scales (often significantly) better than the other approaches.

We also applied our context enhanced search algorithm to uninformed search. The results for breadth-first are given in Table 3. First, we want to stress that breadth-first search is *optimal* in the sense that it returns shortest possible counterexamples. This is not the case for *CE*. However, the results in Table 3 show that the length of the found error traces by *CE* is mostly only marginally longer than the optimal one (around a factor of 2 in the worst case in S_1 and S_2, but mostly much better). Contrarily, the scaling behavior of *CE* is much better than that of breadth-first search. This allows us to solve two more problems on the one hand, and also allows us to solve almost all of the harder problems much faster. In particular, this shows up in the M and N examples, that could be solved within seconds with *CE* (compared to sometimes hundreds of seconds otherwise). Finally, we remark that *UT* is not applicable with breadth-first search, as no distance heuristic is applied. Overall, we conclude that if *short*, but not necessarily *shortest* error traces are desired, breadth-first search should be applied with *CE* because

Table 3. Experimental results for breadth-first search. Abbreviations as in Table 1.

	explored states				runtime in s				trace length			
Exp.	plain	*CE*	ICB_P	ICB_I	plain	*CE*	ICB_P	ICB_I	plain	*CE*	ICB_P	ICB_I
F_5	333	**29**	129	273	0.0	0.0	0.0	0.0	6	6	6	6
F_{10}	5313	**44**	484	3868	0.0	0.0	0.0	0.0	6	6	6	6
F_{15}	34068	**59**	1064	20538	0.4	0.0	0.0	0.3	6	6	6	6
S_1	41517	**19167**	50361	58379	0.1	0.1	0.2	0.3	54	109	59	54
S_2	118075	**52433**	181941	217712	0.4	**0.3**	0.8	0.9	54	109	59	54
S_3	149478	**33297**	230173	264951	0.5	**0.2**	1.1	1.1	54	71	59	54
S_4	1.3e+6	**146094**	3.5e+6	3.7e+6	5.4	**0.7**	18.7	16.2	55	67	60	55
S_5	1.1e+7	**569003**	4.6e+7	4.4e+7	49.8	**3.2**	258.5	227.3	56	73	56	56
S_6	–	**2.5e+6**	–	–	–	**16.2**	–	–	–	**74**	–	–
S_7	–	–	–	–	–	–	–	–	–	–	–	–
M_1	192773	**32593**	273074	116682	4.6	**0.4**	7.4	1.5	**47**	51	50	50
M_2	680288	**75159**	1.7e+6	1.6e+6	19.1	**1.1**	95.2	56.6	50	52	53	50
M_3	740278	**94992**	1.7e+6	1.7e+6	22.0	**1.6**	80.9	76.9	50	54	63	50
M_4	2.6e+6	**189888**	9.7e+6	8.0e+6	87.6	**3.5**	893.7	506.7	53	55	66	53
N_1	361564	**34787**	310157	157610	20.0	**0.7**	15.6	4.3	**49**	56	58	55
N_2	2.2e+6	**81859**	2.4e+6	3.9e+6	399.0	**1.8**	357.6	622.2	52	57	72	52
N_3	2.4e+6	**92729**	2.3e+6	4.2e+6	442.8	**2.5**	275.8	677.9	52	54	71	52
N_4	–	**201226**	–	–	–	**5.9**	–	–	–	**57**	–	–
H_3	448	**315**	1062	954	0.0	0.0	0.0	0.0	22	22	30	24
H_4	4040	**2689**	11702	7228	0.0	0.1	0.0	0.1	**52**	54	64	54
H_5	42340	**19158**	146955	121807	**0.1**	0.2	0.3	0.4	**114**	116	148	148
H_6	377394	**161747**	1.5e+6	1.2e+6	**0.7**	0.8	3.0	2.8	**240**	300	294	278
H_7	3.4e+6	**1.2e+6**	1.5e+7	1.3e+7	7.2	**5.3**	36.8	33.7	**494**	520	634	636
H_8	3.0e+7	**9.2e+6**	–	–	67.2	**44.0**	–	–	**1004**	1302	–	–
H_9	–	–	–	–	–	–	–	–	–	–	–	–

of the better scaling behavior of *CE* on the one hand, and the still reasonable short error traces on the other hand.

To get a deeper insight into the performance of our context enhanced search algorithm in practice, we report average results for our approach applied to various previously proposed heuristics in Table 4. For each heuristic as well as breadth-first and depth-first search, we average the data on the instances that could be solved by all configurations. Furthermore, we give the total number of solved instances.

First, we observe that also on average, *CE* compares favorably to plain directed model checking. The average number of explored states could (sometimes by an order of magnitude) be reduced, which mostly also pays off in overall runtime. Furthermore, except for breadth-first search which returns shortest possible counterexamples, the length of the error traces could be reduced. Compared to the related approaches ICB_P, ICB_I and *UT*, we still observe that the average number of explored states is mostly lower with *CE* (except for the median with *UT* for h^L and h^U). In almost all cases, the average runtime is still much shorter. Apart from breadth-first search, the shortest error traces are obtained with iterative context bounding. However, *CE* scales much better on average, and could solve the most problem instances in *every* configuration. Furthermore, the only configuration that could solve *all* instances is *CE* with the h^U heuristic.

Table 4. Summary of experimental results. Abbreviations: *DFS*: depth-first search, *BFS*: breadth-first search, average: arithmetic means, solved: number of solved instances (out of 27). Uniquely best results in bold fonts for each configuration. Other abbreviations as in Table 1.

	explored states		runtime in s		trace length		solved
	average	median	average	median	average	median	
BFS							
plain	1266489.9	277168.5	53.0	2.7	**78.3**	**52.0**	21
CE	**140644.4**	**43610.0**	**1.1**	**0.6**	91.9	55.5	**23**
ICB_P	4248527.1	291615.5	102.3	5.2	95.7	59.0	20
ICB_I	4133416.8	241331.5	111.5	2.2	89.7	53.5	20
DFS							
plain	445704.1	63712.5	3.6	0.5	37794.3	9624.5	21
CE	**197295.0**	**15688.0**	**1.1**	**0.2**	2308.8	795.5	**22**
ICB_P	3397688.6	409480.0	34.8	2.4	**148.7**	**71.0**	21
ICB_I	2371171.5	155694.0	12.9	1.5	16477.9	1819.5	21
d^U							
plain	469310.8	42692.5	107.9	0.3	30415.8	1949.0	20
CE	**245070.9**	**13186.5**	**1.6**	**0.2**	665.4	230.5	**22**
ICB_P	3503904.9	152689.5	63.8	1.8	**155.0**	**64.0**	21
ICB_I	2380880.4	81524.0	16.5	0.8	892.9	391.5	20
UT	394999.4	23003.0	87.6	0.6	4764.3	1124.5	21
d^L							
plain	701962.7	54742.0	14.9	0.5	16414.1	7725.0	21
CE	**189144.3**	**12181.0**	**1.3**	**0.2**	1391.6	562.0	**22**
ICB_P	2783118.2	199548.0	72.7	3.7	**100.6**	**67.0**	21
ICB_I	1918955.4	105246.0	17.5	0.9	2642.1	798.0	19
UT	344885.2	46509.0	23.8	1.4	13664.1	2521.0	20
h^L							
plain	143536.3	18009.0	4.1	0.4	3327.0	773.5	25
CE	**41090.5**	5205.5	**1.2**	0.3	917.8	108.5	**26**
ICB_P	2075198.1	374834.5	72.5	6.5	**150.5**	**70.5**	21
ICB_I	1052988.1	89065.0	14.1	2.0	1981.0	126.0	21
UT	164821.9	**4972.5**	9.7	0.3	657.8	97.5	25
h^U							
plain	138325.2	12938.0	3.1	0.3	419.6	112.0	26
CE	**22956.1**	6523.0	**1.0**	0.3	213.0	92.0	**27**
ICB_P	1953710.5	145351.0	73.7	7.3	**147.7**	**66.0**	21
ICB_I	965865.2	72437.0	12.7	1.6	302.1	116.0	21
UT	106837.0	**2537.0**	9.6	**0.2**	436.3	80.0	26

Finally, we also compared *CE* with the exact pruning criterion given by Prop. 1. However, it turned out that this exact criterion is very strict in practice, and did not fire in any case. This effectively means that the results for this criterion are the same as the results for plain search, except for a slightly longer runtime due to the preprocessing.

Overall, our evaluation impressively demonstrated the power of directed model checking with interference contexts and multiple open queues. We have observed that the overall model checking performance could (often significantly) be increased for various search methods and distance heuristics on a range of heuristics and real world problems. The question remains on which parameters the performance of the different search algorithms depend, and in which cases they perform best. We will discuss these points in the next section.

5.4 Discussion

Our context-enhanced search algorithm uses several open queues to handle the different levels of interference. In Table 5, we provide additional results about the number of queues and queue accesses for *CE* and *UT*, as well as the number of context switches for iterative context bounding. The data is averaged over all instances of the specific case study.

For our context enhanced search algorithm, we report the number of queues that are needed for the different problems, as well as the number of pushed and popped states of these queues. First, we observe that in the F examples, only one deferred queue (q_1) is needed, which is accessed very rarely. However, the situation changes in the S, M and N examples, where three deferred queues are needed. Deferred states are explored from up to two deferred queues (for d^U and breadth-first search), whereas the last (non-empty) deferred queue is never accessed. Most strikingly, in the H examples, we need six deferred queues, from which most of them are never accessed. Overall, the performance of *CE* also depends on the number of explored deferred states. If there are deferred queues that never have to be accessed at all, the corresponding states do not have to be explored, and the branching factor of the system is reduced.

We applied the useless transitions approach in a multi-queue setting, where *useless* states, i. e., states reached by a useless transition, are maintained in a separate queue. Table 5 shows the number of explored non-useless states (q_0) as well as the number of explored useless states (q_1). We observe that for the well-informed h^L heuristic, q_1 is never accessed except for the H examples, which explains the good performance of *UT* in this case. However, for the coarser d^U heuristic, q_1 is accessed very often, which explains the favorable performance of *CE* over *UT* with d^U.

Finally, let us give some explanations of the performance of the iterative context bound algorithm *ICB* compared to *CE*. The *ICB* approach is guaranteed to minimize the number of context switches, and obviously performs best in systems where not many context switches are needed. Contrarily, if the context has to be switched n times, the whole state space for all context switches smaller than n has to be traversed until an error state is found, which could be problematic if n is high. Table 5 shows the average number n of context switches needed to find an error state in our examples.[2] We observe that, except for the F examples, n is pretty high for ICB_P. Contrarily, in the F examples where the context has to switched only two times, iterative context bounding performs very well. Overall, we conclude from our experiments that the method proposed by Musuvathi and Qadeer works well for programs with rather loose interaction where not many context switches are required. However, in protocols with tight interaction and many required changes of the active threads, directed model checking with interference contexts performs better.

---

[2] As a side remark, the different number of context switches for h^L, d^U and *BFS* with ICB_P and ICB_I are due to the different number of solved instances of these configurations.

Table 5. Average number of queue accesses (for queues $q_0, \ldots, q_6$) for *CE* and *UT*, and average number of context switches for *ICB* per case study. Number of pushed states at the top, number of popped states at the bottom. Abbreviations as in Table 1.

	Accesses with *CE*							Accesses with *UT*		Context Switches	
	q_0	q_1	q_2	q_3	q_4	q_5	q_6	q_0	q_1	ICB_P	ICB_I
h^L heuristic											
F	38	114	0	0	0	0	0	13	24	2	0
	35	1	0	0	0	0	0	7	0		
S	169161	742370	87766	136105	0	0	0	1702	2440	31.6	0
	169144	277922	0	0	0	0	0	1268	0		
M	5585	5687	8598	3455	0	0	0	12308	9137	21	3
	5584	1801	0	0	0	0	0	9693	0		
N	6654	6547	9384	4124	0	0	0	69534	4332	22.33	3
	6652	1941	0	0	0	0	0	51716	0		
H	377962	294737	230682	297175	345419	445245	612451	404205	308105	134.8	15.6
	377935	93051	0	0	0	0	0	404186	204806		
d^U heuristic											
F	38	114	0	0	0	0	0	14	24	2	0
	35	1	0	0	0	0	0	9	0		
S	287161	395163	65564	273596	0	0	0	12746	1042207	31.6	3
	287149	379679	520	0	0	0	0	12746	1030510		
M	9712	7734	11949	5043	0	0	0	23355	115058	21	4
	9708	4902	0	0	0	0	0	23354	83849		
N	10006	7943	11920	6614	0	0	0	16204	109769	21.5	4.75
	10000	4399	0	0	0	0	0	16204	80079		
H	379149	289671	222272	289380	323717	385445	498216	117141	220791	134.8	15.2
	379100	164472	0	0	0	0	0	117141	143929		
BFS											
F	56	114	0	0	0	0	0	n/a	n/a	2	0
	43	1	0	0	0	0	0	n/a	n/a		
S	323745	607706	189050	447035	0	0	0	n/a	n/a	31.6	0
	323704	229784	1111	0	0	0	0	n/a	n/a		
M	50251	56932	86116	30730	0	0	0	n/a	n/a	21	1.25
	50249	47908	0	0	0	0	0	n/a	n/a		
N	55105	55314	92173	39908	0	0	0	n/a	n/a	20.67	1.67
	55103	47546	0	0	0	0	0	n/a	n/a		
H	894952	925034	649694	843886	861079	980240	1476125	n/a	n/a	134.8	20.8
	894927	874677	0	0	0	0	0	n/a	n/a		

6 Conclusion

In this paper, we have introduced context-enhanced directed model checking. This multi-queue search algorithm makes use of interference contexts to determine the degree of relevance of transitions. Our approach is orthogonal to the directed model checking process and can hence be combined with arbitrary heuristics and blind search. Our empirical evaluation impressively shows the potential for various heuristics on large and realistic case studies. We obtain considerable performance improvements compared to plain directed model checking as well as compared to related search algorithms like iterative context bounding or useless transitions.

For the future, it will be interesting to extend and refine our concept of interference contexts. This includes, for example, to take into account the structure of our automaton model more explicitly. In particular, we plan to better adapt our approach to timed automata. Although we are able to handle such systems, our technique is not yet optimized for them as clocks are currently ignored. We expect that taking them into account will further improve our method for that class of systems.

Acknowledgments

This work was partly supported by the German Research Foundation (DFG) as part of the Transregional Collaborative Research Center "Automatic Verification and Analysis of Complex Systems" (SFB/TR 14 AVACS, `http://www.avacs.org/`).

References

1. Edelkamp, S., Schuppan, V., Bosnacki, D., Wijs, A., Fehnker, A., Aljazzar, H.: Survey on directed model checking. In: Peled, D.A., Wooldridge, M.J. (eds.) MoChArt 2008. LNCS, vol. 5348, pp. 65–89. Springer, Heidelberg (2009)
2. Kupferschmid, S., Hoffmann, J., Dierks, H., Behrmann, G.: Adapting an AI planning heuristic for directed model checking. In: Valmari, A. (ed.) SPIN 2006. LNCS, vol. 3925, pp. 35–52. Springer, Heidelberg (2006)
3. Dräger, K., Finkbeiner, B., Podelski, A.: Directed model checking with distance-preserving abstractions. International Journal on Software Tools for Technology Transfer 11(1), 27–37 (2009)
4. Hoffmann, J., Smaus, J.G., Rybalchenko, A., Kupferschmid, S., Podelski, A.: Using predicate abstraction to generate heuristic functions in Uppaal. In: Edelkamp, S., Lomuscio, A. (eds.) MoChArt 2007. LNCS (LNAI), vol. 4428, pp. 51–66. Springer, Heidelberg (2007)
5. Smaus, J.G., Hoffmann, J.: Relaxation refinement: A new method to generate heuristic functions. In: Peled, D.A., Wooldridge, M.J. (eds.) MoChArt 2008. LNCS, vol. 5348, pp. 146–164. Springer, Heidelberg (2009)
6. Edelkamp, S., Leue, S., Lluch-Lafuente, A.: Directed explicit-state model checking in the validation of communication protocols. International Journal on Software Tools for Technology Transfer 5(2), 247–267 (2004)
7. Qian, K., Nymeyer, A.: Guided invariant model checking based on abstraction and symbolic pattern databases. In: Jensen, K., Podelski, A. (eds.) TACAS 2004. LNCS, vol. 2988, pp. 497–511. Springer, Heidelberg (2004)
8. Kupferschmid, S., Hoffmann, J., Larsen, K.G.: Fast directed model checking via russian doll abstraction. In: Ramakrishnan, C.R., Rehof, J. (eds.) TACAS 2008. LNCS, vol. 4963, pp. 203–217. Springer, Heidelberg (2008)
9. Wehrle, M., Helmert, M.: The causal graph revisited for directed model checking. In: Palsberg, J., Su, Z. (eds.) SAS 2009. LNCS, vol. 5673, pp. 86–101. Springer, Heidelberg (2009)
10. Hoffmann, J., Nebel, B.: The FF planning system: Fast plan generation through heuristic search. Journal of Artificial Intelligence Research 14, 253–302 (2001)
11. Helmert, M.: The Fast Downward planning system. Journal of Artificial Intelligence Research 26, 191–246 (2006)
12. Wehrle, M., Kupferschmid, S., Podelski, A.: Useless actions are useful. In: Rintanen, J., Nebel, B., Beck, J.C., Hansen, E. (eds.) Proceedings of the 18th International Conference on Automated Planning and Scheduling (ICAPS 2008), pp. 388–395. AAAI Press, Menlo Park (2008)

13. Wehrle, M., Kupferschmid, S., Podelski, A.: Transition-based directed model checking. In: Kowalewski, S., Philippou, A. (eds.) TACAS 2009. LNCS, vol. 5505, pp. 186–200. Springer, Heidelberg (2009)
14. Musuvathi, M., Qadeer, S.: Iterative context bounding for systematic testing of multithreaded programs. In: Ferrante, J., McKinley, K.S. (eds.) Proceedings of the ACM SIGPLAN 2007 Conference on Programming Language Design and Implementation (PLDI 2007), pp. 446–455. ACM Press, New York (2007)
15. Pearl, J.: Heuristics: Intelligent Search Strategies for Computer Problem Solving. Addison-Wesley, Reading (1984)
16. Hart, P.E., Nilsson, N.J., Raphael, B.: A formal basis for the heuristic determination of minimum cost paths. IEEE Transactions on Systems Science and Cybernetics 4(2), 100–107 (1968)
17. Godefroid, P.: Partial-Order Methods for the Verification of Concurrent Systems — An Approach to the State-Explosion Problem. LNCS, vol. 1032. Springer, Heidelberg (1996)
18. Clarke, E.M., Grumberg, O., Peled, D.A.: Model Checking. The MIT Press, Cambridge (2000)
19. Edelkamp, S., Leue, S., Lluch-Lafuente, A.: Partial-order reduction and trail improvement in directed model checking. International Journal on Software Tools for Technology Transfer 6(4), 277–301 (2004)
20. Kupferschmid, S., Wehrle, M., Nebel, B., Podelski, A.: Faster than Uppaal? In: Gupta, A., Malik, S. (eds.) CAV 2008. LNCS, vol. 5123, pp. 552–555. Springer, Heidelberg (2008)
21. Alur, R., Dill, D.L.: A theory of timed automata. Theoretical Computer Science 126(2), 183–235 (1994)
22. Dierks, H.: Comparing model-checking and logical reasoning for real-time systems. Formal Aspects of Computing 16(2), 104–120 (2004)
23. Krieg-Brückner, B., Peleska, J., Olderog, E.-R., Baer, A.: The UniForM workbench, a universal development environment for formal methods. In: Woodcock, J.C.P., Davies, J., Wing, J.M. (eds.) FM 1999. LNCS, vol. 1709, pp. 1186–1205. Springer, Heidelberg (1999)
24. Lamport, L.: A fast mutual exclusion algorithm. ACM Transactions on Computer Systems 5(1), 1–11 (1987)

Efficient Explicit-State Model Checking on General Purpose Graphics Processors

Stefan Edelkamp[1] and Damian Sulewski[2]

TZI, Universität Bremen, Germany
{edelkamp,sulewski}@tzi.de

Abstract. We accelerate state space exploration for explicit-state model checking by executing complex operations on the graphics processing unit (GPU). In contrast to existing approaches enhancing model checking through performing parallel matrix operations on the GPU, we parallelize the breadth-first layered construction of the state space graph. For efficient processing, the input model is translated to the reverse Polish notation, resulting in a representation as an integer vector. The proposed GPU exploration algorithm then divides into two parallel stages. In the first stage, each state is replaced with a Boolean vector to denote which transitions are enabled. In the second stage, pairs consisting of replicated states and enabled transition IDs are copied to the GPU then all transitions are applied in parallel to produce the successors. Bitstate hashing is used as a Bloom filter to remove duplicates from the set of successors in RAM. The experiments show speed-ups of about one order of magnitude. Compared to state-of-the-art in multi-core model checking software, still advances remain visible.

1 Introduction

In the last few years there has been a remarkable increase in performance and capabilities of graphics processing units (GPUs). Whereas quad-core CPU processors have become already a commonplace, in the years to come core numbers are likely to follow Moore's law. This trend to many-core processors is already realized in graphical processing units. Modern GPUs are not only powerful, but programmable processors featuring high arithmetic capabilities and memory bandwidths. Moreover, high-level programming interfaces have been designed for using GPUs as ordinary computing devices. Current NVIDIA GPUs, for example, feature up to hundreds of scalar processing units per chip, which are directly programmable in C using CUDA[1].

The highly parallel GPU has rapidly gained maturity as a powerful engine for computationally demanding numerical operations. The access of it is streamed, using a kernel function given to every scalar processing unit.

The GPU's rapid increase in both programmability and capability has inspired researchers to map computationally challenging, complex problems to it. These

[1] Compute Unified Device Architecture, see www.nvidia.com/object/cuda_home.html

J. van de Pol and M. Weber (Eds.): SPIN 2010, LNCS 6349, pp. 106–123, 2010.

efforts in general purpose programming on the GPU (also known as GPGPU or $(GP)^2U$ programming)[2] have positioned the GPU as a compelling alternative to traditional microprocessors in high-performance computing. Since the memory transfer between the graphics card and main board (on the express bus) is extremely fast, GPUs have helped to speed-up large-scale computations like sorting [16,24], and computationally intense applications like folding proteins [22], simulating bio-molecular systems [28] or computing prefix sums [18].

This paper applies GPGPU technology to the state space generation for explicit-state model checking. During the construction of the state space, we detect and eliminate duplicates and check a visited state for possible violation of so-called safety properties. Our approach applies breadth-first search (BFS) and can return counter-examples of minimal length. It includes checking enabledness and generating the successors on the GPU. Instead of the delayed elimination of duplicates for supporting large-scale analyses on disk, as proposed in a precursor of this paper [11], in this paper we consider RAM-based model checking with Bloom filters [4] in form of (double) bit-state hash tables [21]. Thus, the (random access) memory for the exploration is mainly limited by the size of the according bitvector. In our approach storing full state information for expanding a state in RAM is optional, as the search frontier is managed on external memory. Eventually, the entire reachable state space has been flushed to disk.

State space construction via BFS is the essential step and the performance bottleneck for checking large models [31,7,2,23,13,32,9]. Besides checking safety properties, variants of BFS generate LTL property counter-examples of minimal length [15]. Moreover, BFS is the basis for distributed (usually LTL) model checking algorithms like OWCTY [30] and MAP [6] as well as for constructing perfect hash functions from disk in so-called semi-external model checking [10].

The proposed state space generation algorithm is divided into two stages, executed on the GPU: 1) Checking enabledness, i.e., testing the applicability of transitions against the current state; 2) Generating the set of successors (one for each enabled transition and explored state). The core reason to operate in two subsequent stages is to maximize space utilization of the graphics card. To please the GPU's computational model, the reverse Polish notation [8] is chosen for achieving a flat bracket-free representation of expressions, since it offers the possibility to concatenate all transition descriptions to one integer vector, yielding a memory- and time-efficient exploration.

After generating the successors, they have to be checked for duplicates against the list of expanded states. This can be done with either a complete method or with an incomplete but usually faster hashing method. We were able to exploit multiple threads running on the CPU for parallelizing the access to the hash table. We preferred partial search methods, because otherwise, for multi-threaded memorization at high-end exploration performance, a non-trivial lock-free hash table implementation would be needed [14].

Our CUDA-driven model checker (CUDMoC) takes the same input format as DIVINE namely, DVE, but shares no code. By changing the parser, however, the

[2] For more insights in GPGPU programming, see www.gpgpu.org

algorithms we propose can be integrated to any other explicit-state model checkers, including SPIN [19]. We also assume CUDA supporting NVIDIA hardware, but there are trends on GPGPU programming with other vendors, too.

For each of the two exploration stages, we obtain significant speed-ups of more than one order of magnitude for analyzing benchmark protocols on the GPU. In BFS, hashing contributes only a small fraction to the overall performance, so that we compute the hash values on the CPU[3].

The paper is structured as follows. We first provide an overview on our GPU architecture. Then, we recall related work in GPU-based state space exploration. Next, we motivate the usage of the reverse Polish notation for efficient processing of the model on the GPU and turn to GPU-based BFS, providing details on transition checking and successor generation. Finally, we present empirical results in benchmark protocols, conclude, and discuss future research avenues.

2 GPU Essentials

Some of the design decisions in our model checking algorithms are closely related to the architecture of GPUs. Thus, insights into this architecture are essential.

GPUs have multiple cores, but the programming and the computational models are different from the ones for multi-core CPUs. GPU programming requires a special compiler, which translates the code to native GPU instructions. Roughly speaking, the GPU architecture is that of a vector computer with the same function running on all processors. The architecture supports different layers for accessing memory. Moreover, nowadays GPUs forbid common writes to a memory cell but support a limited form of concurrent read.

The numbers of cores on the GPU clearly exceed the ones on the CPU, but GPUs are limited to streamed processing. While cores on a multi-core processor work autonomously, the operations of cores on the GPU are strongly correlated.

The G200 chipset – one representative for the NVIDIA GPU technology found on our GTX 280 graphics card – is roughly characterized in Fig. 1. It has 240 cores and one GB global memory. With NVIDIA SLI, Tesla or Fermi technologies (e.g. supplied on the new GTX 480 graphics card), 480 and more cores as well as larger amounts of memory are available.

A scalar *core* is a streaming processor (SP), capable of performing single precision arithmetic. SPs are grouped together with a cache structure and two special function units (performing, e.g., double precision arithmetic) to a streaming multiprocessor (SM). Texture processing clusters (TPCs) form the top level architecture and combine SMs with a second cache.[4] Due to the fact that the cores are similar to an SIMD technology and operate on a lower frequency than the CPU a speed-up comparable to the number of cores is not to be expected.

[3] There is a recent study for advanced incremental hashing in the depth-first search engine of SPIN [25] with visible performance gains, which hardly applies to BFS.

[4] The G200 chipset consists of 10 TPCs, each one containing 3 SMs with 8 SPs, yielding 240 cores on one chip.

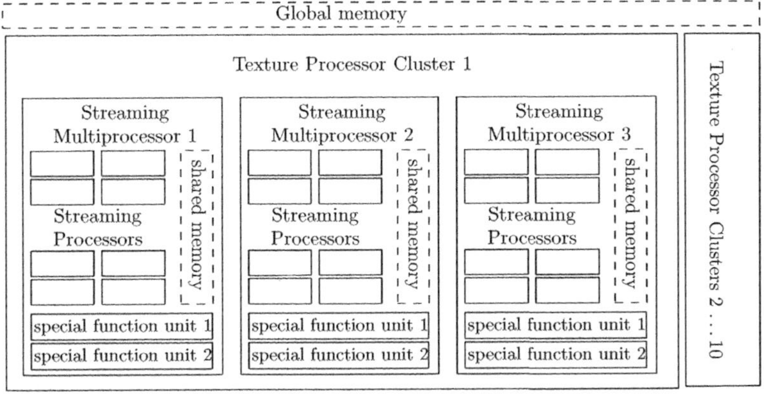

Fig. 1. GPU architecture for G200 chipset on NVIDIA 280 GTX card

Memory is structured hierarchically, starting with the global memory (video RAM, or VRAM). Access to this memory is relatively slow, but can be accelerated through *coalescing*, where adjacent accesses are combined to one. Each SM includes 16 KB of memory (shared RAM or SRAM), shared between all its SPs and accessed at a speed compatible to a register. Additional registers are also located in each SP. Data has to be copied to VRAM to be accessible.

The *kernel* function executed in parallel on the GPU is driven by *threads* that are grouped together in *blocks*. The TPC distributes the blocks on its streaming multiprocessors in such a way that none of the SMs runs more than 1,024 threads. A block is not distributed among different SMs. This way, taking into account that the maximal block size is 512, at most 2 blocks can be executed by one SM. Each TPC schedules 24 threads to be executed in parallel, providing the same chunk of code to all its SMs.

Since all the SPs execute the same line of code, SPs in an *else*-branch are paused, waiting for the SPs in the *if*-branch. After the 24 threads have executed a chunk the next chunks are executed. Blocks are executed sequentially on all the resources available. Threads which are waiting for data can be parked by the TPC, while the SPs work on threads, which have already received the data.

3 Related Work in GPU-Based Exploration

Model checking usually amounts to explore a state space graph. To prevent revisiting of already explored states, all processed states are stored. If a state is generated, it is first checked against the set of stored states. Due to the huge number of states and their large sizes, time and memory demands for analyzing systems rise rapidly. For model checking safety properties, a complete scan of the reachable (possibly reduced) search space suffices.

Explicit graph algorithms utilizing the GPU (with a state space residing in RAM or on disk) were presented, e.g., by [17]. In model checking, however, state space graphs are generated implicitly, by the application of transitions to states, starting with some initial state. Additionally, considering the fundamental difference in the architectures of the processing units solutions developed for multi-core model checking [20], however, hardly transfer to ones for the GPU.

For breadth-first state-space generation on the GPU in artificial intelligence (AI) search challenges like sliding-tile puzzles, speed-ups between factor 10 and 27 wrt. single-core CPU computation [12] were established. Based on computing reversible minimal perfect hash functions on the GPU, one-bit reachability and one-bit BFS algorithms were proposed. Specific perfect hash functions were studied. In solving the two player game Nine-Men-Morris a speed-up factor of over 12 was obtained. Specialized hashing for ranking and unranking states on the GPU and a parallel retrograde analysis on the GPU were applied. Unfortunately, the AI exploration approaches hardly carry over to model checking, as general designs of invertible hash functions – as available for particular games – are yet unknown.

While the precursor of this paper [11] pioneered explicit-state model checking with delayed duplicate detection on the GPU by accelerating state set sorting, in the meantime there have been a number of attempts to exploit the computational power located on the graphics card. In all other GPU-based model checking algorithms we are aware of, however, the state space is generated on the CPU.

For example, GPGPU-based probabilistic model checking [5] boils down to solving linear equations via computing multiple sparse matrix-vector products on the GPU. The mathematical background is parallelizing Jacobi iterations. While the PCTL probabilistic model checking approach accelerates one iterated numerical operation on the GPU, for explicit-state LTL model checking we perform a single scan over a large search space. As a result, we propose a conceptually different algorithm, suited to parallel model checking of large models.

Barnat et al. [1] present a tool that performs CUDA accelerated LTL model checking. They adjust the MAP algorithm to the GPU to detect the presence of accepting cycles. As in bounded model checking [3], the state space may be generated in layers on the CPU, before being transformed into a matrix representation to be processed on the GPU. The speed-ups are visible, but the approach is limited by the memory available on the GPU and able to checking properties in moderately-sized models only.

4 GPU-Based Breadth-First Search

In the following, we provide the essentials for breadth-first explicit-state model checking on the GPU. We show how to test enabledness for a set of states in parallel, and – given all sets of applicable transitions – how to generate the successor state sets accordingly. We restrict to BFS for generating the entire search space, since it is sufficient for verifying the safety properties we are interested in. Even for model checking full LTL, which we do not address in this paper, efficient state space generation via breadth-first search is often a crucial step [10].

We assume a hierarchical memory structure of SRAM (small, but fast parallel access) and VRAM (large, but slow parallel access) located on the GPU, together

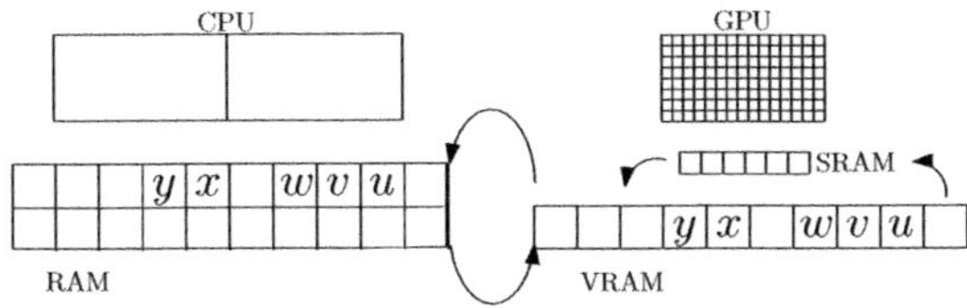

Fig. 2. GPU-based model checking with different sorts of memory and processing cores

with RAM located on the motherboard. The setting, illustrated in Fig. 2, indicates the partition of memory into cells and of processing units into cores.

We observed that duplicate detection and elimination is not as CPU-inefficient in practice as we have expected. This maybe due to the large number of successors that are already eliminated within one BFS layer. In the instances we looked at transition enabledness checking and successor generation were identified as the main performance bottlenecks. To save RAM the BFS search frontier is stored on disk and accessed streamed in blocks corresponding to the size of the VRAM.

The intuition behind our approach is to dispatch a set of operations to the GPU. For each BFS layer, the state space enumeration is divided into two main computational stages that are called in Alg. 1; Stage 1: generation of sets of enabled transitions based on checking the transition guards in parallel; and Stage 2: generation sets of successors based on applying transition effects in parallel.

The pseudo-codes for checking enabledness (Alg. 3) and generating the successors (Alg. 4) reflect that each processing core selects its share based on its group and thread ID. For duplicate detection, a Bloom filter [4] is provided.

In the first stage, a set of enabled transitions is generated by copying the states to the VRAM and replacing them by a bitvector. In the second stage, sets of all possible successors are generated. For each enabled transition a pair, joining the transition ID and the explored state, is copied to the VRAM. Each state is replicated by the number of successors it generates in order to avoid memory to be allocated dynamically. After the generation all duplicates are removed, e.g. by bitstate hashing. For a better compression in RAM, we separate the search frontier from the set of visited states on disk.

4.1 Preparing the Model

To check the transitions enabledness, a representation of them has to be accessible by the GPU cores. While an object-oriented data structure – where each expression in a process is realized as an object linked to its substructures – might be a preferable representation of the model for CPU access, such a representation would be less effective for GPU access.

As described in Section 2, the GPU's memory manager prefers sequential access to the data structures. Moreover, to use coalescing many threads have to access the same memory area in parallel. Hence, in order to speed up the access

Algorithm 1. Breadth-First Search on the GPU

Input: initial state: s_0
Output: set of all reached states: *Closed*

```
Open ← {s0}; Closed ← ∅; Enabled ← ∅; Successors ← ∅;          ;; initialize search
while (Open ≠ ∅)                                      ;; repeat until search terminates
                    Stage 1 - Generate sets of enabled transitions
  while (|Enabled| ≠ |Open|)                   ;; until all frontier states are processed
    VRAM ← {u ∈ Open | VRAM not full}                          ;; Copy nodes to VRAM
    Enabled ← Enabled ∪ GPU-MarkEnabled(VRAM)                       ;; GPU function
                    Stage 2 - Generate sets of successors
  while (Enabled ≠ ∅)                                 ;; Until all transitions processed
    VRAM ← {(t, s) | t ∈ Enabled and s fits t ∈ Open ∧ VRAM not full}
               ;; Move state copies for all enabled transitions of a state to VRAM
    Enabled ← Enabled \ {t}                         ;; remove transitions from Enabled
    Successors ← Successors ∪ GPU-GenerateSuccessors(VRAM)          ;; GPU function
  Open ← ∅;                                                    ;; prepare next layer
  Successors ← Successors ∩ Closed;     ;; remove explored states from successors set
  Closed ← Closed ∪ Successors;                     ;; extend set of explored states
  Open ← Successors;                           ;; add new layer to the search frontier
```

the model, data should reside in the SRAM of each multi-processor. This way a fast randomized access can be granted, while the available space shrinks to at most SRAM size. Another positive aspect of storing the model directly in the SRAM arises from the fast accessibility by all threads of a multi-processor, so that the model has to be copied only once from the VRAM to RAM.

Since the GPU should not access RAM and pointer manipulation on the GPU is limited, it is necessary to rewrite the transition guard labels to be evaluated. This description has to be efficient in terms of memory and evaluation time, since the size of the VRAM is small (compared to the computational power of the GPU). Furthermore, all transitions should be moved into one memory block to take advantage of fast block transfers on the express bus.

Parsing the DVE Language. To use the benchmark protocols provided by the BEEM Library[5] DVE was chosen as an input model representation. The underlying theoretical model of the DVE language is that of communicating finite state machines and consists of several parts, structured hierarchically and identified as global variables and a number of processes on the top level. Processes are divided into local variables, states and transitions, while transitions consist of guards and effects represented by Boolean formula and variable assignments, respectively. Transitions are assigned to particular states and indicate, which state to activate if the transition is enabled. Given the process is in state s only transitions assigned to s should be checked. If a guard evaluates to true, the

[5] See: http://anna.fi.muni.cz/models/

```
byte Slot[1] = {1 };
byte next=0;
process P_0 {
 byte my_place;
 state NCS, p1, p2, p3, CS;
 init NCS;
 trans
 NCS -> p1 { effect my_place = next, next = next+1; },
 p1 -> p2 { guard my_place == 3-1; effect next = next-3; },
 p1 -> p2 { guard my_place != 3-1; effect my_place = my_place%3; },
 p2 -> p3 { guard Slot[my_place] == 1;  },
 p3 -> CS { effect Slot[my_place]=0; },
 CS -> NCS { effect Slot[(my_place+1)%3]=1;};
}
```

Fig. 3. Example of the Anderson (1) protocol in DVE input language

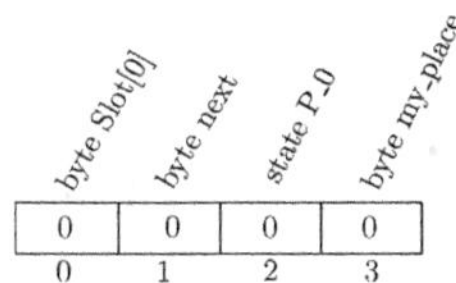

Fig. 4. State vector representing the example in Fig. 3

transition is enabled and the effects should be applied, assigning the process a new state and optionally new values to some global or local variables. The example in Fig. 3 shows the Anderson protocol with only one process. The array *Slot* and the variable *next* are global, while *my_place* is a local variable. The process can be in one of 5 states named as *NCS, p1, p2, p3, CS* where *NCS* is the initial state. Note that transitions 2 and 3 cannot be applied concurrently, due to the fact that only one of the guards can be true.

Based on knowing the grammar, the model description can be parsed and a syntax tree constructed. To store different variable assignments and indicate in which state a process currently is, a byte vector can be used. Fig. 4 describes the state vector assigned to the example in Fig. 3. Necessary space for each global variable is reserved, followed by a byte indicating the current state of each process, and combined with space for the local variables for each process.[6]

The challenge is to store the representation of the transitions efficiently. On the GPU, the *reverse Polish notation* (RPN) [8], i.e., a postfix representation of Boolean and arithmetic expressions, was identified as effective. It is used to represent all guards and effects of the model in one integer array. This array is partitioned into two parts, one for the guards, the other for the effects. A prefix assigns the guards and effects to its processes after creating the array. In addition to the guards, each transition indicates the goal state the process

[6] This representation is equivalent to the one used in the DiVinE model checker.

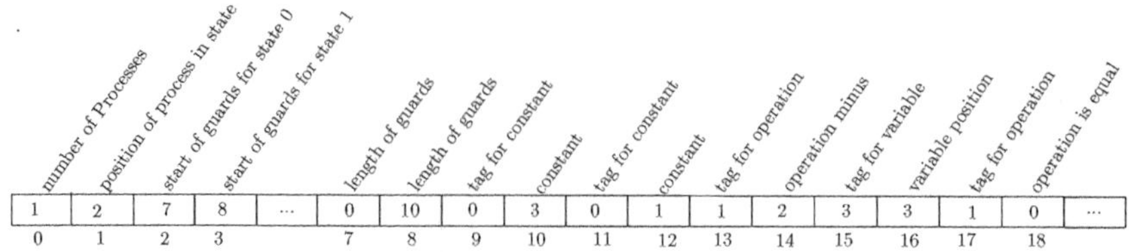

Fig. 5. Fragments of the transition vector representing the example in Fig. 3

will reach after applying the effects. *Tokens* are used to distinguish different elements of the Boolean formulas. Each entry consists of a pair (token,value) identifying the action to take. Consider the guard starting at position 8 of the array presented in Fig. 5 representing the guard of the second transition in the example (`my_place==3-1;`). It is translated to the RPN as an entry of length 10 using tokens for constants, arithmetic operation and variables. Constant tokens, defining also the type of the constant, are followed by the value. Arithmetic tokens identify the following byte as an operator. One special token is the variable token, there is no need for distinction in arrays or variables, since variables are seen as arrays of length 1, so the token defines the type of the variable and is followed by the index to access it in the state.

This yields a pointer-free, compact and flat representation of the transition guards. Converting the protocol to the RPN notation and copying it to the GPU is executed before the model checking process starts. Using this representation a check for enabledness of transitions in a process boils down to 3 steps:

1. Checking the state the process is in, by reading its byte in the state vector.
2. Identify transitions to check by reading the global prefix of the integer vector describing the model.
3. Evaluation of all guards dependent to the actual state and process on a stack.

To enable the transition given its ID, the representation of its effects starting at the position given in the second partition of the array has to be evaluated. The advantage of this approach is to copy all information needed for the model checking process into 1 block. Given that all guards and effects, respectively, are located in adjacent memory cells, we have a streamed access for evaluating a large number of guards.

4.2 State Exploration on the GPU

For accelerating the joint exploration of states, we executed both the enabledness check and the generation of successors on the GPU, parallelizing (the essentials of) the entire model checking process. We exploit the fact that the order of explorations in one BFS-layer does not matter, so that no communication between the threads nor explicit load balancing is required. Each processor is simply assigned to its share and starts operating. Duplicate detection is delayed on the GPU and delegated to the CPU.

Algorithm 2. *CheckGuard*: checking a guard for a state on the GPU

Global: expression vector *transitions*
Input: state vector *state* ; transition ID *trans*
Output: true, if guard evaluation was successful; false, otherwise

```
pos ← start_of_guard(trans);                                  ;; set starting position of guard.
while pos < start_of_guard(trans) + length_of_guard(trans);   ;; while end not reached
  if is_constant(transitions[pos]) push transitions[pos+1] on top of stack;
                                                  ;; constant? just store it on the stack
  if is_variable(transitions[pos]) push state[transitions[pos+1]] on top of stack;
      ;; variable? read the indexed value in the state vector and store it on the stack
  if is_operator(transitions[pos]) pop var1 and var2 from stack;
                                                  ;; operator? get two values from the top
    result ← var1 transitions[pos+1] var2;        ;; apply the indexed operator
    push result on top of stack;                  ;; and store the result on the stack
  pos ← pos + 2;                                  ;; set pointer to the next element
return result;
```

Still, there are remaining obstacles in implementing of a fully-fledged model checker on the GPU. First, the state size may vary during the verification. Fortunately, common model checkers provide upper bounds on the state vector size or induce the maximal size of the state vector once the initial state has been read. Another technical challenge is that the GPU kernel (though being C-like) does not exactly match the sources of the model checker, such that all methods being called have to be ported to CUDA.

Checking Enabledness on the GPU. In the state exploration routine first, all transitions are checked, and then, the enabled ones are fired. Before the execution the transition vector is copied to the SRAM for faster access. All threads access in parallel the VRAM and read the state vector into their registers using coalescing. Then all threads access *transitions*[0] to find the number of processes in the model. Next, all threads access *transitions*[1] to find the state the first process is in. At this point in time, the memory access diverges for the first time. Since processes have reached different states at different positions in the search space, different guards have to be evaluated. This does not harm, since the transition vector is accessible in the SRAM and all access is streamed. After collecting the necessary information, all threads call Alg. 2. A stack consisting of pair entries (token,value) is used to evaluate the Boolean formulas.[7] The checking process boils down to storing the values on the stack, and executing all operations on the two entries on top of the stack. The stack serves as a cache for all operations and if an assignment is found, the value on top of it is written to the state.

[7] The max. stack size is fixed for each protocol and can be extracted from the model.

Algorithm 3. *GPU-MarkEnabled*: GPU kernel for transition enabledness check

Global: integer transition vector *transitions* in reverse Polish notation
Input: state vectors $\{s_1, \ldots, s_k\}$ to check for enabledness
Output: array of transition sets $\{t_1, \ldots, t_k\}$ (overwrites state vectors with bitvectors)

for each group g **do** ;; partially distributed computation
  for each thread p **do in parallel** ;; distributed computation
    $B \leftarrow$ (**false**, ..., **false**) ;; clear enabledness bitvector
    for each possible transition t for $s_{g \cdot sizeof(g)+p}$ **do** ;; select state transitions
      $B[t] \leftarrow CheckGuard(s, t)$;; check enabledness and set according bit
    $s_{g \cdot sizeof(g)+p} \leftarrow B$;; overwrite selected state
return $\{s_1, \ldots, s_k\}$;; return overwritten states to CPU

In the first stage the VRAM is filled with states from the *Open* list. Then, Alg. 3, executed on the GPU, computes a bitvector B of transitions, with bit B_t denoting, whether or not transition t applies. The entire array, whose size is equal to the number of enabled transitions, is initialized to *false*. A bit is set, if a transition is enabled. Each thread reads one single state at a unique position defined by its ID and computes the set of its enabled transitions. For improved VRAM efficiency we allow the vector of transitions to overwrite the states they are applied to. Therefore, we utilize the fact that the number of transitions in a protocol is constant and the number of transitions does not exceed the size of the bitvector representation of a state. For the implementation, after having checked all transitions for enabledness, the bitvectors are copied back to RAM.

To evaluate a postfix representation of a guard, one scan through its representation suffices. The maximal length of a guard times the number of groups thus determines the parallel running time, as for all threads in a group, the check for enabledness is executed concurrently.

Generating the Successors on the GPU. After having fixed the set of applicable transitions for each state, generating the successors on the GPU is relatively simple. First, we replicate each state to be explored by the number of enabled transitions on the CPU. Moreover, we attach the ID of the transition that is enabled together with each state. Then, we move the array of states to the GPU and generate the successors in parallel.

For the application of a transition to a given state, similar to processing the guards, the effect expressions have been rewritten in reverse Polish notation, (cf. Alg. 4). Since this static representation resides in the GPU's VRAM for the entire checking process and since it is addressed by all instances of the same kernel function, its access is fast. The cause is that broadcasting is an integral operation on most graphics cards.

Each state to be explored is overwritten with the result of applying the attached transition, which often results in small changes to the state vector. Finally, all states are copied back to RAM. The run-time is determined by the maximal

Algorithm 4. *GPU-GenerateSuccessors*: GPU kernel for successor generation

Global: transition postconditions effects in reverse Polish notation *effects*
Input: set of pairs (transition,state) $\{\{t_1, s_1\}, \dots \{t_k, s_k\}\}$
Output: set of successors (explored nodes are overwritten)

for each group g **do** ;; Partially distributed computation
  for each thread p **do in parallel** ;; Distributed computation
    $s_{g \cdot sizeof(g)+p} \leftarrow Explore(effects, t_{g \cdot sizeof(g)+p}, s_{g \cdot p})$;; Generate successor
return $\{s_1, \dots, s_k\}$;; Feedback result to CPU

length of an effect times the number of groups, as for all threads in a group we generate the successors in parallel.

Duplicate Checking on (Multiple Cores of) the CPU. Since the successors are generated in parallel, an efficient parallel method is necessary to detect duplicates by checking the current state against the list of explored nodes. Like in the SPIN model checker, we use double bitstate hashing as a default. Looking at the number of states explored, the error probability for tens of gigabytes of main memory is acceptably small. Different options have been proposed to increase coverage [21], including the choice of a new hash function, e.g., from a set of universal ones (our state hash functions borrowed from Rasmus Pagh [26] are universal). To increase space utility, cache-, hash-, and space-efficient Bloom filters have been proposed [29] and compress a static dictionary to its information-theoretic optimum by using a Golomb code. We haven't succeeded in extending them to dynamic case of breadth-first model checking we are interested in. Refinements like sequential hashing with different hash function, or hash compaction are possible but not yet implemented. To parallelize bitstate hashing on multiple CPU cores, the set of successors is partitioned and all partitions are scanned in parallel. In bitstate hashing, a bit set is never cleared. As we conduct BFS, state caches with different replacement strategies are also feasible.

5 Experiments

We implemented our new model checker called CUDA Driven Model Checker (CUDMOC) with gcc 4.3.3. The bitstate table has a capacity of 81,474,836,321 entries consuming 9.7 GB of RAM. Models are taken from the BEEM library [27]. We use a NVIDIA geForce 280 GTX (MSI) graphics card (with one GB VRAM and 240 streaming processors). RAM amounts to 12 GB. The CPU of the system is an Intel Core i7 CPU 920 @ 2.67 GHz providing 8 cores.

The first evaluation in Table 1 analyses the performance of the GPU algorithm compared to the CPU. We used the `-deviceemu` directive of the nvcc compiler to simulate the experiments on the CPU[8]. The table shows that using the GPU for

[8] Earlier experiences showed no significant speed difference between simulating CUDA code with this directive and converting it by hand to, e.g., POSIX threads.

Table 1. Experimental results, cross-comparing different versions of CUDA-driven model checker. Running times given in seconds.

	CUDMOC			
Protocol	1 Core CPU	1 Core + GPU	8 Core + GPU	States
anderson (6)	235	25	20	18,206,914
anderson (8)	1381	669	440	538,493,685
at (5)	404	36	29	31,999,395
at (6)	836	170	119	160,588,070
bakery (7)	296	30	28	29,047,452
bakery (8)	3603	250	182	253,111,016
elevator (2)	334	30	23	11,428,766
fisher (3)	41	10	9	2,896,705
fisher (4)	22	7	7	1,272,254
fisher (5)	1692	126	86	101,027,986
fisher (6)	107	16	13	8,321,728
fisher (7)	4965	555	360	386,281,613
frogs (4)	153	20	17	17,443,219
frogs (5)	2474	203	215	182,726,077
lamport (8)	867	70	49	62,669,266
mcs (5)	896	77	50	60,556,458
mcs (6)	12	7	7	332,544
phils (6)	422	36	27	14,348,901
phils (7)	2103	196	125	71,933,609
phils (8)	1613	105	70	43,046,407

the successor generation results in a mean speed-up (sum of all 1 Core + CPU times / sum of all 1 core + GPU) of 22,456 / 2,638 = 8.51. Column *8 Core + GPU* displays additional savings obtained by utilizing all 8 CPU cores for duplicate detection, operating simultaneously on a partitioned vector of successors. The comparison demonstrates only the influence to the whole model checking process; larger speed-ups were reached by considering only this aspect.

In order to compare CUDMOC with the current state-of-the-art in (multi-core) explicit-state model checking, we additionally performed experiments on the (most recent publicly available) releases of the DIVINE (version 2.2) and SPIN (version 5.2.4) model checker.

DIVINE instances were run with `divine reachability -w N protocol.dve` with N denoting the number of cores to use and aborted when more then 11GB RAM were used. Table 2 shows the comparison in running time of the 1 core and the 8 core versions. Of course, DIVINE is not able tho check some instances due to its exhaustive duplicate detection, it needs to store all visited states in full length, which is less memory efficient than bitstate hashing. One interesting fact in the frogs (5) protocol, is that DIVINE is only able to verify this instance in single-core mode. We assume that the queues, needed to perform communication between the cores consume too much memory. Additionally, we display the number of reached states, to indicated the number of states omitted. In the largest instance, the amount of states omitted is at most 3%.

Table 2. Experimental results, comparing CUDA-driven model checker with DIVINE. Times given in seconds, o.o.m denotes out of memory.

	CUDMOC			DIVINE		
Protocol	1 Core	8 Core	States	1 Core	8 Core	States
anderson (6)	25	20	18,206,914	75	21	18,206,917
at (5)	36	29	31,999,395	118	33	31,999,440
at (6)	170	119	160,588,070	674	189	160,589,600
bakery (7)	30	28	29,047,452	95	26	29,047,471
bakery (8)	250	182	253,111,016	–	-	o.o.m
elevator (2)	30	23	11,428,766	74	21	11,428,767
fisher (3)	10	9	2,896,705	12	3	2,896,705
fisher (4)	7	7	1,272,254	5	1	1,272,254
fisher (5)	126	86	101,027,986	541	141	101,028,339
fisher (6)	16	13	8,321,728	37	10	8,321,728
fisher (7)	555	360	386,281,613	-	-	o.o.m
frogs (4)	20	17	17,443,219	69	15	17,443,219
frogs (5)	203	215	182,726,077	787	-	182,772,126
lamport (8)	70	49	62,669,266	238	68	62,669,317
mcs (5)	77	50	60,556,458	241	68	60,556,519
mcs (6)	7	7	332,544	0	0	332,544
phils (6)	36	27	14,348,901	122	36	14,348,906
phils (7)	196	125	71,933,609	768	-	71,934,773
phils (8)	105	70	43,046,407	405	-	43,046,720

The speed-up averaged over all successful instances is 3,088 / 863 = 3.58 for one core and 632 / 484 = 1.31 for the 8 core implementation[9].

SPIN is also able to manage an exhaustive representation of the closed list, however, due to the memory limitations of an exhaustive search, we decided to compare CUDMOC against SPIN with the bitstate implementation. SPIN has two options for performing reachability, BFS and DFS. Table 3 presents the results in BFS, which has no multi-core implementation. SPIN experiments were performed by calling `spin -a protocol.pm; cc -O3 -DSAFETY -DMEMLIM=12000 -DBFS -DBITSTATE -o pan pan.c; ./pan -m10000000 -c0 -n -w28;`. For the sake of clarity, we also present the number of reached states for both model checkers. We see that the number of states varies extremely for the larger instances. We explain the diversity with the size of the bitstate tables (in SPIN 2^{28} = 268,435,456 entries were chosen, as we could not rise this size because the remaining memory that was occupied by the algorithm). We use *Speed* to denote the number generated states per second; CUDMOC achieves an average speed of 637,279 compared to SPIN with an average speed of 593,598. Although the speed-up is not significant we highlight the fact that CUDMOC stores all the reached states on external memory for later usage, while these states are lost in

[9] DIVINE naturally utilizes all cores for expansion, while CUDMOC uses the additional cores only for duplicate checking.

Table 3. Experimental results, comparing CUDA-driven model checker with SPIN and bitstate storage. Times given in seconds. Column Speed shows the quotient states/time. Protocol mcs 5 was aborted after 10 hours, having generated 6,308,626.

	CUDMoC			SPIN Bitstate BFS		
Protocol	1 Core	Speed	States	1 Core	Speed	States
anderson (6)	25	728,276	18,206,914	26	698,282	18,155,353
anderson (8)	669	804,923	538,493,685	228	618,216	140,953,300
at (5)	36	888,872	31,999,395	40	790,811	31,632,471
at (6)	170	944,635	160,588,070	146	727,404	106,201,110
bakery (7)	30	968,248	29,047,452	29	942,202	27,323,870
bakery (8)	250	1,012,444	253,111,016	156	78,283	12,212,250
elevator (2)	30	380,958	11,428,766	19	601,239	11,423,554
fisher (3)	10	289,670	2,896,705	4	724,170	2,896,681
fisher (4)	7	181,750	1,272,254	2	636,131	1,272,262
fisher (5)	126	801,809	101,027,986	141	614,026	86,577,752
fisher (6)	16	520,108	8,321,728	13	639,997	8,319,972
fisher (7)	555	696,002	386,281,613	242	547,841	132,577,710
frogs (4)	20	872,160	17,443,219	19	916,191	17,407,634
frogs (5)	203	900,128	182,726,077	136	853,619	116,092,290
lamport (8)	70	895,275	62,669,266	8	917,817	7,342,543
mcs (5)	77	786,447	60,556,458	–	–	0
mcs (6)	7	47,506	332,544	1	36,598	36,598
phils (6)	36	398,580	14,348,901	43	333,412	14,336,722
phils (7)	196	367,008	71,933,609	229	297,427	68,110,830
phils (8)	105	409,965	43,046,407	139	304,714	42,355,353

SPIN. Storing the information on external storage in SPIN leads to a slowdown by a factor of 2 and more.

As the SPIN BFS algorithm is not parallelizable, we were forced to compare our implementation to the DFS version of SPIN and bitstate hashing called via `spin -a protocol.pm; cc -O3 -DSAFETY -DMEMLIM=8000 -DBITSTATE -DNCORE=N -DNSUCC -DVMAX=144 -o pan pan.c; ./pan -m10000000 -c0 -n -w27;` (for 1 core), and `./pan -m10000000 -c0 -n -w25;` (for 8 cores) with N denoting the number of cores. Table 4 shows the running times and per node efficiencies for the tested protocols. Since the numbers for the 1 core CUDMoC implementation are identical in table 3, we present only the values for the 8 core implementation here. As we can see, the 8 core implementation of the DFS algorithm is always faster then the CUDMoC implementation. A closer inspection of the number of the visited states reveals that the number of cores has an impact on the size of the bitstate table, thus resulting in different amounts of visited states. In the Anderson (8) protocol, which is the largest checked protocol, CUDMoC identifies 538,493,685 unique states, while the SPIN 8 core implementation reaches 145,028,600 states, omitting nearly 70% of the state space. Additional observations showed that at the beginning of the search the speed is higher, since new states are reached more often, than at the end, where a large amount of reached states has already been explored.

Table 4. Experimental results, comparing CUDA-driven model checker with SPIN and partial state storage. Times given in seconds. Speed denotes states per second.

	CUDMoC		SPIN Bitstate					
Protocol	8 Core	Speed	1 Core	Speed	States	8 Core	Speed	States
anderson (6)	20	910,345	58	313,911	18,206,893	9	2,017,465	18,157,188
anderson (8)	440	1,223,849	1316	275,800	362,954,000	78	1,859,341	145,028,600
at (5)	29	1,103,427	90	355,547	31,999,291	12	2,630,998	31,571,983
at (6)	119	1,349,479	399	339,403	135,422,110	42	2,476,482	104,012,280
bakery (7)	28	1,037,409	48	573,577	27,531,713	8	3,413,837	27,310,696
bakery (8)	182	1,390,719	456	488,071	222,560,800	39	3,062,315	119,430,320
elevator (2)	23	496,902	47	243,165	11,428,769	8	1,427,956	11,423,654
fisher (3)	9	321,856	7	413,815	2,896,707	2	1,448,344	2,896,689
fisher (4)	7	181,750	2	636,128	1,272,256	1	1,272,298	1,272,298
fisher (5)	86	1,174,744	275	367,375	101,028,340	36	2,397,127	86,296,605
fisher (6)	13	640,132	20	416,086	8,321,730	4	2,079,982	8,319,929
fisher (7)	360	1,073,004	1372	281,557	386,296,530	63	2,098,240	132,189,170
frogs (4)	17	1,026,071	26	670,893	17,443,221	5	3,472,759	17,363,799
frogs (5)	215	849,888	289	632,427	182,771,630	24	3,878,232	93,077,570
lamport (8)	49	1,278,964	17	431,974	7,343,562	3	2,447,541	7,342,625
mcs (5)	50	1,211,129	81	358,055	29,002,474	14	2,343,949	32,815,294
mcs (6)	7	47,506	0	–	36,600	0	–	36,948
phils (6)	27	531,440	26	387,130	10,065,395	17	843,330	14,336,624
phils (7)	125	575,468	351	183,494	64,406,569	51	1,217,002	62,067,145
phils (8)	70	614,948	12	766,795	9,201,551	35	1,043,143	36,510,039

6 Conclusion and Discussion

The main purpose of the paper is to show that explicit-state model checking on the GPU has the potential for growing towards an exciting research field. Therefore, we contributed a new model checker for efficient state space generation for featuring explicit-state model checking on the GPU. In the algorithm design successfully attacked two causes of bad CPU performance of the model checker: transition checking and successor generation and exploited a GPU-friendly representation of the model. Bitstate-based duplicate detection has been delayed for, and parallelized on the CPU. The results show noticeable gains, likely to rise on more advanced GPU technologies.

Of course, improving the speed-up is still subject to further research. For example, computing the hash values may be executed in parallel on the GPU, while generating the successor states. We restricted our exposition to BFS. As other algorithms discussed in literature like best-first search for directed model checking may also be streamed, they may to be executed on the GPU.

So far, the model checker works on a modern but ordinary personal computer. The presented algorithm can, however, be extended to computing clusters, e.g. by storing the search on shared external space, dividing a BFS layer into partitions, and expanding them on different nodes of the cluster. For this case, however, duplicate checking has to be synchronised.

In order to lift the analyzes to full LTL, in the future we likely will attach GPU breadth-first search to semi-external model checking. Together with large RAIDs of hard or solid state disks we expect to obtain a high-performance LTL model checker, exploiting the current cutting edges of hardware technology.

References

1. Barnat, J., Brim, L., Ceska, M., Lamr, T.: CUDA accelerated LTL model checking. In: International Conference on Parallel and Distributed Systems (ICPADS), pp. 34–41 (2009)
2. Barnat, J., Brim, L., Šimeček, P., Weber, M.: Revisiting resistance speeds up I/O-efficient LTL model checking. In: Ramakrishnan, C.R., Rehof, J. (eds.) TACAS 2008. LNCS, vol. 4963, pp. 48–62. Springer, Heidelberg (2008)
3. Biere, A., Cimatti, A., Clarke, E., Zhu, Y.: Symbolic model checking without BDDs. In: Cleaveland, W.R. (ed.) TACAS 1999. LNCS, vol. 1579, p. 193. Springer, Heidelberg (1999)
4. Bloom, B.: Space/time trade-offs in hashing coding with allowable errors. Communication of the ACM 13(7), 422–426 (1970)
5. Bosnacki, D., Edelkamp, S., Sulewski, D.: Efficient probabilistic model checking on general purpose graphics processors. In: Păsăreanu, C.S. (ed.) SPIN 2009. LNCS, vol. 5578, pp. 32–49. Springer, Heidelberg (2009)
6. Brim, L., Cerná, I., Moravec, P., Simsa, J.: Accepting predecessors are better than back edges in distributed LTL model-checking. In: Hu, A.J., Martin, A.K. (eds.) FMCAD 2004. LNCS, vol. 3312, pp. 352–366. Springer, Heidelberg (2004)
7. Brizzolari, F., Melatti, I., Tronci, E., Della Penna, G.: Disk based software verification via bounded model checking. In: 14th Asia-Pacific Software Engineering Conference (APSEC), pp. 358–365. IEEE Computer Society, Los Alamitos (2007)
8. Burks, A.W., Warren, D.W., Wright, J.B.: An analysis of a logical machine using parenthesis-free notation. Mathematical Tables and Other Aids to Computation 8(46), 53–57 (1954)
9. Edelkamp, S., Jabbar, S.: Large-scale directed model checking LTL. In: Valmari, A. (ed.) SPIN 2006. LNCS, vol. 3925, pp. 1–18. Springer, Heidelberg (2006)
10. Edelkamp, S., Sanders, P., Šimeček, P.: Semi-external LTL model checking. In: Gupta, A., Malik, S. (eds.) CAV 2008. LNCS, vol. 5123, pp. 530–542. Springer, Heidelberg (2008)
11. Edelkamp, S., Sulewski, D.: Model checking via delayed duplicate detection on the GPU. Technical Report 821, Technische Universität Dortmund (2008); Presented on the 22nd Workshop on Planning, Scheduling, and Design PUK (2008)
12. Edelkamp, S., Sulewski, D.: Perfect hashing for domain-dependent planning on the GPU. In: 20th International Conference on Automated Planning and Scheduling (to appear, 2010)
13. Evangelista, S.: Dynamic delayed duplicate detection for external memory model checking. In: Havelund, K., Majumdar, R., Palsberg, J. (eds.) SPIN 2008. LNCS, vol. 5156, pp. 77–94. Springer, Heidelberg (2008)
14. Gao, H., Hesselink, W.H.: A general lock-free algorithm using compare-and-swap. Inf. Comput. 205(2), 225–241 (2007)
15. Gastin, P., Moro, P.: Minimal counterexample generation in SPIN. In: Bošnački, D., Edelkamp, S. (eds.) SPIN 2007. LNCS, vol. 4595, pp. 24–38. Springer, Heidelberg (2007)

16. Govindaraju, N.K., Gray, J., Kumar, R., Manocha, D.: GPUTeraSort: High performance graphics coprocessor sorting for large database management. In: International Conference on Management of Data (SIGMOD), pp. 325–336 (2006)
17. Harish, P., Narayanan, P.: Accelerating large graph algorithms on the gpu using cuda. In: Aluru, S., Parashar, M., Badrinath, R., Prasanna, V.K. (eds.) HiPC 2007. LNCS, vol. 4873, pp. 197–208. Springer, Heidelberg (2007)
18. Harris, M., Sengupta, S., Owens, J.D.: Parallel prefix sum (scan) with cuda. In: GPU Gems 3. Addison-Wesley, Reading (August 2007)
19. Holzmann, G.: The Spin Model Checker: Primer and Reference Manual. Addison-Wesley, Reading (2004)
20. Holzmann, G., Bosnacki, D.: The design of a multicore extension of the SPIN model checker. IEEE Transactions on Software Engineering 33(10), 659–674 (2007)
21. Holzmann, G.J.: An analysis of bitstate hashing. Formal Methods in System Design 13(3), 287–305 (1998)
22. Jayachandran, G., Vishal, V., Pande, V.S.: Using massively parallel simulations and Markovian models to study protein folding: Examining the Villin head-piece. Journal of Chemical Physics 124(6), 164903–164914 (2006)
23. Lamborn, P., Hansen, E.: Layered duplicate detection in external-memory model checking. In: Havelund, K., Majumdar, R., Palsberg, J. (eds.) SPIN 2008. LNCS, vol. 5156, pp. 160–175. Springer, Heidelberg (2008)
24. Leischner, N., Osipov, V., Sanders, P.: Gpu sample sort. CoRR, abs/0909.5649 (2009)
25. Nguyen, V.Y., Ruys, T.C.: Incremental hashing for Spin. In: Havelund, K., Majumdar, R., Palsberg, J. (eds.) SPIN 2008. LNCS, vol. 5156, pp. 232–249. Springer, Heidelberg (2008)
26. Pagh, R., Rodler, F.F.: Cuckoo hashing. In: Meyer auf der Heide, F. (ed.) ESA 2001. LNCS, vol. 2161, pp. 121–133. Springer, Heidelberg (2001)
27. Pelánek, R.: BEEM: Benchmarks for Explicit Model Checkers. In: Bošnački, D., Edelkamp, S. (eds.) SPIN 2007. LNCS, vol. 4595, pp. 263–267. Springer, Heidelberg (2007)
28. Phillips, J.C., Braun, R., Wang, W., Gumbart, J., Tajkhorshid, E., Villa, E., Chipot, C., Skeel, R.D., Kale, L., Schulten, K.: Scalable molecular dynamics with NAMD. Journal of Computational Chemistry 26, 1781–1802 (2005)
29. Putze, F., Sanders, P., Singler, J.: Cache-, hash-, and space-efficient bloom filters. ACM Journal of Experimental Algorithmics 14 (2009)
30. Ravi, K., Bloem, R., Somenzi, F.: A Comparative Study of Symbolic Algorithms for the Computation of Fair Cycles. In: Johnson, S.D., Hunt Jr., W.A. (eds.) FMCAD 2000. LNCS, vol. 1954, pp. 143–160. Springer, Heidelberg (2000)
31. Stern, U., Dill, D.L.: Using magnetic disk instead of main memory in the murphi verifier. In: Probst, D.K., von Bochmann, G. (eds.) CAV 1992. LNCS, vol. 663, pp. 172–183. Springer, Heidelberg (1993)
32. Verstoep, K., Bal, H., Barnat, J., Brim, L.: Efficient Large-Scale Model Checking. In: 23rd IEEE International Symposium on Parallel and Distributed Processing (IPDPS). IEEE, Los Alamitos (2009)

The SpinJa Model Checker*

Marc de Jonge[1] and Theo C. Ruys[2]

[1] TNO, The Netherlands
marcdejonge@gmail.com
[2] RUwise, The Netherlands
theo.ruys@gmail.com

Abstract. SpinJa is a model checker for PROMELA, implemented in Java. SpinJa is designed to behave similarly to Spin, but to be more easily extendible and reusable. Despite the fact that SpinJa uses a layered object-oriented design and is written in Java, SpinJa's performance is reasonable: benchmark experiments have shown that, in exhaustive mode, SpinJa is about five times slower than the highly optimized Spin. For bitstate verification runs the difference is only a factor of two.

1 Introduction

The Spin model checker [2,10] is arguably one of the most powerful and popular (software) model checkers available. Unfortunately, the highly optimized C code of Spin is difficult to understand and hard to extend. Moreover, the algorithms implemented in Spin cannot be reused in other tools.

This paper presents SpinJa[1] [11], a model checker for PROMELA, implemented in Java. SpinJa is designed to behave similarly to Spin, but to be more easily extendible and reusable.

Related Work. Independently from SpinJa, Mordechai Ben-Ari has started the development of the model checker Erigone [1,8], a model checker for (a subset of) PROMELA, implemented in Ada. Erigone's goal is to facilitate *learning* concurrency and model checking. NIPS [7,9] is another attempt to provide a stand-alone alternative model checker for PROMELA. NIPS uses the virtual machine approach to model checking. Both Erigone and NIPS do not (yet) implement any of Spin's powerful optimization algorithms (e.g., partial order reduction, bitstate hashing, hash compaction) though.

Sec. 2 explains the design and implementation of SpinJa. Sec. 3 reports on a benchmark experiment with SpinJa and Spin. Sec. 4 concludes the paper and discusses future work.

2 SpinJa

SpinJa can be used to check for the absence of deadlocks, assertions, liveness properties and never claims in PROMELA models. SpinJa's verification mode can

* The first version of SpinJa has been developed as part of a MSc project within the Formal Methods & Tools group of the University of Twente, The Netherlands.

[1] SpinJa stands for '*Spin in Java*'. SpinJa rhymes with *ninja*.

J. van de Pol and M. Weber (Eds.): SPIN 2010, LNCS 6349, pp. 124–128, 2010.

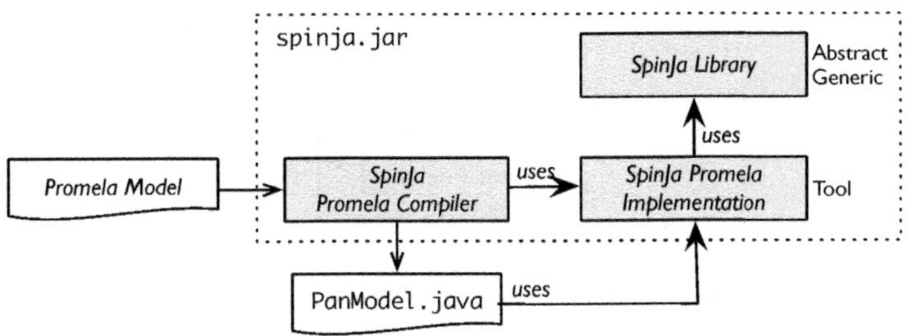

Fig. 1. Architecture of SpinJa

exploit (nested) depth first search (DFS) or breadth first search (BFS). Bitstate hashing and hash compaction modes are also supported. Furthermore, Spin's partial order reduction and statement merging are implemented. SpinJa can also be used for simulation. To enable or disable features, SpinJa uses the same syntax for options as Spin. And the output of SpinJa also mimics Spin: seasoned Spin users should feel right at home.

SpinJa supports a large subset of the PROMELA language. Currently, the following aspects of the PROMELA language are not yet supported: the `unless` statement, `typedef` definitions, non-FIFO communication, and embedded C code.

2.1 Design

The research question behind the development of SpinJa was the following: 'Is it possible to re-implement the core of Spin in Java using an extendible object-oriented design while being competitive in terms of memory consumption and runtime behaviour?' Beforehand – given the folklore about Java's infamous lack of speed, compared to C/C++ – we would have been happy if SpinJa would turn out to be a single order of magnitude slower than Spin.

From the start we have committed ourselves to Java and a clean object-oriented approach. This section only sketches the design of SpinJa; please refer to [3] for a detailed description.

Fig. 1 shows the high-level architecture of SpinJa. SpinJa follows the same principle as Spin: given a PROMELA model as input, a verifier program is generated: `PanModel.java`. The SpinJa library, which is used by `PanModel.java`, consists of two parts: a PROMELA specific part and a generic part. The complete SpinJa package (i.e., compiler and library) is supplied as a single Java jar-file.

For the design and implementation of SpinJa we have adopted the conceptual framework for explicit-state model checkers as developed by Mark Kattenbelt et.al. [5]. This layered framework is more flexible than the 'black box' approach of conventional model checkers. Fig. 2 shows the layered model as implemented in SpinJa. Each layer extends the layer below it and adds more functionality. This is achieved through inheritance. This way the different parts of the model checker are loosely coupled. This increases the maintainability and reusability of the whole system.

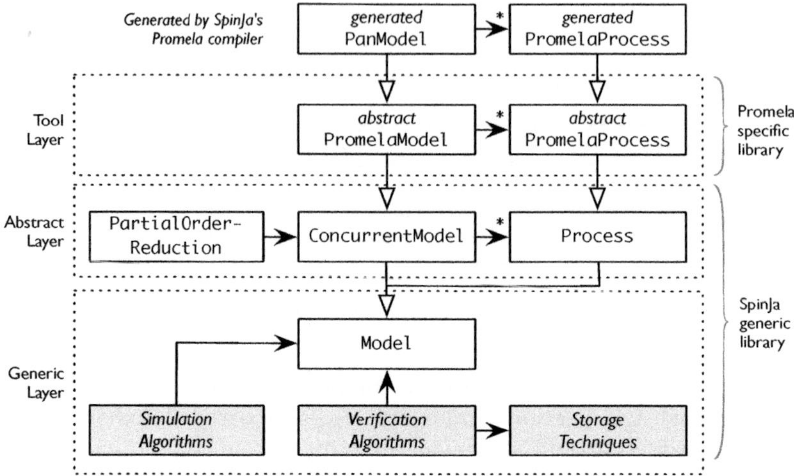

Fig. 2. Layered design of SpinJa

Generic layer. The Generic layer is the lowest layer. A `Model` is responsible for generating all the states at run-time. The `Model` knows how to take `Transitions` from one state to the next. On the basis of just `State` and `Transition` objects, several important algorithms are implemented within the generic layer: search (DFS, BFS) and simulation algorithms, storage methods, hashing methods.
Abstract layer. The Abstract layer extends on the Generic layer by adding concurrency to the model: a `ConcurrentModel` is a collection of `Processes` which are `Model` objects themselves. The class `PartialOrderReduction` changes the way the set of successor transitions of a `ConcurrentModel` are being computed. The Generic and Abstract layers are completely independent from the PROMELA language and could serve as the basis for any explicit-state model checker.
Tool Layer. Within the Tool layer the abstract `PromelaModel` is defined which forms the blueprint for the generated Java verifier `PanModel`. The `PromelaModel`, for example, knows how to create and terminate PROMELA proctypes and how to add `Channel` objects.
Compiler. The SpinJa PROMELA compiler is responsible for translating the PROMELA specification to the generated Java program: `PanModel`. Much effort has been put into implementing the same semantics for PROMELA as Spin does: in almost all cases, the resulting automata of the SpinJa compiler are the same as the ones that Spin produces. Consequently, for most PROMELA models, the number of states and transitions traversed by SpinJa and Spin are the same.

Implementation. The current version of SpinJa is version 0.9. SpinJa is released as open-source under the Apache 2.0 license and is available from [11]. The development took roughly one man year of work (i.e., [4] and [3]). The code base of SpinJa 0.9 consists of 144 files, 25k loc and its size is 1100Kb. By comparison, Spin 5.2.4 consists of 48 files, 48k loc and is 1200Kb and Erigone 2.1.5 consists of 71 files, 8k loc and is 300Kb.

Table 1. Summary of benchmark experiments: SPINJA vs. SPIN (*no* -O2 and *with* -O2). Running times are in seconds.

verification mode	⊘ *states*	⊘ *transitions*	⊘ SPINJA	⊘ SPIN no -O2	⊘ SPIN with -O2	SJA/(S no -O2)	SJA/(S with -O2)
Exhaustive, with POR	4.2×10^6	19.9×10^6	38.7	14.8	8.63	2.6×	4.5×
Exhaustive, no POR	4.2×10^6	20.2×10^6	38.4	13.9	8.06	2.8×	4.8×
Bitstate Hashing (with POR)	4.2×10^6	19.9×10^6	21.3	17.0	10.67	1.3×	2.0×
Hash Compaction (with POR)	4.2×10^6	19.9×10^6	20.5	14.7	8.56	1.4×	2.4×

3 Experiments

As mentioned in Sec. 2, we are interested in how a Java verifier generated by SPINJA compares with the C verifier generated by SPIN with respect to time and memory consumption. In this section we report on a benchmark experiment. For this paper, we have used ten medium size PROMELA models from the BEEM benchmark suite [6]: *at.4*, *elevator2.3*, *fischer.6*, *hanoi.3*, *loyd.2*, *mcs.3*, *peterson.4*, *sorter.3*, *szymanski.4* and *telephony.4*.

We compared SPIN against SPINJA in (i) a default exhaustive safety run, (ii) with partial order reduction (POR) disabled, (iii) in bitstate hashing mode (with -k3 -w31), and (iv) in hash compaction mode. We considered two versions of SPIN's pan verifier: (i) default compilation without optimizations and (ii) a compilation with gcc's -O2 optimization option set. All runs were limited to 1Gb of memory and a depth of 1.2×10^6 steps. All models could be verified completely except for *hanoi.3* which requires an even larger depth. The experiments were run on an Apple MacBook 2.4Ghz Intel Core 2 Duo, with 4Gb of RAM, running Mac OS X 10.5.8, with SPIN 5.2.4, SPINJA 0.9, gcc 4.2.1 and Java 1.6.0_17.

Table 1 summarizes the *averages* (i.e. ⊘) of running the verifiers: the number of states, the number of transitions and the running time (i.e., *user time*) of the verifiers in the various verification modes. Generation and compilation time have not been taken into account. The last two columns list the average speed difference factor between SPINJA and SPIN *without* -O2, and SPINJA and SPIN *with* -O2. Several important observations can be made from Table 1:

- SPIN's performance profits a lot from gcc's -O2 optimization option.
- Using Java for the implementation of a model checker seems acceptable: without -O2, SPIN is less than three times faster than SPINJA.
- SPINJA is surprisingly close to SPIN for the two approximate verification modes: the difference in speed is only a factor of two.

We do not report on the memory consumption of the verifiers in Table 1. The reason for this is that there is no substantial difference between SPINJA and SPIN with respect to memory. In most cases, SPINJA needs slightly less memory than SPIN though.

For a more extensive benchmark comparison between SPIN 5.1.6 and SPINJA 0.8 (under Windows XP and using Microsoft's C compiler) we refer to [3].

4 Conclusions

In this paper we presented SPINJA, a model checker for PROMELA, implemented in Java. Due to its layered, object-oriented design we believe that the design and implementation of SPINJA is clear, readable and extensible. Compared to the highly optimized C-based SPIN, the Java-based SPINJA is clearly slower. For bitstate hashing mode, however, the difference is only a factor of two. To extend the usability of SPINJA further, several improvements are planned:

- Support for the missing PROMELA features.
- Support for modelling languages other than PROMELA.
- Implementation of SPIN's `-DREVERSE`, `-DP_RAND`, `-DT_REVERSE` and `-DT_RANDOM` to increase the coverage of bitstate hashing verification runs.
- Improvement of SPINJA's explicit-state storage algorithms.
- Support for embedding Java code (similar to the support for C code in SPIN); this would make it possible to use SPINJA to model check Java applications.
- Development of a code generator for PROMELA on basis of SPINJA's generated verifier code.

References

1. Ben-Ari, M.: Teaching Concurrency and Model Checking. In: Păsăreanu, C.S. (ed.) SPIN 2009. LNCS, vol. 5578, pp. 6–11. Springer, Heidelberg (2009)
2. Holzmann, G.J.: The SPIN Model Checker – Primer and Reference Manual. Addison-Wesley, Boston (2004)
3. de Jonge, M.: The SpinJ Model Checker. Master's thesis, University of Twente, Enschede, The Netherlands (September 2008)
4. Kattenbelt, M.A.: Towards an Explicit-State Model Checking Framework. Master's thesis, University of Twente, Enschede, The Netherlands (September 2006)
5. Kattenbelt, M.A., Ruys, T.C., Rensink, A.: An Object-Oriented Framework for Explicit-State Model Checking. In: Proc. of VVSS 2007, Eindhoven, The Netherlands, March 2007. pp. 84–92. TUE Computer Science Reports, Nr. 07-04 (2007)
6. Pelánek, R.: BEEM: Benchmarks for Explicit Model Checkers. In: Bošnački, D., Edelkamp, S. (eds.) SPIN 2007. LNCS, vol. 4595, pp. 263–267. Springer, Heidelberg (2007)
7. Weber, M.: An Embeddable Virtual Machine for State Space Generation. In: Bošnački, D., Edelkamp, S. (eds.) SPIN 2007. LNCS, vol. 4595, pp. 168–185. Springer, Heidelberg (2007)
8. ERIGONE, http://code.google.com/p/erigone/
9. NIPS, http://www.ewi.utwente.nl/~michaelw/nips/
10. SPIN, http://spinroot.com/
11. SPINJA, http://code.google.com/p/spinja/

On the Virtue of Patience: Minimizing Büchi Automata*

Rüdiger Ehlers and Bernd Finkbeiner

Reactive Systems Group
Saarland University
{ehlers,finkbeiner}@react.cs.uni-saarland.de

Abstract. Explicit-state model checkers like SPIN, which verify systems against properties stated in linear-time temporal logic (LTL), rely on efficient LTL-to-Büchi translators. A difficult design decision in such constructions is to trade time spent on minimizing the Büchi automaton versus time spent on model checking against an unnecessarily large automaton. Standard reduction methods like simulation quotienting are fast but often miss optimization opportunities. We propose a new technique that achieves significant further reductions when more time can be invested in the minimization of the automaton. The additional effort is often justified, for example, when the properties are known in advance, or when the same property is used in multiple model checking runs. We use a modified SAT solver to perform bounded language inclusion checks on partial solutions. SAT solving allows us to prune large parts of the search space for smaller automata already in the early solving stages. The bound allows us to fine-tune the algorithm to run in limited time. Our experimental results show that, on standard LTL-to-Büchi benchmarks, our prototype implementation achieves a significant further size reduction on automata obtained by the best currently available LTL-to-Büchi translators.

1 Introduction

Minimizing Büchi automata is a fundamental task in automatic verification. Explicit-state model checkers like SPIN [13] translate the specification, given as a formula in linear-time temporal logic (LTL), into a Büchi automaton that corresponds to the negation of the formula. This automaton is composed with the system-under-verification, and the resulting product is checked for counterexample traces. Since the specification is usually much smaller than the system, reducing the automaton generated from the specification even by a small number of states can have a huge impact on the size of the product state space and, hence, on the performance of the model checker.

* This work was supported by the German Research Foundation (DFG) within the program "Performance Guarantees for Computer Systems" and the Transregional Collaborative Research Center "Automatic Verification and Analysis of Complex Systems" (SFB/TR 14 AVACS).

J. van de Pol and M. Weber (Eds.): SPIN 2010, LNCS 6349, pp. 129–145, 2010.

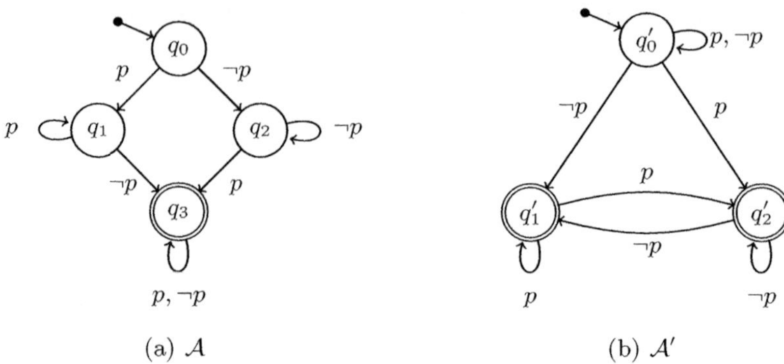

Fig. 1. Two Büchi automata for the LTL formula $(Fp) \wedge (F\neg p)$. The 4-state automaton $\mathcal{A}$ shown on the left was generated by a standard LTL-to-Büchi translator. The equivalent 3-state automaton $\mathcal{A}'$ shown on the right was obtained using our minimization method.

Since minimizing Büchi automata is hard (it includes the universality problem as a special case, which is already PSPACE-hard), the optimization techniques in the literature aim for a compromise between time spent on minimizing the Büchi automaton versus time spent on model checking against an unnecessarily large automaton. In addition to simple local optimizations such as edge label rewriting and the elimination of subautomata without accepting runs, the standard approach is to merge states based on simulation and bisimulation relations (cf. [8,16,12]). Simulation and bisimulation relations can be computed in polynomial time. Optimizing automata by merging similar states is therefore fast, but it often misses optimization opportunities. Consider, for example, the automata shown in Figure 1, which correspond to the LTL formula $\mathsf{F}p \wedge \mathsf{F}\neg p$ over the singleton set $\{p\}$ of atomic propositions. The 4-state automaton $\mathcal{A}$ on the left was generated by a standard LTL-to-Büchi translator: q_0 is the initial state; q_1 represents the case where a p has been seen, but not yet a $\neg p$, and, analogously, q_2 the case where a $\neg p$ has been seen but not yet a p; q_3 represents the case where both obligations have been satisfied. Since none of the four states simulates any other state, standard reduction techniques cannot optimize this automaton any further. There exists, however, an equivalent automaton $\mathcal{A}'$ with just 3 states, shown on the right in Figure 1: an accepting run on a word that contains both p and $\neg p$ simply stays in the initial state q_0' until just before some $p, \neg p$ or $\neg p, p$ sequence occurs and then moves between the accepting states q_1' and q_2' according to the remaining suffix.

Given the complexity of the minimization problem, it seems unlikely that one can improve over the standard reduction techniques without increasing the computation time. However, investing additional time may well be justified. Considering that the specification is often written long before the system design is complete, it is not unrealistic to assume that the optimization of the specification automata can begin hours or even days before the first model checking run. If such additional time is available, can it be used productively to obtain smaller automata that might then, once the verification starts, be used over and over again, when different systems (or, during debugging, multiple versions of the same system) are checked against the same properties?

In this paper, we present a new optimization technique that uses a modified SAT solver to search for a small automaton that accepts the same language as a given reference automaton $\mathcal{A}^+$. For this purpose, we encode a ***candidate automaton*** $\mathcal{A}$ with Boolean variables and check, after each decision made by the solver, whether the current partial variable valuation can still be completed to the representation of an automaton that is equivalent to $\mathcal{A}^+$. It is fairly simple to ensure that the candidate automaton only accepts words that are in the language of $\mathcal{A}^+$, because we can compute the complement $\mathcal{A}^-$ of $\mathcal{A}^+$ (if the starting point is an LTL formula, we simply run the LTL-to-Büchi translator on the negated formula). Then, $\mathcal{L}(\mathcal{A}) \subseteq \mathcal{L}(\mathcal{A}^+)$ corresponds to $\mathcal{L}(\mathcal{A}^-) \cap \mathcal{L}(\mathcal{A}) = \emptyset$, which is easy to check. The challenge, however, is to efficiently check $\mathcal{L}(\mathcal{A}^+) \subseteq \mathcal{L}(\mathcal{A})$, because here the complement would have to be recomputed for every candidate automaton.

We introduce ***bounded*** language containment, an approximative version of language containment, whose precision and computational cost can be fine-tuned so that the check runs in limited time. Bounded language containment between two Büchi automata $\mathcal{A}$ and $\mathcal{A}'$ requires that there exists a constant $b \in \mathbb{N}$ such that for each accepting run π of $\mathcal{A}$ on some word there is a run π' of $\mathcal{A}'$ on the same word such that the number of visits to accepting states in π between two visits of accepting states in π' is bounded by b. We can thus fine-tune the precision of bounded language containment by choosing different values for the bound: higher values result in greater precision, lower values in faster computation. No matter how we choose the bound, however, bounded language containment is always a sound approximation of language containment.

A SAT-based search for the smallest Büchi automaton that accepts the same language as a given reference automaton is slower than applying standard optimization techniques directly on the reference automaton. On automata from LTL-to-Büchi benchmarks [16,8,6], our prototype implementation often runs for several hours. By comparison, it usually only takes seconds to compute some reference automaton. However, the resulting size reduction is remarkable: even for automata obtained by the best currently available LTL-to-Büchi translators, `spot` [5] and `ltl2ba` [10], using various parameter settings on standard benchmarks for LTL-to-Büchi translation, our method improves in 43 out of 94 cases over the smallest automaton found by the LTL-to-Büchi tools, saving as many as 22 out of 28 states in one benchmark.

The remainder of the paper is structured as follows. In the following section, we review preliminaries on Büchi automata and SAT solving. In Section 3, we present our new algorithm for checking language equivalence based on bounded language containment. In Section 4, we integrate this algorithm into the SAT-based search for a small automaton that accepts the same language as a given reference automaton. Our experimental results are reported in Section 5. We conclude the paper in Section 6 with a discussion of the benefits and limitations of our approach in comparison to precise language containment and simulation-based approaches.

2 Preliminaries

2.1 Büchi Automata

A *Büchi automaton* $\mathcal{A} = (Q, \Sigma, \delta, q_0, F)$ consists of a finite set of states Q, a finite alphabet Σ, a transition relation $\delta \subseteq Q \times \Sigma \times Q$ with a designated initial state $q_0 \in Q$, and a set of accepting states $F \subseteq Q$. We refer to the number of states in an automaton as its *size*.

A word over an alphabet Σ is an infinite sequence $w = w_0 w_1 \ldots \in \Sigma^\omega$. A *run* of $\mathcal{A}$ on an infinite word $w = w_0 w_1 \ldots \in \Sigma^\omega$ is an infinite sequence $\pi = \pi_0 \pi_1 \ldots \in Q^\omega$ of states where $\pi_0 = q_0$ and for all $i \in \mathbb{N}_0$, $(\pi_i, w_i, \pi_{i+1}) \in \delta$. A run π is *accepting* iff $\inf(\pi) \cap F \neq \emptyset$, where $\inf(\pi)$ denotes the set of states that occur infinitely often in π. The automaton is *without dead-ends* if every finite prefix of a run can be extended to an accepting run (possibly on a different input word). A word w is accepted by $\mathcal{A}$ iff there exists an accepting run for it. We denote the set of runs of $\mathcal{A}$ on w by $\mathcal{R}(\mathcal{A}, w)$, and the set of accepting runs by $\mathcal{R}_F(\mathcal{A}, w)$. For convenience, we extend the definition of $\mathcal{R}(\mathcal{A}, w)$ to finite prefixes $w \in \Sigma^*$ in the natural way. The set of accepted words is called the *language* $\mathcal{L}(\mathcal{A})$ of the automaton. Two automata $\mathcal{A}, \mathcal{A}'$ are *equivalent* if $\mathcal{L}(\mathcal{A}) = \mathcal{L}(\mathcal{A}')$.

An important application of Büchi automata is model checking for specifications given in *linear-time temporal logic* (LTL). The models of an LTL formula are infinite words over the alphabet $\Sigma = 2^{\mathsf{AP}}$, where AP is a fixed set of atomic propositions. In analogy to Büchi automata, we call the set of words that satisfy an LTL formula ψ the language $\mathcal{L}(\psi)$ of ψ. Model checkers like SPIN use translation algorithms that construct for a given LTL formula ψ a Büchi automaton such that $\mathcal{L}(\psi) = \mathcal{L}(\mathcal{A})$. Several such algorithms are described in the literature (cf. [16,8,10,11]). For a comprehensive introduction to LTL and LTL model checking we refer the reader to standard textbooks on computer-aided verification (cf. [1]).

2.2 SAT Solving

Satisfiability (SAT) is the problem of determining if the variables of a given Boolean formula can be assigned in such a way that the formula evaluates to true. A SAT instance is given as a set of Boolean variables V and a set of clauses C, all of which are of the form $l_1 \vee \ldots \vee l_n$ for some set of literals $l_1, \ldots, l_n$ with $l_i \in V \cup \{\neg v : v \in V\}$ for all $1 \leq i \leq n$. An assignment of the variables to the values in $\mathbb{B} = \{\mathbf{false}, \mathbf{true}\}$ is called valid for $\langle V, C \rangle$ if it leads to the satisfaction of all clauses.

The algorithm presented in this paper is based on *search-based* SAT solving. Search-based SAT solvers maintain a *partial valuation* $V \rightarrow \{\mathbf{false}, \mathbf{true}, \bot\}$

of the variables by assigning to every variable either a truth value in $\mathbb{B}$ or the value $\bot$, indicating that no truth value has been decided for the variable yet. We call a partial evaluation $z' \in (V \to \{\mathbf{false}, \mathbf{true}, \bot\})$ an *extension* of a partial valuation $z \in (V \to \{\mathbf{false}, \mathbf{true}, \bot\})$ if for all $v \in V$ with $z(v) \in \mathbb{B}$, we have $z'(v) = z(v)$. A partial valuation z' is a *completion* of some partial valuation z if z' is an extension of z and every extension of z' is identical to z'.

In every step of the computation, the solver checks if the current decisions already make some clause unsatisfied, i.e., if a partial valuation has been reached where no completion of satisfies the clause. In this case, we say that a ***conflict*** has occurred and the solver ***back-tracks*** some of the decisions already made. Then, modern solvers analyze the cause of the conflict and store a learned clause that prevents the decisions that lead to the conflict from being made again.

SAT solving has been extended with ***non-clausal constraints***, as they occur, for example, in ***satisfiability modulo theory*** solving [2]. The SAT instance is now given as a tuple $\langle V, C, N\rangle$, where the set of variables V and the set of clauses C is defined as before. Additionally, the set of non-clausal constraints $N \subseteq (V \to \{\mathbf{false}, \mathbf{true}, \bot\}) \to \mathbb{B}$ consists of functions that map partial valuations to a truth value indicating whether the partial valuation has a completion satisfying the constraint. Consequently, for a non-clausal constraint $f \in N$ and two partial valuations z, z', where z' is an extension of z, $f(z') = \mathbf{true}$ implies $f(z) = \mathbf{true}$. For SAT with non-clausal constraints, the solver checks, after each decision and for each non-clausal and clausal constraint, whether the current partial valuation can be extended in such a way that the constraint is satisfied. For more background on SAT solving, we refer the interested reader to a recent handbook [4].

3 Checking Language Equivalence

The key component of our minimization algorithm is the efficient test whether some candidate automaton accepts the same language as the reference automaton. As discussed in the introduction, we use a precise test to check whether the language of the candidate automaton is contained in the language of the reference automaton, and an approximative test, called ***bounded*** language containment, to check the opposite direction. These two tests are discussed in the following two subsections.

3.1 Precise Language Containment

The standard way to check if the language of an automaton $\mathcal{A}$ is contained in the language of an automaton $\mathcal{A}'$ is to check whether the intersection of $\mathcal{L}(\mathcal{A})$ with the complement of $\mathcal{L}(\mathcal{A}')$ is empty: $\mathcal{L}(\mathcal{A}) \subseteq \mathcal{L}(\mathcal{A}')$ iff $\mathcal{L}(\mathcal{A}) \cap (\Sigma^\omega \setminus \mathcal{L}(\mathcal{A}')) = \emptyset$.

The drawback of this approach is that the complementation of $\mathcal{A}'$ is expensive: the number of states in the complement automaton is exponential in the number of states of $\mathcal{A}$. In our construction, we use precise language containment for checking whether the language of a candidate automaton $\mathcal{A}$ is contained in the

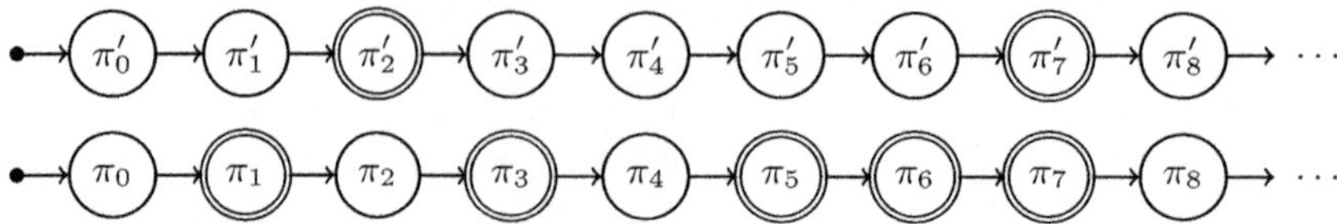

Fig. 2. A pair of runs with an acceptance lag of (at least) 3. The figure shows (prefixes of) runs π and π' of two Büchi automata on the same input word. Visits to accepting states are depicted as double circles. The acceptance lag between π and π' is at least 3, because π has 3 visits to accepting states between the two visits to accepting states of π' in positions 2 and 7.

language of the reference automaton $\mathcal{A}^+$, but not for the opposite direction. In this way, only a single complementation, of the reference automaton $\mathcal{A}^+$ into its complement $\mathcal{A}^-$, is required. Furthermore, if $\mathcal{A}^+$ was obtained from an LTL formula ψ, we obtain $\mathcal{A}^-$ simply by translating the LTL formula $\neg\psi$ to a Büchi automaton.

3.2 Bounded Language Containment

Bounded language containment is an efficient approximative check if the language of an automaton $\mathcal{A}$ is contained in the language of an automaton $\mathcal{A}'$. In addition to the standard language containment condition, that for every word $w \in \Sigma^\omega$ and accepting run $\pi \in \mathcal{R}_F(\mathcal{A}, w)$ in $\mathcal{A}$, there must exist some accepting run $\pi' \in \mathcal{R}_F(\mathcal{A}', w)$ in $\mathcal{A}'$, we require that the number of visits to accepting states in π between two visits to accepting states in π' is bounded by some constant. Formally, the ***acceptance lag*** between a run $\pi = \pi_0\pi_1\ldots$ of $\mathcal{A}$ and a run $\pi' = \pi'_0\pi'_1\ldots$ of $\mathcal{A}'$ is defined as follows:

$$\begin{aligned}\mathrm{lag}(\pi, \pi') = \max\{ & j \in \mathbb{N}_0 : \exists x_1, \ldots, x_j \in \mathbb{N}_0 : (\forall 1 \le i < j : x_i < x_{i+1}) \\ & \wedge (\forall 1 \le i \le j : \pi_{x_i} \in F) \wedge (\forall x_1 \le i \le x_j : \pi'_i \notin F')\}\end{aligned}$$

In the example shown in Figure 2, the acceptance lag is (at least) 3, because π has 3 visits to accepting states (in positions 3, 5, and 6) between the two visits to accepting states of π' in positions 2 and 7.

Clearly, if π is an accepting run and the lag between π and π' is bounded by some constant, then π' is also accepting. Furthermore, if we have a word w that is in the language of $\mathcal{A}$ but not in the language of $\mathcal{A}'$, then the lag between some accepting run of $\mathcal{A}$ on w and an arbitrary run of $\mathcal{A}'$ on w is unbounded: any run of $\mathcal{A}'$ on w is rejecting and, hence, visits the accepting states only finitely often. Thus, if we fix some bound $b \in \mathbb{N}$ and observe that for every word w and every run $\pi \in \mathcal{R}_F(\mathcal{A}, w)$, the lag between π and some run $\pi' \in \mathcal{R}(\mathcal{A}', w)$ is at most b, we can conclude that indeed $\mathcal{L}(\mathcal{A}) \subseteq \mathcal{L}(\mathcal{A}')$.

This observation is the motivation for the definition of bounded language containment, which simultaneously checks the same bound for all words in Σ^ω. For a bound $b \in \mathbb{N}$, we say that the language of $\mathcal{A}$ is ***b-bounded contained*** in the language of $\mathcal{A}'$, denoted by $\mathcal{L}(\mathcal{A}) \subseteq_b \mathcal{L}(\mathcal{A}')$, if, for every word $w \in \Sigma^\omega$ and every $\pi \in \mathcal{R}_F(\mathcal{A}, w)$, there exists some $\pi' \in \mathcal{R}(\mathcal{A}', w)$ such that $\text{lag}(\pi, \pi') \leq b$. We use bounded language containment as a conservative approximation of language containment: for every $b \in \mathbb{N}$, $\mathcal{L}(\mathcal{A}) \subseteq_b \mathcal{L}(\mathcal{A}')$ implies $\mathcal{L}(\mathcal{A}) \subseteq \mathcal{L}(\mathcal{A}')$.

The idea of the bounded language containment checking algorithm we describe next is to encode bounded language containment as a graph reachability problem. The *lag-checking graph* branches according to the possible runs of $\mathcal{A}$ and keeps track of the possible runs of $\mathcal{A}'$ on the same input word. For this purpose, the vertices of the lag-checking graph contain a counter value $f(q')$ for each state q' of $\mathcal{A}'$ that indicates how many visits to accepting states in $\mathcal{A}$ (without visiting accepting states in $\mathcal{A}'$) are left before the paths through q' will exceed the bound on the acceptance lag.

Definition 1. *For two Büchi automata $\mathcal{A} = (Q, \Sigma, \delta, q_0, F)$ and $\mathcal{A}' = (Q', \Sigma, \delta', q'_0, F')$, and a bound $b \in \mathbb{N}$, the* lag-checking graph *$\mathcal{G}(\mathcal{A}, \mathcal{A}', b) = \langle V, E\rangle$ consists of the following set V of vertices and set $E \subseteq V \times \Sigma \times V$ of labelled edges:*

- $V = Q \times (Q' \to \{0, \ldots, b+1\})$
- *For all $(q_1, f_1), (q_2, f_2) \in V$ with $q_2 \in F$, and for all $x \in \Sigma$, we have $((q_1, f_1), x, (q_2, f_2)) \in E$ if and only if $(q_1, x, q_2) \in \delta$ and*
  - *for all $q'_2 \in F'$: if there exist some $q'_1 \in Q'$ with $f_1(q'_1) > 0$ such that $(q'_1, x, q'_2) \in \delta'$, then $f_2(q'_2) = b + 1$, otherwise $f_2(q'_2) = 0$;*
  - *for all $q'_2 \notin F'$: $f_2(q'_2) = \max(\{f_1(q'_1) - 1 : q'_1 \in Q', (q'_1, x, q'_2) \in \delta'\} \cup \{0\})$.*
- *For all $(q_1, f_1), (q_2, f_2) \in V$ with $q_2 \notin F$, and for all $x \in \Sigma$, we have $((q_1, f_1), x, (q_2, f_2)) \in E$ if and only if $(q_1, x, q_2) \in \delta$ and*
  - *for all $q'_2 \in F'$: if there exists some $q'_1 \in Q'$ with $f(q'_1) > 0$ such that $(q'_1, x, q'_2) \in \delta'$, then $f_2(q'_2) = b + 1$, otherwise $f_2(q'_2) = 0$;*
  - *for all $q'_2 \notin F'$: $f_2(q'_2) = \max(\{f_1(q'_1) : q'_1 \in Q', (q'_1, x, q'_2) \in \delta'\})$.*

If $q_0 \notin F$ or $q'_0 \in F$, we call the vertex (q_0, f_0), where $f_0(q'_0) = b + 1$ and $f_0(q') = 0$ for all $q' \in Q' \setminus \{q'_0\}$, the initial vertex; otherwise, the vertex (q_0, f_0), where $f_0(q'_0) = b$ and $f_0(q') = 0$ for all $q' \in Q' \setminus \{q'_0\}$, is the initial vertex. Additionally, we call the vertices (q, f), where $f(q') = 0$ for all $q' \in Q'$, the final vertices.

Figure 3 shows, as an example, the lag-checking graph $\mathcal{G}(\mathcal{A}, \mathcal{A}', 1)$ for the automata $\mathcal{A}$ and $\mathcal{A}'$ from Figure 1 and bound 1. Since every reachable vertex has some non-zero counter, there exists, for every run on $\mathcal{A}$, a run of $\mathcal{A}'$ on the same input word such that the acceptance lag is bounded by 1. We formalize the meaning of the node labels in the following lemmas.

Lemma 2. *Let $w = w_0 \ldots w_{k-1} \in \Sigma^*$ be a finite word, $\mathcal{A} = (Q, \Sigma, \delta, q_0, F)$ and $\mathcal{A}' = (Q', \Sigma, \delta', q'_0, F')$ be two Büchi automata, $\pi = \pi_0 \ldots \pi_k$ be a prefix of a run of $\mathcal{A}$, and $b > 0$ be some bound. For any number $c > 0$ and state $q' \in Q'$,*

- *if there exists some path $(q_0, f_0) \xrightarrow{w_0} (q_1, f_1) \xrightarrow{w_1} \ldots \xrightarrow{w_{k-1}} (q_k, f_k)$ in $\mathcal{G}(\mathcal{A}, \mathcal{A}', b)$ from the initial vertex (q_0, f_0), such that $q_i = \pi_i$, for all $i \in \{0, \ldots, k\}$, and $f_k(q') = c$,*

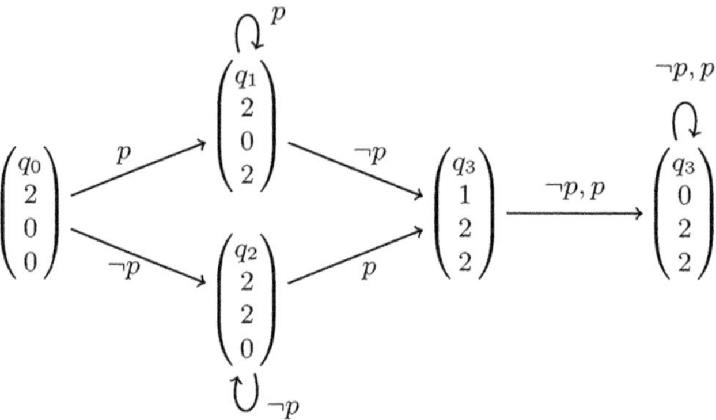

Fig. 3. Example lag-checking graph that shows that language of the automaton depicted on the left in Figure 1 is 1-bounded contained in the language of the automaton depicted on the right in Figure 1. In each vertex (q, f) of the lag-checking graph, the values of q, $f(q'_0)$, $f(q'_1)$ and $f(q'_2)$ are shown (from top to bottom). No final vertex (i.e., no vertex (q, f) with $f(q') = 0$ for all $q' \in Q'$) is reachable.

- *then there exists a run prefix* $\pi' = \pi'_0 \ldots \pi'_k$ *in* $\mathcal{R}(\mathcal{A}', w)$ *with* $\pi'_k = q'$ *such that* $\text{lag}(\pi, \pi') \leq b$ *and* $b - c + 1$ *visits to* F *have occurred along* π *after the last visit to an accepting state in* π'.

Lemma 3. *Let* $w = w_0 \ldots w_{k-1} \in \Sigma^*$ *be a finite word,* $\mathcal{A} = (Q, \Sigma, \delta, q_0, F)$ *and* $\mathcal{A}' = (Q', \Sigma, \delta', q'_0, F')$ *be two Büchi automata,* $\pi = \pi_0 \ldots \pi_k$ *be a prefix of a run of* $\mathcal{A}$*, and* $b > 0$ *be some bound. For any number* $c > 0$ *and state* $q' \in Q'$,

- *if there exists a run prefix* $\pi' = \pi'_0 \ldots \pi'_k$ *in* $\mathcal{R}(\mathcal{A}', w)$ *with* $\pi'_k = q'$ *such that* $\text{lag}(\pi, \pi') \leq b$ *and* $b - c + 1$ *visits to* F *have occurred along* π *after the last visit to an accepting state in* π',
- *then there exists some path* $(q_0, f_0) \xrightarrow{w_0} (q_1, f_1) \xrightarrow{w_1} \ldots \xrightarrow{w_{k-1}} (q_k, f_k)$ *in* $\mathcal{G}(\mathcal{A}, \mathcal{A}', b)$ *from the initial vertex* (q_0, f_0)*, such that* $q_i = \pi_i$*, for all* $i \in \{0, \ldots, k\}$*, and* $f_k(q') \geq c$.

The lemmas are easy to prove by induction over the length of w, π and π' and a case split on the four possible combinations of whether $\pi_k \in F$ and $\pi'_k \in F'$ hold or not. We use the two lemmas to reduce the bounded language containment check to a reachability property of the lag-checking graph:

Theorem 4. *Let* $\mathcal{A}$ *and* $\mathcal{A}'$ *be two Büchi automata such that* $\mathcal{A}$ *has no dead-ends, and let* $b \in \mathbb{N}$ *be some bound. The following two conditions are equivalent:*

1. $\mathcal{L}(\mathcal{A}) \subseteq_b \mathcal{L}(\mathcal{A}')$;
2. *in the lag-checking graph* $\mathcal{G}(\mathcal{A}, \mathcal{A}', b)$*, no final vertex is reachable from the initial node.*

The reachability of the final nodes can be checked by a simple depth-first or breadth-first graph traversal.

4 SAT-Based Minimization of Büchi Automata

We now describe a SAT-based algorithm for finding a small Büchi automaton that accepts the same language as a given reference automaton $\mathcal{A}^+$. We use a SAT solver to determine if, for a given number of states n, there is some automaton $\mathcal{A}$ that is equivalent to $\mathcal{A}^+$. For this purpose, we encode the candidate automata symbolically using Boolean variables and search for a valuation that corresponds to an automaton that passes the equivalence check defined in the previous section. We start by defining, in the following subsection, the Boolean encoding of the candidate automata. In Sections 4.2 and 4.3 we adapt the language containment tests from the previous section to this setting.

4.1 Boolean Encodings of Büchi Automata

We give a Boolean encoding for a candidate automaton $\mathcal{A} = (Q, \Sigma, \delta, q_0, F)$ over a given alphabet Σ and with a given number of states $n = |Q|$. Without loss of generality, we assume $Q = \{1, \ldots, n\}$ and $q_0 = 1$. It remains to encode the transition relation δ and the set F of accepting states.

For every pair $q, q' \in Q$ of states and input letter $s \in \Sigma$, we define a boolean variable $\langle q, s, q' \rangle_\delta$ indicating whether $(q, s, q') \in \delta'$. Likewise, for all states $q \in Q$, a boolean variable $\langle q \rangle_F$ is used for representing whether the state is accepting or not.

Checking if there exists an automaton $\mathcal{A}$ with n states and $\mathcal{L}(\mathcal{A}) = \mathcal{L}(\mathcal{A}^+)$ can be done by iterating over all possible transition relations δ and sets of final states F. For every combination of δ and F, we check whether the language of $\mathcal{A}$ with these values of δ and F is the same as the language of $\mathcal{A}^+$. For our encoding, the overall search space thus has a size of $2^{n^2|\Sigma|+n}$. We can assume that $\mathcal{A}^+$ has more than n states as otherwise the problem is trivial to solve (by taking $\mathcal{A} = \mathcal{A}^+$).

In the remainder of this section, we describe how to modify a SAT solver to search for smaller equivalent Büchi automata over this Boolean encoding. For this purpose we adapt the language equivalence check developed in the previous section to work on ***partially specified automata***, given by the partial valuation of the variables $\langle\cdot\rangle_\delta$ and $\langle\cdot\rangle_F$ provided by the SAT solver during the search.

This allows the SAT solver to recognize conflicts early. A commonly occurring situation is, for example, that the candidate automaton has a self-loop in an accepting initial state and, as a result, accepts words that are not in the language of $\mathcal{A}^+$. In this case, the decision procedure should be able to identify this situation already after only the two corresponding bits have been set of **true**.

We split the language equivalence $\mathcal{L}(\mathcal{A}) = \mathcal{L}(\mathcal{A}^+)$ into its two language containment relations. For $\mathcal{L}(\mathcal{A}) \subseteq \mathcal{L}(\mathcal{A}^+)$, we adapt the precise language containment check from Section 3.1, for $\mathcal{L}(\mathcal{A}^+) \subseteq \mathcal{L}(\mathcal{A})$ the bounded language containment check from Section 3.2. The two constructions are explained in the following subsections.

4.2 Checking $\mathcal{L}(\mathcal{A}) \subseteq \mathcal{L}(\mathcal{A}^+)$

As discussed in Section 3.1, we reduce $\mathcal{L}(\mathcal{A}) \subseteq \mathcal{L}(\mathcal{A}^+)$ to checking whether the intersection of $\mathcal{L}(\mathcal{A})$ with the complement of $\mathcal{L}(\mathcal{A}^+)$ is empty.

During the search for a satisfying variable valuation, we perform the test already on partially specified automata, i.e., when for some transitions it is not (yet) known whether they are contained in the transition relation or not, and for some states it is not (yet) known whether they are contained in the set of accepting states. Thus, we need to be able to check if the candidate automaton can be completed in a way such that (bounded) language containment holds.

In order to check language containment for a partially specified candidate automaton, we interpret the "undecided" value $\perp$ in a partial valuation as **false**. Since this eliminates any transitions and accepting states that are not required by the partial valuation, we thus obtain the candidate automaton with the *least* language that is compatible with the decisions made so far.

If the intersected language is non-empty, we also provide the SAT solver with a conflict clause. For this purpose, the emptiness check on the intersection automaton, which searches for a lasso path from the initial state to some loop that contains an accepting state, annotates every state in the intersection automaton with the predecessor state encountered during the search. When an accepting lasso is found, this annotation is used to traverse the lasso backwards. By collecting the negations of the literals in the SAT instance corresponding to the transitions on the lasso and the literal for the accepting state, we extract a conflict clause, which is used by the learning scheme of the SAT solver to avoid a repetition of the decisions that have allowed the language of the candidate automaton to become too large.

4.3 Checking $\mathcal{L}(\mathcal{A}^+) \subseteq \mathcal{L}(\mathcal{A})$

We check $\mathcal{L}(\mathcal{A}^+) \subseteq \mathcal{L}(\mathcal{A})$ using the bounded language containment test described in Section 3.2. In order to apply the test to partially specified candidate automata, we interpret the "undecided" value $\perp$ in a partial valuation as **true**, and thus obtain the candidate automaton with the *greatest* language that is compatible with the decisions made so far.

If the bounded language containment test $\mathcal{L}(\mathcal{A}^+) \subseteq_b \mathcal{L}(\mathcal{A})$ fails, we again supply the SAT solver with a cause for the conflict in order to benefit from its learning scheme. The test fails when a final vertex is reachable in the lag-checking graph $\mathcal{G}(\mathcal{A}^+, \mathcal{A}, b)$. We collect the labels $x \in \Sigma$ observed along the path from the initial vertex to some final vertex and report all SAT variables set to **false** corresponding to these alphabet symbols, along with all variables for final states that are set to **false**.

4.4 Symmetry Breaking

The concept of symmetry breaking has been identified to be indispensable for the efficient solution of many SAT problems [15]. Symmetry breaking prunes the search space of a SAT solver by adding constraints that remove some solutions that are isomorphic to others which are not pruned away. In the case of Büchi automaton minimization, for example, swapping two states in the automaton results in an automaton that is isomorphic to the original one.

For the purposes of this work, we break symmetry only partially as it has been observed that this is often faster than performing total symmetry breaking [15], where in the pruned state space, only one representative of each equivalence class of the automata equivalent under isomorphism remains. This is done by choosing some order over the variables and adding a (non-clausal) constraint to the SAT problem that for n being the number of states of the candidate automaton, for every $i \in \{1, \ldots, n-1\}$, swapping the ith and $(i+1)$th state does not result in an automaton that is lexicographically smaller with respect to this bit order.

5 Experimental Evaluation[1]

We have evaluated the automaton minimization approach presented in this paper on three benchmark sets from the literature, which have previously been used to evaluate and compare LTL-to-Büchi translators:

- The 27 specifications from the paper "Efficient Büchi Automata from LTL Formulae" by Fabio Somenzi and Roderick Bloem [16].
- The 12 specifications from the paper "Optimizing Büchi Automata" by Kousha Etessami and Gerard J. Holzmann [8].
- 55 LTL properties built from the specification patterns in the paper "Property Specification Patterns for Finite-state Verification" by Matthew B. Dwyer, George S. Avrunin and James C. Corbett [6].

We have implemented a single-threaded prototype tool on top of the SAT solver `minisat v.1.12b` [7]. Our tool reads in a reference automaton $\mathcal{A}^+$ and its complement $\mathcal{A}^-$ over some fixed alphabet Σ (using SPIN never-claim syntax) and checks, for some given bound $b \in \mathbb{N}$ and size $n \in \mathbb{N}$, whether there exists a Büchi automaton $\mathcal{A}$ with n states such that $\mathcal{L}(\mathcal{A}) \subseteq \mathcal{L}(\mathcal{A}^+)$ and $\mathcal{L}(\mathcal{A}^+) \subseteq_b \mathcal{L}(\mathcal{A})$ (assuming that $\mathcal{L}(\mathcal{A}^+) = \Sigma^\omega \setminus \mathcal{L}(\mathcal{A}^-)$). All benchmarks were performed on a computer with AMD Opteron 2.8Ghz processors running Linux. In our experiments, we have used bounds between 1 and 8.

Our goal has been to start with Büchi automata that have already been optimized by the best currently available methods. Starting with the LTL formulas from the benchmark suites, we therefore applied the two best currently available LTL-to-Büchi converters [14], namely `spot v.0.5a` [5] and `ltl2ba v.1.1` [10] to compute the automata $\mathcal{A}^+$ and $\mathcal{A}^-$. The `spot` tool combines several approaches and optimizations for the conversion process in one program; we applied all 15 different parameter combinations and took for every specification the smallest automata encountered for some tool/parameter combination. In total,

[1] Details and a downloadable implementation of the approach can be found at `http://react.cs.uni-saarland.de/tools/nbwminimizer`

this scheme resulted in $94 \cdot 16 \cdot 2$ calls to LTL-to-Büchi converters. In two of these cases, running spot required more than 5 minutes due to a expensive optimization. In these cases, we aborted the run and took the best automaton found by some other run instead. All in all, the computation of the Büchi automata took about 60 minutes on the computer mentioned above.

Table 1 shows the running times of our prototype tool on a typical (but rather small) specification from the third benchmark set. For some smaller values of the bound and number of states in the candidate automaton, the solver ran too quickly to measure its running time with the Linux `time` utility. On the other hand, needlessly large values of n and b can delay the termination of the

Table 1. Running times (in seconds) of our prototype tool for the specification $(\mathsf{G}\neg s) \vee \mathsf{F}(s \wedge (\neg r \mathsf{U}(t \vee \mathsf{G}\neg r)))$, inducing automata sizes of $|\mathcal{A}^+| = 6$ and $|\mathcal{A}^-| = 3$. Gray table cells represent cases in which the solver found out that the instance is satisfiable, i.e., some smaller automaton has been found. The respective tables for all 94 benchmarks can be found at `http://react.cs.uni-saarland.de/tools/nbwminimizer`.

# states / bound	1	2	3	4	5	6	7	8
1	0.0	0.0	0.0	0.0	0.0	0.0	0.0	0.0
2	0.0	0.0	0.0	0.0	0.0	0.02	0.0	0.01
3	0.01	0.03	0.05	0.1	0.1	0.1	0.12	0.11
4	0.52	1.15	2.21	1.33	1.07	2.35	2.74	2.05
5	0.3	1.03	27.28	10.24	56.41	59.21	80.2	80.1

Table 2. Overview table of the experimental evaluation, grouped by benchmark suites

	[16]	[8]	[6]
# Automata in benchmark suites	27	12	55
# Cases for which a smaller automaton was found	7	0	36
# Cases for which no smaller automaton was found	20	10	15
# Cases for which a smaller automaton was found but it is not known if it is the smallest one (w.r.t. the maximum bound of 8)	2	0	2
# Cases for which it is unknown if there exists a smaller automaton	0	2	4
Maximum size saving:	3 out of 5	–/–	22 out of 28
Average size saving:	7.28%	0.0%	24.0%
Mean computation times (Scheme A):	85669.87 s	83711.1 s	194558.8 s
Mean computation times (Scheme B):	4454.274 s	7203.017 s	4850.677 s
Minimum ratio between $\mathcal{A}^+$ and $\mathcal{A}^-$:	1/2	2/3	1/2
Median ratio between $\mathcal{A}^+$ and $\mathcal{A}^-$:	2/2	2/2	5/3
Maximum ratio between $\mathcal{A}^+$ and $\mathcal{A}^-$:	5/4	6/6	28/5

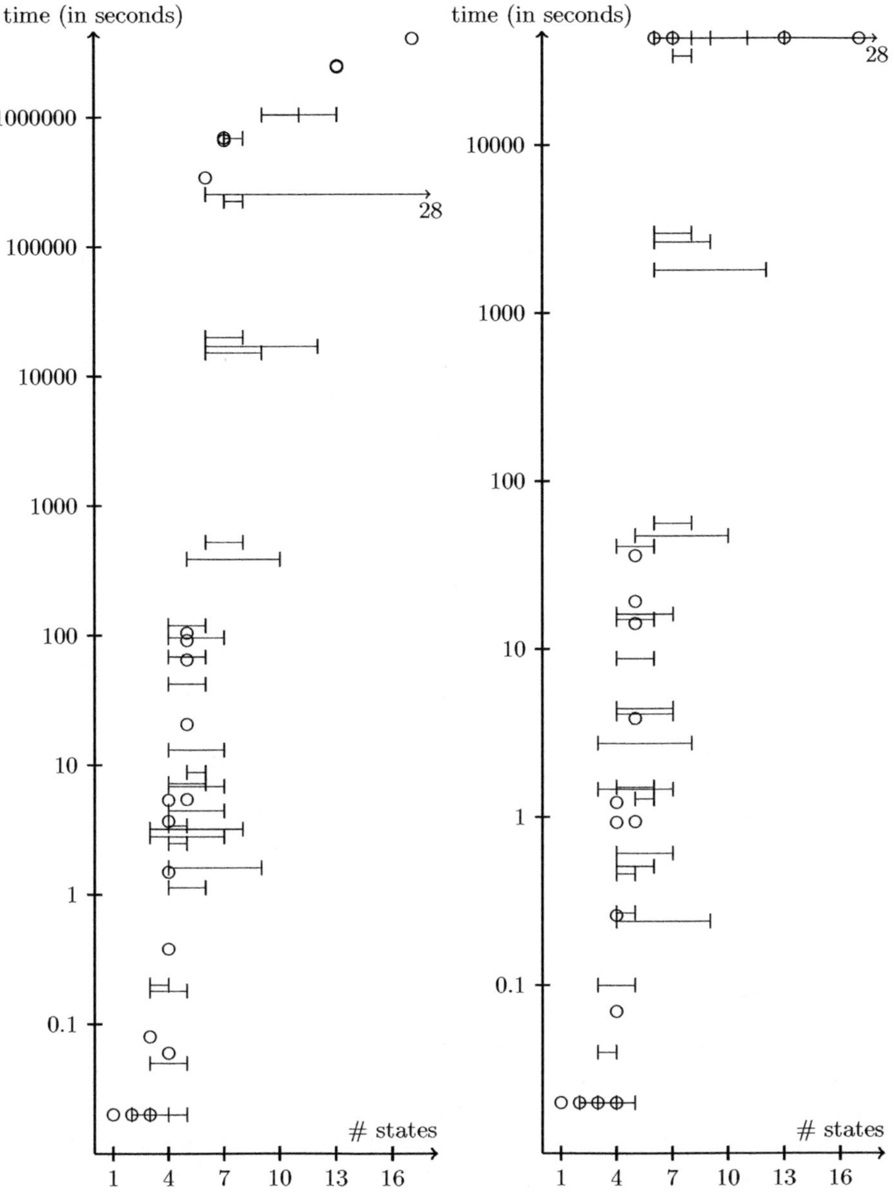

Fig. 4. Running times (in seconds, Y-axis) and automata sizes (in number of states, X axis) for the 95 specifications in our experimental evaluation. The left table corresponds to evaluation scheme A, the right table to scheme B. Automata whose sizes were not reduced by our technique are denoted by a circle, bars indicate the original and reduced sizes of the automata whenever a smaller automaton was found.

SAT solver unnecessarily. Thus, for a meaningful application of the solver in practice, an *evaluation scheme* is necessary, which fixes how the solver runs for the individual bound and target state number values are combined to an overall Büchi automaton size reduction program. We propose two such schemes here:

- **Scheme A:** The solver is applied repeatedly to the state number/bound pairs $(1,1),(1,2),\ldots,(1,8),(2,1),(2,2),\ldots$ until we obtain the result that the SAT instance is satisfied (so a smaller automaton is found) or until the results for all state number/bound pairs have been computed.
- **Scheme B:** We assume that for all state number/bound pairs, the SAT solving instances are started in parallel (taking for granted that we have sufficiently many computers at hand). Once the minimal state number (for the chosen maximal bound of 8) can be deduced from the results obtained so far, all remaining SAT solving runs are stopped. Here, the computation time is defined to be the time after which the solver runs are stopped.

In both cases, we have chosen a timeout of 12 hours and a memory limit of 2 GB for the individual runs of the SAT solver. Table 2 contains an overview of the results for these two schemes, grouped by the benchmark sets. In all of the cases, the smallest automata we found have been obtained already with a bound of 2. Furthermore, in most cases where a smaller Büchi automaton was found, this was already the case with a bound of 1. Additionally, for only 8 out of the 94 specifications considered, the maximum time of 12 hours per SAT solver run was insufficient to decide whether the input automaton was already the smallest equivalent one (with respect to the maximum bound of 8), which shows that the technique presented in this paper is indeed useful.

Finally, we discuss the scalability of our approach. Figure 4 correlates the original and reduced sizes of the automata for the specifications considered with the running times of the reduction process using the schemes described above. It can be seen that the running time of our technique is roughly exponential in the number of states. However, the figure shows that with this investment in terms of computation time, significant size savings are possible.

6 Discussion

In this paper, we have presented a new approach for the optimization of Büchi automata that allows for significant further size reductions over standard techniques when more time can be invested in the minimization of the automaton. The new approach is based on a combination of bounded language containment checking, which allows us to fine-tune the precision and efficiency of the check, and SAT solving, which allows us to prune large parts of the search space for smaller automata already in the early solving stages. We conclude the paper by discussing the limits of the approach and its relation to simulation-based optimization methods.

A limitation of the approach is that bounded language containment is only an approximation of language containment. Figure 5 shows two equivalent automata for which the bounded language containment check $\mathcal{L}(\mathcal{A}) \subseteq_b \mathcal{L}(\mathcal{A}')$ fails.

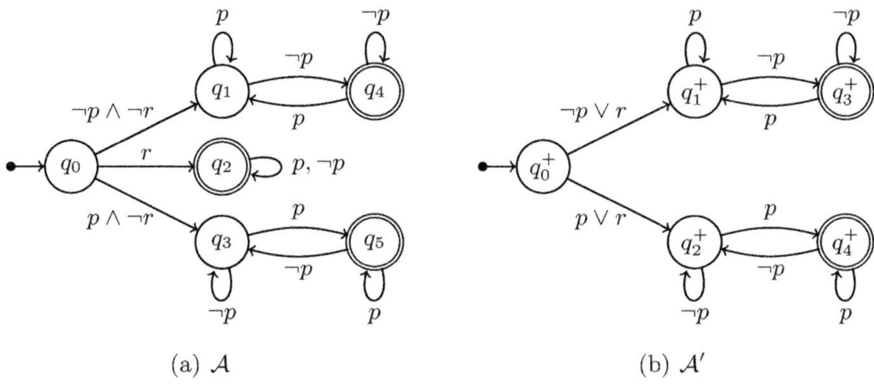

Fig. 5. Two Büchi automata, $\mathcal{A}$ and $\mathcal{A}'$ that are language equivalent, but not bounded language equivalent: $\mathcal{L}(\mathcal{A}) = \mathcal{L}(\mathcal{A}')$, but $\mathcal{L}(\mathcal{A}) \not\subseteq_b \mathcal{L}(\mathcal{A}')$ for every $b \in \mathbb{N}$. For the word $w = \{r\}\{p\}^{(b+1)}\emptyset^{(b+1)}\{p\}^\omega$, the acceptance lag between the unique accepting runs for this word is b, for every $b \in \mathbb{N}$.

Consider the word $w = \{r\}\{p\}^{(b+1)}\emptyset^{(b+1)}\{p\}^\omega$ for some value of $b \in \mathbb{N}$. Regardless of the actual choice of b, the word is clearly accepted by both automata. The acceptance lag between the unique accepting runs for this word is b. Thus, for all $b \in \mathbb{N}$, there exists a witness for the fact that $\mathcal{L}(\mathcal{A}) \not\subseteq_b \mathcal{L}(\mathcal{A}')$, showing that bounded language containment is sound but not complete.

In practice, of course, this limitation matters very little, since, in order to limit the running time, the test cannot be used with arbitrarily large bounds. In fact, our experimental evaluation shows that the approach is already very useful for small bounds. This success can be explained by the fact the bounded language containment check, which is the only part of the approach which can make it incomplete, has several nice properties. First of all, if the reference automaton is a safety automaton (a safety automaton is a Büchi automaton with only accepting states), then even for a bound of 1, we never miss a smaller safety automaton in the search process. This can easily be seen from the fact that the acceptance lag between an accepting run of the candidate automaton and an accepting run of the reference automaton is always 0 (as all states are accepting). Thus, our technique is complete for the minimization of safety automata, which is itself a PSPACE-complete problem.

Furthermore, the approach is complete with respect to previous approaches to the minimization of Büchi automata. In [9], the usage of *fair simulation* for approximating Büchi automaton language containment is discussed. In this setting, language containment can be proven by showing that a *simulation parity game* is winning for the *duplicator* player. From the structure of this parity game and the fact that parity games are memoryless determined, it can immediately be deduced that the duplicator player can only win if it is able to mimic an accepting run in the reference automaton $\mathcal{A}^+$ by some accepting run in the candidate automaton $\mathcal{A}$ such that the acceptance lag is below $|\mathcal{A}^+| \cdot |\mathcal{A}|$. Thus, by setting the bound in our approach to this value, we do not miss automata that would be found using fair bisimulation. Furthermore, in our technique, one direction of the language containment check is precise and by using SAT solving as the reasoning backbone, the limitations of bisimulation quotienting for fair simulation in the classical approaches are avoided.

Note that our approach ***strictly*** subsumes simulation-based methods (for fair, delayed and direct simulation). One such example is given in Figure 1: states q'_1 and q'_2 do not simulate state q_3. As a result, simulation-based methods cannot reduce the 4-state automaton $\mathcal{A}$ to the 3-state automaton $\mathcal{A}'$.

Acknowledgements

The authors want to thank Alexandre Duret-Lutz from the spot team for the support with the specifications and the converter.

References

1. Baier, C., Katoen, J.P.: Principles of Model Checking. MIT Press, Cambridge (2008)
2. Barrett, C., Sebastiani, R., Seshia, S., Tinelli, C.: Satisfiability Modulo Theories. In: [4], pp. 825–885
3. Berry, G., Comon, H., Finkel, A. (eds.): CAV 2001. LNCS, vol. 2102, pp. 233–242. Springer, Heidelberg (2001)
4. Biere, A., Heule, M., van Maaren, H., Walsh, T. (eds.): Handbook of Satisfiability. IOS Press, Amsterdam (2009)
5. Duret-Lutz, A., Poitrenaud, D.: Spot: An extensible model checking library using transition-based generalized büchi automata. In: DeGroot, D., Harrison, P.G., Wijshoff, H.A.G., Segall, Z. (eds.) MASCOTS, pp. 76–83. IEEE Computer Society, Los Alamitos (2004)
6. Dwyer, M.B., Avrunin, G.S., Corbett, J.C.: Property specification patterns for finite-state verification. In: Ardis, M. (ed.) Proceedings of the 2nd Workshop on Formal Methods in Software Practice (FMSP 1998), pp. 7–15. ACM Press, New York (1998)
7. Eén, N., Sörensson, N.: An extensible SAT-solver. In: Giunchiglia, E., Tacchella, A. (eds.) SAT 2003. LNCS, vol. 2919, pp. 502–518. Springer, Heidelberg (2004)
8. Etessami, K., Holzmann, G.J.: Optimizing Büchi automata. In: Palamidessi, C. (ed.) CONCUR 2000. LNCS, vol. 1877, pp. 153–167. Springer, Heidelberg (2000)
9. Etessami, K., Wilke, T., Schuller, R.A.: Fair simulation relations, parity games, and state space reduction for büchi automata. In: Orejas, F., Spirakis, P.G., van Leeuwen, J. (eds.) ICALP 2001. LNCS, vol. 2076, pp. 694–707. Springer, Heidelberg (2001)
10. Gastin, P., Oddoux, D.: Fast LTL to Büchi automata translation. In: [3], pp. 53–65
11. Gerth, R., Peled, D., Vardi, M.Y., Wolper, P.: Simple on-the-fly automatic verification of linear temporal logic. In: Dembinski, P., Sredniawa, M. (eds.) PSTV. IFIP Conference Proceedings, vol. 38, pp. 3–18. Chapman & Hall, Boca Raton (1995)

12. Giannakopoulou, D., Lerda, F.: From states to transitions: Improving translation of LTL formulae to Büchi automata. In: Peled, D.A., Vardi, M.Y. (eds.) FORTE 2002. LNCS, vol. 2529, pp. 308–326. Springer, Heidelberg (2002)
13. Holzmann, G.: The Spin model checker: primer and reference manual. Addison-Wesley Professional, Reading (2003)
14. Rozier, K.Y., Vardi, M.Y.: LTL satisfiability checking. In: Bošnački, D., Edelkamp, S. (eds.) SPIN 2007. LNCS, vol. 4595, pp. 149–167. Springer, Heidelberg (2007)
15. Sakallah, K.A.: Symmetry and Satisfiability. In: [4], pp. 289–338
16. Somenzi, F., Bloem, R.: Efficient Büchi automata from LTL formulae. In: Emerson, E.A., Sistla, A.P. (eds.) CAV 2000. LNCS, vol. 1855, pp. 248–263. Springer, Heidelberg (2000)

Enacting Declarative Languages Using LTL: Avoiding Errors and Improving Performance

Maja Pešić[1], Dragan Bošnački[2], and Wil M.P. van der Aalst[1]

[1] Department of Mathematics and Computer Science,
Eindhoven University of Technology,
P.O. Box 513, NL-5600 MB, The Netherlands
{m.pesic,w.m.p.v.d.aalst}@tue.nl
[2] Department of Biomedical Engineering,
Eindhoven University of Technology,
P.O. Box 513, NL-5600 MB, The Netherlands
dragan@win.tue.nl

Abstract. In our earlier work we proposed using the declarative language DecSerFlow for modeling, analysis and enactment of processes in autonomous web services. DecSerFlow uses constraints specified with Linear Temporal Logic (LTL) to implicitly define possible executions of a model: any execution that satisfies all constraints is possible. Hence, a finite representation of all possible executions is retrieved as an automaton generated from LTL-based constraints. Standard model-checking algorithms for creating Büchi automata from LTL formulas are not applicable because of the requirements posed by the proper execution of DecSerFlow (and LTL-based process engines). On the one hand, LTL handles *infinite words* where each element of the word can refer to *zero or more propositions*. On the other hand, each execution of a DecSerFlow model is a *finite* sequence of *single events*. In this paper we adopt an existing approach to *finite-word* semantics of LTL and propose the modifications of LTL and automata generation algorithm needed to handle occurrences of *single events*. Besides eliminating errors caused by the 'multiple properties - single events' mismatch, the proposed adjustments also improve the performance of the automata generation algorithms dramatically.

1 Introduction

In our previous work [1] we proposed using DecSerFlow for the specification, verification, monitoring, and orchestration (i.e. execution) of web services in the context of business processes. DecSerFlow uses constraints to implicitly specify in which order tasks can be executed. Constraints are rules specified on two levels. First, there is a graphical representation which is similar to other graphical process modeling approaches: tasks are represented as rectangles and constraints as special lines between tasks. Second, Linear Temporal Logic (LTL) [5] is used for the formal specification of the semantics of these constraints. The graphical

J. van de Pol and M. Weber (Eds.): SPIN 2010, LNCS 6349, pp. 146–161, 2010.

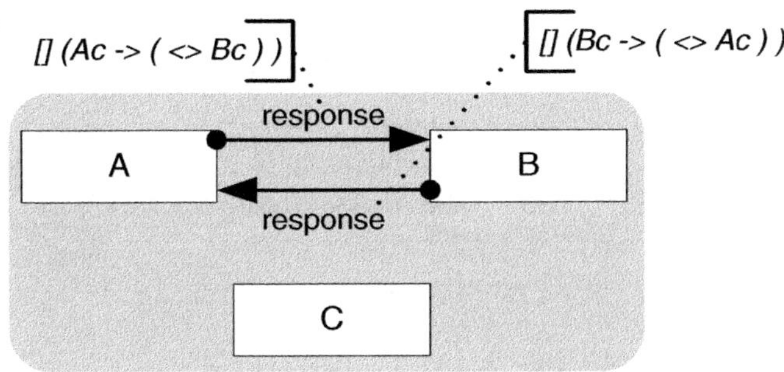

Fig. 1. A DecSerFlow model

representation of a DecSerFlow model improves the readability of models, while LTL expressions enable verification, monitoring and deadlock-free execution.

Figure 1 shows an illustrative example of a DecSerFlow model. This model contains tasks A, B and C, and two ***response*** constraints. The first constraint specifies that each successfully completed execution of task A must eventually be followed by at least one successfully completed execution of task B, which is formally defined with the LTL formula $\Box(A_c \Rightarrow \Diamond B_c)$. The second constraint specifies that each successfully completed execution of task B must eventually be followed by at least one successfully completed execution of task A, which is formally defined by the LTL formula $\Box(B_c \Rightarrow \Diamond A_c)$. Note that DecSerFlow uses the notion of events related to execution of a task: scheduling, starting, completing, canceling, delegating, etc. For example, starting, canceling and completing the execution of some task T is denoted by T_s, T_x and T_c, respectively. This increases the expressive power of the language.

The DecSerFlow language is supported by the DECLARE system, which enables modeling, verification and enactment of LTL-based models, e.g., DecSerFlow models. Note that this system cannot directly be used to enact web services. Instead it can be used for manual execution of declarative models, where the user manually executes each step in the process. DECLARE is an open source system and it can be downloaded from `http://declare.sf.net`.

Using LTL for formalization of constraints makes DecSerFlow a truly declarative process modeling language, which increases flexibility [1] needed for autonomous web services. On the one hand, procedural process models lack flexibility because they explicitly specify all possible executions (i.e., orderings of tasks). On the other hand, DecSerFlow models are more flexible because all possible executions are specified implicitly, as all executions that satisfy all constraints in the model. A finite representation of all possible executions is obtained from LTL specifications of DecSerFlow constraints by means of generating automata for LTL formulas. Algorithms for generating automata that represent exactly all traces that satisfy an LTL formula have been developed in the field of model checking [5]. Note that, in DecSerFlow, we do not use automata generated from LTL specifications of constraints for model checking in the sense

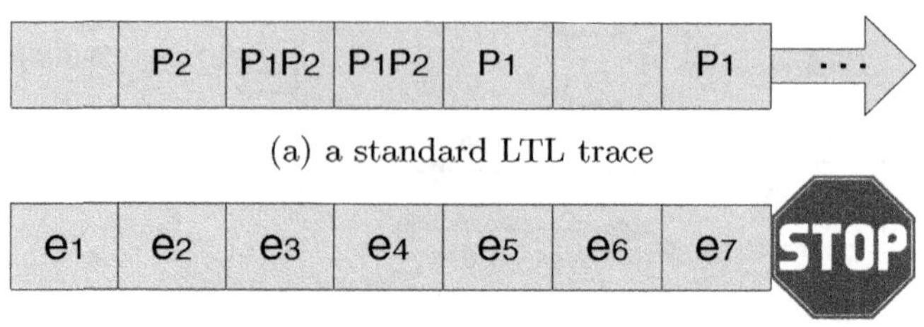

(a) a standard LTL trace

(b) a DecSerFlow execution trace

Fig. 2. LTL for DecSerFlow

of checking if the model satisfies certain properties. Instead, we use the generated automata for detecting errors caused by conflicting constraints, execution monitoring, and ensuring deadlock-free execution of models of web services [11].

Typically, LTL and model-checking techniques are used to verify properties of a given model. DecSerFlow uses LTL to define possible executions, as sequences of executed events. For example, one possible execution of the model shown in Figure 1 is executing (i.e., starting and completing) task C three times, which is specified as $\sigma = C_s, C_c, C_s, C_c, C_s, C_c$. There are *two important differences* between the 'standard' LTL and the LTL applied to DecSerFlow models, as illustrated in Figure 2.

The first difference between standard LTL and DecSerFlow LTL is the length of execution traces (i.e., words). On the one hand, standard LTL considers infinite traces, as shown in Figure 2(a). On the other hand, Figure 2(b) shows that the execution of process instances (e.g. a customer order or service request) eventually terminates. Hence, the infinite semantics of standard LTL [5] cannot be applied to DecSerFlow models. In order to apply LTL to finite traces, we adopt a simple and efficient approach originally proposed by Giannakopoulou et al. [7].

The second difference between standard LTL and the DecSerFlow LTL is the semantics of elements in a trace. Standard LTL assumes that one element of the trace can refer to more than one *proposition*. For example, it is possible to monitor two properties: (P_1) the motor temperature is higher than 80 degrees and (P_2) the speed of the turbine is higher than 150 km/h. As Figure 2(a) shows, each element of the trace could then refer to: (1) none of the two properties, i.e., neither P_1 nor P_2 hold, (2) only property P_1 holds, (3) only property P_2 holds, or (4) properties P_1 and P_2 both hold. In the case of execution traces of DecSerFlow models one proposition refers to one event, e.g., starting task C (C_s). Therefore, we may safely assume that only one proposition holds at one moment, i.e., each of the elements of the trace refers to exactly one event, as shown in Figure 2(b).

Due to these differences, using standard LTL and automata generation algorithm may cause errors when it comes to the verification, monitoring and deadlock-free execution of DecSerFlow models. In this paper we show how the *semantics* of standard LTL and the automata generation can be adjusted for declarative languages like DecSerFlow. Besides elimination of errors, the proposed adjustments improve the performance of the algorithm, both with respect to the size of the automata and the processing time. We will use the model shown in Figure 1 as a running example.

The remainder of this paper is organized as follows. We start by describing how LTL and automata generated from LTL are used in DecSerFlow. In Section 3 we sketch how the finite trace semantics can be applied to LTL and generated automata, by using the approach described in [7]. Section 4 describes how the LTL semantics and the algorithm for generating automata must be changed in order to be applicable to sequences of *single events*. The results of experiments testing the performance of proposed changes are presented in Section 5. Finally, related work is discussed in Section 6 and Section 7 concludes the paper.

2 LTL and Automata for Finite Traces

DecSerFlow uses LTL for finite traces [7] to formally specify constraints. Just like in standard LTL, a well-formed LTL formula can use standard logical operators ($!$, $\wedge$ and $\vee$) and several additional temporal operators: $\bigcirc$ (next), U (until), W (weak until), V (release), $\Box$ (always) and $\Diamond$ (eventually). The finite trace semantics is reflected in the way propositions and the until (U) operator are defined. A proposition is a finite sequence and the index i in the until (U) has the upper bound n:

Definition 1 (LTL for finite traces [7]). *Given a finite set of atomic propositions P, every $p \in P$ is a well-formed LTL formula. If Φ and Ψ are well-formed LTL formulas, then* `true`*,* `false`*, $!\Phi$, $\Phi \wedge \Psi$, $\Phi \vee \Psi$, $\Box\Phi$, $\Diamond\Phi$, $\bigcirc\Phi$, $\Phi U \Psi$, $\Phi V \Psi$ and $\Phi W \Psi$ are also well-formed LTL formulas. An interpretation of an LTL formula is a set of finite traces $\sigma = \sigma_1, \sigma_2, \ldots$ over 2^P (sets of propositions). We write σ^i for the suffix of σ starting at position i, i.e., $\sigma^i = \sigma_i, \sigma_{i+1}, \ldots$. The semantics of LTL is defined as follows:*

- $\sigma \models p$ *iff* $p \in \sigma_1$, *for* $p \in P$
- $\sigma \models \Phi \vee \Psi$ *iff* $(\sigma \models \Phi) \vee (\sigma \models \Psi)$
- $\sigma \models !\Phi$ *iff* $\sigma \not\models \Phi$
- $\sigma \models \bigcirc\Phi$ *iff* $\sigma^2 \models \Phi$
- $\sigma \models \Phi \wedge \Psi$ *iff* $(\sigma \models \Phi) \wedge (\sigma \models \Psi)$
- $\sigma \models \Phi U \Psi$ *iff* $(\exists_{1 \leq i \leq n} : (\sigma^i \models \Psi \wedge (\forall_{1 \leq j < i} : \sigma^j \models \Phi)))$

Also, abbreviations are used:

- $\Phi \Rightarrow \Psi$ *for* $!\Phi \vee \Psi$
- $\Diamond\Phi$ *for* `true`$U\Phi$
- $\Phi W \Psi$ *for* $(\Phi U \Psi) \vee (\Box\Phi)$
- `true` *for* $\Phi \vee !\Phi$
- $\Box\Phi$ *for* $!\Diamond!\Phi$
- $\Phi V \Psi$ *for* $!(!\Phi U !\Psi)$
- `false` *for* `!true`

DecSerFlow does not directly use LTL for constraint specification. Instead, constraints are created from constraint templates. Each template has a unique name and graphical representation and its semantics is formalized by an LTL formula. Although DecSerFlow has more than twenty constraint templates, new templates can be easily added to the language. Hence, any LTL formula can be used in DecSerFlow. For the detailed description of the full list of DecSerFlow templates we refer the reader to [11].

A widely exploited property of LTL is the fact that for every LTL formula a finite state automaton (cf. Definition 2) can be generated, such that the language (i.e., all accepted traces) of this automaton exactly represents all traces that satisfy the formula. In the field of model-checking, various algorithms are proposed for generating automata from LTL formulas. Some examples of these algorithms can be found in [5,8,3,4,7]. In the remainder of this paper we use the algorithm for generating finite automata for finite traces presented in [7]. We will refer to this algorithm as to the `BASIC` algorithm.

Definition 2 (Finite automaton (*FA*)). *Finite automaton FA is a five-tuple* $\langle A, S, T, S_0, S_F \rangle$ *such that A is the* alphabet, *S is the finite set of* states, $T \subseteq S \times A \times S$ *it the* transition relation, $S_0 \subseteq S$ *is the set of* initial states, *and* $S_F \subseteq S$ *is the set of* accepting states. *We say that:*

- *A run of FA is a sequence* $\delta = s_1 a_1 s_2 \ldots a_{n-1} s_n$ *such that* $(s_i, a_i, s_{i+1}) \in T$ *and* $s_1 \in S_0$.
- *A run* δ *is accepting if* $s_n \in S_F$.
- *A FA accepts a finite trace* $\sigma = \langle e_1, e_2, \ldots, e_m \rangle$ *if there exists an accepting run* $\delta = s_1 e_1 s_2 \ldots e_{m-1} s_m$ *of FA.*

All algorithms (including the `BASIC` algorithm) are based on expanding a graph node into a set of nodes, which will eventually become states of the automaton [5,8,3,4,7]. Each node has several fields [5]. Field *ID* is a unique identification for the node; Field *INCOMING* contains the set of nodes that lead to this node; Field *NEW* contains the set of formulas that must hold in the current node but have not yet been processed, i.e., this node must make these formulas true; Field *OLD* contains the set of formulas that have already been processed; Field *NEXT* contains the set of formulas that must hold at all immediate successors of this node. The `BASIC` algorithm consists of several basic steps:

1. The original LTL formula is rewritten to a normal form.
2. A graph of nodes is created by the recursive method *expand*, which is briefly sketched in Algorithm 2.1. Formulas from the field NEW are processed one by one (line 14), by breaking down the formulas to the level of propositions. Formulas aUb, aVb and $a \vee b$ are broken down by creating two new nodes (following special rules) and expanding them further (lines 24-27). Formula $a \wedge b$ is resolved by adding a and b to the field NEW and further expanding the current node (lines 29-31). While processing a literal f (lines 16-23), a conflict occurs and the current node is discarded if the field OLD of the current node already contains $!f$ (lines 17 and 18). When there is no conflict, f is added to the field OLD and the current node is further expanded (lines 20 and 21). Expanding a specific node finishes when all formulas have been processed, i.e., the NEW field is empty (lines 2-12). If an equal node is already in the GRAPH, then this (equal) node is updated with data for the current node (lines 3-6). Otherwise, the current node is added to the GRAPH, a new node is created and expanded with the current NODE in the field INCOMING. All formulas from the field NEXT of the current node are copied in the field NEW of the created node(lines 7-11).

3. A finite automaton is created in the following manner: (1) created nodes become states in the automaton, (2) automaton edges are defined by the INCOMING field of each state, (3) labels on edges are defined by literals stored in the field OLD, and (4) finite acceptance of states is imposed, ensuring that an accepting node does not have any unprocessed until (U) formulas in the NEXT field.

The procedure for creating graph nodes in the `BASIC` algorithm is also part of several algorithms [5,8,3,4,7]. The main difference is in the way acceptance of nodes (i.e., states) is determined in the last step. On the one hand, standard algorithms impose infinite acceptance which ensures that, whenever a node contains pUq, some successor node will contain q [5]. On the other hand, the `BASIC` algorithm imposes finite acceptance by ensuring that an accepting trace satisfies all required eventualities, i.e., the NEXT field does not contain any unprocessed until (U) formulas [7].

A finite representation of all possible executions of a DecSerFlow model (i.e., all executions that satisfy all constraints in the model) is obtained by generating the *model automaton* from the *model formula*. The model formula F for a model featuring n constraints given by the LTL formulas $f_1, f_2, \ldots, f_n$ is a conjunction of those LTL formulas, i.e., $F = f_1 \wedge f_2 \wedge \ldots \wedge f_n$. For example, the *model formula* for the DecSerFlow model shown in Figure 1 is a conjunction of formulas for the two ***response*** constraints, as shown in Figure 3(a). Figure 3(b) shows the Büchi automaton generated by the `BASIC` algorithm for this model formula. Hence, the language (i.e., all accepted traces) of this automaton represents all possible executions of the DecSerFlow model from Figure 1. Automaton states are represented by circles such that a single border marks a non-accepting state, whereas a double border denotes an accepting state. Transitions are represented as directed labeled arcs between states. The arc without a source state marks the initial state.

Automata generated from DecSerFlow models can be used for multiple purposes [1,11]. For example, the *model automaton* and automata generated for each constraint can be used to monitor the state of a model instance (we call one execution of a model an instance) and constraints during execution. This is done by checking if the trace satisfies the model, i.e., if the automaton accepts the trace. Naturally, when processing the instance (execution) state the model automaton is used, and when processing states of constraints, automata generated from LTL specifications are used. Note that the generated automata are non-deterministic, and we say that an automaton accepts a trace if the trace can be 'replayed' on the automaton in such a way that an accepting state is reached [1]. Given the current execution trace of an instance, the instance or constraint state is determined as follows:

- If the trace is accepted by the automaton, then the instance/constraint is *satisfied*.
- The instance/constraint is *temporarily violated* if the current trace is not accepted but it is a prefix of a trace accepted by the automaton. In other words, the instance/constraint is *temporarily violated* if the current trace

Algorithm 2.1. BASIC algorithm: expanding the graph of nodes

```
function expand(NODE, GRAPH)
if NODE.NEW = ∅ then {*finished processing node*}
  if ∃A ∈ GRAPH : equal(NODE, A) then {*equivalent node already processed*}
    update_existing(NODE,A); {*just update the existing node*}
    return GRAPH;
  else
    GRAPH ⇐ GRAPH ∪ {NODE}; {*add NODE to GRAPH*}
    NEWNODE ⇐ createNewNode(); {*create NEWNODE*}
    NEWNODE.INCOMING ⇐ {NODE};
    NEWNODE.NEW ⇐ NODE.NEXT;
    return expand(NEWNODE, GRAPH); {*expand NEWNODE*}
  end if
else
  f ⇐ getFormula(NODE.NEW); {*get the next formula for processing*}
  NODE.NEW ⇐ NODE.NEW \ {f};
  if (f ∈ P∨!f ∈ P) ∨ (f = true ∨ f = false) then {*f is a literal*}
    if (f = false) ∨ (!f ∈ NODE.OLD) then {*a contradiction in NODE*}
      return GRAPH {*discard current NODE*}
    else
      NODE.OLD ⇐ NODE.OLD ∪ {f}
      return expand(NODE,GRAPH)
    end if
  end if
  if f = aUb, aVb, or a ∨ b then
    NODE1 ⇐ create1(f, NODE); {*depending the current operator in f*}
    NODE2 ⇐ create2(f, NODE); {*depending the current operator in f*}
    return expand(NODE2,expand(NODE1, GRAPH));
  end if
  if f = a ∧ b then
    NODE.NEW ⇐ NODE.NEW ∪ {a, b};
    return expand(NODE,GRAPH);
  end if
end if
end expand;
```

can be ‘replayed’ on the automaton, but all possible replay scenarios lead to non-accepting state.

- If the trace is neither accepted by the automaton nor it is a prefix of an accepted trace, then the instance/constraint is *(permanently) violated.* In other words, the instance/constraint is *violated* if the current trace can not be ‘replayed’ on the automaton at all.

In addition to state monitoring, the model automaton can be used to ensure a deadlock-free execution and to verify service models. On the one hand, if the service execution were driven by the model automaton, deadlocks would be eliminated. On the other hand, we have developed verification procedures that

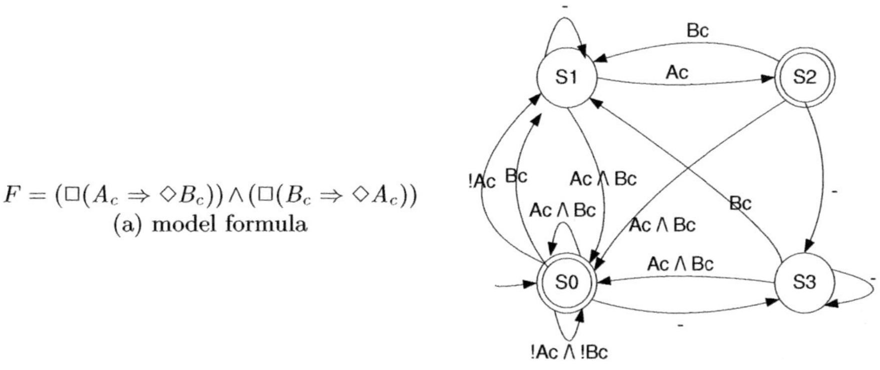

(b) model automaton generated using the `BASIC` algorithm

Fig. 3. Retrieving a finite representation of all possible executions of the model shown in Figure 1. Note that the absence of an edge label, denoted with "-", is equivalent to the label `true`.

can detect two types of errors based on model automata. First, a dead task is a model task that can never be executed because its completion is never allowed by transition labels. Second, a model has a conflict if the generated automaton is empty, i.e., it has no states and its language is empty. The DECLARE system uses the above described procedures for model verification, monitoring states of instances and constraints and ensuring the deadlock-free execution [11].

3 Applying the Finite Traces Semantics

As explained in Section 1, an execution trace of a web service is a *finite* sequence, i.e., $\sigma = p_1, p_2, \ldots p_n$. Using automata generated for infinite traces can create problems if used for finite executions of DecSerFlow models.

Consider, for example, the situation when the DecSerFlow model shown in Figure 1 is executed by executing task A, i.e., the execution trace is

$$\sigma = A_s, A_c. \tag{1}$$

The model automaton shown in Figure 3(b) suggests that σ satisfies the model because it brings the model automaton to the accepting state S_2 by triggering transitions '$!A_c$' and 'A_c': $S_0 \xrightarrow[(!A_c)]{A_s} S_1 \xrightarrow[(A_c)]{A_c} S_2$. (The labels in parentheses below the transition arrows denote the actual edge labels of the automaton that match the actions above the arrows.)

If the finite semantics of the until (U) operator is assumed, trace σ given in (1) does not satisfy the model formula shown in Figure 3(a). This is because event A_c is not followed by event B_c by the end of the trace (note that this is required by the response constraint of the model in Figure1). Hence, trace σ does not

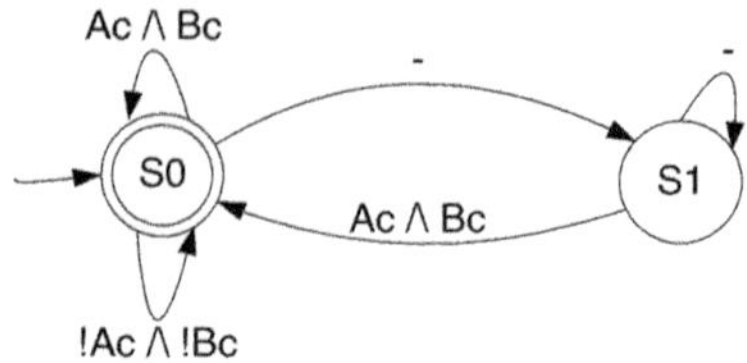

Fig. 4. The BASIC^{FIN} model automaton for model shown in Figure 1

satisfy the model shown in Figure 1. However, as explained in Section 2, the model automaton shown in Figure 3(b) suggests otherwise: trace σ satisfies the model because it brings the model automaton to the accepting state S_2.

To avoid this type of errors, the algorithm for automata generation must be adjusted to finite traces, as described in [7]. The infinite semantics of LTL is reflected in the fact that i does not have an upper bound in the definition of the until (U) operator: $\exists_{1 \le i} : \ldots$ (cf. Section 2). The manner in which the infinite acceptance is imposed in the standard algorithm is described in Section 2. As described in [7], finite semantics must be reflected in the upper bound n of i in the until operator: $\sigma \models \varphi U \psi$ if and only if $(\exists_{1 \le i \le n} : (\sigma^i \models \psi \wedge (\forall_{1 \le j < i} : \sigma^j \models \varphi))$. The main change in the algorithm is the way accepting conditions are imposed: a finite trace is accepting only if it satisfies all required eventualities (i.e., untils). Formulas that still need to be satisfied are stored in the field NEXT. Therefore, only if the NEXT field of a node does not contain any until (U) formulas, the automaton state generated from this node is accepting [7]. In the remainder of this paper we will use BASIC^{FIN} to denote the algorithm presented in [8] and modified for finite traces as described in [7]. We will refer to the automaton generated by the BASIC^{FIN} algorithm as to the BASIC^{FIN} automaton. Figure 4 shows the BASIC^{FIN} automaton generated for the model formula given in Figure 3(a). Indeed, this automaton suggests that trace σ does not satisfy the model from Figure 1, because this trace brings the automaton to the non-accepting state S_1: $S_0 \xrightarrow[(!A_c \wedge !B_c)]{A_s} S_0 \xrightarrow[(-)]{A_c} S_1$.

4 Applying the 'Single Event' Semantics

In standard LTL, traces are defined over 2^P, which means that σ is a sequence of sets of propositions ($\forall_{1 \le i} : \sigma_i \subseteq P$). Hence, each element σ_i of a trace is a *set of atomic propositions*. The fact that one element of a trace can refer to multiple properties in standard LTL is semantically expressed in the way the proposition is defined: $\sigma \models p$ if and only if $p \in \sigma_1$ (cf. Section 2). As explained in Section 1, execution trace of a web service is a sequence of ***single*** events/propositions: $\forall_{1 \le i \le n} : \sigma_i \in P$. In order to adjust the semantics of LTL to traces where each element refers to exactly one event, i.e. proposition, we must check if the proposition ***is*** the first element of the trace: $\sigma \models p$ if and only if $p = \sigma_1$.

Algorithm 4.1. Detecting a contradiction in the 'single events' algorithm

```
1: function expand(NODE, GRAPH)
2: ...
3: if (f ∈ P∨!f ∈ P) ∨ (f = true ∨ f = false) then
4:    if ( f = false) ∨ (!f ∈ node.OLD) ∨ (l ∈ P ∧ f ≠ l ∧ l ∈ node.OLD) then
5:       return GRAPH
6:    else
7:       NODE.OLD ⇐ NODE.OLD ∪ f
8:       return expand(NODE,GRAPH)
9:    end if
10: end if
11: ...
12: end expand;
```

Automata that consider traces containing sets of propositions can create problems in DecSerFlow. For example, consider the $\texttt{BASIC}^{FIN}$ model automaton shown in Figure 4 and an instance of the model (cf. Figure 1 on page 147) with the execution trace σ given in (1). As explained in Section 3, this automaton suggests that the instance is not satisfied because trace σ brings the automaton to the non-accepting state S_1. Moreover, because an accepting state is reachable (i.e., accepting state S_0 is reachable from S_1 via transition $A_c \wedge B_c$), this automaton suggests that the instance is only temporarily violated. However, because events are triggered ***one by one***, transition $A_c \wedge B_c$ can never be taken. Hence, the state of this instance is actually ***permanently violated*** because an accepting state can no longer be reached.

In order to eliminate this error, we must adjust the algorithm to consider sequences of single events in the following way. The most important change is strengthening the contradiction test in Algorithm 2.1 (lines 16-18). As described in Section 2, literals that belong to the field *OLD* will become labels on the transitions in the generated automaton. Therefore, if the processed formula f is a literal, contradiction occurs and the current node is discarded if the (negation of f ($!f$) is already in the field *OLD* (lines 13 and 14).

Algorithm 4.1 shows how contradiction requirements must be strengthened in order to reflect the single event property. The additional requirement is: if we are processing a proposition f and another proposition $l \neq f$ is already in the field *OLD*, then this is also a contradiction (line 3). Further, the handling of contradictions and regular situations stays the same: the current node is discarded when a contradiction is detected. Otherwise, further expansion of the current node in the graph is continued. In what follows $\texttt{BASIC}_{SE}^{FIN}$ denotes Algorithm 4.1.

In addition to strengthening the contradiction requirement, labels on transitions can be displayed in a more concise way. If a label contains one positive proposition and an arbitrary number of negative propositions (e.g., $A_c \wedge !B_c \wedge !C_c$), it can be replaced by a shorter label containing only the positive proposition (e.g., A_c). This is because the latter is implied by the former. Note that making labels shorter is not necessary from the semantical and correctness perspective, but it significantly improves readability.

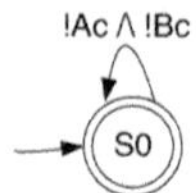

Fig. 5. The $\texttt{BASIC}_{SE}^{FIN}$ model automaton for model shown in Figure 1

Figure 5 shows the $\texttt{BASIC}_{SE}^{FIN}$ automaton generated for the model formula given in Figure 3(a). ("SE" in the subscript refers to single event.) This automaton correctly indicates that an instance with trace σ is ***permanently violated*** because σ is neither accepted by the automaton, nor it is a prefix of a trace accepted by this automaton. Moreover, tasks A and B can never be executed (i.e., these are dead tasks) because the language of this automaton does not accept traces that contain A_c or B_c. This is because, as soon as either A or B would be executed, no finite execution would be able to satisfy ***both response*** constraints from the model shown in Figure 1.

4.1 Correctness Arguments

In this section we give a brief discussion of the correctness of the single event Algorithm 4.1 $\texttt{BASIC}_{SE}^{FIN}$. Algorithm 2.1, $\texttt{BASIC}^{FIN}$, can also be used to generate automata that accept only single-event traces satisfying a given model formula F. To this end we need to add a restrictive conjunct to F. Thus, to rule out all multiple-event traces, we run $\texttt{BASIC}^{FIN}$ on the formula $R \wedge F$, where $a_1, a_2, \ldots, a_n \in P$ are the events that appear in F, and $R = \Box \bigwedge_{i,j} !(a_i \wedge a_j)$ where $1 \leq i \leq n$, $1 \leq j \leq n$ and $i \neq j$.

For the correctness of the standard algorithm $\texttt{BASIC}^{FIN}$ we rely on [5,8]. Hence, we can establish the correctness of the single-event algorithm $\texttt{BASIC}_{SE}^{FIN}$ by showing the following: for each run $\mathcal{R}_2$ of the algorithm $\texttt{BASIC}_{SE}^{FIN}$ applied to a given model formula F, there exists a run $\mathcal{R}_1$ of algorithm $\texttt{BASIC}^{FIN}$ applied to the formula $R \wedge F$, such that the automata produced by $\mathcal{R}_2$ and $\mathcal{R}_1$ are equivalent, i.e., they accept the same language. Moreover, to each state of the automaton generated by $\texttt{BASIC}_{SE}^{FIN}$ there corresponds an equivalence class of states in the automaton generated by $\texttt{BASIC}^{FIN}$.

To show this, we construct a run $\mathcal{R}_1$ of algorithm $\texttt{BASIC}^{FIN}$ as we trace the run $\mathcal{R}_2$ of algorithm $\texttt{BASIC}_{SE}^{FIN}$. In $\texttt{BASIC}_{SE}^{FIN}$ run $\mathcal{R}_2$ is applied to F', which is the normal form of F. (For the definition of a normal form see, for example, [8].) Run $\mathcal{R}_1$ simulates $\mathcal{R}_2$ in a "stuttering" manner, i.e., multiple steps of $\mathcal{R}_1$ can correspond to a single step of $\mathcal{R}_2$. Algorithm $\texttt{BASIC}^{FIN}$ is actually applied on the normal form of $R \wedge F$, where F is rewritten to its normal form F' and R is rewritten into $R' = \texttt{false}\ V \bigwedge_{i,j}(!a_i \vee !a_j)$ such that $1 \leq i \leq n$, $1 \leq j \leq n$ and $i \neq j$. In $\mathcal{R}_1$ we process R' before F'. It is straightforward to check that a sequence of node transformations as a result of the processing of R' in $\mathcal{R}_1$ leads to insertion of $n-1$ literals of the form $!a_i$ in the field OLD of each generated node [5]. This ensures that at most one positive proposition a_k can be added to the OLD field of each node, such that $!a_k \notin OLD$. Adding the second positive proposition a_l ($l \neq k$) will automatically invoke a contradiction in the original sense because the OLD field already contains the negation $!a_l$.

At each point one can prove that the following invariant holds for the parallel execution of $\mathcal{R}_1$ and $\mathcal{R}_2$. Let run $\mathcal{R}_2$ discard its current node n_2, because field OLD contains proposition l (lines 4-5 in $\texttt{BASIC}_{SE}^{FIN}$) different from the currently processed formula/proposition f. Then field OLD of node n_1, currently considered by run $\mathcal{R}_1$, contains $!f$. As a consequence, $\mathcal{R}_1$ also discards the node (because of contradiction) and in this way rules out a possible multiple event transition in the automaton.

Besides that, one can show that for each action by $\mathcal{R}_1$ that adds a new node n_1 to the set of nodes (lines 7-11 in $\texttt{BASIC}^{FIN}$), there exists an action of $\mathcal{R}_2$ that adds a corresponding node n_2. Both n_1 and n_2 contain in OLD only one literal without negation and this literal is the same in both nodes. Nodes n_1 and n_2 will be transformed into equivalent states in the resulting automata. Vice versa, each node added by $\mathcal{R}_2$ corresponds to an equivalent node added by $\mathcal{R}_1$.

5 Experiments

We performed experiments to measure the effects of the 'single events' adjustments on the performance of the $\texttt{BASIC}_{SE}^{FIN}$ algorithm compared to the $\texttt{BASIC}^{FIN}$ algorithm. We run $\texttt{BASIC}^{FIN}$ with LTL formulas which were conjoined with a corresponding restrictive conjunct R, as introduced in Section 4.1 above, i.e., $R = \Box \bigwedge_{i,j} !(a_i \wedge a_j)$ where $1 \leq i \leq n$, $1 \leq j \leq n$ and $i \neq j$. Using such modified formulas can be seen as a high-level implementation of the single event restriction, i.e., without modification of the algorithm $\texttt{BASIC}^{FIN}$ and its implementation.

We used the testing method based on randomly generated LTL formulas presented in [3,8]. Each test set consists of F randomly generated LTL formulas of length L with N propositional variables. Temporal operators U and V are generated with the probability P. A formula of length L is generated in the following way:

- $\boldsymbol{L} = 1$ Randomly generate a propositional variable using a uniform distribution.
- $\boldsymbol{L} = 2$ Randomly generate a unary operator from the set $\{!, \bigcirc\}$. Apply the generated unary operator to a random formula of $L = 1$.
- $\boldsymbol{L} > 2$ Randomly generate an operator from the set $\{!, \bigcirc, \vee, \wedge, U, V\}$. The probability to generate either U or V is $\frac{P}{2}$ and $\frac{1-P}{4}$ to generate the other operators. If the chosen operator is unary, it is applied to a random formula of $L = 1$. If the chosen operator is binary, it is applied to two random formulas: one of length S and the other of length $L - S - 1$. S is generated randomly using a uniform distribution between 1 and $L - 2$ inclusive.

We performed tests on ten sets containing $F = 100$ randomly generated formulas of varying lengths with 5 propositional variables ($N = 5$) and the probability of $\frac{1}{2}$ to select operators U and V. In each test set, formulas had different lengths: $L \in \{5, 10, 15, 20, 25, 30, 35, 40, 45, 50\}$. As mentioned above, for each formula f,

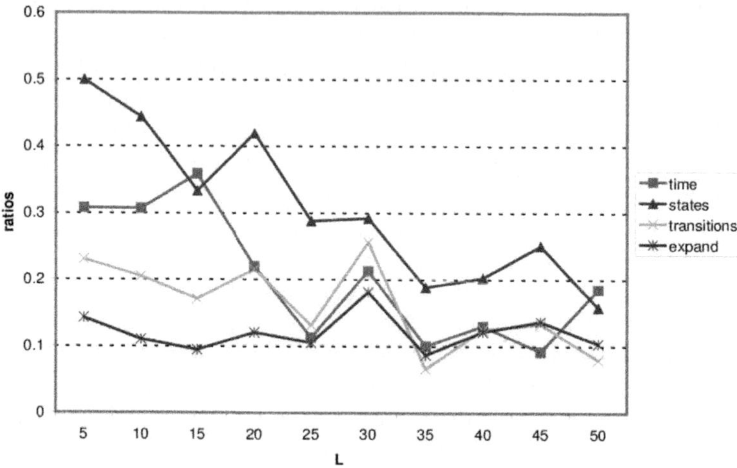

Fig. 6. The ratio of number of states, number of transitions, number of node expansions, and generation time between the $\texttt{BASIC}_{SE}^{FIN}$ and $\texttt{BASIC}^{FIN}$ algorithms for $F = 100$ randomly generated formulas of various lengths L, with $N = 5$ and $P = \frac{1}{2}$

we apply directly $\texttt{BASIC}_{SE}^{FIN}$ to f, whilst $\texttt{BASIC}^{FIN}$ is applied to the f extended with its corresponding restricting conjunct to ensure the single event semantics.

When evaluating algorithms for generating automata from LTL formulas, it is a common practice to consider the size of the automaton (i.e., number of states and transitions) and the total time needed to generate the automaton [3,8]. In addition to measuring the automata size and processing time, we have measured the number of times the procedure for *expanding* a node was invoked. This is because strengthening the contradiction requirements with the single event property causes the algorithm to abandon more expansion paths in the graph. Hence, the *expand* procedure is typically invoked fewer times.

Figure 6 presents the ratio between the corresponding results of the $\texttt{BASIC}_{SE}^{FIN}$ algorithm and the $\texttt{BASIC}^{FIN}$ algorithm. The results show that the low level implementation of the single event semantics, featured in $\texttt{BASIC}_{SE}^{FIN}$, significantly improves the performance by reducing the processing time, automata size, and number of invocations of the *expand* procedure. For example, only 10% of the original time is needed to process a formula of length 35 and 45. A lower number of invocations of procedure *expand* results in shorter processing times. The typical automaton size is also reduced because transitions referring to more than one property are eliminated.

Figure 6 shows that effects become more significant as the length of the formula increases up to the value $L = 25$. With further increase of the formula length, it seems that the effect begins to stabilize.

Each improvement of the performance with the $\texttt{BASIC}_{SE}^{FIN}$ algorithm is important for enactment of declarative models. This is because the model formula of a DecSerFlow model is generated as a conjunction of all constraints and, hence, it can be much longer than typical formulas used in model checking. If $L(f)$ denotes length of LTL formula f, then the length of model formula $F = c_1 \wedge c_2 \wedge \ldots \wedge c_n$ of a DecSerFlow model with n constraints specified with LTL formulas $c_1, c_2, \ldots, c_n$ is $L(F) = n - 1 + \sum_{i=1}^{n} L(c_i)$. For example, the length of model formula F (cf. Figure 3(a)) is $L(F) = 2 - 1 + \sum_{i=1}^{2} 5 = 11$, because the length of each ***response*** constraint in the model shown in Figure 1 is $L(c) = 5$.

6 Related Work

In our previous work, we proposed using DecSerFlow for declarative specification of web service processes [1]. The $\mathcal{S}$CIFF language is another declarative language [2], which is based on abductive logic programming. While DecSerFlow and $\mathcal{S}$CIFF are similar with respect to their declarative approach to process modeling, both languages have some specific advantages. $\mathcal{S}$CIFF has more expressive power and is more efficient while checking constraints on executed traces (i.e., a posteriori) [11]. However, $\mathcal{S}$CIFF cannot ensure a deadlock-free execution at run-time. Moreover, the adjustments proposed in this paper enable detection of more sophisticated model errors and improve efficiency.

DecSerFlow uses LTL for formal specification of constraints and automata generated from LTL formulas for retrieving the final representation of all possible model executions as all executions that satisfy model constraints. LTL is extensively used in the field of model checking and algorithms for automata generation from LTL formulas based on [5] are proposed in this field. Moreover, improving the performance of these algorithms is an important topic in the field [3,8,4]. While these approaches improve the performance of the original algorithm, which works with the standard LTL, changes proposed in this paper improve the performance by limiting the LTL to sequences of single events.

The problem of applying finite trace semantics to standard LTL has been addressed by other researchers. The approach presented in [10] considers only safety properties and generating finite-trace automata for monitoring running programs. Adjustments of the algorithm for automata generation to finite traces is given in [7]. We use this approach because it does not limit the expressiveness of DecSerFlow [7].

Standard LTL considers properties, rather than events, which means that zero or more properties can hold at any point of time. Methods for model checking for event-based systems use several approaches to LTL for sequences of single events. In [12], an approach is proposed for specifying events indirectly in terms of edges. Edges do not relate directly to occurrence of event, but capture changes of truth/false values of atomic propositions. The Tracta model-checking approach [6] for analysis of concurrent systems uses the special kind of LTL for sequences of single actions: Action Linear Temporal Logic (ALTL). However, this approach uses the Büchi automata following the standard automata-theoretic approach to verification and focuses on solving issues related to hierarchical systems using the Compositional Reachability Analysis (CRA) [6]. ALTL is extended for ***fluent model checking*** in [9]. Here, instead of using each event occurrence, time intervals between action initiation and termination are considered. A special model-checking procedure is proposed for fluent actions. This procedure uses Büchi automata, but avoids the need for using the synchronous product operation [9].

7 Conclusions

Using standard LTL and Büchi automata for enacting DecSerFlow models can cause errors and inefficiencies. This is because of two important differences between the standard model-checking problem and the execution processes based on a declarative language like DecSerFlow. This paper describes how the standard LTL and algorithm for automata generation can be adapted in order to fit two special properties of DecSerFlow. Both the adjustments for finite traces described by Giannakopoulou et al. in [7], and the adjustments for sequences for single events described in Section 4 must be used in order to avoid errors. Because automata are generated for the DecSerFlow model formula (which is a conjunction of formulas for all constraints), the performance of the algorithm becomes a potential bottleneck. For the special class of problems where properties hold one at a time, results of our experiments show that the proposed adjustments also significantly decrease the processing time and size of automata. Processing times are reduced for more than one order of magnitude. Since the enactment of declarative languages like DecSerFlow requires the repeated execution of this procedure (each time some activity is started or completed), this is highly relevant.

References

1. van der Aalst, W.M.P., Pesic, M.: DecSerFlow: Towards a Truly Declarative Service Flow Language. In: Bravetti, M., Núñez, M., Zavattaro, G. (eds.) WS-FM 2006. LNCS, vol. 4184, pp. 1–23. Springer, Heidelberg (2006)
2. Alberti, M., Chesani, F., Gavanelli, M., Lamma, E., Mello, P., Montali, M., Storari, S., Torroni, P.: Computational Logic for Run-Time Verification of Web Services Choreographies: exploiting the SOCS-SI tool. In: Bravetti, M., Núñez, M., Zavattaro, G. (eds.) WS-FM 2006. LNCS, vol. 4184, pp. 58–72. Springer, Heidelberg (2006)
3. Daniele, M., Giunchiglia, F., Vardi, M.Y.: Improved Automata Generation for Linear Temporal Logic. In: Halbwachs, N., Peled, D.A. (eds.) CAV 1999. LNCS, vol. 1633, pp. 249–260. Springer, Heidelberg (1999)
4. Gastin, P., Oddoux, D.: Fast LTL to Büchi Automata Translation. In: Berry, G., Comon, H., Finkel, A. (eds.) CAV 2001. LNCS, vol. 2102, pp. 53–65. Springer, Heidelberg (2001)
5. Gerth, R., Peled, D., Vardi, M.Y., Wolper, P.: Simple On-The-Fly Automatic Verification of Linear Temporal Logic. In: Proceedings of the Fifteenth IFIP WG6.1 International Symposium on Protocol Specification, Testing and Verification XV, London, UK, pp. 3–18. Chapman & Hall, Ltd., Boca Raton (1996)
6. Giannakopoulou, D.: Model Checking for Concurrent Software Architectures. PhD Thesis, University of London, London, The United Kingdom (1999)

7. Giannakopoulou, D., Havelund, K.: Automata-Based Verification of Temporal Properties on Running Programs. In: ASE 2001: Proceedings of the 16th IEEE International Conference on Automated Software Engineering, Washington, DC, USA, pp. 412–416. IEEE Computer Society, Los Alamitos (2001)
8. Giannakopoulou, D., Lerda, F.: From States to Transitions: Improving Translation of LTL Formulae to Büchi Automata. In: Peled, D.A., Vardi, M.Y. (eds.) FORTE 2002. LNCS, vol. 2529, pp. 308–326. Springer, Heidelberg (2002)
9. Giannakopoulou, D., Magee, J.: Fluent Model checking for event-based systems. In: Proceedings of the 9th European Software Engineering Conference Held Jointly with 11th ACM SIGSOFT International Symposium on Foundations of Software Engineering (ESEC/FSE-11), pp. 257–266. ACM, New York (2003)
10. Latvala, T.: Efficient Model Checking of Safety Properties. In: Ball, T., Rajamani, S.K. (eds.) SPIN 2003. LNCS, vol. 2648, pp. 74–88. Springer, Heidelberg (2003)
11. Montali, M., Pesic, M., van der Aalst, W.M.P., Chesani, F., Mello, P., Storari, S.: Declarative specification and verification of service choreographies. ACM Trans. Web. 4(1), 1–62 (2010)
12. Paun, D.O., Chechik, M.: Events in Linear-Time Properties. In: Proceedings of the 4th IEEE International Symposium on Requirements Engineering (RE 1999). LNCS, pp. 123–132. IEEE Computer Society, Los Alamitos (1999)

Nevertrace Claims for Model Checking

Zhe Chen and Gilles Motet

LATTIS & LAAS-CNRS, INSA, Université de Toulouse
135 Avenue de Rangueil, 31077 Toulouse, France
{zchen,gilles.motet}@insa-toulouse.fr

Abstract. We propose the `nevertrace` claim, which is a new construct for specifying the correctness properties that either finite or infinite *execution traces* (i.e., *sequences of transitions*) that should *never* occur. In semantics, it is neither similar to `never` claim and `trace` assertion, nor a simple combination of them. Furthermore, the theoretical foundation for checking `nevertrace` claims, namely the Asynchronous-Composition Büchi Automaton Control System (AC-BAC System), is proposed. The major contributions of the `nevertrace` claim include: a powerful construct for formalizing properties related to transitions and their labels, and a way for reducing the state space at the design stage.

1 Introduction

The SPIN (Simple Promela INterpreter) model checker is an automated tool for verifying the correctness of asynchronous distributed software models [1,2,3]. System models and correctness properties to be verified are both described in Promela (Process Meta Language). This paper is based on SPIN Version 5.2.5, released on 17th April 2010.

Promela supports various constructs for formalizing different classes of properties. The most powerful constructs are the `never` claim, the `trace` and `notrace` assertions. The `never` claim specifies the properties on sequences of *states*, while the `trace` and `notrace` assertions specify the properties on sequences of *transitions of simple channel operations*, i.e., simple send and receive operations on message channels, where a *transition* is a statement between two states. However, we observed that the existing constructs cannot specify properties on *full sequences of transitions*, apart from the transitions of simple channel operations.

In this paper, we propose the `nevertrace` claim, which is a new claim construct for specifying correctness properties related to *all types of transitions* and their *labels*. A `nevertrace` claim specifies the properties that either finite or infinite *execution traces* (i.e., *sequences of transitions*) that should *never* occur. A `nevertrace` claim could be *nondeterministic*, and performed at *every single execution step* of the system.

Literally, it seems that the `nevertrace` claim combines the `never` claim and the `trace` assertion. However, we will show that, in semantics, it is neither similar to any of them, nor a simple combination of them.

The major contributions of this construct include the following two aspects:

J. van de Pol and M. Weber (Eds.): SPIN 2010, LNCS 6349, pp. 162–179, 2010.

First, the nevertrace claim provides a powerful construct for formalizing properties related to transitions and their labels. Furthermore, the nevertrace claim can be used to express the semantics of some existing constructs in Promela.

Second, the nevertrace claim provides a way for reducing the state space at the design stage. We observed that variables are always used for two objectives: functional computation, or implicitly recording the execution trace for verification. The nevertrace claim can reduce the usage of variables for marking the execution trace. The decreased number of variables can reduce the state space.

The paper is organized as follows. In Section 2, the existing constructs in Promela are recalled to facilitate further discussion and comparison. In Section 3, the nevertrace claim is proposed and illustrated by example. The theoretical foundation for checking nevertrace claims, namely the Asynchronous-Composition Büchi Automaton Control System (AC-BAC System), is presented in Section 4. Then in Section 5 we show how to express some constructs in Promela using nevertrace claims. We discuss related work in Section 6 and conclude in Section 7.

To illustrate some constructs in Promela and our new construct in the sequel, we use a simple Promela model (see Listing 1.1) as an example. This model contains two channels (c2s and s2c), three processes (two clients and a server) and four types of messages. Client 1 can send msg1 through the channel c2s, and receive ack1 from the channel s2c, and repeat the procedure infinitely. Client 2 does the similar with msg2 and ack2. There are nine labels in the model, e.g., again at Line 7, c2srmsg at Line 23. The variable x counts the number of messages in the channel c2s, thus is used for functional computation.

2 Constructs for Formalizing Properties in SPIN

Promela supports the following constructs for formalizing correctness properties, of which numerous examples could be found in the monographs [3,4].

- Basic assertions. A *basic assertion* is of the form assert(expression).
- End-state labels. Every label name that starts with the prefix end is an *end-state label.*
- Progress-state labels. Every label name that starts with the prefix progress is a *progress-state label.*
- Accept-state labels. Every label name that starts with the prefix accept is an *accept-state label.*
- Never claims. A never claim specifies either finite or infinite system behavior that should *never* occur.
- Trace assertions. A trace assertion specifies properties about sequences of simple send and receive operations on message channels.
- Notrace assertions. A notrace assertion specifies the opposite of a trace assertion, but uses the same syntax.

Note that never claims could be nondeterministic, whereas trace and notrace assertions must be deterministic. Furthermore, Promela also supports Linear Temporal Logic (LTL) formulas, which are converted into never claims for verification [5].

Listing 1.1. A Promela Model of Client and Server

```
mtype = {msg1, msg2, ack1, ack2};
chan c2s = [2] of {mtype};
chan s2c = [0] of {mtype};
int x = 0;

active proctype client1() {
again:
c2ssmsg1:   c2s!msg1;
x_inc:      x = x+1;
            s2c?ack1;
            goto again;
}

active proctype client2() {
again:
c2ssmsg2:   c2s!msg2;
x_inc:      x = x+1;
            s2c?ack2;
            goto again;
}

active proctype server() {
c2srmsg:  do
          :: c2s?msg1;
x_dec1:      x = x-1;
             s2c!ack1;
          :: c2s?msg2;
x_dec2:      x = x-1;
             s2c!ack2;
          od;
}
```

To facilitate the comparison in the sequel, we recall first the semantics of `notrace` assertions through a simple example.

The following `notrace` assertion specifies the property that there should *not* exist a sequence of send operations on the channel `c2s` that contains two consecutive `c2s!msg1`. Note that, for `notrace` assertions, an error is reported, if the assertion is matched completely. Note that only the send operations on the channel `c2s` are within the scope of this check, and other statements are ignored.

```
notrace {  /* containing two consecutive c2s!msg1 */
S0:
      if
        :: c2s!msg1 -> goto S1;
        :: c2s!msg2 -> goto S0;
      fi;
S1:
      if
        :: c2s!msg1;
        :: c2s!msg2 -> goto S0;
      fi;
/* S2 */
}
```

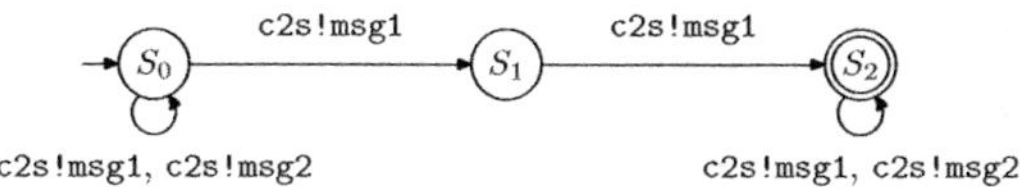

Fig. 1. The Nondeterministic Automaton of `notrace` Assertion

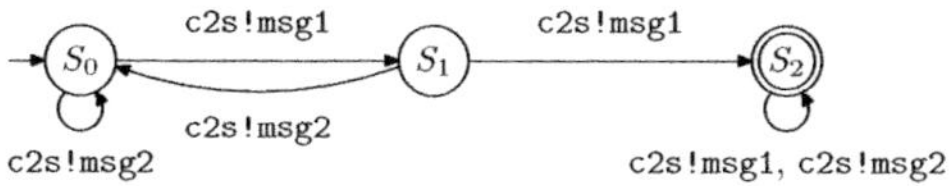

Fig. 2. The Deterministic Automaton of `notrace` Assertion

The model in Listing 1.1 violates this assertion, since sequences containing two consecutive `c2s!msg1` are feasible. These sequences cause the termination of the `notrace` assertion.

We observed that `notrace` assertions could be also constructed from LTL formulas. The procedure reuses the technique that translates LTL formulas into `never` claims [5]. Note that `never` claims specify Nondeterministic Finite Automata (NFA). Thus, an additional step of manually determinizing NFA [6] is needed, since a `notrace` assertion must be deterministic.

For this example, we can convert the LTL formula `<>(c2s!msg1 -> X c2s!msg1)` into an NFA in Fig. 1. Note that the condition statement `(1)` (or `true`) was replaced by all send operations on the channel `c2s` in the model. To obtain a deterministic `notrace` assertion, we have to manually determinize the NFA to a Deterministic Finite Automaton (DFA) and minimize the DFA. The result is shown in Fig. 2. Finally, we can write the above assertion according to the established DFA.

3 Nevertrace Claims

In this section, we will propose the `nevertrace` claim. A `nevertrace` claim may contain control-flow constructs and *transition expressions*, whose major ingredient is the *label expression*. Thus, we will present three new constructs.

3.1 Label Expressions

In a program or model (e.g., Promela model), some statements have labels. A statement may have several labels. A *label* name in a model contains only the following characters: digits (`0` to `9`), letters (`a` to `z`, `A` to `Z`), and underscore (_). We assume that all the unlabeled statements have the empty string (denoted by ϵ) as its default label name.

A *label expression* is a regular expression for matching label names. The label expression reuses a subset of the characters of POSIX-extended regular

Table 1. Special Characters in Label Expressions

Symbol	Meaning over the Alphabet [0-9A-Za-z_]
.	A *dot* matches any single character.
( )	*Parentheses* group a series of patterns into a new pattern.
[ ]	A *character class* matches any character within the brackets. If the first character is a *circumflex* [^], it matches any character except the ones within the brackets. A *dash* inside the brackets indicates a character range, e.g., [a-d] means [abcd], [^a-d] means [0-9A-Ze-z_].
{ }	If the braces contain one number, it indicates the exact number of times the previous pattern can match. While two numbers indicate the minimum and maximum number of times.
*	A *Kleene star* matches zero or more copies of the previous pattern.
+	A *positive closure* matches one or more copies of the previous pattern.
?	A *question mark* matches zero or one copy of the previous pattern.
|	An *alternation* operator matches either the previous pattern or the following pattern.
	Additional Symbols
(^)	If the first character is a *circumflex* (^), it matches any string except the ones expressed by the expression within the parentheses.
#	A *hash mark* matches any string over the alphabet, i.e., [0-9A-Za-z_]*.

expressions[1], and adds some new symbols. The special characters are listed in Table 1, where the additional symbols in the bottom part are not included in POSIX-extended regular expressions. All the characters other than the special characters listed in Table 1, including digits, letters and underscore, match themselves. Also note that the interpretation of these symbols is over the restricted alphabet [0-9A-Za-z_].

For example, in Listing 1.1, the label expression `c2ssmsg#` matches the labels starting with `c2ssmsg`, i.e., `c2ssmsg1` and `c2ssmsg2`. The expression `(^c2ss#)` matches all labels in the model other than those starting with `c2ss`. The empty string ϵ could be matched by `a{0}`, where `a` could be other letters or any digit.

Let us consider the complexity of deciding whether a label name is matched by a label expression. It is well known that a Deterministic Finite Automaton (DFA) can be effectively constructed from a regular expression [6]. In the label expression, most of the special characters are reused from regular expressions. It is easy to see, the additional characters also produce DFA's. For example, `(^)` means constructing the complementation of a regular language (and its DFA) [6]. Therefore, a DFA can be also effectively constructed from a label expression.

It is also well known that the membership problem for regular languages (accepted by DFA's) can be decided in linear time [6]. Therefore, the membership problem for label expressions can be also decided in linear time. This means, given a label name l of length n, whether l is matched by a label expression can be decided in linear time $O(n)$. This shows that label expressions are feasible in practice.

[1] POSIX-extended regular expressions are widely used in Unix applications.

3.2 Transition Expressions

An *atomic transition expression* is of the form `procname[pid]$lblexp`, and may take three arguments. The first optional argument is the name of a previously declared `proctype procname`. The second optional argument is an expression enclosed in brackets, which provides the process identity number `pid` of an active process. The third required argument `lblexp` is a *label expression*, which matches a set of label names in the model. There must be a symbol $ between the second and the third arguments.

Given a transition and its labels, an atomic transition expression `procname [pid]$lblexp` matches the transition (i.e., returns *true*), if the transition belongs to the process `procname[pid]`, and *at least one of the labels* is matched by the label expression `lblexp`. We should notice that the first two arguments are only used to restrict the application domain of the label expression.

A *transition expression* contains one or more atomic transition expressions connected by propositional logic connectives. It can be defined in Backus-Naur Form as follows:

```
t ::= a | (!t) | (t && t) | (t || t) | (t -> t)
```

where `t` is transition expression, and `a` is atomic transition expression.

Given a transition and its labels, a transition expression matches the transition (i.e., returns *true*), if the propositional logic formula is evaluated to *true* according to the values of its atomic transition expressions. Note that the transition expression is side effect free. That is, it does not generate new system behavior, just like condition statements.

For example, in Listing 1.1, the (atomic) transition expression `client1[0] $c2ssmsg#` matches all transitions that have a label starting with `c2ssmsg` in the process 0 of type `client1`, i.e., the statement with label `c2ssmsg1` at Line 8. The transition expression `(client2[1]$(c2s#)) && $again#` matches all transitions that have a label starting with `c2s` and a label starting with `again`, in the process 1 of type `client2`, i.e., the statement with two labels `again` and `c2ssmsg2` at Line 16.

In an atomic transition expression, the second arguments (together with the brackets) can be omitted, if there is only one active process of the type specified by the first argument, or the transition expression is imposed on all active processes of the type. The first and the second arguments (together with the brackets) can be both omitted, if the transition expression is imposed on all active processes. But note that the symbol $ cannot be omitted in any case.

For example, in Listing 1.1, the transition expression `client1[0]$c2ssmsg#` is equivalent to `client1$c2ssmsg#`. The transition expression `$c2ssmsg#` matches the transitions that have a label starting with `c2ssmsg` in all active processes, i.e., the statements at Lines 8 and 16.

The reader may find that the atomic transition expression is syntactically similar to the remote label reference in Promela, except the symbol $. Note that, at first, there are two superficial differences: (1) the first argument of the remote label reference cannot be omitted, (2) the third argument of the remote label reference should be an existing label name, rather than a label expression. Furthermore, we will show later that they have different semantics in their corresponding claims.

Let us consider the complexity of deciding whether a transition is matched by a transition expression.

For *atomic transition expressions*, we showed that the membership problem for label expressions (the third argument) can be decided in linear time $O(n)$. As mentioned, the first two arguments only check the owner of the label, so do not affect the complexity. Thus, given a transition with several labels of the total length n, whether it is matched by an atomic transition expression can be decided in linear time $O(n)$. That is, the membership problem for atomic transition expressions can be also decided in linear time $O(n)$.

Suppose a *transition expression* has i atomic transition expressions and j logic connectives, then the membership problem can be decided in $i \cdot O(n) + O(j)$ time. Since i, j are constants for a given transition expression, the membership problem can be decided in linear time $O(n)$. This shows that transition expressions are feasible in practice.

3.3 Nevertrace Claims

A `nevertrace` claim specifies the properties that either finite or infinite *execution traces* (i.e., *sequences of transitions*) that should *never* occur. A `nevertrace` claim could be *nondeterministic*, and performed at *every single execution step* of the system.

A `nevertrace` claim may contain only control-flow constructs and *transition expressions*. A `nevertrace` claim can contain end-state, progress-state and accept-state labels with the usual interpretation in `never` claims. Therefore, it looks like a `never` claim, except the keyword `nevertrace` and allowing transition expressions instead of condition statements.

An example of `nevertrace` claim for the model in Listing 1.1 is as follows:

```
nevertrace {  /* ![]( $x_inc -> <> $x_dec#) */
T0_init:
    if
    :: (!$x_dec# && $x_inc) -> goto accept_S4
    :: $# -> goto T0_init
    fi;
accept_S4:
    if
    :: (!$x_dec#) -> goto accept_S4
    fi;
}
```

In the example, the claim specifies the property that increasing `x` always leads to decrease `x` later. In other words, if one of the transitions labeled `x_inc` is executed, then one of the transitions that have a label starting with `x_dec` will be executed in the future. By the way, if we replace `$x_inc` by `$x_i#nc#`, or replace `$x_dec#` by `server[2]$x_dec#`, for this model, the resulting claim is equivalent to the above one.

A `nevertrace` claim is performed as follows, starting from the initial system state. One transition expression of the claim process is executed each time after the system executed a transition. If the transition expression matches the *last executed transition*, then it is evaluated to *true*, and the claim moves to one of the next possible statements. If the claim gets stuck, then this means that the undesirable behavior cannot be matched. Therefore, no error is reported.

For a rendezvous communication, the system executes an atomic event in which two primitive transitions are actually executed at a time, one send operation and one receive operation. In this case, we assume that the send operation is executed before the receive operation in an atomic rendezvous event.

An error is reported, if the full behavior specified could be matched by any feasible execution. The violation can be caught as termination of the claim, or an acceptance cycle, just like `never` claims. Note that all the transitions of the model are within the scope of the check.

In the example, it is easy to see that there exists no violation, since the `nevertrace` claim cannot be matched completely.

Note that it is hard to express this property using existing constructs in Promela. For example, `trace` or `notrace` assertions are not capable of expressing this property, since they can only specify properties on simple channel operations. The three types of special labels do not have this power neither.

Fortunately, `never` claims can express this property by introducing new variables to implicitly record the information about execution traces. For instance, we introduce two boolean variables `a`, `b`. After each statement labeled `x_inc`, we add the statements "`a=1; a=0;`", which let `a` be 1 once. After each statement labeled `x_dec#`, we add the statements "`b=1; b=0;`", which let `b` be 1 once. Then the property can be expressed as LTL formula `[](a -> <>b)`. The negation of this formula can be converted into a `never` claim that specifies the required property.

However, please note that the additional variables quadruple the state space (different combinations of `a` and `b`), and make the program malformed and harder to read. In contrast, the `nevertrace` claim is more economic, since it takes full advantage of the transition information (e.g., control-flow states and their labels) that is already tracked as part of the state space in the verification mode of SPIN.

An interesting thing is that `nevertrace` claims could be also converted from LTL formulas. In the example, a `never` claim can be generated from the LTL formula `![]($x_inc -> <>$x_dec#)` by SPIN. Then we can obtain the `nevertrace` claim above by replacing the condition statement `(1)` or `true` by `$#` matching all transitions. This fact can facilitate the use of `nevertrace` claims in practice.

Finally, let us consider the syntax definition of `nevertrace` claims. There are various ways to modify the grammar of Promela to take into account the `nevertrace` claim. For example, we can add the following productions into the grammar of Promela.

```
unit     :  nevertrace ;

nevertrace  : NEVERTRACE body ;

expr     :  PNAME '[' expr ']' '$' expr_label
    | PNAME '$' expr_label
    | '$' expr_label
    ;
```

Here `unit`, `body` and `expr` are existing nonterminals in the grammar of Promela, thus we only extend the grammar by appending the new productions. The productions for the nonterminal `expr_label` are omitted, since its syntax is clearly specified in Table 1.

4 Theory for Checking Nevertrace Claims

In this section, we propose the theory of *asynchronous-composition Büchi automaton control systems.* Then we will show the connection between the theory and the checking of `nevertrace` claims by example.

4.1 The Asynchronous Composition of Büchi Automata

At first, we recall the classic definition of Büchi automata [7,8].

Definition 1. *A* (nondeterministic) Büchi automaton *(simply automaton) is a tuple $A = (Q, \Sigma, \delta, q_0, F)$, where Q is a finite set of* states, *Σ is a finite* alphabet, *$\delta \subseteq Q \times \Sigma \times Q$ is a set of* named transitions, *$q_0 \in Q$ is the* initial state, *$F \subseteq Q$ is a set of* accepting states. *For convenience, we denote the set of* transition names *also by δ.* □

Note that the concept of transition name is introduced. A transition in δ is of the form $p_k : (q, a, q')$, where p_k is the *name* of the transition. In the transition diagram, a transition $p_k : (q, a, q') \in \delta$ is denoted by an arc from q to q' labeled $p_k : a$.

Given a set of automata, they execute asynchronously, but may synchronize on rendezvous events. We assume that the send operation is executed before the receive operation in an atomic rendezvous event. Formally, we define their asynchronous composition as follows.

Let $N = \{n_1, ..., n_k\} \subseteq \mathbb{N}$ be a countable set with cardinality k, and for each $n_j \in N$, S_{n_j} be a set. We define the *Cartesian product* as:

$$\prod_{n_j \in N} S_{n_j} = \{(x_{n_1}, x_{n_2}, ..., x_{n_k}) \mid \forall j \in \{1, ..., k\}, x_{n_j} \in S_{n_j}\}$$

For each $j \in \{1, ..., k\}$, we denote the j-th component of the vector $q = (x_{n_1}, x_{n_2}, ..., x_{n_k})$ by the projection $q[j]$, i.e., $q[j] = x_{n_j}$.

Definition 2. *The* asynchronous composition $A = \prod_{n\in N} A_n$ *of a countable collection of Büchi automata* $\{A_n = (Q_n, \Sigma_n, \delta_n, q_n, F_n)\}_{n\in N}$ *is a Büchi automaton*

$$A = (\prod_{n\in N} Q_n, \Sigma, \delta, \prod_{n\in N} q_n, F)$$

where $\Sigma = \bigcup_{n\in N} \Sigma_n$,

$$\delta = \{p_k : (q, a, q') \mid \exists n_i \in N, a \in \Sigma_{n_i} \wedge p_k : (q[i], a, q'[i]) \in \delta_{n_i}, \\ and\ \forall n_j \in N, n_j \neq n_i \rightarrow q[j] = q'[j]\}$$

$F = \{q \in \prod_{n\in N} Q_n \mid \exists n_i \in N, q[i] \in F_{n_i}\}$. □

We interpret the asynchronous composition as the expanded version which fully expands all possible values of the variables in the state space (see Appendix A of [3]). The executability of a transition depends on its source state.

4.2 The Asynchronous-Composition BAC System

An Asynchronous-Composition Büchi Automaton Control System (AC-BAC System) consists of an asynchronous composition of Büchi automata and a Büchi controlling automaton. The controlling automaton controls all the transitions of the primitive components in the composition. Thus, the alphabet of the controlling automaton equals the set of transition names of the controlled automata.

Definition 3. *Given an asynchronous composition of a set of Büchi automata* $A = \prod_{n\in N} A_n$, *a* (Büchi) controlling automaton *over* A *is* $A_c = (Q_c, \Sigma_c, \delta_c, q_c, F_c)$ *with* $\Sigma_c = \bigcup_{n\in N} \delta_n$. *The global system is called an* Asynchronous-Composition Büchi Automaton Control System *(AC-BAC System).* □

The controlling automaton is used to specify the sequences of transitions that should *never* occur, since a controlling automaton accepts sequences of transitions.

We compute the *meta-composition* of an asynchronous composition and a controlling automaton. In the *meta-composition*, a transition is allowed iff it is in the asynchronous composition and allowed by the controlling automaton. The name "*meta-composition*" denotes that the controlling automaton is at a higher level, since it treats the set of transitions rather than the alphabet. We formally define the *meta-composition* ($\vec{\cdot}$ operator) as follows.

Definition 4. *The* meta-composition *of an asynchronous composition* $A = (Q, \Sigma, \delta, q_0, F)$ *and a controlling automaton* $A_c = (Q_c, \Sigma_c, \delta_c, q_c, F_c)$ *is a Büchi automaton:*

$$A' = A \vec{\cdot} A_c = (Q \times Q_c, \Sigma, \delta', (q_0, q_c), (F \times Q_c) \cup (Q \times F_c))$$

where for each $q_i, q_l \in Q$, $q_j, q_m \in Q_c$ *and* $a \in \Sigma$, *we have* $p_k : ((q_i, q_j), a, (q_l, q_m)) \in \delta'$ *iff* $p_k : (q_i, a, q_l) \in \delta$ *and* $(q_j, p_k, q_m) \in \delta_c$. □

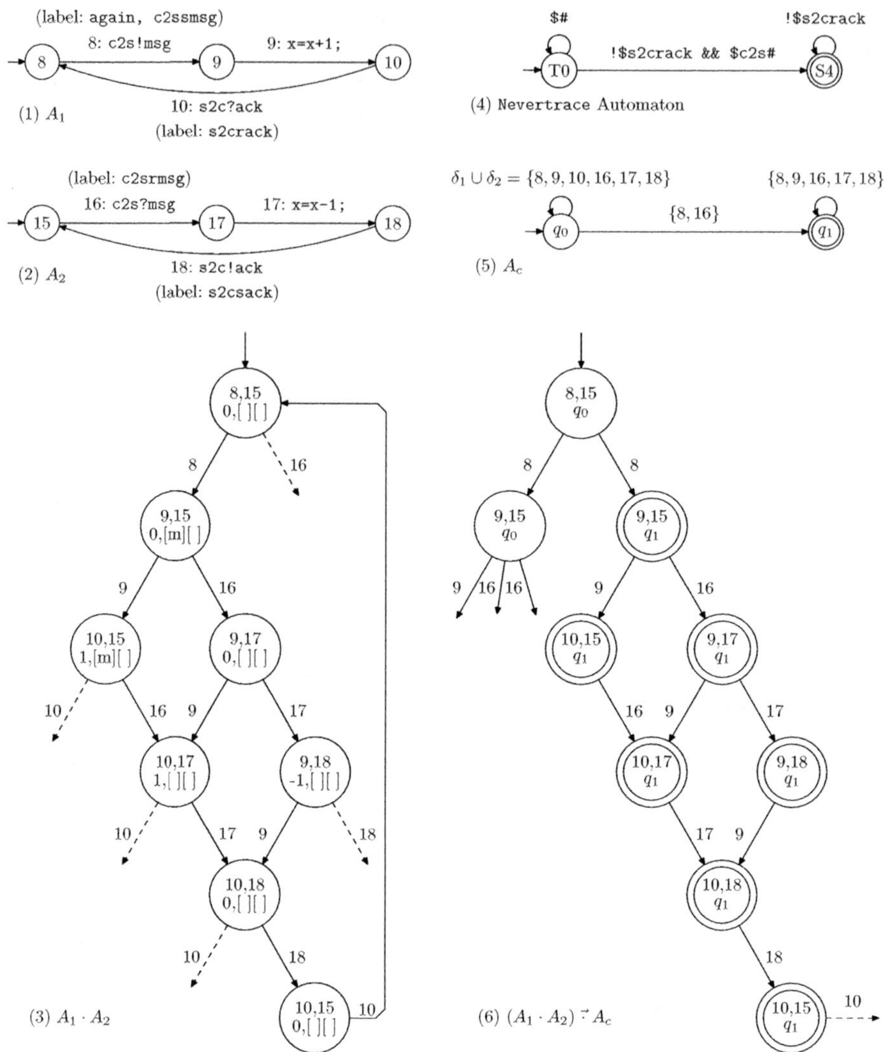

Fig. 3. An Example of Asynchronous-Composition BAC System

If we let $\{A_n\}_{n \in N}$ contain only a single primitive automaton, i.e., $|N| = 1$, the definition will express the meta-composition over a single automaton.

We observe that A has feasible sequences of transitions accepted by A_c (or A matches A_c), iff the language accepted by the meta-composition is not empty. This fact will be used for checking `nevertrace` claims.

Note that the emptiness problem for meta-compositions is decidable. It is well known that the emptiness problem for Büchi automata is decidable [8]. Since the meta-composition is a Büchi automaton, checking its emptiness is also decidable.

It is worth noting that the controlling automaton specifies properties on transitions rather than states, which is the major difference between our theory and Vardi and Wolper's automata theoretical framework for model checking.

4.3 From Nevertrace Claims to AC-BAC Systems

We will show at first how to translate a model with a `nevertrace` claim into an AC-BAC system. Let us consider a simple example in Listing 1.2 consisting of a client and a server.

Listing 1.2. A Simplified Promela Model of Client and Server

```
1  mtype = {msg, ack};
2  chan c2s = [2] of {mtype};
3  chan s2c = [0] of {mtype};
4  int x = 0;
5
6  active proctype client() {
7  again:
8  c2ssmsg:    c2s!msg;
9              x = x+1;
10 s2crack:    s2c?ack;
11             goto again;
12 }
13
14 active proctype server() {
15 c2srmsg:  do
16           :: c2s?msg;
17              x = x-1;
18 s2csack:     s2c!ack;
19           od;
20 }
```

Figures 3 (1) and (2) show the automata A_1, A_2 describing the behavior of the client and the server, respectively. Each transition between two control-flow states is labeled by its transition name (may be related to line number and control-flow state etc.) and statement. For example, 8 is the transition name between the states 8 and 9.

The asynchronous composition $A_1 \cdot A_2$ is shown in Fig. 3(3). A system state consists of four elements: the control-flow states of A_1 and A_2, the value of `x` and the contents of the channel `c2s`. Note that the dashed transitions are not executable at their corresponding states, although themselves and omitted subsequent states are part of the composition. That is, the figure contains exactly the reachable states in the system. At the bottom of the figure, the transitions labeled 18 and 10 constitute a handshake.

Let us consider the following `nevertrace` claim:

```
nevertrace {  /* ![]( $c2s# -> <> $s2crack) */
T0_init:
    if
    :: (!$s2crack && $c2s#) -> goto accept_S4
    :: $# -> goto T0_init
    fi;
accept_S4:
```

```
    if
    :: (!$s2crack) -> goto accept_S4
    fi;
}
```

The claim specifies the property that any operation on channel c2s always leads to receive ack from the channel s2c later. In other words, if one of the transitions that have a label starting with c2s is executed, then one of the transitions labeled s2crack will be executed in the future.

Figure 3(4) shows the automaton specified by the nevertrace claim. Figure 3(5) shows the controlling automaton specified by the nevertrace automaton. For example, the transition expression (!$s2crack && $c2s#) matches the transitions 8 and 16.

The automata in Figures 3 (3) and (5) constitute an AC-BAC system, which is established from the model and the nevertrace claim. The next step is to check whether the asynchronous composition $A_1 \cdot A_2$ matches the claim A_c.

The meta-composition $(A_1 \cdot A_2) \vec{\cdot} A_c$ is shown in Fig. 3(6) (To save space, the state space starting from the state (9,15,q_0) is not drawn). The state of the controlling automaton is added into the system state. In the meta-composition, a transition is allowed, iff it is in $(A_1 \cdot A_2)$ and allowed by A_c. Note that the transition 10 is blocked, since it is not allowed by the state q_1 of A_c. It is easy to see there does not exist any acceptance cycle, thus the ω-language accepted by the meta-composition is empty. This means, no counterexample can be found, and the system satisfies the required correctness property.

To conclude, checking nevertrace claims is equivalent to the emptiness problem for meta-compositions. A nevertrace claim is violated if and only if the meta-composition is not empty. As we mentioned, the emptiness problem for meta-compositions is decidable. Therefore, checking nevertrace claims is feasible in practice. Furthermore, the emptiness of meta-compositions can be checked on-the-fly, using the technique for checking never claims [9].

5 On Expressing Some Constructs in SPIN

In this section, we will show how to express the semantics of some constructs in Promela using nevertrace claims, although the major objective of the nevertrace claim is expressing a new class of properties rather than replacing them.

5.1 Expressing Notrace Assertions

There are various ways to convert a notrace assertion into a nevertrace claim. As an example, let us consider the notrace assertion in Section 2. We can construct an NFA in Fig. 4 which specifies the same property as the DFA in Fig. 2 of the notrace assertion for the model in Listing 1.1.

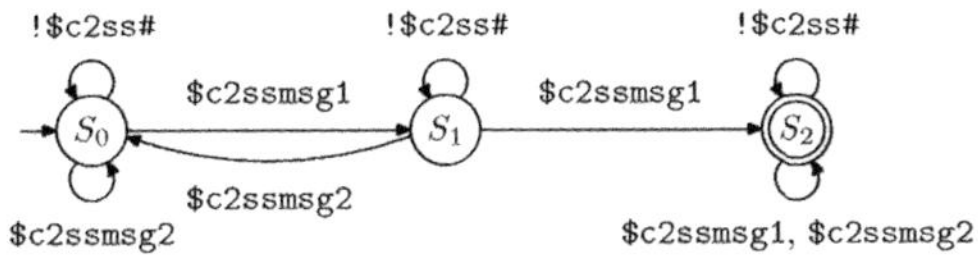

Fig. 4. The Nondeterministic Automaton of `nevertrace` Claim

A `nevertrace` claim can be written according to the automaton.

```
nevertrace {  /* containing two consecutive c2s!msg1 */
S0:
      if
        :: $c2ssmsg1 -> goto S1;
        :: $c2ssmsg2 -> goto S0;
        :: (!$c2ss#) -> goto S0;
      fi;
S1:
      if
        :: $c2ssmsg1;
        :: $c2ssmsg2 -> goto S0;
        :: (!$c2ss#) -> goto S1;
      fi;
/* S2 */
}
```

It is easy to see, we used the following rules to convert the `notrace` assertion into a `nevertrace` claim.

First, in the system model, all send operations of message `msg` on a channel `ch` must have a label `chsmsg`, while all receive operations of message `msg` on the channel must have a label `chrmsg`. The labels of all statements other than channel operations should not start with the names of declared channels.

Second, in the `notrace` assertion, (1) replace `ch!msg` by `$chsmsg`, `ch?msg` by `$chrmsg`; (2) for each state, add new transition expressions to match the statements outside the scope of the `notrace` assertion. In the example, for each state, we add a transition from the state to itself with the transition expression `(!$c2ss#)`, since only send operations on the channel `c2s` are within the scope of the `notrace` assertion.

5.2 Expressing Remote Label Reference

The predefined function `procname[pid]@label` is a remote label reference. It returns a nonzero value only if the next statement that can be executed in the process `procname[pid]` is the statement with `label`.

It seems that `procname[pid]@label` can be also used as a transition expression, if replacing `@` by `$`. However, there is a little difference in semantics. The remote label reference is evaluated over the next statement of the process `procname[pid]`, but the transition expression is evaluated over the last executed transition, which does not necessarily belong to the process `procname[pid]`.

5.3 Expressing the Non-progress Variable

The predefined non-progress variable `np_` holds the value *false*, if at least one running process is at a control-flow state with a progress-state label. It is used to detect the existence of non-progress cycles.

It seems that the variable `np_` is equivalent to our transition expression `!$progress#`. However, there is a little difference. The variable `np_` is evaluated over all the running processes, but the transition expression is evaluated over the last executed process.

5.4 Expressing Progress-State Labels

There are two types of progress cycles. A ***weak*** progress cycle is an infinite execution cycle that contains at least one of the progress-state labels, which denotes reaching some progress-state labels infinitely often. A ***strong*** progress cycle is a weak progress cycle with the requirement that each statement with a progress-state label in the cycle must be executed infinitely often.

Promela supports only the weak progress cycle, whereas our `nevertrace` claim can express the strong progress cycle.

As an example, let us consider the model in Listing 1.3 consisting of two processes `p1` and `p2`. Note that `p1` does not execute any statement, but waits at the label `progress` for ever.

Listing 1.3. A Promela Model of Two Processes

```
chan ch = [0] of {bool};

active proctype p1() {
                  bool x;
   progress:      ch?x;
}

active proctype p2() {
   bool x = 0;
   do
      :: x==0; x=1;
      :: x==1; x=0;
   od;
}
```

In the verification mode of SPIN, none (weak) non-progress cycle is found, both with or without fairness condition[2]. All executions are weak progress cycles, since `p1` stays for ever at a progress-state label.

In contrast, we can find a strong non-progress cycle using the following `nevertrace` claim, which can be constructed from the LTL formula

[2] The (weak) fairness in SPIN means, if the executability of an executable statement never changes, it will eventually be executed. The strong fairness means, if a statement becomes executable infinitely often, it will eventually be executed [3].

<>[]!$progress#. If we modify a never claim generated from the LTL formula by SPIN, remember to replace the condition statement (1) or true by $# matching all transitions.

```
nevertrace { /* strong non-progress cycle detector */
T0_init:
    if
    :: (!$progress#) -> goto accept_S4
    :: $# -> goto T0_init
    fi;
accept_S4:
    if
    :: (!$progress#) -> goto accept_S4
    fi;
}
```

Note that the evaluation of transition expressions is over the last executed transition, and all the executable transitions do not have a progress-state label. Therefore, strong non-progress cycles can be detected as counterexamples.

5.5 Expressing Accept-State Labels

There are two types of acceptance cycles. A *weak* acceptance cycle is an infinite execution cycle that contains at least one of the accept-state labels, which denotes reaching some accept-state labels infinitely often. A *strong* acceptance cycle is a weak acceptance cycle with the requirement that each statement with an accept-state label in the cycle must be executed infinitely often.

Promela supports only the weak acceptance cycle, whereas our nevertrace claim can express the strong acceptance cycle.

As an example, let us replace the label progress by accept in the model of Listing 1.3. Note that p1 does not execute any statement, but waits at the label accept for ever.

In the verification mode of SPIN, a (weak) acceptance cycle is found, both with or without fairness condition. All executions are weak acceptance cycles, since p1 stays for ever at an accept-state label. Therefore, (weak) acceptance cycles can be detected as counterexamples.

In contrast, we cannot find any strong acceptance cycle using the following nevertrace claim, which can be constructed from the LTL formula []<>($accept#). If we modify a never claim generated from the LTL formula by SPIN, remember to replace the condition statement (1) or true by $# matching all transitions.

```
nevertrace  { /* strong acceptance cycle detector */
T0_init:
    if
    :: $accept# -> goto accept_S9
```

```
    :: $# -> goto T0_init
    fi;
accept_S9:
    if
    :: $# -> goto T0_init
    fi;
}
```

Note that the evaluation of transition expressions is over the last executed transition, and all the executable transitions do not have an acceptance-state label. Therefore, there is no strong acceptance cycle.

6 Related Work

In the previous section, we mentioned some differences between `nevertrace` claims and some constructs in Promela. In this section, we would like to summarize the comparison with the most powerful two constructs in Promela, `never` claims and `notrace` assertions.

The major differences between `nevertrace` claims and `never` claims are obvious. They are used to specify properties on sequences of ***transitions*** (execution traces) and sequences of ***states***, respectively. A `nevertrace` claim is performed after executing a transition, whereas a `never` claim is started from the initial system state. A `nevertrace` claim is evaluated over the last executed transition, whereas a `never` claim is evaluated over the current system state. Thanks to their different focuses, they can be used together in a model checker to achieve stronger power.

`Nevertrace` claims and `notrace` (also `trace`) assertions are both about execution traces, their major differences are as follows.

1. They have different scopes of checking. `Nevertrace` claims consider all transitions, whereas only simple send/receive operations are within the scope of `notrace` assertions. Furthermore, only the channel names that are specified in a `notrace` assertion are considered to be within its scope. All other transitions are ignored.
2. The `notrace` assertion cannot contain random receive, sorted send, or channel poll operations. But these can be also tracked by a `nevertrace` claim.
3. The `notrace` assertion must be deterministic, whereas the `nevertrace` claim could be nondeterministic, just like the `never` claim.
4. The `notrace` assertion does not execute synchronously with the system, but executes only when events of interest occur. Whereas the `nevertrace` claim executes synchronously with the system, just like the `never` claim.

7 Conclusion

In this paper, we proposed the `nevertrace` claim, which is a new construct for specifying the correctness properties that either finite or infinite *execution traces* (i.e., ***sequences of transitions***) that should ***never*** occur. The Asynchronous-Composition Büchi Automaton Control System (AC-BAC System) provides the theoretical foundation for checking `nevertrace` claims. We showed that the `nevertrace` claim and its checking problem are feasible in practice.

One important future work is to implement the `nevertrace` claim. Then empirical data could be collected to show whether and how much the `nevertrace` claim can reduce the state space and decrease checking time in practice, comparing with checking the same properties specified by existing constructs in SPIN. Another research direction is to make the checking of `nevertrace` claims compatible with partial order reduction technique.

References

1. Holzmann, G.J., Peled, D.: The state of SPIN. In: Alur, R., Henzinger, T.A. (eds.) CAV 1996. LNCS, vol. 1102, pp. 385–389. Springer, Heidelberg (1996)
2. Holzmann, G.J.: The model checker SPIN. IEEE Transactions on Software Engineering 23(5), 279–295 (1997)
3. Holzmann, G.J.: The SPIN Model Checker: Primer and Reference Manual. Addison-Wesley Professional, Reading (2003)
4. Ben-Ari, M.: Principles of the SPIN Model Checker. Springer, Heidelberg (2008)
5. Gastin, P., Oddoux, D.: Fast LTL to Büchi automata translation. In: Berry, G., Comon, H., Finkel, A. (eds.) CAV 2001. LNCS, vol. 2102, pp. 53–65. Springer, Heidelberg (2001)
6. Hopcroft, J.E., Ullman, J.D.: Introduction to Automata Theory, Languages, and Computation. Addison-Wesley, Reading (1979)
7. Büchi, J.R.: On a decision method in restricted second order arithmetic. In: Proceedings of the International Congress on Logic, Methodology, and Philosophy of Science, pp. 1–11. Stanford University Press, Stanford (1960)
8. Thomas, W.: Automata on infinite objects. In: Handbook of Theoretical Computer Science. Formal Models and Semantics, vol. B, pp. 133–191. Elsevier Science Publishers B.V, Amsterdam (1990)
9. Gerth, R., Peled, D., Vardi, M.Y., Wolper, P.: Simple on-the-fly automatic verification of linear temporal logic. In: Dembinski, P., Sredniawa, M. (eds.) Proceedings of the 15th IFIP WG6.1 International Symposium on Protocol Specification, Testing and Verification, pp. 3–18. Chapman & Hall, Boca Raton (1995)

A False History of True Concurrency: From Petri to Tools

Javier Esparza

Institut für Informatik, Technische Universität München
Boltzmannstr. 3, 85748 Garching, Germany

Abstract. I briefly review the history of the unfolding approach to model checking.

Carl Adam Petri passed away on July 2, 2010. I learnt about his death three days later, a few hours after finishing this text. He was a very profound and highly original thinker, and will be sadly missed. This note is dedicated to his memory.

In some papers and talks, Moshe Vardi has described the history of the automata-theoretic approach to model checking, the verification technique that inspired the SPIN model checker and other tools. He traces it back to the work of theoreticians like Büchi, Prior, Trakhtenbrot and others, whose motivations were surprisingly far away from the applications that their ideas found down the line. Inspired by this work, in this note I briefly present the origins of the unfolding approach to model checking [21], a branch of the automata-theoretic approach that alleviates the state-explosion problem caused by concurrency.

Since the unfolding approach is based on the theory of *true concurrency*, describing its origins requires to speak about the origin of true concurrency itself. However, here I only touch upon those aspects of the theory that directly inspired the unfolding approach. This leaves many important works out, and so this is a very partial and "false" history of true concurrency.

The theory of true concurrency starts with two fundamental contributions by Carl Adam Petri, described in detail by Brauer and Reisig in an excellent article [11]. Both were a result of Petri's interest in analyzing the connection between mathematical, abstract computing machines, and their physical realizations. In his dissertation "Kommunikation mit Automaten", defended in 1962, Petri observes that the performance of a physically implemented Turing machine will degrade over time if the machine uses more and more storage space, because in this case signals have to travel longer and longer distances over longer and longer wires. To solve this problem he proposes an *asynchronous* architecture in which the storage space can be extended while the machine continues to operate. In the dissertation this abstract machine is described with the help of several semi-formal representations, but three years later Petri has already distilled the first mathematical formalism for asynchronous computation, and, arguably, the beginning of concurrency theory: Petri nets.

J. van de Pol and M. Weber (Eds.): SPIN 2010, LNCS 6349, pp. 180–186, 2010.

Petri's second contribution is an analysis of the notion of execution of a machine as a sequence of global states, or as a sequence of events ordered by their occurrence times with respect to some global clock. He observes that global states or global clocks are again a mathematical construct that cannot be "implemented": since information can only travel at finite speed, no part of a system can know the state of all its components at a certain moment in time.[1] He proposes to replace executions by ***nonsequential processes***, sets of events ordered not by the time at which they occur, but by the ***causality relation***, which is independent of the observer. The theory of nonsequential processes, subsequently developed by Goltz, Reisig, Best, Devillers, and Fernández, among others [26,8,9], distinguishes a system that concurrently executes two events a and b (usually denoted by $a \parallel b$ in process algebra) from a system that chooses between executing a and then b, or b and then a, (usually denoted by $a.b + b.a$): they have the same executions, namely ab and ba, but different nonsequential processes. In fact, $a \parallel b$ is not equivalent to any sequential system, and hence the name "truly concurrent semantics" or "true concurrency."

The next important step was due to Nielsen, Plotkin, and Winskel [51] in the early 80s. Recall that the executions of a system can be bundled together into a *computation tree*: the tree of events in which the nodes are the global states, and the children of a state are the states that the system may possibly reach next (where "next" implicitly assumes a global clock). Similarly, Nielsen, Plotkin, and Winskel showed how to bundle the nonsequential processes of the system into the ***unfolding*** of the system, a truly-concurrent branching-time semantics.[2] Incidentally, their motivation was to extend Scott's thesis (stating that the functions between datatypes computable by sequential programs are the continuous functions) to concurrent programs. The theory of unfoldings was further developed by Engelfriet, Nielsen, Rozenberg, Thiagarajan, Winskel, and others in [52,53,60,61,18].

All this research was taking place in the area of semantics, with semantic goals: to provide a precise, formal definition of the behaviour of a concurrent system that could be used as a reference object to prove the correctness of, for instance, proof systems à la Hoare. The success of model checking introduced a new way of looking at semantics: semantical objects were not only mathematical objects that allowed to formally prove the correctness or completeness of proof systems; they could also be constructed and stored in a computer, and used to automatically check behavioural properties. More precisely, model checking suggested to construct and store an increasingly larger part of the (usually infinite) computation tree until all global states have been visited (which was bound to happen for systems with finitely many global states). By the end of the 80s model checking had already achieved significant success. However, it faced the state-explosion problem: the number of states of the system could grow very quickly

[1] This can be taken a bit further: relativity theory shows that if the parts of a system move with respect to each other there is no physical notion of a global moment in time.

[2] "Unfolding" is not the term used in [51].

as a function of the size of the system itself. One of the causes of the problem was concurrency: the number of global states of a system with n concurrent components, each of them with m local states, can be as large as m^n.

The state-explosion problem was attacked by Ken McMillan in his PhD Thesis "Symbolic Model Checking", where he famously proposed the use of Binary Decision Diagrams as a data structure for storing and manipulating sets of states. But the thesis also contains a second idea: instead of computing an initial part of the computation tree containing all global states (a *complete prefix*), McMillan suggests to construct a complete prefix *of the unfolding*. The unfolding of a concurrent system contains the same information as the computation tree, but encoded in a different way: where the computation tree represents all global states explicitly, as different nodes of a graph, the unfolding represents them implicitly, as the tuples of local states satisfying a certain condition. McMillan was the first to observe that this implicit representation provided a line of attack on the state-explosion problem, due to the smaller size of the implicit representation [45,46,47]. He showed how to algorithmically construct a complete prefix of the unfolding, and provided convincing experimental evidence that this approach contributed to solving the state-explosion problem. Thanks to McMillan's ideas, the unfolding moved from being a mathematical object, born out of abstract work on the nature of concurrency, into a data structure for compactly representing the set of global states of a concurrent system.

McMillan's approach, however, still faced two problems. First, while the complete prefix of the unfolding constructed by his algorithm was usually much more compact than a complete prefix of the computation tree, it could also be exponentially *bigger* in the worst case. Second, McMillan's algorithms could only check specific problems, like deadlock freedom or conformance. Both problems were overcome in the next years. Improved algorithms for constructing complete prefixes were described in [49,22,23,31,32,35,36,38,24], and extensions to (almost) arbitrary properties expressible in Linear Temporal Logic (LTL) were presented in [16,19,20].

Since 2000 the algorithms for constructing complete prefixes have been parallelized [33,55] and distributed [5]. Initially developed for systems modeled as "plain" Petri nets, the unfolding approach has been extended to high-level Petri nets [37,55], symmetrical Petri nets [17], unbounded Petri nets [1], nets with read arcs [59,4], time Petri nets [25,14,15,58],products of transition systems [22] automata communicating through queues [44], networks of timed automata [10,12], process algebras [43], and graph transformation systems [3,2]. It has been implemented many times [55,56,33,42,50,29,31,20] and applied, among other problems, to conformance checking [48], analysis and synthesis of asynchronous circuits [39,41,40], monitoring and diagnose of discrete event systems [7,6,13,27], and analysis of asynchronous communication protocols [44]. Two unfolders available online are Mole and PUNF, developed and maintained by Stefan Schwoon and Victor Khomenko, respectively [57,34].

The unfolding approach to model checking is another example of how theoretical considerations about the nature of computation, and the relation between ideal and physical machines, have evolved into a pragmatic technique for the automatic verification of concurrent systems.

Acknowledgments

Many thanks to Stefan Schwoon for helpful suggestions.

References

1. Abdulla, P.A., Iyer, S.P., Nylén, A.: Unfoldings of unbounded Petri nets. In: Emerson, E.A., Sistla, A.P. (eds.) CAV 2000. LNCS, vol. 1855, pp. 495–507. Springer, Heidelberg (2000)
2. Baldan, P., Chatain, T., Haar, S., König, B.: Unfolding-based diagnosis of systems with an evolving topology. In: van Breugel, F., Chechik, M. (eds.) CONCUR 2008. LNCS, vol. 5201, pp. 203–217. Springer, Heidelberg (2008)
3. Baldan, P., Corradini, A., König, B.: Verifying finite-state graph grammars: An unfolding-based approach. In: Gardner, P., Yoshida, N. (eds.) CONCUR 2004. LNCS, vol. 3170, pp. 83–98. Springer, Heidelberg (2004)
4. Baldan, P., Corradini, A., König, B., Schwoon, S.: McMillan's complete prefix for contextual nets. In: Jensen, K., van der Aalst, W.M.P., Billington, J. (eds.) Transactions on Petri Nets and Other Models of Concurrency I. LNCS, vol. 5100, pp. 199–220. Springer, Heidelberg (2008)
5. Baldan, P., Haar, S., König, B.: Distributed unfolding of Petri nets. In: Aceto, L., Ingólfsdóttir, A. (eds.) FOSSACS 2006. LNCS, vol. 3921, pp. 126–141. Springer, Heidelberg (2006)
6. Benveniste, A., Fabre, E., Jard, C., Haar, S.: Diagnosis of asynchronous discrete event systems, a net unfolding approach. IEEE Transactions on Automatic Control 48(5), 714–727 (2003)
7. Benveniste, A., Haar, S., Fabre, E., Jard, C.: Distributed monitoring of concurrent and asynchronous systems. In: Amadio, R.M., Lugiez, D. (eds.) CONCUR 2003. LNCS, vol. 2761, pp. 1–26. Springer, Heidelberg (2003)
8. Best, E., Devillers, R.R.: Sequential and concurrent behaviour in Petri net theory. Theoretical Computer Science 55(1), 87–136 (1987)
9. Best, E., Fernández, C.: Nonsequential Processes. EATCS Monographs on Theoretical Computer Science. Springer, Heidelberg (1988)
10. Bouyer, P., Haddad, S., Reynier, P.-A.: Timed unfoldings for networks of timed automata. In: Graf and Zhang [28], pp. 292–306
11. Brauer, W., Reisig, W.: Carl Adam Petri and "Petri nets". Fundamental Concepts in Computer Science 3, 129–139 (2009)
12. Cassez, F., Chatain, T., Jard, C.: Symbolic unfoldings for networks of timed automata. In: Graf and Zhang [12], pp. 307–321
13. Chatain, T., Jard, C.: Symbolic diagnosis of partially observable concurrent systems. In: de Frutos-Escrig, D., Núñez, M. (eds.) FORTE 2004. LNCS, vol. 3235, pp. 326–342. Springer, Heidelberg (2004)
14. Chatain, T., Jard, C.: Time supervision of concurrent systems using symbolic unfoldings of time Petri nets. In: Pettersson, P., Yi, W. (eds.) FORMATS 2005. LNCS, vol. 3829, pp. 196–210. Springer, Heidelberg (2005)

15. Chatain, T., Jard, C.: Complete finite prefixes of symbolic unfoldings of safe time Petri nets. In: Donatelli, S., Thiagarajan, P.S. (eds.) ICATPN 2006. LNCS, vol. 4024, pp. 125–145. Springer, Heidelberg (2006)
16. Couvreur, J.-M., Grivet, S., Poitrenaud, D.: Designing a LTL model-checker based on unfolding graphs. In: Nielsen, M., Simpson, D. (eds.) ICATPN 2000. LNCS, vol. 1825, p. 123. Springer, Heidelberg (2000)
17. Couvreur, J.-M., Grivet, S., Poitrenaud, D.: Unfolding of products of symmetrical Petri nets. In: Colom, J.-M., Koutny, M. (eds.) ICATPN 2001. LNCS, vol. 2075, pp. 121–143. Springer, Heidelberg (2001)
18. Engelfriet, J.: Branching processes of Petri nets. Acta Informatica 28, 575–591 (1991)
19. Esparza, J., Heljanko, K.: A new unfolding approach to LTL model checking. In: Welzl, E., Montanari, U., Rolim, J.D.P. (eds.) ICALP 2000. LNCS, vol. 1853, pp. 475–486. Springer, Heidelberg (2000)
20. Esparza, J., Heljanko, K.: Implementing LTL model checking with net unfoldings. In: Dwyer, M.B. (ed.) SPIN 2001. LNCS, vol. 2057, pp. 37–56. Springer, Heidelberg (2001)
21. Esparza, J., Heljanko, K.: Unfoldings - A Partial-Order Approach to Model Checking. EATCS Monographs in Theoretical Computer Science. Springer, Heidelberg (2008)
22. Esparza, J., Römer, S.: An unfolding algorithm for synchronous products of transition systems. In: Baeten, J.C.M., Mauw, S. (eds.) CONCUR 1999. LNCS, vol. 1664, pp. 2–20. Springer, Heidelberg (1999)
23. Esparza, J., Römer, S., Vogler, W.: An improvement of McMillan's unfolding algorithm. Formal Methods in System Design 20(3), 285–310 (2002)
24. Esparza, J., Schröter, C.: Reachability analysis using net unfoldings. In: Proceeding of the Workshop Concurrency, Specification & Programming 2000. Informatik-Bericht 140, vol. II, pp. 255–270. Humboldt-Universität zu, Berlin (2000)
25. Fleischhack, H., Stehno, C.: Computing a finite prefix of a time Petri net. In: Esparza, J., Lakos, C.A. (eds.) ICATPN 2002. LNCS, vol. 2360, pp. 163–181. Springer, Heidelberg (2002)
26. Goltz, U., Reisig, W.: The non-sequential behaviour of Petri nets. Information and Control 57(2/3), 125–147 (1983)
27. Grabiec, B., Traonouez, L.-M., Jard, C., Lime, D., Roux, O.H.: Diagnosis using unfoldings of parametric time Petri nets. In: Proceedings of FORMATS 2010 (to appear, 2010)
28. Graf, S., Zhang, W. (eds.): ATVA 2006. LNCS, vol. 4218. Springer, Heidelberg (2006)
29. Grahlmann, B.: The PEP tool. In: Grumberg [30], pp. 440–443
30. Grumberg, O. (ed.): CAV 1997. LNCS, vol. 1254. Springer, Heidelberg (1997)
31. Heljanko, K.: Using logic programs with stable model semantics to solve deadlock and reachability problems for 1-safe Petri nets. Fundamenta Informaticae 37(3), 247–268 (1999)
32. Heljanko, K.: Model checking with finite complete prefixes is PSPACE-complete. In: Palamidessi [54], pp. 108–122
33. Heljanko, K., Khomenko, V., Koutny, M.: Parallelisation of the Petri net unfolding algorithm. In: Katoen, J.-P., Stevens, P. (eds.) TACAS 2002. LNCS, vol. 2280, pp. 371–385. Springer, Heidelberg (2002)
34. Victor Khomenko. PUNF — Petri net unfolder, `http://homepages.cs.ncl.ac.uk/victor.khomenko/tools/`

35. Khomenko, V., Koutny, M.: LP deadlock checking using partial order dependencies. In: Palamidessi [54], pp. 410–425
36. Khomenko, V., Koutny, M.: Towards an efficient algorithm for unfolding Petri nets. In: Larsen, K.G., Nielsen, M. (eds.) CONCUR 2001. LNCS, vol. 2154, pp. 366–380. Springer, Heidelberg (2001)
37. Khomenko, V., Koutny, M.: Branching processes of high-level Petri nets. In: Garavel, H., Hatcliff, J. (eds.) TACAS 2003. LNCS, vol. 2619, pp. 458–472. Springer, Heidelberg (2003)
38. Khomenko, V., Koutny, M., Vogler, W.: Canonical prefixes of Petri net unfoldings. Acta Informatica 40(2), 95–118 (2003)
39. Khomenko, V., Koutny, M., Yakovlev, A.: Detecting state encoding conflicts in STG unfoldings using SAT. Fundamenta Informaticae 62(2), 221–241 (2004)
40. Khomenko, V., Koutny, M., Yakovlev, A.: Logic synthesis for asynchronous circuits based on STG unfoldings and incremental SAT. Fundamenta Informaticae 70(1-2), 49–73 (2006)
41. Khomenko, V., Madalinski, A., Yakovlev, A.: Resolution of encoding conflicts by signal insertion and concurrency reduction based on STG unfoldings. In: ACSD, pp. 57–68. IEEE Computer Society, Los Alamitos (2006)
42. König, B., Kozioura, V.: AUGUR - A tool for the analysis of graph transformation systems. Bulletin of the EATCS 87, 126–137 (2005)
43. Langerak, R., Brinksma, E.: A complete finite prefix for process algebra. In: Halbwachs, N., Peled, D.A. (eds.) CAV 1999. LNCS, vol. 1633, pp. 184–195. Springer, Heidelberg (1999)
44. Lei, Y., Iyer, S.P.: An approach to unfolding asynchronous communication protocols. In: Fitzgerald, J.S., Hayes, I.J., Tarlecki, A. (eds.) FM 2005. LNCS, vol. 3582, pp. 334–349. Springer, Heidelberg (2005)
45. McMillan, K.L.: Using unfoldings to avoid the state explosion problem in the verification of asynchronous circuits. In: Probst, D.K., von Bochmann, G. (eds.) CAV 1992. LNCS, vol. 663, pp. 164–177. Springer, Heidelberg (1993)
46. McMillan, K.L.: Symbolic Model Checking. Kluwer Academic Publishers, Dordrecht (1993)
47. McMillan, K.L.: A technique of state space search based on unfolding. Formal Methods in System Design 6(1), 45–65 (1995)
48. McMillan, K.L.: Trace theoretic verification of asynchronous circuits using unfoldings. In: Wolper, P. (ed.) CAV 1995. LNCS, vol. 939, pp. 180–195. Springer, Heidelberg (1995)
49. Melzer, S., Römer, S.: Deadlock checking using net unfoldings. In: Grumberg [30], pp. 352–363
50. Melzer, S., Römer, S., Esparza, J.: Verification using PEP. In: Nivat, M., Wirsing, M. (eds.) AMAST 1996. LNCS, vol. 1101, pp. 591–594. Springer, Heidelberg (1996)
51. Nielsen, M., Plotkin, G.D., Winskel, G.: Petri nets, event structures and domains. Theoretical Computer Science 13(1), 85–108 (1981)
52. Nielsen, M., Rozenberg, G., Thiagarajan, P.S.: Behavioural notions for elementary net systems. Distributed Computing 4, 45–57 (1990)
53. Nielsen, M., Rozenberg, G., Thiagarajan, P.S.: Transition systems, event structures and unfoldings. Information and Computation 118(2), 191–207 (1995)
54. Palamidessi, C. (ed.): CONCUR 2000. LNCS, vol. 1877. Springer, Heidelberg (2000)
55. Schröter, C., Khomenko, V.: Parallel LTL-X model checking of high-level Petri nets based on unfoldings. In: Alur, R., Peled, D.A. (eds.) CAV 2004. LNCS, vol. 3114, pp. 109–121. Springer, Heidelberg (2004)

56. Schröter, C., Schwoon, S., Esparza, J.: The model-checking kit. In: van der Aalst, W.M.P., Best, E. (eds.) ICATPN 2003. LNCS, vol. 2679, pp. 463–472. Springer, Heidelberg (2003)
57. Stefan Schwoon. Mole — a Petri net unfolder, `http://www.lsv.ens-cachan.fr/~schwoon/tools/mole/`
58. Traonouez, L.-M., Grabiec, B., Jard, C., Lime, D., Roux, O.H.: Symbolic unfolding of parametric stopwatch petri nets. In: Proceedings of ATVA 2010 (to appear, 2010)
59. Vogler, W., Semenov, A.L., Yakovlev, A.: Unfolding and finite prefix for nets with read arcs. In: Sangiorgi, D., de Simone, R. (eds.) CONCUR 1998. LNCS, vol. 1466, pp. 501–516. Springer, Heidelberg (1998)
60. Winskel, G.: Event structures. In: Brauer, W., Reisig, W., Rozenberg, G. (eds.) APN 1986. LNCS, vol. 255, pp. 325–392. Springer, Heidelberg (1987)
61. Winskel, G.: An introduction to event structures. In: de Bakker, J.W., de Roever, W.-P., Rozenberg, G. (eds.) Linear Time, Branching Time and Partial Order in Logics and Models for Concurrency. LNCS, vol. 354, pp. 364–397. Springer, Heidelberg (1989)

Analysing Mu-Calculus Properties of Pushdown Systems

Matthew Hague and C.-H. Luke Ong

Oxford University Computing Laboratory
Matthew.Hague@comlab.ox.ac.uk, Luke.Ong@comlab.ox.ac.uk

Abstract. Pushdown systems provide a natural model of software with recursive procedure calls. We provide a tool (PDSolver) implementing an algorithm for computing the winning regions of a pushdown parity game and its adaptation to the direct computation of modal μ-calculus properties over pushdown systems. We also extend the algorithm to allow backwards, as well as forwards, modalities and allow the user to restrict the control flow graph to configurations reachable from a designated initial state. These extensions are motivated by applications in dataflow analysis. We provide two sets of experimental data. First, we obtain a picture of the general behaviour by analysing random problem instances. Secondly, we use the tool to perform dataflow analysis on real-world Java programs, taken from the DaCapo benchmark suite.

1 Introduction

Pushdown systems — finite-state transition systems equipped with a stack — have received a lot of interest in the software verification community. They accurately model the control flow of recursive programs (such as C and Java), and are ideal for algorithmic analysis. Pushdown systems have played a key role in the automata-theoretic approach to software model checking [1,10,14]. Considerable progress has been made in the implementation of scalable model checkers of pushdown systems. These tools (e.g. Bebop [11] and Moped [10]) are an essential back-end component of such model checkers as SLAM [12].

The modal μ-calculus is a highly expressive specification language (subsuming all standard temporal logics). Walukiewicz showed that modal μ-calculus model checking of pushdown systems is EXPTIME-complete [5], although no tools have been implemented. Previously, we gave the first algorithm that does not always suffer from an exponential explosion [4]. We introduce a tool (PDSolver) providing the first implementation of this algorithm. We also extend the technique to allow backwards modalities — which are needed for certain dataflow properties — and allow the analysis to be restricted to reachable configurations.

We provide two sets of experimental data in support of the tool. First, we give a picture of the behaviour of the tool on arbitrary inputs by analysing randomly generated problem instances. Secondly, we consider a specific application to dataflow analysis of pushdown systems extracted from real-world examples from the DaCapo Benchmarks [9]. This second set of experiments is an application of Steffen's work on dataflow analysis and model checking [3]. The tool can

J. van de Pol and M. Weber (Eds.): SPIN 2010, LNCS 6349, pp. 187–192, 2010.

be downloaded from `http://web.comlab.ox.ac.uk/people/Matthew.Hague/pdsolver.html`.

Related Work. There are several pushdown reachability checkers available, e.g., Bebop [11] and Moped [10]. Reps *et al.* have developed dataflow analysis tools based on *weighted* pushdown systems [14]. To the best of our knowledge, ours is the first tool for evaluating modal μ-calculus with backwards modalities. Steffen *et al.* have implemented dataflow analysis as model checking in jABC [2], although no work has been published extending jABC to pushdown systems.

2 Preliminaries

A ***pushdown system*** is a triple $\mathbb{P} = (\mathcal{P}, \mathcal{D}, \Sigma_\perp)$ where $\mathcal{P}$ is a set of control states, $\Sigma_\perp := \Sigma \cup \{\perp\}$ is a finite stack alphabet (we assume $\perp \notin \Sigma$) and $\mathcal{D} \subseteq \mathcal{P} \times \Sigma_\perp \times \mathcal{P} \times \Sigma_\perp^*$ is a set of rules. As is standard, we assume the bottom-of-stack symbol $\perp$ is neither pushed onto, nor popped from, the stack. A *configuration* is a pair $\langle p, w\rangle$ with $p \in \mathcal{P}$ and $w \in \Sigma^* \perp$. We have $\langle p, aw\rangle \rightarrow \langle p', w'w\rangle$ whenever $(p, a, p', w') \in \mathcal{D}$. Let $\mathcal{C}$ be the set of all pushdown configurations.

For a set AP of atomic propositions and a disjoint set $\mathcal{Z}$ of variables, formulas of the ***modal μ-calculus*** are (with $x \in AP$, $\Lambda \subseteq AP$ and $Z \in \mathcal{Z}$):

$$\varphi := x \mid \neg x \mid Z \mid \varphi \wedge \varphi \mid \varphi \vee \varphi \mid [\Lambda]\varphi \mid \langle\Lambda\rangle\varphi \mid \overline{[\Lambda]}\varphi \mid \overline{\langle\Lambda\rangle}\varphi \mid \mu Z.\varphi \mid \nu Z.\varphi \ .$$

Thus we assume formulas are in ***positive form***. The semantics of a formula φ are given with respect to a ***valuation*** of free variables $V : \mathcal{Z} \rightarrow \mathcal{P}(\mathcal{C})$ and atomic propositions $\rho : AP \rightarrow \mathcal{P}(\mathcal{C})$. The ***denotation*** $[\![\varphi]\!]^{\mathbb{P}}_{V,\rho}$ of a formula is the set of all satisfying configurations. A configuration c satisfies $\langle\Lambda\rangle\varphi$ iff $\exists x \in \Lambda.c \in \rho(x) \wedge \exists c'.c \rightarrow c' \wedge c' \in [\![\varphi]\!]^{\mathbb{P}}_{V,\rho}$ and c satisfies $[\Lambda]\varphi$ iff $(\exists x \in \Lambda.c \in \rho(x)) \Rightarrow (\forall c'.c \rightarrow c' \Rightarrow c' \in [\![\varphi]\!]^{\mathbb{P}}_{V,\rho})$. The operators $\overline{[\Lambda]}$ and $\overline{\langle\Lambda\rangle}$ are their backwards time counterparts. The μ and ν operators specify greatest and least fixed points (for details we refer the reader to Bradfield and Stirling [6]). We may also interpret propositions as actions: a configuration satisfies a proposition if leaving the configuration executes the action. Hence $[\Lambda]\varphi$ holds if φ holds after all Λ actions.

3 Algorithm and Implementation

Algorithm. We present the full algorithm separately [7] and provide a summary here. Sets of configurations are represented using a kind of automata over words [1]. Broadly speaking, when representing $[\![\varphi]\!]^{\mathbb{P}}_{V,\rho}$, we have $\langle p, w\rangle \in [\![\varphi]\!]^{\mathbb{P}}_{V,\rho}$ if the word w is accepted from the state (p, φ) of the automaton.

The algorithm recurses over subformulas. For propositions x or variables Z the automaton representing its valuation is either given or already computed. For $\varphi = \varphi_1 \wedge \varphi_2$, we introduce the state (p, φ) for each control state p and add transitions combining the transitions from (p, φ_1) and (p, φ_2). Similarly for $\vee$.

We use, for $[\Lambda]$ and $\langle\Lambda\rangle$, standard backwards reachability techniques [1]. E.g., for $\langle\Lambda\rangle\varphi$, we have all configurations a step in front of $[\![\varphi]\!]^{\mathbb{P}}_{V,\rho}$. The extension to backwards modalities is similar, but uses an adaptation of forwards reachability [10]. To restrict the analysis to the reachable configurations, we first use the efficient algorithm of Schwoon [10] to obtain the set of reachable configurations, then restrict our results by taking the conjunction with this set. The $\overline{[\Lambda]}$ modality is an exception: we compute $\overline{[\Lambda]}(\varphi \vee \neg \mathit{reachable})$. This is not needed for $[\Lambda]$ since any successor of a reachable state is itself reachable.

For fixed points we use a trick called ***projection***, introduced by Cachat [13]. This ingenious technique allows us to compute a fixed point of φ by repeatedly computing φ. We refer to our previous work for details [4].

The algorithm is exponential in the number of control states and the sizes of the formula and the (automaton) representations of V and ρ. With backwards modalities, it is also exponential in the size of the alphabet.

Implementation. We provide an explicit state implementation using OCaml and apply two main optimisations. The first is to identify subformulas whose denotation will not change when iterating the computation of a fixed point, and then store the computed value to speed up subsequent iterations. Secondly, there are cases where an automaton state should behave similarly for all characters except a few. We introduce ***default*** transitions that can be taken on reading a character a whenever there are no other a-transitions. This is important for backwards modalities as it greatly reduces the cost of an n^2 loop. These transitions need to be dealt with carefully by the other procedures.

4 Experimental Results[1]

Random Instances. We generated 395 model checking instances. Each PDS of size n, ranging from 5 to 450, has n states and n characters (giving between 25 and 250k pairs $\langle p, a \rangle$) and between n^2 and $2n^2$ transitions ((p, a, p', w) where $|w|$ is uniformly 0, 1 or 2). Each formula has a maximum connective depth of 5, a minimum fixed point depth of 2, lengths between 7 and 22 and up to 5 literals. Each proposition has a 10% probability of holding at a given pair of control state and top of stack character. Furthermore, each bound variable occurs within at least one $[\Lambda]$ or $\langle \Lambda \rangle$ operator. Note we only use forwards modalities and $\Lambda = AP$. The figure above shows the terminating results, plotted using the tool ***R***. In 120 instances the algorithm timed out after 30 minutes, with a failure rate of 23% at $0 \leq n \leq 50$ rising to 50% at $400 \leq n \leq 450$. Hence, difficult instances can occur even on small pushdown systems. Never-the-less, in the next section, we show that useful properties can be checked on large systems.

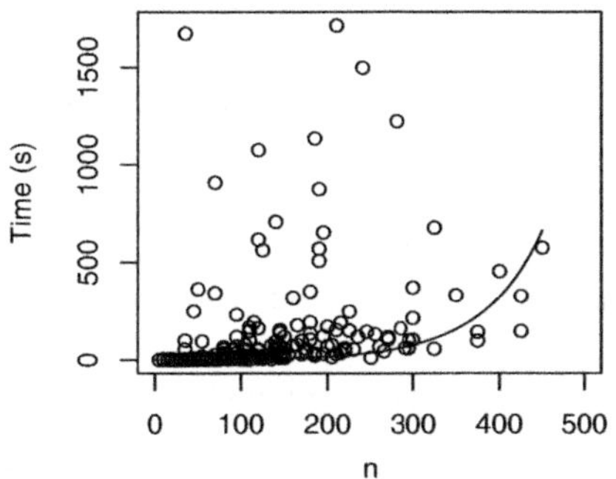

[1] All tests were run on a 2.4Ghz, quad core Intel Xeon with 12Gb of RAM.

Dataflow Analysis. Steffen advocates using modal μ-calculus model checkers for dataflow analysis [3]. This approach provides real-life test cases, taken from the DaCapo Benchmarks [9] (Version 9.12). We consider the ***optimal placement of computations*** problem. Intuitively, all modifications of a variable should happen as early as possible, provided they are necessary. For example, take the program

```
main () { i = [value]; a(); b(); }
a() { [computation not including i] }
b() { print(i); }
```

where `a()` may cause the program to fail. The only optimal placement of the computation of `i` is just before `b()`. An earlier computation is unnecessary if `a()` fails. We tested this example with our tool, obtaining the expected result.

Recalling Steffen, define the "always globally" operators $AG_{\Lambda}\varphi = \nu X.(\varphi \wedge [\Lambda]X)$ and $\overline{AG}_{\Lambda}\varphi = \nu X.(\varphi \wedge \overline{[\Lambda]}X)$. Fix a variable i and let M be the set of actions modifying i and U the set using i. For a set S, S^c denotes the complement. The proposition *end* marks the end of the computation. A necessary computation is one which will always be used and an optimal computation point is one at which earlier computations are unnecessary. This property is bi-directional. Let

$$\varphi_{nec} = AG_{U^c}(\neg end \wedge [M \cap U^c]false) \text{ and } \varphi_{ocp} = \varphi_{nec} \wedge \overline{[M^c]}(\overline{AG}_{M^c}\neg\varphi_{nec}) \ .$$

We chose parts of the Avrora (A) and the FOP (F) benchmarks and extracted pushdown control flow graphs with a supplementary tool based on Soot [8]. Polymorphic method calls may call any implementing procedure. We assume that all calls may result in an exception (e.g. RuntimeExceptions), hence each call is followed by an exception handling branch. Finally, data values are ignored.

For each benchmark, we chose a non-local variable with several use/define statements. Table 1 shows the results. The final columns give the size of the denotation representation. Each example had three control states. The number of control points is $|\Sigma|$. Since φ_{ocp} contains backwards modalities, the problem is exponential in $|\Sigma|$. Because $\overline{[\Lambda]}$ is computationally intensive, we evaluated $\neg\varphi_{ocp}$ rather than φ_{ocp}. In all tests, we only consider reachable configurations. Since we only consider one variable per test, program slicing could considerably increase performance. We do not perform this optimisation; instead we take the opportunity to test our tool on large systems, and obtain encouraging results.

Table 1. Optimal computation point analysis of several Java examples

Example	Control Points	Pushdown Rules	Time (s)	States	Transitions
RegisterTestAction (A)	3k	4k	14	509	19k
ELFDumpAction (A)	6k	7k	40	724	32k
ExampleFO2PDF (F)	17k	24k	95	1724	90k
ExampleDOM2PDF (F)	18k	25k	132	1753	95k
DisassembleAction (A)	54k	75k	1525	6215	296k
CFGAction (A)	90k	12k	3946	9429	500k

5 Conclusion and Future Work

We introduced the first tool for evaluating modal μ-calculus formulas over pushdown systems. We support forwards and backwards modalities and a restriction to reachable configurations. We tested random and real-life examples, demonstrating the tool's potential as a component of a pushdown analysis framework.

For forwards reachability, Schwoon's optimisations lead to significant performance gains. We may attempt to extend these techniques to operators like AG. Applying the optimisations to the full algorithm, however, may prove difficult. We may also use BDDs to represent the transition relation of the multi-automata.

Another avenue is to develop the dataflow analysis applications of our tool, by providing an improved translation from Java and exploiting optimisations such as program slicing or counter-example guided abstraction refinement.

Since ours is the first tool of its kind, we have no comparative data. For certain specific applications, we may perform a comparison with suitable tools; however, we are unaware of any such tools for the examples considered here.

Acknowledgments. We thank Vijay D'Silva for recommending Steffen [3], Oege De Moor for suggesting DaCapo, and Georg Weissenbacher for his comments.

References

1. Bouajjani, A., Esparza, J., Maler, O.: Reachability analysis of pushdown automata: Application to model-checking. In: Mazurkiewicz, A., Winkowski, J. (eds.) CONCUR 1997. LNCS, vol. 1243, pp. 135–150. Springer, Heidelberg (1997)
2. Lamprecht, A., Margaria, T., Steffen, B.: Data-flow analysis as model checking within the jabc. In: Mycroft, A., Zeller, A. (eds.) CC 2006. LNCS, vol. 3923, pp. 101–104. Springer, Heidelberg (2006)
3. Steffen, B.: Data flow analysis as model checking. In: Ito, T., Meyer, A.R. (eds.) TACS 1991. LNCS, vol. 526, pp. 346–365. Springer, Heidelberg (1991)
4. Hague, M., Ong, C.-H.L.: Winning regions of pushdown parity games: A saturation method. In: Bravetti, M., Zavattaro, G. (eds.) CONCUR 2009. LNCS, vol. 5710, pp. 384–398. Springer, Heidelberg (2009)
5. Walukiewicz, I.: Pushdown processes: Games and model checking. In: Alur, R., Henzinger, T.A. (eds.) CAV 1996. LNCS, vol. 1102, pp. 62–74. Springer, Heidelberg (1996)
6. Bradfield, J.C., Stirling, C.P.: Modal logics and mu-calculi: An introduction. In: Handbook of Process Algebra, pp. 293–330 (2001)
7. Hague, M., Ong, C.H.L.: A saturation method for the modal mu-calculus with backwards modalities over pushdown systems. arXiv:1006.5906v1 [cs.FL] (2010)
8. Vallée-Rai, R., Hendren, L., Sundaresan, V., Lam, P., Gagnon, E., Co, P.: Soot - a Java optimization framework. In: CASCON 1999, pp. 125–135 (1999)
9. Blackburn, S.M., et al.: The DaCapo benchmarks: Java benchmarking development and analysis. In: OOPSLA 2006, pp. 169–190 (2006)
10. Schwoon, S.: Model-checking Pushdown Systems. PhD thesis, Technical University of Munich (2002)

11. Ball, T., Rajamani, S.K.: Bebop: A symbolic model checker for boolean programs. In: Havelund, K., Penix, J., Visser, W. (eds.) SPIN 2000. LNCS, vol. 1885, pp. 113–130. Springer, Heidelberg (2000)
12. Ball, T., Rajamani, S.K.: The SLAM project: Debugging system software via static analysis. In: POPL 2002, pp. 1–3 (2002)
13. Cachat, T.: Higher order pushdown automata, the caucal hierarchy of graphs and parity games. In: Baeten, J.C.M., Lenstra, J.K., Parrow, J., Woeginger, G.J. (eds.) ICALP 2003. LNCS, vol. 2719, pp. 556–569. Springer, Heidelberg (2003)
14. Reps, T., Schwoon, S., Jha, S., Melski, D.: Weighted pushdown systems and their application to interprocedural dataflow analysis. Sci. Comput. Program. 58(1-2), 206–263 (2005)

Time-Bounded Reachability in Distributed Input/Output Interactive Probabilistic Chains

Georgel Calin[1], Pepijn Crouzen[1], Pedro R. D'Argenio[2], E. Moritz Hahn[1], and Lijun Zhang[3]

[1] Department of Computer Science, Saarland University, Saarbrücken, Germany
[2] FaMAF, Universidad Nacional de Córdoba, Córdoba, Argentina
[3] DTU Informatics, Technical University of Denmark, Denmark

Abstract. We develop an algorithm to compute timed reachability probabilities for distributed models which are both probabilistic and nondeterministic. To obtain realistic results we consider the recently introduced class of (strongly) distributed schedulers, for which no analysis techniques are known.

Our algorithm is based on reformulating the nondeterministic models as parametric ones, by interpreting scheduler decisions as parameters. We then apply the PARAM tool to extract the reachability probability as a polynomial function, which we optimize using nonlinear programming.

Keywords: Distributed Systems, Probabilistic Models, Nondeterminism, Time-Bounded Reachability.

1 Introduction

This paper considers the computation of reachability probabilities for compositional models with probabilistic and nondeterministic behavior. Such models arise, for instance, in the field of distributed algorithms, where probabilistic behavior is often used to break symmetries in the system. Nondeterminism may appear through the uncertain order of events occurring in different processes or to model freedom of design or unspecified behavior within a process.

Traditional analysis techniques for probabilistic models with nondeterminism compute the maximal and minimal probability to reach a set of configurations by considering all possible resolutions of the nondeterminism [2]. Recently it has been shown that this approach may lead to unrealistic results for models of distributed systems or algorithms [15]. The problem is that the traditional approach allows processes to use non-local information to influence their decisions.

As a running example we will use a simple coin-flip experiment. One player repeatedly flips a coin, while a second player (nondeterministically) guesses the outcome (See Fig. 1). We are interested in the probability that the second player manages to guess correctly at least once within t rounds. Intuitively this probability is $1 - \left(\frac{1}{2}\right)^t$, but it has been shown that standard analysis methods will produce a probability of 1 for any $t > 0$ [15]. The issue is that, from a ***global***

J. van de Pol and M. Weber (Eds.): SPIN 2010, LNCS 6349, pp. 193–211, 2010.

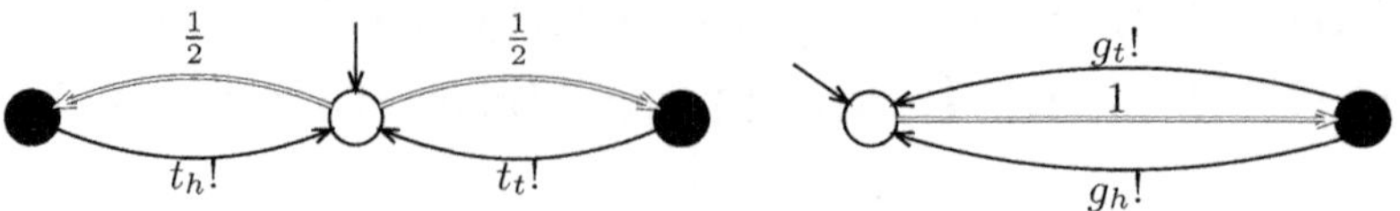

The coin-flip is depicted on the left-hand side and the coin-guess on the right-hand side. Initial states are indicated by incoming arrows; interactive transitions are labelled with their actions and probabilistic transitions $s \Rightarrow \mu$ are depicted by arrows from s to the support of μ, where each such arrow is labelled with the associated probability. Probabilistic transitions are required to synchronise in the composition.

Fig. 1. Basic I/O-IPC Models of the Repeated Coin-Flip Experiment

point of view, the optimal resolution of the nondeterministic guess simply uses the outcome of the coin-flip as a guide and this way always guesses correctly.

Distributed schedulers restrict the resolution of nondeterminism by enforcing that *local* decisions of the processes are based only on local knowledge [15]. For our example, this means that the guesser is not allowed to base the guess on the outcome of the coin-flip. We will see that this leads to realistic results for the probability of attaining a correct guess. Strongly distributed schedulers, in addition, ensure that the relative probability of choosing between two different components does not change with time, provided these components remain idle and uninformed of the progress of the rest of the system.

When considering distributed (or strongly distributed) schedulers, bounds for reachability probabilities are both undecidable and unapproximable in general [14]. However *time-bounded* reachability probabilities, i.e., the probability to reach a set of configurations within a specified time-period, can be computed. For distributed schedulers, this is due to the fact that optimal solutions in this setting can be computed by only taking into account the subset of deterministic distributed schedulers, which is finite if the system under consideration is finite and acyclic. Nonetheless, the theoretical complexity of this problem is exponential in the number of states. The case of strongly distributed schedulers turns out to be more difficult. In this setting, optimal solutions may lie on pure probabilistic schedulers [15]. Therefore, exploring all possible solutions is not an option, and hence its decidability was unknown until now.

In this paper, we propose to reduce the problem of computing time-bounded reachability probabilities for distributed, probabilistic, and nondeterministic models, under distributed (or strongly distributed) schedulers to a nonlinear optimization problem, more precisely, to a polynomial optimization problem. Since polynomial programming is decidable [5], it turns out that time-bounded reachability probabilities under strongly distributed schedulers is also decidable. We use as our modeling vehicle the formalism of ***input/output interactive probabilistic chains*** (see Section 2). The computation of time-bounded reachability probabilities is achieved by reformulating the models as parametric Markov chains (see Section 5), where the parameters are the decisions of the schedulers and the distributed model is ***unfolded*** up to the specified time-point (see Section 6). The time-bounded reachability probability can now be expressed as a polynomial function and we can compute bounds for it by optimizing the function under certain constraints.

While for distributed schedulers the only restriction on the variables of the polynomials is that appropriately grouped they form a distribution (i.e. all variables take values between 0 and 1 and each group of variables sum up to 1), the case of strongly distributed schedulers requires some additional and more complex restrictions, the optimal value of the property being calculated through more involved nonlinear programming techniques.

In Sections 2 to 5 we recall the necessary background, lifted to the newly introduced setting of input/output interactive probabilistic chains. From Section 6 onwards we present our novel algorithm to compute time-bounded reachability for input/output interactive probabilistic chains.

All proofs can be found in an extended version of this paper [4].

2 Input/Output Interactive Probabilistic Chains

Interactive probabilistic chains (IPCs) are state-based models that combine discrete-time Markov chains and labelled transition systems [9]. IPCs can be used to compositionally model probabilistic systems. An important feature of the IPC formalism is that probabilistic transitions and action-labelled transitions are handled orthogonally. As our modeling vehicle we use input/output interactive probabilistic chains (I/O-IPCs), a restricted variant of IPCs with a strict separation between local and non-local behavior. The restriction of IPCs to I/O-IPCs follows the one of interactive Markov chains to I/O-IMCs in the continuous-time setting [3]. The separation between local and non-local behavior is achieved by partitioning the I/O-IPC actions in *input*, *output*, and *internal* actions. In this section we briefly introduce the necessary I/O-IPC definitions.

Let *Dist*(X) be the set of all probability distributions over the finite set X.

Definition 1. *A basic I/O-IPC $\mathcal{P}$ is a quintuple $\langle S, A, \rightarrow_{\mathcal{P}}, \Rightarrow_{\mathcal{P}}, \hat{s}\rangle$, where:*
– S is a finite set of states with $\hat{s} \in S$ the initial state;
– $A = A^I \cup A^O \cup A^{int}$ is a finite set of actions, consisting of disjoint sets of input actions (A^I), output actions (A^O), and internal actions (A^{int});
– $\rightarrow_{\mathcal{P}} \subseteq S \times A \times S$ is the set of interactive transitions;
– $\Rightarrow_{\mathcal{P}} : S \rightharpoonup Dist(S)$ is a partial function representing the set of probabilistic transitions.
Input actions are suffixed by "?", output actions by "!" and we require that an I/O-IPC is input-enabled, i.e. for each state s and each input action a there is at least one state s' such that $(s, a, s') \in \rightarrow_{\mathcal{P}}$. We also require that the I/O-IPC is action-deterministic, *that is, for each state s and each action a there is at most one state s' such that $(s, a, s') \in \rightarrow_{\mathcal{P}}$. Finally we require that every state has at least one outgoing, internal, output, or probabilistic transition.*

We say that an I/O-IPC is *closed* if it has no input actions, i.e., $A^I = \emptyset$. Note that the requirement of action-determinism is introduced only to simplify the theoretical framework around schedulers. Nondeterministic choices between input transitions can be handled in a similar way as nondeterministic choices between output or internal transitions [15].

Given an action a, we use the shorthand notation $s \xrightarrow{a}_{\mathcal{P}} s'$ for an interactive transition $(s, a, s') \in \rightarrow_{\mathcal{P}}$ of any I/O-IPC $\mathcal{P}$. Given a distribution μ over the states of $\mathcal{P}$ we use the shorthand notation $s \Rightarrow_{\mathcal{P}} \mu$ for $(s, \mu) \in \Rightarrow_{\mathcal{P}}$. We often leave out the subscript when it is clear from the context.

2.1 Parallel Composition

Distributed I/O-IPCs are obtained through parallelizing ("||") simpler I/O-IPCs.

Definition 2. *Two I/O-IPCs $\mathcal{P}$ and $\mathcal{Q}$ are composable if $A^O_{\mathcal{P}} \cap A^O_{\mathcal{Q}} = A_{\mathcal{P}} \cap A^{int}_{\mathcal{Q}} = A^{int}_{\mathcal{P}} \cap A_{\mathcal{Q}} = \emptyset$. If $\mathcal{P}$ and $\mathcal{Q}$ are composable then $\mathcal{C} := \mathcal{P} \| \mathcal{Q}$ will be the I/O-IPC*

$$\langle S_{\mathcal{P}} \times S_{\mathcal{Q}}, A^I_{\mathcal{C}} \cup A^O_{\mathcal{C}} \cup A^{int}_{\mathcal{C}}, \rightarrow_{\mathcal{C}}, \Rightarrow_{\mathcal{C}}, (\hat{s}_{\mathcal{P}}, \hat{s}_{\mathcal{Q}}) \rangle,$$

where $A^O_{\mathcal{C}} := A^O_{\mathcal{P}} \cup A^O_{\mathcal{Q}}$, $A^I_{\mathcal{C}} := \left(A^I_{\mathcal{P}} \cup A^I_{\mathcal{Q}}\right) \setminus A^O_{\mathcal{C}}$, $A^{int}_{\mathcal{C}} = A^{int}_{\mathcal{P}} \cup A^{int}_{\mathcal{Q}}$ and the transition relations are

$$\begin{aligned}
\rightarrow_{\mathcal{C}} = \{(s,t) \xrightarrow{a}_{\mathcal{C}} (s',t) |\ s \xrightarrow{a}_{\mathcal{P}} s',\ a \in A_{\mathcal{P}} \setminus A_{\mathcal{Q}}\} \\
\cup \{(s,t) \xrightarrow{a}_{\mathcal{C}} (s,t') |\ t \xrightarrow{a}_{\mathcal{Q}} t',\ a \in A_{\mathcal{Q}} \setminus A_{\mathcal{P}}\} \\
\cup \{(s,t) \xrightarrow{a}_{\mathcal{C}} (s',t') |\ s \xrightarrow{a}_{\mathcal{P}} s',\ t \xrightarrow{a}_{\mathcal{Q}} t',\ a \in A_{\mathcal{P}} \cap A_{\mathcal{Q}}\} \\
\Rightarrow_{\mathcal{C}} = \{(s,t) \Rightarrow_{\mathcal{C}} (\mu_s \times \mu_t) |\ s \Rightarrow_{\mathcal{P}} \mu_s\ \wedge\ t \Rightarrow_{\mathcal{Q}} \mu_t\}
\end{aligned}$$

with $\mu_s \times \mu_t$ denoting the product distribution on $S_{\mathcal{P}} \times S_{\mathcal{Q}}$.

Parallel composition can be extended to any finite set $\mathcal{C}$ of I/O-IPCs in the usual way. Let $\#\mathcal{C}$ denote the number of basic *components of $\mathcal{C}$.*

The result of synchronizing an input action with an output action through I/O-IPC parallelization will be an output action in the resulting model.

2.2 Vanishing and Tangible States

The use of distinct probabilistic and instantaneous transitions separates the concerns of time and interaction. In essence, it allows us to specify interactions between components which are instantaneous and do not have to be modeled with explicit time steps. We say that internal and output transitions are *immediate* and that probabilistic transitions are *timed*. We now assume that immediate transitions always take precedence over timed transitions. This assumption is known as the *maximal progress* assumption [19]. This separation between immediate and timed transitions is also reflected in the system states.

Definition 3. *A state is called vanishing if at least one outgoing immediate transition is enabled in it. If only probabilistic actions are enabled in a state then it is called tangible.*

The black-colored nodes in Fig. 1 and 2 are vanishing states, while the rest are all tangible states. For simplicity, in our current study we consider only models that

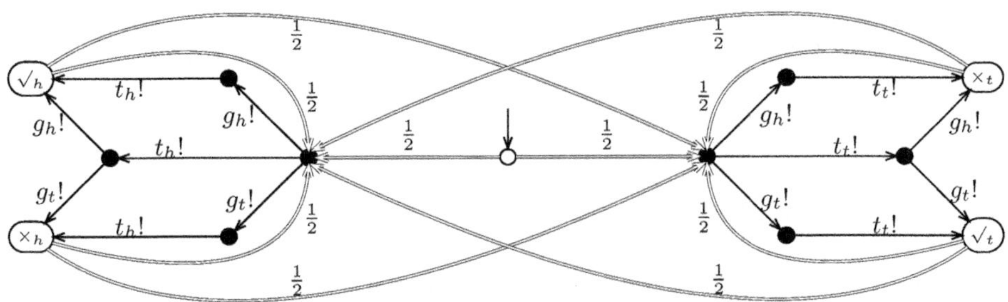

In the labelled states, the two I/O-IPCs in Fig. 1 distribute over the next states according to their possible combined choices. Otherwise, the output actions are interleaved. The flip matching the guess is represented by the $\surd$-labelled "goal" states.

Fig. 2. Distributed I/O-IPC Model of the Repeated Coin-Flip Experiment

do not exhibit Zeno behaviour (i.e. loops consisting of only immediate actions are not reachable/present in the distributed model).

2.3 Paths

An I/O-IPC *path* describes one possible *run* of the I/O-IPC. In such a run, we start in a particular state, follow a transition to another state, and so forth.

Definition 4. *Given an I/O-IPC* $\mathcal{P} = \langle S, A, \rightarrow, \Rightarrow, \hat{s}\rangle$, *a finite path of* $\mathcal{P}$ *of length* $n \in \mathbb{N}$ *is a sequence* $s_0 a_0 s_1 a_1 \ldots a_{n-1} s_n$ *where states* ($s_i \in S$ *for* $i \in [0, n]$) *and either actions or distributions* ($a_i \in A \cup Dist(S)$, *for* $i \in [0, n-1]$) *are interleaved. For consecutive states* s_i *and* s_{i+1} *we find that either* $a_i \in A$ *and* $(s_i, a_i, s_{i+1}) \in \rightarrow$ *or* $a_i \in Dist(S)$, s_i *is tangible,* $(s_i, a_i) \in \Rightarrow$, *and* $a_i(s_{i+1}) > 0$. *An infinite path of* $\mathcal{P}$ *is an infinite sequence* $s_0 a_0 s_1 a_1 \ldots$ *interleaving states and actions/distributions. We denote the last state of a finite path* σ *as* $last(\sigma)$.

For studying time-bounded reachability, we need a notion of *time*. We follow the definition of time in IPCs and say that only *probabilistic* transitions take time, while interactive transitions are considered to take place immediately [8].

Definition 5. *The* elapsed time *along a finite path* σ, *notation* $\mathsf{t}(\sigma)$, *is defined recursively, for states* s, *actions* a *and distributions* μ *over states:* $\mathsf{t}(s) = 0$, $\mathsf{t}(\sigma a s) = t(\sigma)$, *and* $\mathsf{t}(\sigma \mu s) = t(\sigma) + 1$.

2.4 Schedulers

We now wish to associate paths of an I/O-IPC with probabilities. The usual strategy is to define the probability of a path as the multiplication of the probabilities of its transitions. To define such a probability for paths in an I/O-IPC we need some way of resolving the nondeterministic choice between interactive transitions in vanishing states of an I/O-IPC. For all states $s \in S$, let $A^{en}_{s,\mathcal{P}} = \{a \in A^O \mid \exists s'.s \xrightarrow{a} s'\} \cup \{a \in A^{int} \mid \exists s'.s \xrightarrow{a} s'\}$ be the set of enabled immediate actions for s.

Definition 6. *A scheduler for an I/O-IPC* $\mathcal{P}$ *is a function* $\eta_{\mathcal{P}} : Paths(\mathcal{P}) \rightarrow Dist(A_{\mathcal{P}})$*, such that positive probabilities are assigned only to actions enabled in the last state of a path:* $\eta_{\mathcal{P}}(\sigma)(a) > 0$ *implies that* $a \in A^{en}_{last(\sigma),\mathcal{P}}$.

If $\mathcal{P}$ is closed, then a scheduler determines the probability to observe a certain path, which also allows us to define time-bounded reachability probabilities. We give the details, in the context of distributed schedulers, in Section 4.

3 I/O-IPC Nondeterminism Resolution

As we have seen, the probability of reaching a set of goal states in a distributed I/O-IPC depends on how the nondeterminism of chosing an action is handled. By assigning probabilities to the available actions, a scheduler can be seen as a refinement of the I/O-IPC such that the induced model becomes deterministic. It can thus be said that a scheduler enables us to determine reachability probabilities in a deterministic fashion.

However, the class of all schedulers for the model of a distributed system contains schedulers that are unrealistic in that they allow components of the system to use non-local information to guide their local decisions. To overcome this problem, ***distributed*** schedulers have been introduced, that restrict the possible choices of a scheduler to make them more realistic in a distributed setting [15]. Distributed schedulers have originally been introduced for (switched) probabilistic input/output automata [7] and we adapt them here for our input/output interactive probabilistic chains formalism.

To illustrate the necessity of distributed schedulers, consider the game described in Fig. 2 where an unbiased coin is repeatedly flipped and guessed by two independent entities at the same time. We are interested in the probability to reach the set of states labelled $\surd$ within a specified number t of timed (probabilistic) steps. This is exactly the probability that the guessing player guesses correctly within at most t tries. Intuitively, for each flip/guess turn, the guessing player should guess right with one half probability – the flip is probabilistic and its outcome should be hidden to the guesser.

However, it is clear that in the composed model there is a scheduler that arrives with probability one at a $\surd$ state within one timed step. This scheduler chooses the action g_h if the flip yields heads and g_t if the flip yields tails, thereby always winning. The purpose of distributed schedulers is to make sure that the decision between g_h and g_t is made only based on *local* information.

3.1 Distributed Schedulers

The main principle of distributed schedulers is to use a separate scheduler for each of the components of the system such that each has access only to their own scheduling history. To be able to reason about *local* information we first introduce path projections.

Given any distributed I/O-IPC $\mathcal{C} = \mathcal{P}_1 \| \ldots \| \mathcal{P}_n$ and a path $\sigma \in Paths(\mathcal{C})$, the projection $\sigma[\mathcal{P}_i]$ of σ on $\mathcal{C}$'s i-th basic component is given by:

- $(\hat{s}_\mathcal{C})[\mathcal{P}_i] = \pi_i(\hat{s}_\mathcal{C})$
- $(\sigma a s)[\mathcal{P}_i] = \begin{cases} \sigma[\mathcal{P}_i] & \text{if } a \notin A_{\mathcal{P}_i} \\ (\sigma[\mathcal{P}_i])a(\pi_i(s)) & \text{if } a \in A_{\mathcal{P}_i} \end{cases}$
- $(\sigma(\mu_1 \times \cdots \times \mu_n)s)[\mathcal{P}_i] = (\sigma[\mathcal{P}_i])\mu_i(\pi_i(s))$.

where $\pi_i((s_1, \ldots, s_n)) = s_i$ for all $(s_1, \ldots, s_n) \in S_\mathcal{C}$.

A *local* scheduler for $\mathcal{P}$ is simply any scheduler for $\mathcal{P}$ as given by Def. 6. A local scheduler resolves the nondeterminism arising from choices between enabled output and internal actions in one of the components. However, nondeterminism may also arise from the interleaving of the different components. In other words, if for some state in a distributed I/O-IPC, two or more components have enabled immediate actions, then it must be decided which component acts first. This decision is made by the *interleaving scheduler.*

Definition 7. *Given a distributed I/O-IPC* $C = \mathcal{P}_1 \| \ldots \| \mathcal{P}_n$*, an interleaving scheduler* $\mathcal{I} : Paths(\mathcal{C}) \to Dist(\{\mathcal{P}_1, \ldots, \mathcal{P}_n\})$ *is defined for paths* σ *such that* $last(\sigma)$ *is vanishing. The interleaving scheduler* $\mathcal{I}$ *chooses probabilistically an enabled component of the distributed system, i.e., we have that* $\mathcal{I}(\sigma)(\mathcal{P}_i) > 0$ *implies* $A^{en}_{last(\sigma[\mathcal{P}_i]),\mathcal{P}_i} \neq \emptyset$.

Local schedulers and an interleaving scheduler yield a *distributed scheduler.*

Definition 8. *Given a distributed I/O-IPC* $\mathcal{C} = \mathcal{P}_1 \| \ldots \| \mathcal{P}_n$*, local schedulers* $\eta_{\mathcal{P}_1}, \ldots, \eta_{\mathcal{P}_1}$*, and interleaving scheduler* $\mathcal{I}$*, the associated* distributed scheduler *is the function* $\eta_\mathcal{C} : Paths(\mathcal{C}) \to Dist(A_\mathcal{C})$ *such that, for all* $\sigma \in Paths(\mathcal{C})$ *with* $last(\sigma)$ *vanishing and for all* $a \in A_\mathcal{C}$*:*

$$\eta_\mathcal{C}(\sigma)(a) = \sum_{i=1}^{n} \mathcal{I}(\sigma)(\mathcal{P}_i) \cdot \eta_{\mathcal{P}_i}(\sigma[\mathcal{P}_i])(a)$$

We denote the set of all distributed schedulers as *DS*.

3.2 Strongly Distributed Schedulers

Although the class of distributed schedulers already realistically restricts the local decisions of processes in a distributed setting, in certain cases there exist distributed schedulers, where the interleaving schedulers are too powerful. In essence, the problem is that a distributed scheduler may use information from a component $\mathcal{P}_1$ to decide how to pick between components $\mathcal{P}_2$ and $\mathcal{P}_3$. In certain settings this is unrealistic. To counter this problem strongly distributed schedulers have been introduced [15].

Given any two components $\mathcal{P}_i$, $\mathcal{P}_j$ of a distributed I/O-IPC $\mathcal{C} = \mathcal{P}_1 \| \ldots \| \mathcal{P}_n$, consider the following property: for all σ, σ' such that $\sigma[\mathcal{P}_i] = \sigma'[\mathcal{P}_i]$ and $\sigma[\mathcal{P}_j] = \sigma'[\mathcal{P}_j]$, if $\mathcal{I}(\sigma)(\mathcal{P}_i) + \mathcal{I}(\sigma)(\mathcal{P}_j) \neq 0$ and $\mathcal{I}(\sigma')(\mathcal{P}_i) + \mathcal{I}(\sigma')(\mathcal{P}_j) \neq 0$ then

$$\frac{\mathcal{I}(\sigma)(\mathcal{P}_i)}{\mathcal{I}(\sigma)(\mathcal{P}_i) + \mathcal{I}(\sigma)(\mathcal{P}_j)} = \frac{\mathcal{I}(\sigma')(\mathcal{P}_i)}{\mathcal{I}(\sigma')(\mathcal{P}_i) + \mathcal{I}(\sigma')(\mathcal{P}_j)}. \tag{1}$$

Definition 9. *A scheduler η is strongly distributed if it is distributed and the restriction in Eq.* (1) *holds for the interleaving scheduler $\mathcal{I}$ of η.*

We denote the set of all strongly distributed schedulers as *SDS*. The intuition behind strongly distributed scheduler is that the choices the interleaving scheduler makes between two components $\mathcal{P}_i$, $\mathcal{P}_j$ should be consistent with respect to the local paths of $\mathcal{P}_i$, $\mathcal{P}_j$. If for two global paths, the local paths of $\mathcal{P}_i$, $\mathcal{P}_j$ are identical, then the probability of choosing $\mathcal{P}_i$ under the condition that we choose either $\mathcal{P}_i$ or $\mathcal{P}_j$ should be identical for both global paths.

Strongly distributed schedulers are useful depending on which system is considered for study [15]. When analyzing an auctioning protocol, for example, where each component models one of the bidders, then the order in which the bidders interact with the auctioneer should not leak information that can be used to the advantage of the other bidders. In such a situation, strongly distributed schedulers would provide more adequate worst-case/best-case probabilities.

However, if the interleaving scheduler should have access to the history of the components (as it might be the case for a kernel scheduler on a computer) then distributed schedulers should be considered, as the strongly distributed version might rule out valid possibilities.

4 Induced Probability Measure

When all the nondeterministic choices in a distributed I/O-IPC are scheduled, we end up with a probability measure on sets of paths of the I/O-IPC.

We define this probability measure in a similar way as is done for IPCs [23]. We fix a closed distributed I/O-IPC $\mathcal{C} = \mathcal{P}_1 \| \dots \| \mathcal{P}_n$ with state space $S_\mathcal{C}$, actions $A_\mathcal{C}$, and initial state $\hat{s}$. The *cylinder* induced by the finite path σ is the set of infinite paths $\sigma^\uparrow = \{\sigma' \mid \sigma' \text{ is infinite and } \sigma \text{ is a prefix of } \sigma'\}$. Let the set of cylinders generate the σ-algebra on infinite paths of $\mathcal{C}$.

Definition 10. *Let η be a scheduler for $\mathcal{C}$. The* probability measure induced by η *on the set of infinite paths is the unique probability measure P_η such that, for any state s in $S_\mathcal{C}$, any action a in $A_\mathcal{C}$ and any distribution $\mu \in Dist(S_\mathcal{C})$:*

$$P_\eta(s^\uparrow) = \begin{cases} 1 & \textit{if } s = \hat{s} \\ 0 & \textit{otherwise} \end{cases}$$

$$P_\eta(\sigma a s^\uparrow) = \begin{cases} P_\eta(\sigma^\uparrow) \cdot \eta(\sigma)(a) & \textit{if last}(\sigma) \textit{ is vanishing and last}(\sigma) \xrightarrow{a} s \\ 0 & \textit{otherwise} \end{cases}$$

$$P_\eta(\sigma \mu s^\uparrow) = \begin{cases} P_\eta(\sigma^\uparrow) \cdot \mu(s) & \textit{if last}(\sigma) \textit{ is tangible and last}(\sigma) \Rightarrow \mu \\ 0 & \textit{otherwise} \end{cases}$$

We are now ready to define time-bounded reachability for I/O-IPCs.

Definition 11. *Given an I/O-IPC $\mathcal{P}$ with an initial distribution, a set of goal states $\mathcal{G}$ and a time-bound $t \in \mathbb{N}$, we have that the probability to reach $\mathcal{G}$ within t time-steps, denoted $P_\eta(\Diamond^{\leq t}\mathcal{G})$, is:*

$$P_\eta(\Diamond^{\leq t}\mathcal{G}) = P_\eta(\bigcup\{\sigma^\uparrow \mid t(\sigma) \leq t \textit{ and last}(\sigma) \in \mathcal{G}\})$$

5 Parametric Markov Models

To compute probabilities for time-bounded reachability we will transform distributed I/O-IPCs into parametric Markov models (see Section 6). In this section we give a brief overview of parametric Markov chains [10,17,16].

Let S be a finite set of states. We let $V = \{x_1, \ldots, x_n\}$ denote a set of variables with domain $\mathbb{R}$. An ***assignment*** ζ is a function $\zeta : V \to \mathbb{R}$. A ***polynomial*** g over V is a sum of monomials $g(x_1, \ldots, x_n) = \sum_{i_1,\ldots,i_n} a_{i_1,\ldots,i_n} x_1^{i_1} \cdots x_n^{i_n}$ where each $i_j \in \mathbb{N}_0$ and each $a_{i_1,\ldots,i_n} \in \mathbb{R}$. A ***rational function*** f over V is a fraction $f(x_1, \ldots, x_n) = f_1(x_1, \ldots, x_n)/f_2(x_1, \ldots, x_n)$ of two polynomials f_1, f_2 over V.

Let $\mathcal{F}_V$ denote the set of rational functions from V to $\mathbb{R}$. Given $f \in \mathcal{F}_V$ and an assignment ζ, we let $\zeta(f)$ denote the rational function obtained by substituting each occurrence of $x \in V$ with $\zeta(x)$.

Definition 12. *A parametric Markov chain (PMC) is a tuple $\mathcal{D} = (S, \hat{s}, \mathbf{P}, V)$ where S is a finite set of states, $\hat{s}$ is the initial state, $V = \{v_1, \ldots, v_n\}$ is a finite set of parameters and $\mathbf{P}$ is the probability matrix $\mathbf{P} : S \times S \to \mathcal{F}_V$.*

The generalization of the probability matrix $\mathbf{P}$ to k steps is given below.

Definition 13. *Given a PMC $\mathcal{D} = (S, \hat{s}, \mathbf{P}, V)$, the k-step probability matrix $\mathbf{P}_k$, $k \in \mathbb{N}$, is defined recursively for any $k' > 1$ and states $s, s' \in S$:*

$$\mathbf{P}_0(s, s') = \begin{cases} 1 \text{ if } s = s' \\ 0 \text{ if } s \neq s' \end{cases}$$

$$\mathbf{P}_{k'}(s, s') = \sum_{s'' \in S} \mathbf{P}_{k'-1}(s, s'') \cdot \mathbf{P}(s'', s')$$

6 Parametric Interpretation

By having the scheduler η fixed, P_η together with the scheduled I/O-IPC $\mathcal{C}$ would become deterministic. To be more specific, by treating the interleaving and local scheduler decisions as unknowns we arrive at analyzing parametric Markov chains, the parameters being precisely the decisions that the interleaving and local schedulers perform.

We have seen in Section 4 that fixing the scheduler of a distributed I/O-IPC induces a probability measure on paths. Our approach is now to fix the scheduler ***parametrically***, i.e., by treating the probabilities chosen by the interleaving and local schedulers as parameters. We will show that this ***unfolding*** of the I/O-IPC induces a PMC (see Section 5) whose states are paths of the distributed I/O-IPC. To make sure the induced PMC is finite we generate it only for paths up to a specific time-bound t. We then prove that computing the probability to reach a set of states within t time-units for the I/O-IPC is equivalent to computing time-unbounded reachability for the induced PMC.

To give an idea of how this unfolding works, consider again the repeated coin-flip experiment, depicted in Fig. 1 and 2. Intuitively it should hold that

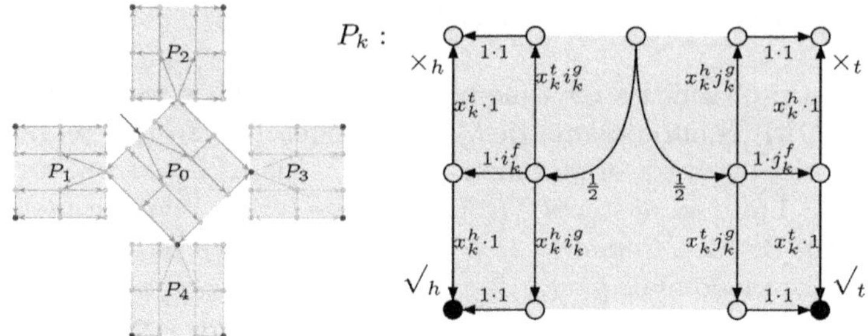

Fig. 3. Repeated Coin-Flip Experiment (PMC scheme up to time 2: all transitions are parametric. Interleaving is used for making the model more compact.)

$Pr(\Diamond^{\leq 2}\{\surd_h, \surd_t\}) = 3/4$ if we assume the guessing player has no information about the outcome of each coin-flip. Since the guessing player must win within two steps he has two chances to guess correctly. The first guess yields a probability of $\frac{1}{2}$ to win, while for the case that the first guess is incorrect (probability $\frac{1}{2}$) there is another opportunity to guess correctly with probability $\frac{1}{2}$. This brings the overall probability to win within two steps to $\frac{1}{2} + \frac{1}{2} \cdot \frac{1}{2} = \frac{3}{4}$.Fig. 3 describes the unfolding of the distributed I/O-IPC from Fig. 2 up to time-point 2. On the right-hand side we see the structure of the PMC for one time-step. The unfolding up to 2 time steps is shown schematically on the left-hand side, where each square represents a copy of the structure on the right-hand side.

The local scheduler decisions in this case for each repeating structure P_k are x_k^h, x_k^t s.t. $x_k^h + x_k^t = 1$ and the interleaving scheduler decisions are $i_k^g, i_k^f, j_k^g, j_k^f$ s.t. $i_k^g + i_k^f = j_k^g + j_k^f = 1$. Here x_k^h, for example, denotes the probability assigned by the local scheduler for the guesser to pick "heads" for a local path ending in a "heads" vs. "tail" choice. The parameters i_k^g, i_k^f (as well as j_k^g, j_k^f) denote the probabilities the interleaving scheduler assigns to the "guessing" model and the "flipping" model respectively, for a given global path which enables them both.

Now, $Pr(\Diamond^{\leq 2}\{\surd_h, \surd_t\})$ can be computed as the sum of the cumulated probabilities on the paths leading to $\{\surd_h, \surd_t\}$ states by using the given unfolding in Fig. 3 and the above parameter restrictions:

$$\tfrac{1}{2}\Big(x_0^h \cdot i_0^g + i_0^f \cdot x_0^h + (x_0^t \cdot i_0^g + i_0^f \cdot x_0^t) \cdot \big[\tfrac{1}{2}(x_1^h \cdot i_1^g + i_1^f \cdot x_1^h) + \tfrac{1}{2}(x_1^t \cdot j_1^g + j_1^f \cdot x_1^t)\big]\Big) +$$
$$\tfrac{1}{2}\Big(x_0^t \cdot j_0^g + j_0^f \cdot x_0^t + (x_0^h \cdot j_0^g + j_0^f \cdot x_0^h) \cdot \big[\tfrac{1}{2}(x_2^h \cdot i_2^g + i_2^f \cdot x_2^h) + \tfrac{1}{2}(x_2^t \cdot j_2^g + j_2^f \cdot x_2^t)\big]\Big) =$$
$$\tfrac{1}{2}(x_0^h + x_0^t \cdot (\tfrac{1}{2}x_1^h + \tfrac{1}{2}x_1^t)) + \tfrac{1}{2}(x_0^t + x_0^h \cdot (\tfrac{1}{2}x_2^h + \tfrac{1}{2}x_2^t)) = \tfrac{3}{4}$$

We now define the above interpretation of choices via parameters formally.

Definition 14. *Let $S_{\mathcal{C}}^t \subseteq Paths(\mathcal{C})$ be the set of all paths with time-length $\leq t$ in a closed, distributed I/O-IPC $\mathcal{C} = \mathcal{P}_1 \| \ldots \| \mathcal{P}_n$ which does not exhibit Zeno-behaviour. Define the parameters set V by*

$$V = \{\ y_\sigma^i \mid \sigma \in S_{\mathcal{C}}^t, 1 \leq i \leq \#\mathcal{C}, A_{last(\sigma[\mathcal{P}_i]),\mathcal{P}_i}^{en} \neq \varnothing\} \cup$$
$$\{\ x_{\sigma[\mathcal{P}_i]}^a \mid \sigma \in S_{\mathcal{C}}^t, 1 \leq i \leq \#\mathcal{C}, a \in A_{last(\sigma[\mathcal{P}_i]),\mathcal{P}_i}^{en}\}$$

and let $\mathbf{P}$ *match the induced probability measure, namely for any path* $\sigma \in S^t_{\mathcal{C}}$*, any state* s *of* $\mathcal{C}$*, any action* a *of* $\mathcal{C}$ *and any distribution* μ *over the states of* $\mathcal{C}$*:*

$$\begin{array}{ll} \mathbf{P}(\sigma, \sigma a s) = y^i_\sigma \cdot x^a_{\sigma[\mathcal{P}_i]} & \text{if } \mathit{last}(\sigma) \text{ is vanishing, } \mathit{last}(\sigma) \xrightarrow{a} s,\ a \in A^{en}_{\mathit{last}(\sigma[\mathcal{P}_i]),\mathcal{P}_i} \\ \mathbf{P}(\sigma, \sigma \mu s) = \mu(s) & \text{if } \mathit{last}(\sigma) \text{ is tangible, } \mathrm{t}(\sigma) < t,\ \mathit{last}(\sigma) \Rightarrow \mu \\ \mathbf{P}(\sigma, \sigma) = 1 & \text{if } \mathit{last}(\sigma) \text{ is tangible, } \mathrm{t}(\sigma) = t. \end{array}$$

All other transition probabilities are zero. The unfolding of the I/O-IPC $\mathcal{C}$ *up to time bound* t *is then the PMC* $\mathcal{D} = (S^t_{\mathcal{C}}, \hat{s}_{\mathcal{C}}, \mathbf{P}, V)$*. Given a set of states* $\mathcal{G}$ *of* $\mathcal{C}$*, we write* $\overline{\mathcal{G}}$ *for the paths in* $S^t_{\mathcal{C}}$ *that end in a state in* $\mathcal{G}$*, but never visit a state in* $\mathcal{G}$ *on the way.*

The finiteness of $S^t_{\mathcal{C}}$ and V is guaranteed by the exclusion of infinite chains consisting of only immediate actions, as it implies that for each state in $\mathcal{C}$ a tangible state is reachable within a finite number of non-probabilistic steps.

The variables in Def. 14 can be restricted to ensure that they represent valid scheduler decisions in the following way:

$$\begin{cases} 0 \le v \le 1 & \text{if } v \in V \\ \sum_{a \in A} x^a_{\sigma[\mathcal{P}_i]} = 1 & \text{if } \sigma \in S^t_{\mathcal{C}};\ 1 \le i \le \#\mathcal{C} \text{ with } A = A^{en}_{\mathit{last}(\sigma[\mathcal{P}_i]),\mathcal{P}_i} \\ \sum_{i \in I} y^i_\sigma = 1 & \text{if } \sigma \in S^t_{\mathcal{C}};\ I = \{i \mid 1 \le i \le \#\mathcal{C}, \mathit{last}(\sigma[P_i]) \text{ vanishing}\} \end{cases} \tag{2}$$

We write $\zeta \vdash (2)$ if the assignment $\zeta : V \to [0,1]$ satisfies (2) and by $\zeta(\mathbf{P}_k(\hat{s}, \sigma))$ we denote $\mathbf{P}_k(\hat{s}, \sigma)$ with all variables substituted according to the assignment ζ. I/O-IPC path probabilities are related to k-step transition probabilities of the induced PMC by the following.

Lemma 1. *For a closed, distributed I/O-IPC* $\mathcal{C}$*, let* $\mathcal{D}$ *be as in Def. 14. Then*
(i) For every distributed scheduler η *there is an assignment* $\zeta \vdash (2)$ *such that for all* $\sigma \in S^t_{\mathcal{C}}:\ P_\eta(\sigma^\uparrow) = \zeta(\mathbf{P}_k(\hat{s}, \sigma))$ *where* k *is the length of* σ*.*
(ii) Reciprocally, for every assignment $\zeta : V \to [0,1]$ *with* $\zeta \vdash (2)$ *there is a distributed scheduler* η *such that for all* $\sigma \in S^t_{\mathcal{C}}:\ P_\eta(\sigma^\uparrow) = \zeta(\mathbf{P}_k(\hat{s}, \sigma))$*.*

We can now reformulate the bounded reachability problem for I/O-IPCs under distributed schedulers as an unbounded reachability problem for the associated induced PMC – which is also bounded in a sense as it is acyclic and has precisely the same depth as the given time-bound.

Theorem 1. *Time-bounded reachability for an I/O-IPC* $\mathcal{C}$ *under distributed schedulers is equivalent to checking time-unbounded reachability on the PMC* $\mathcal{D} = (S^t_{\mathcal{C}}, \hat{s}_{\mathcal{C}}, \mathbf{P}, V)$ *as in Def. 14 for assignments that satisfy* (2)*:*

$$\sup_{\eta \in DS} P_\eta(\Diamond^{\le t} \mathcal{G}) = \sup_{\zeta \vdash (2)} \zeta(P_{\mathcal{D}}(\Diamond \overline{\mathcal{G}})) \text{ and } \inf_{\eta \in DS} P_\eta(\Diamond^{\le t} \mathcal{G}) = \inf_{\zeta \vdash (2)} \zeta(P_{\mathcal{D}}(\Diamond \overline{\mathcal{G}})).$$

To extend this result to strongly distributed schedulers we must further restrict the variables of the induced PMC such that the allowed assignments match the strongly distributed schedulers. First we introduce new variables which represent the conditional probabilities in (1). For every i, j, $1 \le i, j \le \#\mathcal{C}$, $i \ne j$, and $\sigma \in S^t_{\mathcal{C}}$, define a new variable $z^{i,j}_{\sigma[\mathcal{P}_i],\sigma[\mathcal{P}_j]} \notin V$. Notice that two different $\sigma, \sigma' \in S^t_{\mathcal{C}}$ may induce the same variable if $\sigma[\mathcal{P}_i] = \sigma'[\mathcal{P}_i]$ and $\sigma[\mathcal{P}_j] = \sigma'[\mathcal{P}_j]$. We write V_z for the set of all such variables $z^{i,j}_{\sigma[\mathcal{P}_i],\sigma[\mathcal{P}_j]}$.

Using these new variables we impose new restrictions on the variables in the induced PMC of a distributed I/O-IPC.

$$z^{i,j}_{\sigma[\mathcal{P}_i],\sigma[\mathcal{P}_j]}(y^i_\sigma + y^j_\sigma) = y^i_\sigma \quad \text{if } 1 \leq i,j \leq \#\mathcal{C},\ i \neq j, \text{ and } \sigma \in S^t_{\mathcal{C}} \tag{3}$$

Theorem 2. *Time-bounded reachability for an I/O-IPC $\mathcal{C}$ under strongly distributed schedulers is equivalent to time-unbounded reachability of the parametric Markov chain $\mathcal{D} = (S^t_{\mathcal{C}}, \hat{s}_{\mathcal{C}}, \mathbf{P}, V \cup V_z)$ resulted through unfolding as in Def. 14 under the assumptions* (2) *and* (3)*:*

$$\sup_{\eta \in SDS} P_\eta(\Diamond^{\leq t}\mathcal{G}) = \sup_{\zeta \vdash (2),(3)} \zeta(P_{\mathcal{D}}(\Diamond \overline{\mathcal{G}})) \text{ and } \inf_{\eta \in SDS} P_\eta(\Diamond^{\leq t}\mathcal{G}) = \inf_{\zeta \vdash (2),(3)} \zeta(P_{\mathcal{D}}(\Diamond \overline{\mathcal{G}})).$$

7 Algorithm

Time-unbounded reachability probabilities for PMCs can be computed using the tool PARAM, which, since our PMC models are acyclic, results in analyzing a set of polynomial functions over the given variables. These polynomial functions can then be optimized under the constraints given by (2) and – for strongly distributed schedulers – (3) using standard numerical solvers.

We now present our algorithm to compute extremal time-bounded reachability probabilities for distributed I/O-IPCs. The following inputs are required: a closed, distributed I/O-IPC $\mathcal{C}$ which exhibits no Zeno-behavior, a time-bound t, and a set of goal states $\mathcal{G}$. The following steps are sequentially executed:

1. The I/O-IPC is unfolded up to time-bound t, yielding a PMC (see Def. 14). Additional linear constraints on the parameters are provided to ensure that all scheduler decisions lie in the interval $[0, 1]$ and that specific sets of parameters sum up to 1. In the case of strongly distributed schedulers, non-linear constraints are also generated as described in Thm. 2.
2. The time-unbounded reachability probability for the set of goal states $\mathcal{G}$ is calculated parametrically for the PMC generated in step 1 using the PARAM tool [16]. The result is a polynomial function.
3. The polynomial function generated in step 2 is optimized under the constraints generated in step 1 using non-linear programming. We have used the *active-set* algorithm [13,18] provided by the *fmincon* function of Matlab[1], but any non-linear programming tool can in principle be used.

An overview of this tool-chain is presented in Fig. 4. The tool which unfolds the I/O-IPC and generates a PMC together with linear and non-linear constraints is still under development. We have, however generated PMC models and constraints semi-automatically for several case studies which we present next.

[1] See http://www.mathworks.com

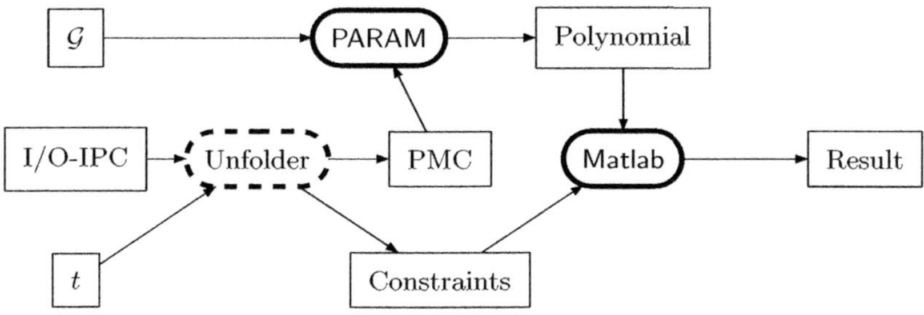

Fig. 4. The Envisioned Tool-Chain: ellipses represent tools, boxes represent data, where dashed ellipses represent tools that are currently in development

8 Case Studies

In this section we apply our algorithm to three case studies. Since the unfolder tool, which translates distributed I/O-IPCs into PMCs and constraints, is still under development we have generated PMCs and constraints for these cases in a semi-automatic way. The PARAM tool has been run on a computer with a 3 Ghz processor and 1 GB of memory, while Matlab was run on a computer with two 1.2 Ghz processors and 2 GB of memory. All I/O-IPC and PMC models are available from the authors.

8.1 Mastermind

In the game of Mastermind [1] one player, the *guesser*, tries to find out a *code*, generated by the other player, the *encoder*. The code consists of a number of tokens of fixed positions, where for each token one color (or other labelling) out of a prespecified set is chosen. Colors can appear multiple times.

Each round, the guesser guesses a code. This code is compared to the correct one by the encoder who informs the guesser on a) how many tokens were of the correct color *and* at the correct place and b) how many tokens were *not* at the correct place, *but* have a corresponding token of the same color in the code.

Notice that the decisions of the encoder during the game are deterministic, while the guesser has the choice between all valid codes. We assume that the encoder chooses the code probabilistically with a uniform distribution over all options. The guesser's goal is to find the code as fast as possible and ours to compute the maximal probability for this to happen within t rounds.

We formalize the game as follows: we let n be the number of tokens of the code and m the number of colors. This means there are m^n possible codes. Let $\mathcal{O}$ denote the set of all possible codes. We now informally describe the I/O-IPCs which represent the game. The guesses are described by actions $\{g_o \mid o \in \mathcal{O}\}$, whereas the answers are described by actions $\{a_{(x,y)} \mid x, y \in [0, n]\}$.

Table 1. Results of Mastermind Case Study

Settings			PMC			PARAM			NLP	
n	m	t	$\#S$	$\#T$	$\#V$	Time(s)	Mem(MB)	$\#V$	Time(s)	Pr
2	2	2	197	248	36	0.0492	1.43	17	0.0973	0.750
2	2	3	629	788	148	0.130	2.68	73	0.653	1.00
3	2	2	1545	2000	248	0.276	5.29	93	1.51	0.625
3	2	3	10953	14152	2536	39.8	235	879	1433	1.00
2	3	2	2197	2853	279	0.509	6.14	100	2.15	0.556

The guesser $\mathcal{G}$ repeats the following steps: From the initial state, $s_\mathcal{G}$ it first takes a probabilistic step to state $s'_\mathcal{G}$ and afterwards the guesser returns to the initial state via one of m^n transitions, each labelled with an output action $g_o!$. In both states the guesser receives answers $a_{(x,y)}?$ from the encoder and for all answers the guesser simply remains in the same state, except for the answer $a_{(n,n)}$ which signals that the guesser has guessed correctly. When the guesser receives this action it moves to the absorbing state $s''_\mathcal{G}$.

The encoder $\mathcal{E}$ is somewhat more complex. It starts by picking a code probabilistically, where each code has the same probability $\frac{1}{m^n}$. Afterwards the encoder repeats the following steps indefinitely. First it receives a guess from the guesser, then it replies with the appropriate answer and then it takes a probabilistic transition. This probabilistic step synchronizes with the probabilistic step of the guesser, which allows us to record the number of rounds the guesser needs to find the code.

The Mastermind game is the composition $\mathcal{C} := \mathcal{G}||\mathcal{E}$ of the two basic I/O IPCs. Using the tool described in Section 7 we can now reason about the maximal probability $Pr(\Diamond^{\leq t} s''_\mathcal{G})$ to break the code within a prespecified number t of guesses. We consider here the set of all distributed schedulers as we obviously want that the guesser uses only local information to make its guesses. If we were to consider the set of all schedulers the maximum probability would be 1 for any time-bound as the guesser would immediately choose the correct code with probability 1. If only two components are considered, condition (1) has no effect and every distributed scheduler is also strongly distributed. Therefore we omit the analysis under strongly distributed schedulers for this case study.

Results are given in Table 1. In addition to the model parameters (n, m), the time bound (t) and the result (Pr) we provide statistics for the various phases of the algorithm. For the unfolded PMC we give the number of states ($\#S$), transitions ($\#T$), and variables ($\#V$). For the PARAM tool we give the time needed to compute the polynomial, the memory required, and the number of variables that remain in the resulting polynomial. Finally we give the time needed for Matlab to optimize the polynomial provided by PARAM under the linear constraints that all scheduler decisions lie between 0 and 1. For this case study we generated PMC models and linear constraints semi-automically given the parameters n, m, and t.

8.2 Dining Cryptographers

The dining cryptographers problem is a classical anonymity problem [6]. The cryptographers must work together to deduce a particular piece of information using their local knowledge, but at the same time each cryptographers' local knowledge may not be discovered by the others. The problem is as follows: three cryptograpers have just finished dining in a restaurant when their waiter arrives to tell them their bill has been paid anonymously. The cryptographers now decide they wish to respect the anonimity of the payer, but they wonder if one of the cryptographers has paid or someone else. They resolve to use the following protocol to discover whether one of the cryptographers paid, without revealing which one.

We depict part of the I/O-IPC models in Fig. 5. On the right-hand side we have the I/O-IPC $\mathcal{F}$ that simply decides who paid (actions p_i) and then starts the protocol. Each cryptographer has a probability of $\frac{1}{6}$ to have paid and there is a probability of $\frac{1}{2}$ that none of them has paid. On the left-hand side of Fig. 5 we see part of the I/O-IPC $\mathcal{G}_1$ for the first cryptographer. Each cryptographer flips a fair coin such that the others cannot see the outcome. In Fig. 5 we only show the case where cryptographer one flips heads. Each cryptographer now shows his coin to himself and his right-hand neighbour (actions h_i for heads and t_i for tails). This happens in a fixed order. Now, again in a fixed order, they proclaim whether or not the two coins they have seen were the same or different (actions s_i for same and d_i for different). However, if a cryptographer has paid he or she will *lie* when proclaiming whether the two coins were identical or not. In Fig. 5 we show the case where cryptographer one has not paid, so he proclaims the truth. Now we have that if there is an even number of "different" proclamations, then all of the cryptographers told the truth and it is revealed that someone else paid. If, on the other hand, there is an odd number of "different" proclamations, one of the cryptographers must have paid the bill, but it has been shown that there

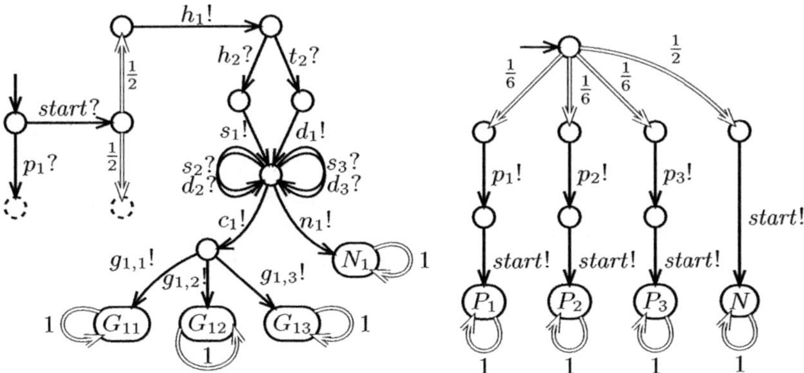

Fig. 5. Part of the I/O-IPC model $\mathcal{G}_1$ (left) of the first dining cryptographer and the I/O-IPC $\mathcal{F}$ (right) that probabilistically decides who has actually paid

Table 2. Results of Dining Cryptographers Case Study

	PMC			PARAM			NLP	
Property	$\#S$	$\#T$	$\#V$	Time(s)	Mem(MB)	$\#V$	Time(s)	Pr
(4)	294	411	97	9.05	4.11	24	0.269	1.00
(5), top	382	571	97	9.03	4.73	16	0.171	0.167
(5), bottom	200	294	97	8.98	4.14	0	N/A	1/3

is no way for the other two cryptographers to know which one has paid. In our model the cryptographer first attempts to guess whether or not a cryptographer has paid (actions c_i to guess that a cryptographer has paid, action n_i if not). In case the cryptographer decides a cryptographer has paid, he guesses which one (action $g_{i,j}$ denotes that cryptographer i guesses cryptographer j has paid.

We can see that a "run" of the distributed I/O-IPC $\mathcal{C} = \mathcal{F} \| \mathcal{G}_1 \| \mathcal{G}_2 \| \mathcal{G}_3$ takes two time-units, since there is one probabilistic step to determine who paid and one probabilistic step where all coins are flipped simultaneously. We are interested in two properties of this algorithm: first, all cryptographers should be able to determine whether someone else has paid or not. We can express this property, for example for the first cryptographer, as a reachability probability property:

$$P(\Diamond^{\leq 2}\{P_1, P_2, P_3\} \times \{G_{11}, G_{12}, G_{13}\} \times S_2 \times S_3 \cup \{N\} \times \{N_1\} \times S_2 \times S_3) = 1. \quad (4)$$

S_2 and S_3 denote the complete I/O-IPC state spaces of the second and third cryptographer. For the other cryptographers we find similar properties. Secondly, we must check that the payer remains anonymous. This means that, in the case that a cryptographer pays, the other two cryptographers cannot guess this fact. We can formulate this as a conditional reachability probability:

$$\frac{P(\Diamond^{\leq 2}\{P_2\} \times \{G_{12}\} \times S_2 \times S_3 \cup \{P_3\} \times \{G_{13}\} \times S_2 \times S_3)}{P(\Diamond^{\leq 2}\{P_2, P_3\} \times S_1 \times S_2 \times S_3)} = \frac{1}{2}. \quad (5)$$

I.e., the probability for the first cryptographer to guess correctly who paid – under the condition that one of the other cryptographers paid – is one half.

Table 2 shows the results for the dining cryptographers case study. We compute the conditional probability in (5) by computing the top and bottom of the fraction separately. We can see that both properties (4) and (5) are fulfilled. Table 2 also lists statistics on the tool performances and model sizes as described for Table 1. Note especially that the third reachability probability was computed directly by PARAM. I.e., this probability is independent of the scheduler decisions and PARAM was able to eliminate all variables.

8.3 Randomized Scheduler Example

For the class of strongly distributed schedulers it may be the case that the maximal or minimal reachability probability can not be attained by a deterministic scheduler, i.e., a scheduler that always chooses one action/component with probability one. As our final case study we use a small example of such an I/O-IPC

Table 3. Results of Randomized Scheduler Case Study
([‡] For certain settings, Matlab reports a maximal probability of 0.500)

PMC			PARAM		NLP		
$\#S$	$\#T$	$\#V$	Time(s)	Mem(MB)	$\#V$	Time(s)	Pr
13	23	12	0.00396	1.39	11	0.241	0.545[†]

as depicted by Fig. 4 in [15]. In this example the maximal reachability probability for deterministic strongly distributed schedulers is $\frac{1}{2}$, while there exists a randomized strongly distributed scheduler with reachability probability $\frac{13}{24}$.

Table 3 shows the result of applying our tool chain to this example. We see that we can find a scheduler with maximal reachability probability 0.545, which is even greater than $\frac{13}{24}$. Note that we can express the maximal reachability probability as a time-bounded property because the example is acyclic. However, for this case, the result from Matlab depends on the initial assignment given to the solver. For certain initial assignments the solver returns a maximal probability of only 0.500. This indicates that further investigation is required in the appropriate nonlinear programming tool for our algorithm.

9 Related Work

The problem that global schedulers may be too optimistic or pessimistic in the verification of distributed, probablistic, and nondeterministic systems has been noted in several different settings [20,21,22,15]. One approach to resolve this issue is to use *partial-information* schedulers [11]. Using partial-information schedulers allows the hiding of information that a global scheduler should not realistically use. However, this approach still assumes there is only one global scheduler, instead of several local schedulers as presented in this paper. For the class of memoryless partial-information schedulers, the extremal long-run average outcomes of tasks can be calculated by reformulating the problem as a non-linear programming problem [11]. A testing pre-order for distributed models with probabilistic and nondeterministic choices has been suggested which is aimed at realistically representing the power of schedulers in a distributed setting [12]. In this context, reachability probabilities (under a particular scheduler) are defined in a similar way as in our paper, but no algorithm to compute extremal probabilities or to compute the pre-order is given. It would be very interesting to study whether this pre-order [12] indeed preserves extremal time-bounded reachability probabilities when lifted to the setting of I/O-IPCs.

10 Conclusion

In this paper we have presented an algorithm to compute maximal and minimal time-bounded reachability probabilities for I/O-IPCs under distributed schedulers or strongly distributed schedulers. The core principle of our algorithm is to reformulate the problem as a polynomial optimization problem under linear and, in the case of strongly distributed schedulers, polynomial constraints.

The main drawback of our approach is that the PMC induced in our algorithm grows exponentially with the size of the original model and the specified time-bound, as the state space of the PMC consists of all paths of the original model, up to a time-bound. However, no other algorithm exists that can compute properties of distributed models under (strongly) distributed schedulers.

In several areas improvements can be made. First, it can be investigated if special purpose algorithms can be used for the specific type of non-linear programming problems we encounter in our context. Secondly, the memory-usage may be optimized by using the fact that in our setting we see only polynomial functions and do not make use of rational polynomial functions.

Acknowledgments. This work was partly supported by the German Research Council (DFG) as part of the Transregional Collaborative Research Center "Automatic Verification and Analysis of Complex Systems" (SFB/TR 14 AVACS) (see `www.avacs.org` for more information), the DAAD-MinCyT project "Quantitative Techniques for Dependable Distributed Systems (QTDDS)", and the ANPCyT-PICT 26135 "Verification of Probabilistic Distributed Systems". Lijun Zhang received partial support from *MT-LAB*, a VKR Centre of Excellence.

References

1. Ault, L.H.: Das Mastermind-handbuch. Ravensburger Buchverlag (1982)
2. Bianco, A., de Alfaro, L.: Model checking of probabilistic and nondeterministic systems. In: FOSSACS 1995, pp. 499–513 (1995)
3. Boudali, H., Crouzen, P., Stoelinga, M.: A compositional semantics for dynamic fault trees in terms of interactive Markov chains. In: Namjoshi, K.S., Yoneda, T., Higashino, T., Okamura, Y. (eds.) ATVA 2007. LNCS, vol. 4762, pp. 441–456. Springer, Heidelberg (2007)
4. Calin, G., Crouzen, P., Hahn, E.M., D'Argenio, P., Zhang, L.: Time-bounded reachability in distributed input/output interactive probabilistic chains. Reports of SFB/TR 14 AVACS 64, SFB/TR 14 AVACS (June 2010)
5. Canny, J.: Some algebraic and geometric computations in PSPACE. In: STOC, pp. 460–469 (1988)
6. Chaum, D.: The dining cryptographers problem: unconditional sender and recipient untraceability. Journal of Cryptology 1(1), 65–75 (1988)
7. Cheung, L., Lynch, N., Segala, R., Vaandrager, F.: Switched probabilistic I/O automata. In: Liu, Z., Araki, K. (eds.) ICTAC 2004. LNCS, vol. 3407, pp. 494–510. Springer, Heidelberg (2005)
8. Coste, N., Garavel, H., Hermanns, H., Hersemeule, R., Thonnart, Y., Zidouni, M.: Quantitative evaluation in embedded system design: validation of multiprocessor multithreaded architectures. In: DATE, pp. 88–89 (2008)
9. Coste, N., Hermanns, H., Lantreibecq, E., Serwe, W.: Towards performance prediction of compositional models in industrial GALS designs. In: Bouajjani, A., Maler, O. (eds.) Computer Aided Verification. LNCS, vol. 5643, pp. 204–218. Springer, Heidelberg (2009)
10. Daws, C.: Symbolic and parametric model checking of discrete-time Markov chains. In: Liu, Z., Araki, K. (eds.) ICTAC 2004. LNCS, vol. 3407, pp. 280–294. Springer, Heidelberg (2005)

11. de Alfaro, L.: The verification of probabilistic systems under memoryless partial–information policies is hard. In: Proceedings of the Workshop on Probabilistic Methods in Verification (1999)
12. Georgievska, S., Andova, S.: Retaining the probabilities in probabilistic testing theory. In: Ong, L. (ed.) FOSSACS 2010. LNCS, vol. 6014, pp. 79–93. Springer, Heidelberg (2010)
13. Gill, P., Murray, W., Wright, M.: Practical optimization. Academic Press, London (1981)
14. Giro, S., D'Argenio, P.R.: Quantitative model checking revisited: neither decidable nor approximable. In: Raskin, J.-F., Thiagarajan, P.S. (eds.) FORMATS 2007. LNCS, vol. 4763, pp. 179–194. Springer, Heidelberg (2007)
15. Giro, S., D'Argenio, P.R.: On the expressive power of schedulers in distributed probabilistic systems. ENTCS 253(3), 45–71 (2009)
16. Hahn, E.M., Hermanns, H., Wachter, B., Zhang, L.: PARAM: A model checker for parametric Markov models. In: Touili, T., Cook, B., Jackson, P. (eds.) CAV 2010. LNCS, vol. 6174. Springer, Heidelberg (2010)
17. Hahn, E.M., Hermanns, H., Zhang, L.: Probabilistic reachability for parametric Markov models. In: STTT (2010)
18. Han, S.: A globally convergent method for nonlinear programming. Journal of Optimization Theory and Applications 22 (1977)
19. Hermanns, H.: Interactive Markov Chains. LNCS, vol. 2428. Springer, Heidelberg (2002)
20. Lowe, G.: Representing nondeterministic and probabilistic behaviour in reactive processes. Technical Report PRG-TR-11-93, Oxford Univ. Comp. Labs (1993)
21. Morgan, C., McIver, A., Seidel, K., Massink, M.: Refinement-oriented probability for CSP. Formal Aspects of Computing 8, 617–647 (1996)
22. Segala, R.: Modeling and verification of randomized distributed real–time systems. PhD thesis, MIT (1995)
23. Zhang, L., Neuhäußer, M.R.: Model checking interactive Markov chains. In: Esparza, J., Majumdar, R. (eds.) TACAS 2010. LNCS, vol. 6015, pp. 53–68. Springer, Heidelberg (2010)

An Automata-Based Symbolic Approach for Verifying Programs on Relaxed Memory Models

Alexander Linden and Pierre Wolper

Institut Montefiore, B28
Université de Liège
B-4000 Liège, Belgium
{linden,pw@montefiore.ulg.ac.be}

Abstract. This paper addresses the problem of verifying programs for the relaxed memory models implemented in modern processors. Specifically, it considers the TSO (Total Store Order) relaxation, which corresponds to the use of store buffers. The proposed approach proceeds by using finite automata to symbolically represent the possible contents of the store buffers. Store, load and commit operations then correspond to operations on these finite automata.

The advantage of this approach is that it operates on (potentially infinite) sets of buffer contents, rather than on individual buffer configurations. This provides a way to tame the explosion of the number of possible buffer configurations, while preserving the full generality of the analysis. It is thus possible to check even designs that exploit the relaxed memory model in unusual ways. An experimental implementation has been used to validate the feasibility of the approach.

1 Introduction

Modern multiprocessor systems do not implement the traditional *Sequential Consistency* [1] (SC) model of memory access. This fact is usually referred to by describing these processors as implementing ***relaxed memory models*** that permit executions not allowed in SC. Thus verification tools such as SPIN that are based on the SC model do not reliably verify programs to be run on widely used current processors. It is quite disturbing to observe that even simple mutual exclusion algorithms such as Peterson's do not run correctly on a standard modern multicore computer. This situation is nevertheless mostly hidden from the programmer since process synchronization is done through system provided functions, which are correctly implemented, forcing memory synchronization if needed. This is a safe approach, but leads to a suboptimal use of multicores. Having tools for analyzing programs with respect to the implemented relaxed memory models would be of great help in designing code that does not unduly force synchronization. It would also be most useful for checking that code designed for the SC memory model can be safely ported to processors implementing relaxed memory models or, if needed for minimally correcting such code.

The exact memory model that is implemented varies and deciphering processor documentation on this topic is, to put it mildly, quite challenging. However, the

J. van de Pol and M. Weber (Eds.): SPIN 2010, LNCS 6349, pp. 212–226, 2010.

topic is being more and more studied and clear models of memory access models have been proposed. These models can be either axiomatic, giving constraints on possible memory accesses, or operational, giving a program-like description of the shared memory model. Of these models, one of the most studied is the ***Total Store Order*** (TSO) model. It has a simple axiomatics characterization and a clear equivalent operational description in terms of store buffers. In TSO, processor writes are buffered and each processor reads the last value written to its buffer, while others only see the values committed to main memory. This model was the one implemented in SPARC processors [2] and [3] and closely corresponds to the one implemented in X86 processors [4]. Furthermore, store buffers are an essential ingredient of even more relaxed memory models [5] and thus being able to analyze TSO is an important stepping stone in developing verification tools for relaxed memory models. This paper will thus exclusively focus on TSO.

Since TSO can be modeled by a memory accessed through buffers, an obvious approach to verifying programs under this memory model is to explicitly include the store buffers in the program being analyzed. This has of course already been tried, but requires overcoming two problems. The first is that there is no natural bound on the size of the buffers, the second is the explosion in the number of states due to the introduction of store buffers. For the first problem, one can arbitrarily bound the size of the buffers, which, at best, leads to verification that is unsatisfactorily hardware dependent. For the second problem, various techniques such as SAT based bounded model-checking have been tried with some success [6], but at the cost of limits on what can be verified.

In this paper, we develop an approach inspired by the techniques developed in [7] for verifying systems with unbounded buffers. The main idea is that, since a buffer content can be viewed as a word, sets of buffer contents are languages that can be represented by finite automata. This allows infinite sets of contents to be represented and manipulated by operations on automata. Of course, in a step by step exploration of the state space, infinite sets of buffer contents will never be generated. Acceleration techniques are thus required and these take the form of algorithms for directly computing the possible contents of buffers after repeating a program cycle an arbitrary number of times.

Compared to the general problem of analyzing programs using unbounded buffers, the specific case of TSO buffers offers both simplifications and added difficulties. The main simplification is that each process only writes to a single buffer, which makes a separate representation of each buffer the natural choice. Among the difficulties are the operations on the store buffers, which are not quite like those on communication buffers. Indeed, if a store is very much like a buffer write and a commit to memory is similar to a buffer read, a load operation is special. Indeed, it should retrieve the most recently written value and, when there is a choice of such values, a repeated read should yield an identical result. One of our contributions is thus to define these operations precisely when applied to sets of store buffer contents and to show how they can be implemented. Another is adapting the cycle iteration acceleration technique to the specific context of store buffers.

To validate our approach we have built an experimental implementation to test the feasibility of the proposed method. Our implementation uses the BRICS automata manipulation package [8] and has allowed us to fully verify (or find errors) in simple synchronization protocols. Since each process writes to its own buffer, the cycle iteration acceleration needs to favor progress by a single process. Partial-order verification techniques [9], and in particular "sleep sets", have been helpful with respect to this. Indeed, it turned out that using sleep sets yielded a significant performance improvement by avoiding the repeated detection of the same cycle from different global control points.

The verification problem we consider has already been addressed in several papers going back at least a decade. In [10] the problem is clearly defined and it is shown that behaviors possible under TSO but not SC can be detected by an explicit state model checker. Later work, [6], uses SAT-based bounded model checking with success for detecting errors with respect to relaxed memory executions. A more recent paper [11] aims at distinguishing programs that can safely be analyzed under SC, even if run in a relaxed memory model environment. Finally, [12] proves decidability and undecidability results for relaxed memory models considering store buffers to be infinite. In this it is very close to our work, but its goal is purely theoretical and it proceeds by reducing the problem to lossy buffer communication. This is very elegant for obtaining decidability results, but of uncertain value for doing actual verification. Indeed, the reduction to lossy buffers implies an elaborate coding of buffer contents. In contrast, our approach works with a direct representation of the store buffer contents and is oriented towards doing actual verification. To our knowledge, it is the first verification technique for relaxed memory models allowing the full generality coming from unbounded store buffer contents.

2 Concurrent Programs and Memory Models

We consider a very simple model of concurrent programs in which a fixed set of finite-state processes interact through a shared memory. A concurrent program is thus defined by a finite set $\mathcal{P} = \{p_1, \ldots, p_n\}$ of processes and a finite set $\mathcal{M} = \{m_1, \ldots, m_k\}$ of memory locations. The memory locations can hold values from a data domain $\mathcal{D}$. The initial content of the memory is given by a function $\mathcal{I} : \mathcal{M} \to \mathcal{D}$.

Each process p_i is defined by a finite set $\mathcal{L}(p_i)$ of control locations, an initial location $\ell_0(p_i) \in \mathcal{L}(p_i)$, and transitions between control locations labeled by operations from a set $\mathcal{O}$. A transition of a process p_i is thus an element of $\mathcal{L}(p_i) \times \mathcal{O} \times \mathcal{L}(p_i)$, usually written as $\ell \xrightarrow{op} \ell'$. The set of operations contains the following memory operations:

- $store(p_i, m_j, d)$, i.e. process p_i stores value $d \in \mathcal{D}$ to memory location m_j (note that since transitions are process specific, mentioning the process in the operation is redundant, but will turn out to be convenient),
- $load(p_i, m_j, d)$, i.e. process p_i loads the value stored in m_j and checks that its value is d. If the stored value is different from d, the transition is not possible.

Table 1. Intra-processor forwarding, given in [13]

initially: x = y = 0;	
Processor 1	Processor 2
$store(p_1, x, 1)$	$store(p_2, y, 1)$
$load(p_1, x, 1)$	$load(p_2, y, 1)$
$load(p_1, y, 0)$	$load(p_2, x, 0)$

The SC semantics of such a concurrent program is the usual interleaving semantics in which the possible behaviors are those that are interleavings of the executions of the various processes and in which stores are immediately visible to all processes.

In TSO, each process sees the result of its loads and stores exactly in the order it has performed them, but other processes can see an older value than the one seen by the process having performed a store. This leads to executions that are not possible in SC. For instance, in the program given in Table 1, both processes could terminate their executions, whereas under SC semantics, either p_1 or p_2 will find the value 1 when performing the last load operation. TSO is thus also referred to as the *store* $\rightarrow$ *load* order relaxation.

To define TSO formally, one uses the concepts of ***program order*** and ***memory order*** [2,14]. Program order, $<_p$ is a partial order in which the instructions of each process are ordered as executed, but instructions of different processes are not ordered with respect to each other. Memory order, $<_m$, is a total order on the memory operations, which is fictitious but characterizes what happens during relaxed executions.

Let l denote any load operation, s any store operation, l_a a load operation on location a, and s_a a store operation on location a. Furthermore, let $val(l)$ or $val(s)$ be the value returned (stored) by a memory operation. A TSO execution is then one for which there exists a memory order satisfying the following constraints:

1. $\forall l_a, l_b : l_a <_p l_b \Rightarrow l_a <_m l_b$
2. $\forall l, s : l <_p s \Rightarrow l <_m s$
3. $\forall s_a, s_b : s_a <_p s_b \Rightarrow s_a <_m s_b$
4. $val(l_a) = val(\max_{<_m}\{s_a \mid s_a <_m l_a \vee s_a <_p l_a\})$. If there is no such a s_a, $val(l_a)$ is the initial value of the corresponding memory location.

The first three rules specify that the memory order has to be compatible with the program order, except that a store can be postponed after a load, i.e. the *store* $\rightarrow$ *load* order relaxation. The last rule specifies that the value retrieved by a load is the one of the last store in memory order that precedes the load in memory or in program order, the latter ensuring that a process can see the last value it has stored. If there is no such store, the initial value of that memory location is loaded.

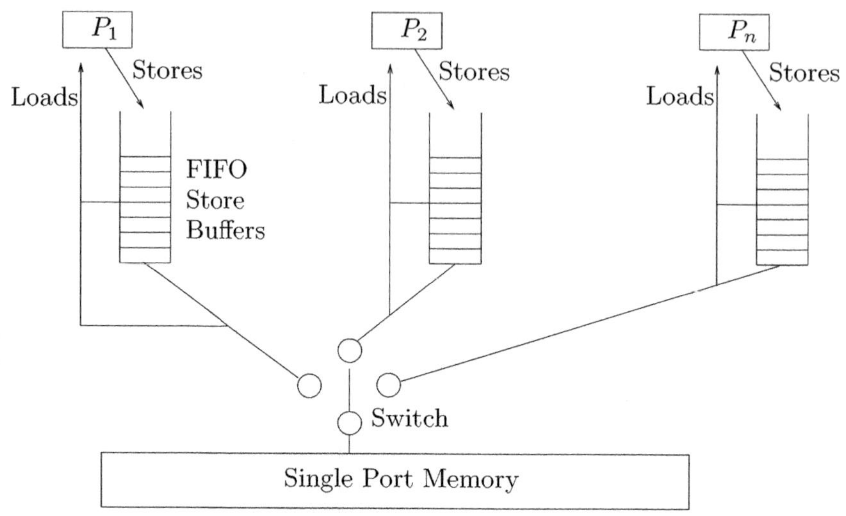

Fig. 1. Operational definition of TSO of Appendix K of [2]

For example, the following is a valid TSO memory order for the program of Table 1 that allows the program to terminate: $load(p_1, x, 1)$, $load(p_1, y, 0)$, $load(p_2, y, 1)$, $load(p_2, x, 0)$, $store(p_1, x, 1)$, $store(p_2, y, 1)$. Note that in SC, memory order has to be fully compatible with program order, and thus this memory order is not possible.

The characterization of TSO we have just given is useful in dealing with TSO axiomatically, but not adapted for applying state-space exploration verification techniques. Fortunately, there exists a natural equivalent operational description of TSO. In this description (see Fig. 1), stores from each process are buffered and eventually committed to main memory in an interleaved way. When a process executes a load, it reads the most recent value in its store buffer or, if there is none, the value present in the shared memory.

This model can be formalized as follows. One introduces a set

$$\mathcal{B} = \{b_{p_1}, \ldots, b_{p_n}\}$$

of store buffers, one for each process[1]. A global state is thus composed of the content of the memory, and, for each process, a control location and a store buffer. The content $[b_p]$ of a buffer b_p is then a word in $(\mathcal{M}, \mathcal{D})^*$ and the program executes load and store operations on these buffers. Furthermore a *commit* operations that removes the oldest store operations from a buffer and writes the corresponding value to memory can nondeterministically be executed at all times. The precise semantics of these operations can be described as follows.

[1] Note that we introduce a buffer per *process* rather than by *processor*. This is a safe approach for verification since it allows more behaviors than a model in which some processes share the same buffer. Furthermore, when analyzing a program it is usually impossible to know which processes will run on the same processor.

store operation: *store*(p, m, d):

$$[b_p] \leftarrow [b_p](m, d).$$

load operation: *load*(p, m, d):

Let $[b_p] = (m_1, d_1)(m_2, d_2) \dots (m_f, d_f)$ and let $i = \max\{j \in \{1 \dots f\} \mid m_j = m\}$. If i exists, then the result of the load is the test $d_i == d$. If not, it is the result of the test $[m] == d$, where $[m]$ denotes the content of the memory location m.

commit operation: *commit*(p):

Let $[b_p] = (m_1, d_1)(m_2, d_2) \dots (m_f, d_f)$. Then, if $[b_p] \neq \varepsilon$, the result of the commit operation is

$$[b_p] \leftarrow (m_2, d_2) \dots (m_f, d_f)$$

and

$$[m_1] \leftarrow d_1.$$

If $[b_p] = \varepsilon$, the commit operation has no effect.

Finally, in programs we will also use an operation *sync* whose effect is to commit to memory the full content of all buffers.

3 Representing Sets of Buffer Contents

If store buffers are unbounded, introducing them leads to a potentially infinite state space. Furthermore, even if store buffers are bounded, they very quickly lead to unmanageably large state spaces, even for very simple programs.

To cope with this problem, we turn to the techniques that have been proposed in [15] and in [7] to represent sets of buffer contents by finite automata. In this approach, sets of possible buffer contents are represented by finite automata and the state-space of the system is explored by manipulating sets of possible contents for each control location as a single object. It is clear that while exploring the state-space of a system, one can combine into a single representation the buffer contents corresponding to identical control locations. However, this will only lead to finite sets of contents being represented as a single object, whereas real gains can only come from manipulating together infinite sets of buffer contents. For achieving this, acceleration techniques are needed. Similarly to what is done in the previously cited work, we will focus on cycles in the program code and provide algorithms for directly computing the effect of iterating a sequence of operations and unbounded numbers. Before turning to this, we will first introduce the representation of sets of buffer contents by automata and see how load store and commit operations can be extrapolated to operations on automata representing sets of buffer contents.

We represent the possible contents of each buffer by a separate automaton over the alphabet $\mathcal{M} \times \mathcal{D}$ and use the following definition.

Definition 1. *A buffer automaton associated to a process p is a finite automaton $A_p = (S, \Sigma, \Delta, S_0, F)$, where*

- *S is a finite set of states,*
- *$\Sigma = \mathcal{M} \times \mathcal{D}$ is the alphabet of buffer elements,*
- *$\Delta \subseteq S \times (\Sigma \cup \{\varepsilon\}) \times S$ is the transition relation,*
- *$S_0 \subseteq S$ is a set of initial states, and*
- *F is a set of final states.*

A buffer automaton A_p represents a set of buffer contents $L(A_p)$, which is the language of the words accepted by the automaton according to the usual definition.

We have defined buffer automata to be nondeterministic, but for implementation purposes we will usually work with reduced deterministic automata. In this case, the transition relation becomes a transition function $\delta : S \times \Sigma \to S$ and the set of initial states becomes a single state s_0.

Operations on buffers can be extrapolated to operations on buffer automata as follows.

store operation: *store*(p, m, d)**:**

The result of the operation is an automaton A'_p such that

$$L(A'_p) = L(A_p) \cdot \{(m, d)\}$$

One thus simply concatenates that new stored value to all words in the language of the automaton.

load operation: *load*(p, m, d)**:**

Load operations are nondeterministic since a buffer automaton can represent several possible buffer contents. Thus it is possible that a load operation can succeed on some represented buffer contents and fail on others. If this is the case, the load operation must lead to a state in which the set of possible buffer contents has been restricted to those on which the load operation succeeds.

For a load operation to succeed, the tested value must be found either in the store buffer or in main memory. Precisely, a load operation succeeds when at least one of the following two conditions is satisfied:

1. The language

$$L_1 = L(A_p) \cap (\Sigma^* \cdot (m, d) \cdot (\Sigma \backslash \{(y, v) \mid y \neq m \wedge v \in \mathcal{D}\})^*)$$

is nonempty.

2. The language

$$L_2 = L(A_p) \cap (\Sigma \backslash \{(m, v) \mid v \in \mathcal{D}\})^*$$

is nonempty and $[m] = d$.

The load operation then leads to a state with a modified store buffer automaton A'_p such that

$$L(A'_p) = L_1 \cup L_2$$

if $[m] = d$ and

$$L(A'_p) = L_1$$

otherwise. Of course, if $L_1 \cup L_2 = \emptyset$, the load operation is simply not possible.

commit operation: *commit*(p)**:**

For the commit operation, we first extract the stores that can be committed to memory. These are the stores (m, α) such that

$$(m, \alpha) \in \text{first}(L(A_p)),$$

where first(L) denotes the language of the first symbols of the words of L. Since there can be more than one such store, we need to modify the store buffer automaton according to the committed store (m, α). We have

$$L(A'_p((m, \alpha))) = \text{suffix}^1(L(A_p) \cap ((m, \alpha) \cdot \Sigma^*)),$$

where $\text{suffix}^1(L)$ denotes the language obtained by removing the first symbol of the words of L.

4 State Space Exploration and Cycle Detection

Our state-space exploration algorithm is based on a classical depth-first search. The major modification we introduce is the detection of cycles and an acceleration technique for directly computing the effect of repeatedly executing a detected cycle. The cycles we detect are those that only modify a single store buffer. This might seem restrictive, but notice that the use of store buffers introduces a lot of independence between processes and experiments show that considering only single process cycles is sufficient. The independence induced by store buffers has however a drawback, which is that it makes the same cycles possible from many different global control locations. Proceeding naively thus results in detecting the same cycle many times over, which is unnecessary and very wasteful. To avoid this, we used the sleep set partial order reduction of [9]. This reduction avoids re-exploring transitions after executing other independent transitions. In general, the sleep set reduction does not reduce the number of states visited, but only the number of transitions followed. This is already very valuable when working with automata symbolic representations, since these increase the cost of comparing states. Furthermore, the fact that we are working with sets of states and not individual states does make sleep sets yield a reduction of the size of the state graph that needs to be explored, as we will illustrate by an example further down.

In the sleep set exploration algorithm, a set of transitions, called a sleep set, is associated with each state. Initially, the sleep set is empty. Once a transition is executed, it is added to the sleep set of the resulting state, but transitions in the sleep set that are not independent with respect to the executed transition are removed. Transitions in the sleep set associated to a state are not executed from that state. The basic depth-first search algorithm using sleep sets is given in Algorithm 1 and Algorithm 2. We will use a crude but sufficient notion of independence. In a state s,

1. transitions of the same process are never independent;
2. transitions of different processes other than *commit* or *sync* are always independent;
3. a *commit(p)* transition of a process p is independent with the transitions of a process p', provided that, for every memory location m affected by this *commit* operation, either p' does not use m, or p' has a value for m in its store buffer, i.e., all words of the language $L(A_p)$ contain an occurrence of (m, v) for some $v \in \mathcal{D}$.
4. a *sync* operation is not independent with any other transition.

Algorithm 1. Initialization of depth first search

1: init(Stack)
2: init(H) /* Table of visited states */
3: s_0 = initial state
4: $s_0.Sleep = \emptyset$
5: push s_0 onto Stack
6: DFS()

What we add to this is cycle detection and acceleration. Cycle detection is done when there is a state on the current search stack that only differs from the state being generated by the content of one store buffer. The modified recursive procedure called within the initialization process is the procedure given in Algorithm 3, DFS()_cycle().

First, we need to define when a state is included in another. A state s is included in another state s' if

1. s and s' are identical with respect to control locations and memory content, and
2. for each process p, $L(A_p(s))$ is included in $L(A_p(s'))$

Next, we need to make explicit the `cycleCondition(ss,s)` predicate. For this predicate to be true, three conditions have to be satisfied by the pair of global states ss, s. Remembering that global states are composed of the control location of each process, the content of the memory and the buffer automata of each process, these conditions can be defined as follows.

1. s and ss are identical, except for the store buffer automaton of a single process p.

Algorithm 2. Recursive DFS() procedure using sleep sets

```
s = top(Stack)
if (s ∈ H) then
    T_executed = enabled(s) \ H(s).Sleep
    s.Sleep = s.Sleep ∩ H(s).Sleep
    H(s).Sleep = s.Sleep
else
    enter s in H
    T_executed = ∅
end if
T = (enabled(s) \ s.Sleep) \ T_executed
for all t ∈ T do
    ssucc = succ(s,t)
    ssucc.Sleep = {tt | tt ∈ s.Sleep ∧ (t, tt) independant in s}
    push ssucc onto Stack
    DFS()
end for
pop(Stack)
```

2. The languages represented by the store buffer automaton of p in ss can be extended to match the language of the store buffer automaton of p in s, i.e. there exists a word w such that $(L(A_p(s)) = L(A_p(ss)) \cdot \{w\}$.
3. The store buffer automaton obtained for s is ***load equivalent*** to the one of ss, i.e. the results of loads will be the same, whether starting from s or ss. Since the only difference between $L(A_p(s))$, and $L(A_p(ss))$ is the suffix w, this will be verified by checking the following condition. For all memory locations m for which there is a store operation $store(p, m, v)$ in w, let v_{last} be the value in the last store operation in w. Then the operation $load(p, m, v_{last})$ must be simultaneously possible in both s and ss and must not modify the store buffer automata $A_p(s)$ and $A_p(ss)$.

Finally, once a possible cycle content w has been detected and the conditions for a cycle are satisfied, we need to store the buffer automaton representing the buffer contents that can be obtained by repeating the cycle, eventually interleaved with previously detected cycles. For a language L, let $W_i^c(L)$ be the maximal sets of suffixes of words in L that can be repeated while remaining in L, i.e. each $W_i^c(L)$ is a maximal set such that $L \cdot (W_i^c(L))^* \subseteq L$. In practice, one computes the $W_i^c(L)$ as the languages that allow an accepting state to be reached from itself. The modified store buffer automaton will then be the automaton $A_p^{cycle}(ss)$ accepting $\bigcup_i L(A_p(ss)) \cdot (W_i^c(L(A_p(ss)) \cup \{w\})^*$. The operation `cycle(`$ss, s$`)` of our search algorithm thus simply replaces the store buffer automaton for process p in state s by the automaton $A_p^{cycle}(ss)$.

Algorithm 3. Recursive DFS_cycle() procedure using sleep sets, cycle detection and acceleration

```
s = top(Stack)
/* Go through stack from top to bottom */
for all ss in (Stack \ top(Stack)) do
   if (cycleCondition(ss,s)) then
      s = cycle(ss,s)
      break
   end if
end for
if (∃sI ∈ H | s ⊆ sI) then
   iSleep = ⋂_{∀sI∈H|s⊆sI} H(sI).Sleep
   T_executed = enabled(s) \ iSleep
   s.Sleep = s.Sleep ∩ iSleep
   if (s ∈ H) then
      H(s).Sleep = s.Sleep
   else
      enter s in H
   end if
else
   enter s in H
   T_executed = ∅
end if
T = (enabled(s) \ s.Sleep) \ T_executed
for all t ∈ T do
   ssucc = succ(s,t)
   ssucc.Sleep = {tt | tt ∈ s.Sleep ∧ (t,tt) independant in s}
   push ssucc onto Stack
   DFS_cycle()
end for
pop(Stack)
```

Example 1. We illustrate the state-space reduction that can be obtained by the use of sleep sets. Fig. 2 shows the control graph of two processes p_0 and p_1. In Fig. 3, part of the global state graph of this system is shown. In state 4, a cycle has been detected for the store buffer of p_0, yielding

$$(x,1)((x,0)(x,1))^*$$

as set of possible contents. In state 6, the buffer has become

$$(x,1)(x,0)(x,1)((x,0)(x,1))^*,$$

and thus, state 6 is included in state 4. In state 5, if we don't add the transition $st(p_0,x,1)$ (which led to state 6) to the sleep set of state 7, we will end up

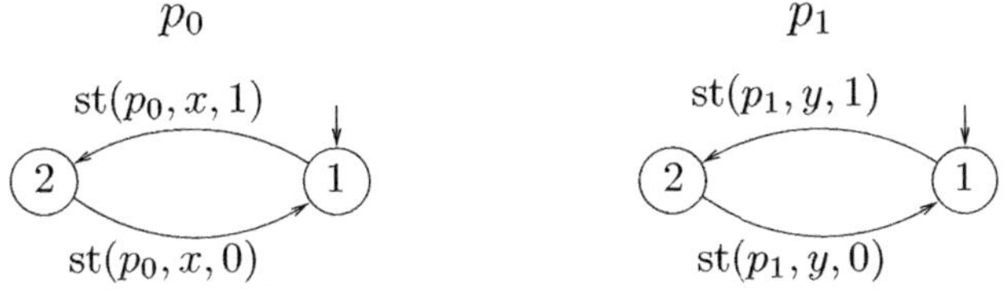

Fig. 2. Control graphs of two processes p_0 and p_1

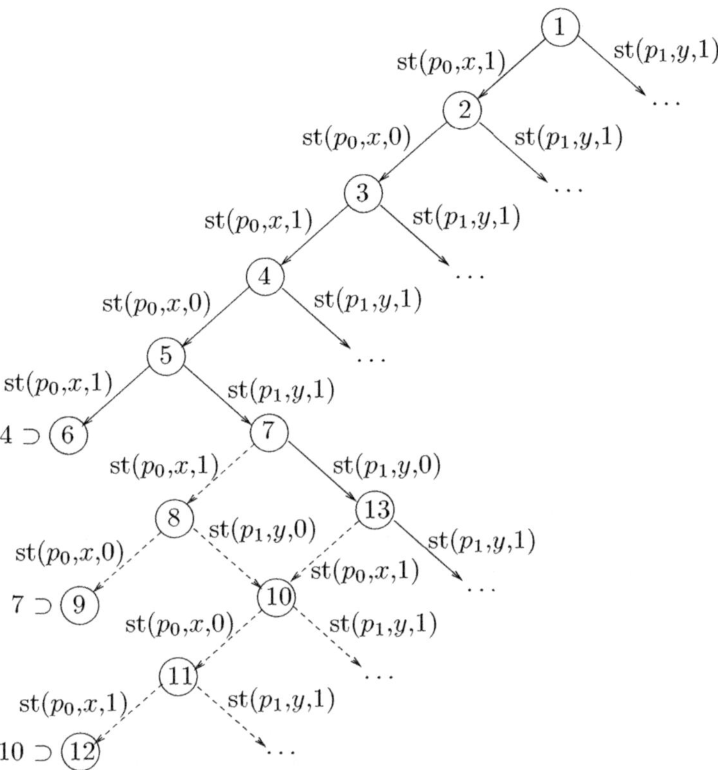

Fig. 3. Global exploration graph showing reduction using sleep sets

generating states 8 and 9 before detecting any state inclusion and add many more states to the search graph.

5 Experimental Results

We have implemented our method in a prototype tool. This tool takes as input a slightly modified (the *store, load and sync* instructions have been added) and simplified version of Promela. The prototype has been implemented in Java, and uses the BRICS automata-package [8] to handle our store-buffers.

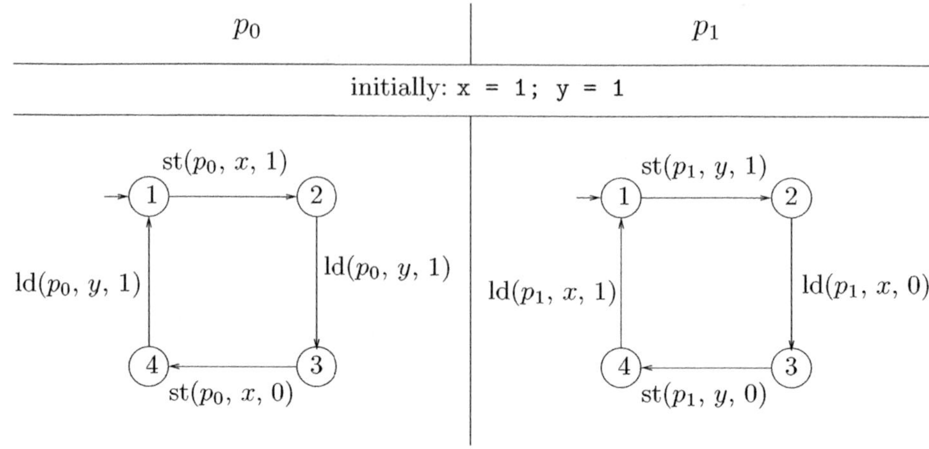

Fig. 4. Example program unlocking a cycle

We have tested our implementation on several programs and protocols. One of our test programs is a program (see Fig. 4)[2] where the first process may cycle indefinitely from the initial state, but where the second depends on the global memory being modified to be able to move. Indeed, p_0 can directly cycle indefinitely, writing the infinite sequence $(x,1)(x,0)(x,1)(x,0)(x,1)(x,0)\ldots$ to its store buffer. This cycle is detected and all possible contents of p_0's store buffer represented. Then, the process p_1 can, once the cycle in the buffer of p_0 is established, "consume" this cycle, which unlocks its own cycle. For example, a global state such as $(1,1,0,0,((x,1)(x,0))^*,((y,1)(y,0))^*)$ (where the notation is $(p_0,\ p_1,\ m_1,\ m_2,\ b_0,\ b_1)$) will eventually be reached. Consuming means that store operations are committed to the global memory, without the process itself doing any action.

Moreover, under SC, if both processes are in state 4, the program is in a deadlock. In TSO, there is the possibility of deadlock, but it is also possible for the program to continue (if there are buffered store operations), and thus the values of x and y may change value. Interestingly, both behaviors have also been observed while running a C implementation of this program on a dual core processor.

Other classical algorithms often analyzed in the context of relaxed memory models are Dekker's and Peterson's algorithm for mutual exclusion. We have considered single entry and repeated entry versions of these algorithms. In the single entry version, the two processes attempt to enter into their critical section only once. Verifying this can be done with our implementation, as well as with other tools, such as those of [6], [5] or [16]. Verification becomes more difficult when considering the repeated entry version. In these versions, both processes attempt to enter their critical section an arbitrary number of times. Using our prototype, we could complete the exploration, finding the errors, or, when ap-

[2] For readability, the operations *store* and *load* are written as *st* and *ld*.

Table 2. Experimental results for Dekker's and Peterson's Algorithm for mutual exclusion

Dekker (2 Proc)	States Stored	States Visited	Time	Max Depth	Nb Errors
single entry	183	301	2,446 s	22	2
single entry + sync	111	161	1,194 s	22	0
repeated entry	3236	6231	22,881 s	785	36
repeated entry + sync	343	631	3,016 s	79	0

Peterson (2 Proc)	States Stored	States Visited	Time	Max Depth	Nb Errors
single entry	120	173	1,969 s	15	2
single entry + sync	54	66	0,399 s	13	0
repeated entry	355	432	3,097 s	50	10
repeated entry + sync	65	92	0,392 s	22	0

propriately adding *sync* operations, showing the absence of errors. In Table 2, we give experimental results for Dekker's and Peterson's algorithms, both for the single entry and the repeated entry versions, with and without the *sync* operations needed to make them correct.

All experiments were obtained by running our Java-program on a 2.0GHz Intel Core Duo laptop running Ubuntu Linux.

6 Conclusions

Compared to earlier methods used to verify programs under relaxed memory models, ours differs by the techniques being used (automata-based symbolic methods) and the scope of the verification that can be done. Indeed, whereas other methods such as those of [17] are limited to very short executions, we analyse arbitrarily long executions. This is clearly not always necessary for detecting errors, but can be essential for robustly establishing correctness in tricky situations.

A natural question about an approach like the one presented in this paper is how well it can scale up. We do not yet have significant data, but our approach will most likely never be usable for large programs. However, this is not the drawback it might at first seem to be. Indeed, while writing larger programs, one uses synchronization primitives that isolate the programmer from the complexity of relaxed memory models. Verifying under relaxed memory will thus only be needed for the rather small programs that implement these primitives, and we believe that this can be handled.

References

1. Lamport, L.: How to make a multiprocessor computer that correctly executes multiprocess programs. IEEE Trans. Computers 28(9), 690–691 (1979)
2. SPARC International, Inc., C.: The SPARC architecture manual: version 8. Prentice-Hall, Inc., Upper Saddle River (1992)

3. SPARC International, Inc., C.: The SPARC architecture manual (version 9). Prentice-Hall, Inc., Upper Saddle River (1994)
4. Owens, S., Sarkar, S., Sewell, P.: A better x86 memory model: x86-TSO. In: Berghofer, S., Nipkow, T., Urban, C., Wenzel, M. (eds.) TPHOLs 2009. LNCS, vol. 5674, pp. 391–407. Springer, Heidelberg (2009)
5. Mador-Haim, S., Alur, R., Martin, M.: Plug and play components for the exploration of memory consistency models. Technical report, University of Pennsylvania (2010)
6. Burckhardt, S., Alur, R., Martin, M.M.K.: Checkfence: checking consistency of concurrent data types on relaxed memory models. In: Ferrante, J., McKinley, K.S. (eds.) Proceedings of the ACM SIGPLAN 2007 Conference on Programming Language Design and Implementation, San Diego, California, USA, June 10-13, pp. 12–21. ACM, New York (2007)
7. Boigelot, B., Godefroid, P., Willems, B., Wolper, P.: The power of QDDs (extended abstract). In: Van Hentenryck, P. (ed.) SAS 1997. LNCS, vol. 1302, pp. 172–186. Springer, Heidelberg (1997)
8. Møller, A.: Package dk.brics.automaton (2001-2009) (DFA/NFA Java implementation), `http://www.brics.dk/automaton/`
9. Godefroid, P.: Partial-Order Methods for the Verification of Concurrent Systems. LNCS, vol. 1032. Springer, Heidelberg (1996)
10. Park, S., Dill, D.L.: An executable specification, analyzer and verifier for rmo (relaxed memory order). In: SPAA 1995: Proceedings of the Seventh Annual ACM Symposium on Parallel Algorithms and Architectures, pp. 34–41. ACM, New York (1995)
11. Burckhardt, S., Musuvathi, M.: Effective program verification for relaxed memory models. In: Gupta, A., Malik, S. (eds.) CAV 2008. LNCS, vol. 5123, pp. 107–120. Springer, Heidelberg (2008)
12. Atig, M.F., Bouajjani, A., Burckhardt, S., Musuvathi, M.: On the verification problem for weak memory models. In: Hermenegildo, M.V., Palsberg, J. (eds.) Proceedings of the 37th ACM SIGPLAN-SIGACT Symposium on Principles of Programming Languages, POPL 2010, Madrid, Spain, January 17-23, pp. 7–18. ACM, New York (2010)
13. Intel Corporation: Intel®64 and IA-32 Architectures Software Developer's Manual. Specification (2007), `http://www.intel.com/products/processor/manuals/index.htm`.
14. Loewenstein, P., Chaudhry, S., Cypher, R., Manovit, C.: Multiprocessor memory model verification. In: AFM (Automated Formal Methods), FLOC Workshop (2006), `http://fm.csl.sri.com/AFM06/`, `http://www.scientificcommons.org/43465152`
15. Boigelot, B., Wolper, P.: Symbolic verification with periodic sets. In: Dill, D.L. (ed.) CAV 1994. LNCS, vol. 818, pp. 55–67. Springer, Heidelberg (1994)
16. Hangal, S., et al.: TSOtool: A program for verifying memory systems using the memory consistency model. In: 31st International Symposium on Computer Architecture (ISCA 2004), Munich, Germany, June 19-23, pp. 114–123. IEEE Computer Society, Los Alamitos (2004)
17. Yang, Y., Gopalakrishnan, G., Lindstrom, G., Slind, K.: Analyzing the intel itanium memory ordering rules using logic programming and sat. In: Geist, D., Tronci, E. (eds.) CHARME 2003. LNCS, vol. 2860, pp. 81–95. Springer, Heidelberg (2003)

Context-Bounded Translations for Concurrent Software: An Empirical Evaluation*

Naghmeh Ghafari[1], Alan J. Hu[2], and Zvonimir Rakamarić[2]

[1] Critical Systems Labs, Vancouver, BC, Canada
naghmeh.ghafari@cslabs.com
[2] Department of Computer Science, University of British Columbia, Canada
{ajh,zrakamar}@cs.ubc.ca

Abstract. Context-Bounded Analysis has emerged as a practical automatic formal analysis technique for fine-grained, shared-memory concurrent software. Two recent papers (in CAV 2008 and 2009) have proposed ingenious translation approaches that promise much better scalability, backed by compelling, but differing, theoretical and conceptual advantages. Empirical evidence comparing the translations, however, has been lacking. Furthermore, these papers focused exclusively on Boolean model checking, ignoring the also widely used paradigm of verification-condition checking. In this paper, we undertake a methodical, empirical evaluation of the three main source-to-source translations for context-bounded analysis of concurrent software, in a verification-condition-checking paradigm. We evaluate their scalability under a wide range of experimental conditions. Our results show: (1) The newest, CAV 2009 translation is the clear loser, with the CAV 2008 translation the best in most instances, but the oldest, brute-force translation doing surprisingly well. Clearly, previous results for Boolean model checking do not apply to verification-condition checking. (2) Disturbingly, confounding factors in the experimental design can change the relative performance of the translations, highlighting the importance of extensive and thorough experiments. For example, using a different (slower) SMT solver changes the relative ranking of the translations, potentially misleading researchers and practitioners to use an inferior translation. (3) SMT runtimes grow exponentially with verification-condition length, but different translations and parameters give different exponential curves. This suggests that the practical scalability of a translation scheme might be estimated by combining the size of the queries with an empirical or theoretical measure of the complexity of solving that class of query.

1 Introduction

The original application for model checking was concurrent software, in the form of protocols (e.g., [7,18]), and concurrent software continues to be a major impetus for model checking. With changes in technology, new versions of the software model checking problem emerge. Currently, due to architectural and electrical constraints, Moore's Law is manifesting itself via an exponential growth in processor cores per chip,

* This work was supported by a Microsoft Research Graduate Fellowship and the Natural Science and Engineering Research Council of Canada.

J. van de Pol and M. Weber (Eds.): SPIN 2010, LNCS 6349, pp. 227–244, 2010.

rather than the formerly exponential improvements in single-threaded performance. The result is a push for vastly greater levels of fine-grained, shared-memory concurrent software — in addition to classical message-passing and coarse-grained protocol-level concurrency — even in the most mundane applications. Such software needs verification.

It is possible, of course, to model check such software directly, and several pioneering systems provide that capability (e.g., [13,19,10,32]). The state space is the cross product of all program variables, stacks, heaps, and program counters for all threads, and this state space can be explored as a transition system. The obvious challenge is extreme state explosion (if variable domains, stacks, and memories are modeled as finite) and/or theoretical undecidability (if any are modeled as infinite).

Context-Bounded Analysis (CBA) [26] promises a way around these challenges. Analogously to bounded model checking [6], the user specifies an integer constant that bounds the maximum number of execution contexts (i.e., periods of a thread running between context swaps) to be considered, and all concurrent executions up to that bound are analyzed. The downside, of course, is that if a bug requires more than that bound to manifest, it will be missed. The upside is that CBA reduces the analysis of concurrent software (under the context bound) to the analysis of sequential software. In theory, the advantage is that CBA is NP-complete [25,23], whereas full concurrent software analysis is undecidable (even with finite variable domains and no heap, due to the call stack). In practice, CBA has proven its ability to detect hard concurrency bugs in real software, and many approaches rely on context-bounding to tackle the complexity of concurrent software (e.g., [26,27,24,17,30,21,20]).

The original CBA paper [26] used a source-to-source translation of concurrent to sequential program text, and subsequent work has followed that approach. The approach enables CBA to exploit all of the tools and algorithms for verification of sequential software, e.g., including the use of logics and decision procedures for reasoning about unbounded data domains, arrays, and heap-allocated memory. Recent papers by Lal and Reps [22] and by La Torre, Madhusudan, and Parlato [31] have proposed two ingenious and radically different source-to-source translations for CBA. These translations are more general than the original, but more importantly, they offer compelling theoretical and conceptual arguments for much better scalability. In Lal and Reps's paper (henceforth referred to as LR in this paper), the key theoretical advance is the elimination of the exponential cross-product of the local states of the threads, at the expense of introducing multiple non-deterministic symbolic variables to guess the values of the shared global variables at context switches. La Torre, Madhusudan, and Parlato's paper (LMP in this paper) retains the theoretical advantage of LR, but adds "laziness" — instead of non-deterministic guesses, variables can assume only those values that are actually possible during a real concurrent execution — at the expense of needing to recompute the values of local variables at context switches. (More on both translations in Section 2.) Both papers support their arguments with runtimes on a handful of small Boolean programs, e.g., the popular "Windows NT Bluetooth driver"-derived example [26].

Given the very different approaches, with differing trade-offs (local state cross-product vs. symbolic variables vs. recomputation), and limited experiments (small Boolean programs model-checked with Moped [15]), it is hard to draw more general conclusions about what will work well in practice, under differing conditions. In particular, finite-state (or PDA) model-checking of highly abstracted Boolean programs (e.g., [2,15,9]) is only one of the major approaches for automatic formal software verification. Another main paradigm is verification-condition (VC) generation[1], with the resulting VC checked by a SAT or SMT solver (e.g., [16,3,5,29,28] for program verification, and [8,1] for bug finding). SAT/SMT solvers behave very differently from the BDDs used in Boolean model checking, so experimental results in the VC-checking paradigm are especially needed.

This paper addresses those needs. We undertake a methodical, empirical evaluation of the three main source-to-source translations for context-bounded analysis of concurrent software, in a VC-checking paradigm. We consider the LMP approach, the LR approach, and a straightforward generalization of the translation given in the original CBA paper [26]. We evaluate how they perform under vastly more experimental conditions than previous work, and also measure scalability versus program length, which was not done before. Some of the results are surprising (e.g., older methods outperforming newer ones), and some are disturbing (e.g., the extent that confounding factors can influence results). Taken altogether, our results highlight the crucial importance of extensive experimental evaluation, provide practical guidance for using context-bounded analysis in a VC-checking paradigm, and outline pitfalls and questions for further research as these and other translations are developed and improved.

2 Context-Bounded Translations

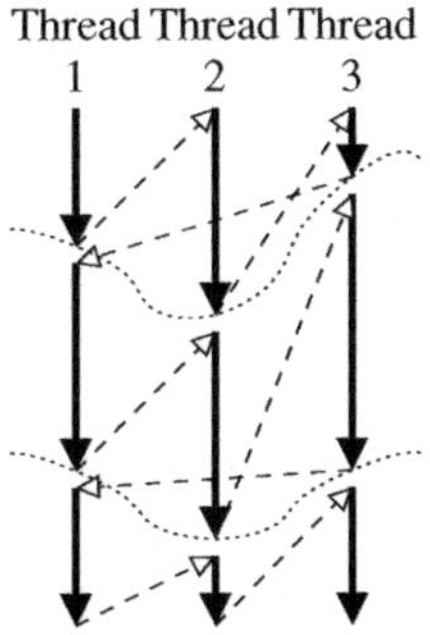

We use a standard model of shared-memory concurrent software. There are T threads, each with its own local variables and program code. The only communication between threads is via a set of global shared variables, which all threads can read or write. (Writes to a global occur atomically: when a thread writes to a global, the new value is immediately visible to all threads.) At all times, exactly one thread is running. At a context switch, the current thread relinquishes control to another thread (determined by the scheduling policy), which proceeds to execute starting from wherever it last gave up control, with whatever values its local variables had at that time and the current values of the global variables. Context switches occur non-deterministically at any point in time. The figure to the right shows the concurrent execution of three threads. The program code executed by each thread is depicted by the sequence of dark, vertical arrows. Each of those arrows represents one "context" — an uninterrupted period when one thread runs its code. The dashed arrows represent context switches, which occur non-deterministically, and transfer control to a different thread.

Thread Thread Thread
1 2 3

When a context switch occurs, which thread runs next is determined by a scheduling policy. Two policies are common in CBA: round-robin and arbitrary. In round-robin scheduling, the context switch is always to the numerically next thread, modulo T. Hence, execution proceeds in a series of rounds, during which each thread gets a

[1] A brief introduction to VC generation is given in Appendix A.

chance to execute once at its turn. In the preceding figure, the schedule is round-robin, and the dotted curved lines demarcate the three rounds. In arbitrary scheduling, a context switch can jump to any thread, non-deterministically chosen. Obviously, the schedules permitted by round-robin with K rounds is a subset of the arbitrary schedules with $K \cdot T$ contexts. Conversely, the schedules permitted by round-robin with K rounds is a superset of the arbitrary schedules with K contexts, since a thread can execute zero instructions before another context switch occurs, so each round of round-robin can simulate one context of an arbitrary-scheduled thread. Between these two bounds, neither policy dominates the other.

We now survey the three main source-to-source translations for CBA under this model. For space reasons, we give only some brief intuition for each.

2.1 Explicit Program Counter (EPC)

We dub our first translation "Explicit Program Counter" (EPC). This is the obvious, brute-force approach and is a straightforward generalization of the original CBA paper [26] (where they restricted themselves to two context switches in order to permit an efficient implementation via the procedure call mechanism).

For the EPC translation, the state of the sequential program includes all of the local variables, including the program counters, of all of the threads. The code of the sequential program consists of the code of all of the threads combined into a single program. However, at each possible location for a context switch (i.e., between every adjacent pair of accesses to global variables), we insert code that can non-deterministically decide to simulate a context switch. The context switch code consists of choosing the next thread to run (based on the scheduling policy), and then jumping to the correct location in that thread based on its stored program counter. The sequential program starts executing at the beginning of $Thread_1$ for round-robin or with a non-deterministic jump to the beginning of an arbitrary thread for arbitrary scheduling. An auxiliary variable k counts how many contexts have run. The sequential program terminates when k reaches the context bound K, or when all threads have executed all of their code.

This translation is simple and has linear static and dynamic code size versus the concurrent program. However, at each point during execution, the program state consists of the cross-product of all local variables and the global variables, potentially producing a complexity blow-up.

2.2 Lal-Reps CAV 2008 (LR)

The LR translation eliminates the EPC complexity blow-up, at the expense of introducing symbolic prophesy variables to guess the values of results that are not yet known. The basic construction is to execute each thread one-by-one in its entirety, in sequence, i.e., all of $Thread_1$, then all of $Thread_2$, then all of $Thread_3$, etc. Accordingly, the static and dynamic code size are unchanged from the original program. Furthermore, since each thread executes in its entirety, without interruption from the others, there is no need to keep the local state of a thread after it is done, thereby eliminating the blow-up of the local state cross-product.

The construction in the preceding paragraph would produce wrong results, since it ignores the fact that in the concurrent program, a context switch could occur at any point and change the value of global variables. Worse, because we are executing the threads sequentially one after another, the results computed by the other threads might not be known until much later in the sequential execution!

The solution is to create K copies of the global variables, where K is the bound on the number of round-robin rounds. The ith copy contains the values of the global variables during the ith scheduling round. Since we will not know what values these variables will contain until the program completes, we initialize all K copies with non-deterministic symbolic values. An auxiliary variable k in each thread keeps track of which round is executing; all accesses to globals are indexed through k. A context switch during the execution of a thread, therefore, consists simply of increasing k, which results in a switch to the correct set of global variables for that round. Hence, at each possible location for a context switch, we insert code that non-deterministically increases k. At the end of the program, we use `assume` statements to enforce that the results in the copy of the globals at the end of round i are equal to the non-deterministic symbolic values we used to initialize the copy of the globals for the start of round $i+1$. In effect, the translation is computing symbolic summaries for each round and stitching them together via `assume` statements at the end.

Note that this construction is intrinsically round-robin. Because the threads are executed in order $1,\ldots,T$, where T is the number of threads, the values of the globals in each round pass automatically from any $Thread_t$ to $Thread_{t+1}$. The symbolic values and stitching are required only between rounds.

2.3 La Torre-Madhusudan-Parlato CAV 2009 (LMP)

Because LR is constructing symbolic summaries from unconstrained symbolic values, it might explore expensive, infeasible regions of the state space, only to eliminate them in the end using the `assume` statements. LMP avoids this problem by introducing "laziness" — instead of non-deterministic guesses, variables can assume only those values that are actually possible during a real concurrent execution. (For comparison purposes, the LMP paper also introduces an eager translation similar to the LR translation. In this paper, LMP refers to their lazy translation.)

LMP with a bound of K contexts starts with a non-deterministic schedule $t_1,\ldots,t_K$, where $t_i \in [1,\ldots,T]$ contains the identity of the thread to execute during the ith context. As in LR, there are K copies of the global variables, but these are assigned only as their values are computed. Like EPC, execution in the LMP translation follows the same order as the concurrent execution — a context switch is an actual jump to the next thread in the schedule. Unlike EPC, however, the local state of a thread is completely discarded when context-switching away from it, thereby eliminating the local-state cross-product blow-up. How can a thread resume where it left off after a context switch? The solution is to recompute the thread's local state! In other words, the context-switch code is considerably more complicated, as it will re-execute a thread from the beginning each time a context switch to it occurs, but during re-execution, the values of the global variables at earlier context switches are already known. In the presence of non-determinism, correctness of this construction is not obvious, since the recomputed local state might be different from the one that occurred when last executing in this thread — a subtle correctness argument is needed to show that no additional behaviors are introduced. The resulting translation has the best attributes of both LR (no local-state blow-up) and EPC (no exploration of infeasible states), but at a cost: a blow-up in the length of the dynamic code paths that must be executed/analyzed. The LMP paper provides some experimental results showing the translation greatly outperforming their version of LR, but only in the Boolean model checking paradigm, and on only two small examples: an artificial example specifically constructed to illustrate the benefit of laziness,[2] and the aforementioned "Bluetooth driver" benchmark. How the methods compare as program size grows, and under the VC-checking paradigm, are open questions.

3 Experimental Methodology and Results

Obviously, the ultimate test of these translations is their performance in the wild on real software. In our experience applying CBA to real, industrial code [21], a crucial factor was scalability to larger code sizes, so the paramount dimension for our experiments is scalability with respect to code length. For scalability benchmarking, however, real code has a fatal flaw: the code length is not scalable.

Accordingly, we crafted a microbenchmark that is scalable along the three key problem parameters: the number of threads T, the context bound K, and the length of the program code in each thread L. To avoid confounding factors, we distilled our benchmark to only the essentials:

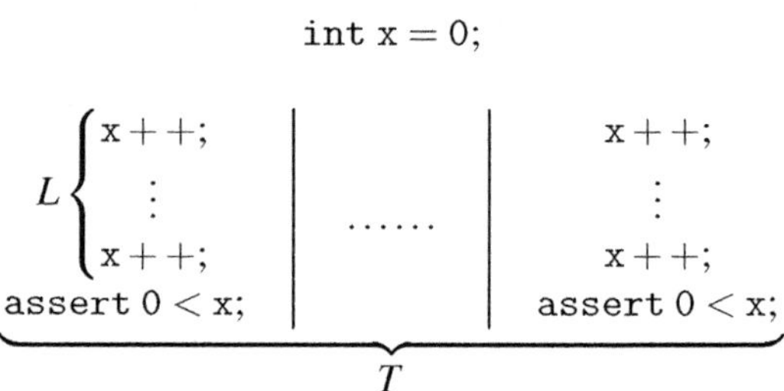

The benchmark has a shared global variable x, which is initialized to 0. Then, T threads are spawned. Each thread consists of L increments of x followed by an assertion that checks if x is greater than 0. Despite its simplicity, this microbenchmark still has the key elements of the concurrent software model: local state (the program counters), shared global state x, and long data-dependency chains that grow with code size and must be inspected in order to prove the assertions, capturing an essential aspect of program scaling. The microbenchmark does not have procedures or loops — in the VC-checking paradigm, these are handled via invariants. Note that this particular microbenchmark could easily be solved via other means, since it has a small finite state

[2] In their "permutation" example, an interlock serializes two threads, the first thread zeroes out 16 bits, and the second thread computes all permutations of the 16 bits. With laziness, the bits are all zero, so the permutation is vacuous; without laziness, the second thread explodes.

space. That is not the point. This is a "test tube" experiment, to identify and eliminate confounding factors while measuring scalability. If a translation scales poorly on this benchmark, it will not fare well on real code.

For each of the three translations, we encoded in BoogiePL [12] multiple instances of this benchmark by varying its T, K, and L parameters. BoogiePL is the input language of the BOOGIE verifier [3], which generates a verification-condition (VC) from the input program. The VC generation in BOOGIE is performed using a variation of the standard *weakest precondition* transformer [14]. This translation is linear in the input code size; combined with the linear static code-size expansion of the three translations, all three translations produce linear-size VCs, albeit with differing complexity (LMP the most complex; LR the simplest). We checked the VCs generated from our benchmarks using the Z3 SMT solver [11], except where indicated otherwise. The experiments were performed on four identical machines (Intel Xeon 5160 at 3GHz with 2GB RAM), running Z3 continuously for weeks. We report the solver's running times, and the time out is set to 2 hours.

As an additional sanity check, we also performed experiments on the Bluetooth driver example [26]. The original benchmark has two threads: an "adder" and a "stopper". We artificially scale T by adding adder threads. We artificially scale code length by repeating (i.e. copy-pasting) the body of the adder threads; the parameter L denotes the number of such repetitions.

Figs. 1–10 present our main results. Details and interpretation of each experiment are in the accompanying captions. Full experimental data and complete results graphs are available at `http://people.cs.ubc.ca/~naghmehg/spin2010-results`.

4 Conclusions

The primary, practical take-away conclusion of this paper is that LMP is not competitive in the VC-checking paradigm. This radical reversal of recently published results highlights the difference of Boolean model checking versus VC-checking. Both are important, and our experiments show that they need different translations.

Our experiments suggest that LR is likely the best translation for the VC-checking paradigm, under most experimental conditions, and with current state-of-the-art SMT solvers. LR is also particularly easy to implement, making it our recommendation for VC-checking-based research prototypes for CBA. Surprisingly, the superiority of LR to LMP holds even with arbitrary schedules, when LR is at an artificial disadvantage. Given that LR with K round-robin *rounds* outperforms LR with K arbitrary contexts, there is no efficiency argument for using arbitrary schedules.

Another surprise was how well the brute-force EPC translation did, beating LMP in almost all experiments and LR in a few. In the VC-checking paradigm, the power of SMT and SAT solvers to quickly prune irrelevant parts of the search space and to propagate information in any direction perhaps lessens the benefit of translation insights like laziness or state space reductions, benefits that might make a big difference for a Boolean model checker. However, SMT/SAT solver performance is quirky, highly dependent on heuristics, and hard to predict.

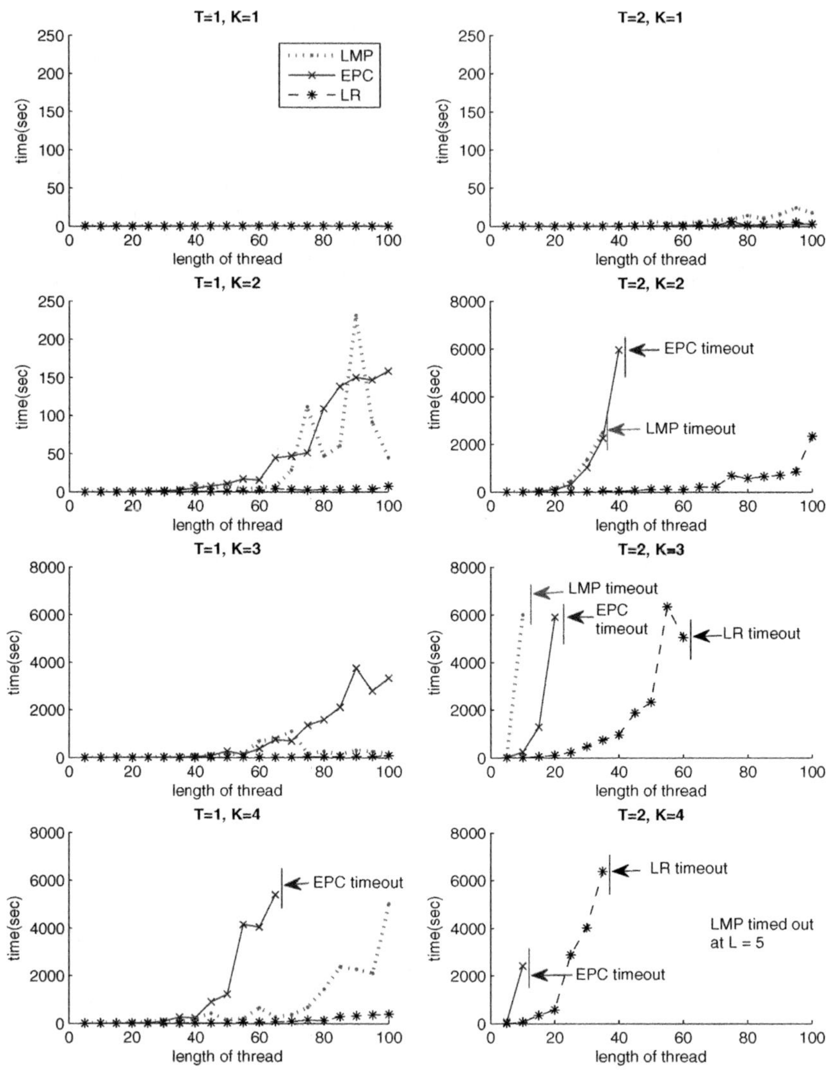

Fig. 1. Baseline Comparison. This and Fig. 2 show a representative sample of our baseline comparison (round-robin scheduling, Z3 as SMT solver), with the number of threads $T \in [1, \ldots, 4]$ (going across the pages), the context bound $K \in [1, \ldots, 4]$ (going down the page), and the length of each thread's program code L going from $5, 10, \ldots$ up to 100. (Caption continues on next page.)

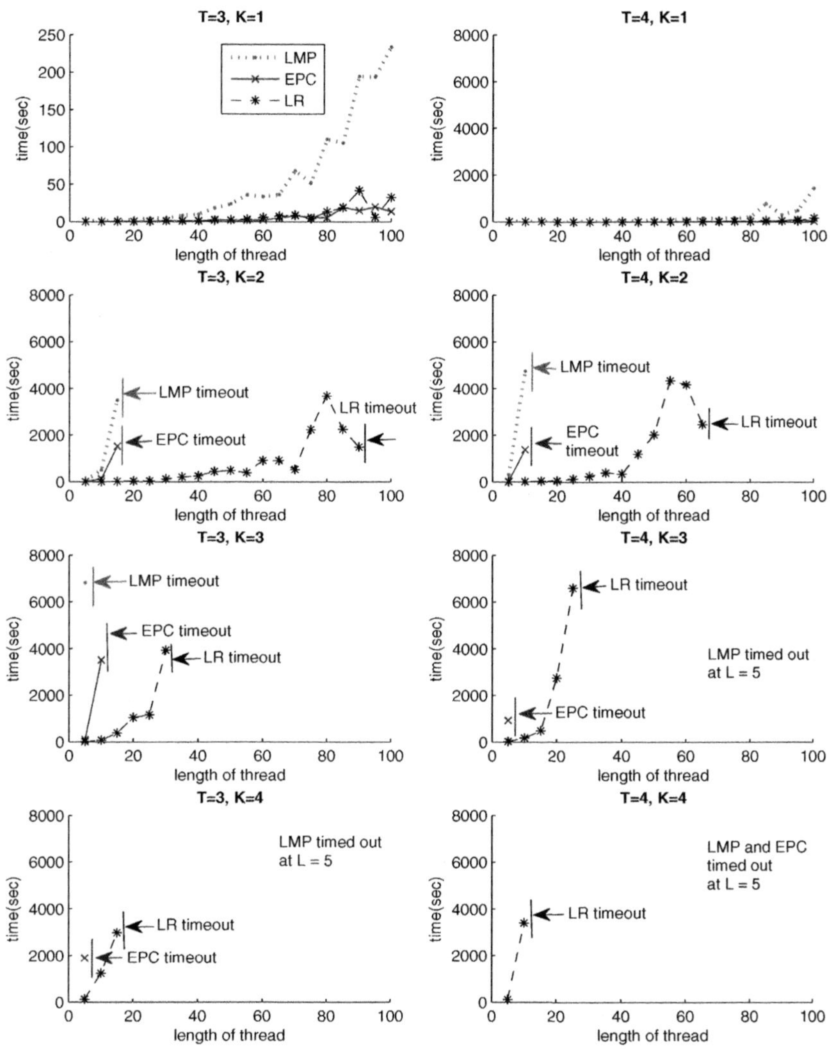

Fig. 2. Baseline Comparison (cont'd). Surprisingly, LR beats LMP, contrasting with the results in [31], and furthermore, even EPC beats LMP. The different experimental conditions in [31] likely explain this reversal: (1) While EPC and LMP do not suffer particularly under round-robin scheduling, LR has an intrinsic advantage. (2) In the VC-checking paradigm, the benefit of laziness is unclear, since the solver can propagate information in any direction. (3) On the other hand, LMP's longer dynamic code paths generate more complex VCs.

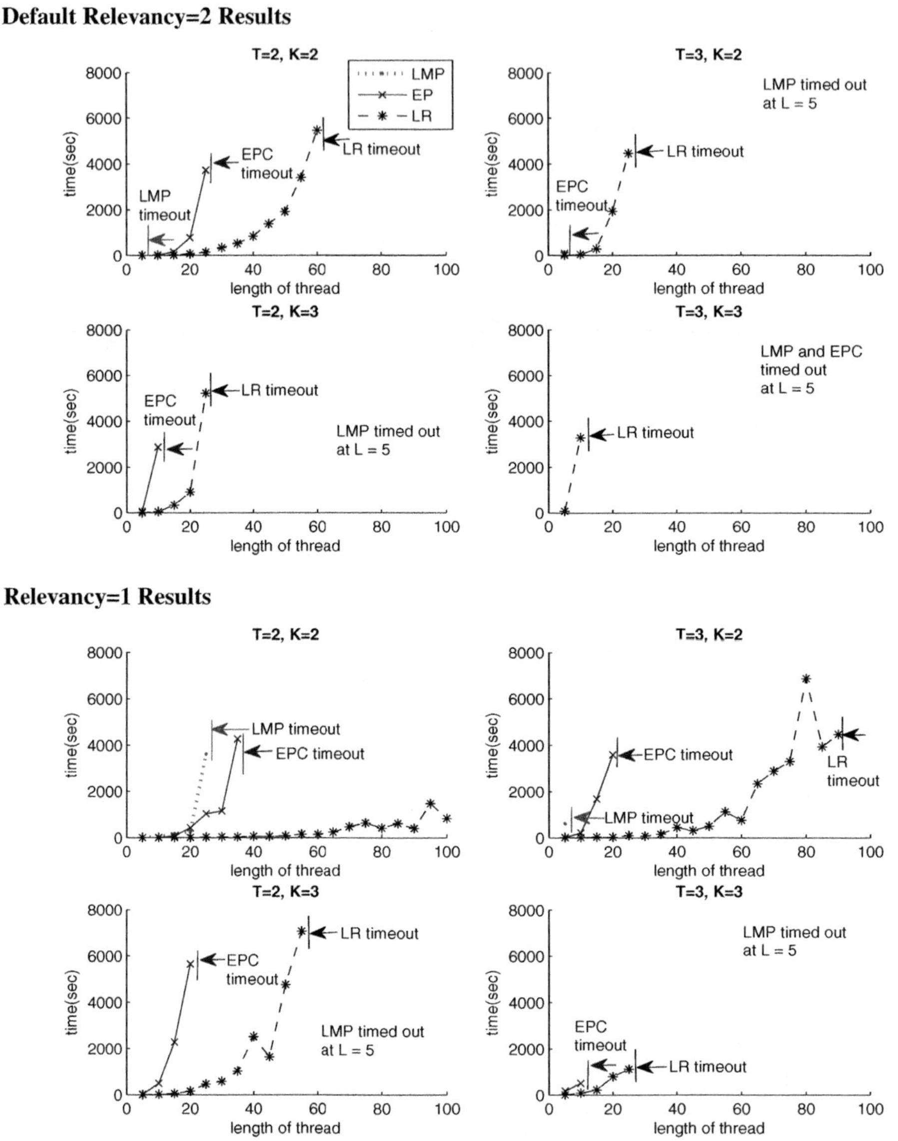

Default Relevancy=2 Results

Relevancy=1 Results

Fig. 3. Sensitivity to Z3 Parameter Tuning. For the baseline results, we had performed informal tuning of Z3 parameters. The only setting that we changed from the defaults was "relevancy propagation heuristic" that affects quantifier instantiation and assertion of atoms in the solver. We set it to 0 for best performance. Given the surprising results, though, it was imperative to run with different relevancy settings, to ensure we had not inadvertently biased our experiments. For space reasons, we show only four graphs, for $T, K \in [2,3]$, the smallest non-degenerate (T or $K = 1$) cases. The results are qualitatively the same: LR wins; LMP loses.

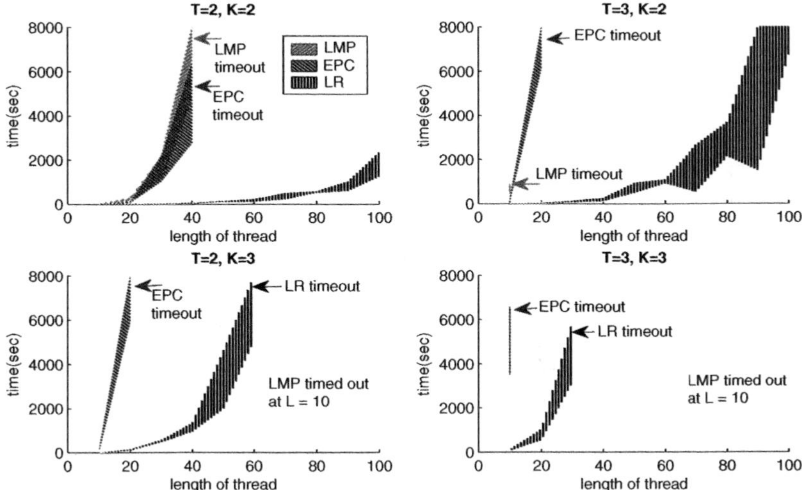

Fig. 4. Sensitivity to Random Perturbation. SMT solvers, like SAT solvers, are notoriously temperamental. To assess the robustness of our results, we repeated all of the baseline experiments three additional times, with different random number seeds. These graphs show the range of performance across different seeds. Although times vary considerably, there is almost no overlap between the translations. We can conclude that the baseline results are robust.

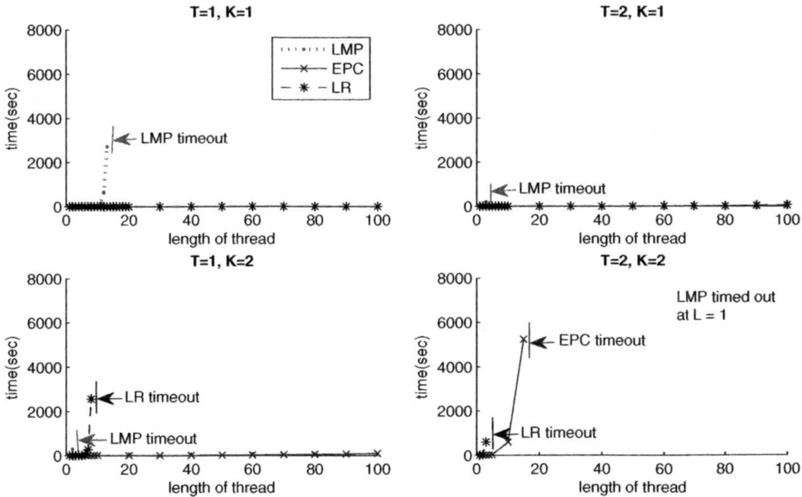

Fig. 5. Sensitivity to SMT Solver. A key question is whether our results are specific to Z3. We undertook to re-run our experiments with all publicly available SMT solvers that can handle the needed logic. Because BOOGIE generates VCs with quantifiers, the only other suitable solver from the 2009 SMT Competition is CVC3 [4]. Performance was much worse, so we have results only for the smallest values of T and K. Disturbingly, the performance order changes: EPC is the clear winner in these experiments. The choice of SMT solver determines which translation performs best! Experimental evaluation, therefore, should always include multiple solvers, or at least the fastest one available. Using a slower solver can produce misleading results.

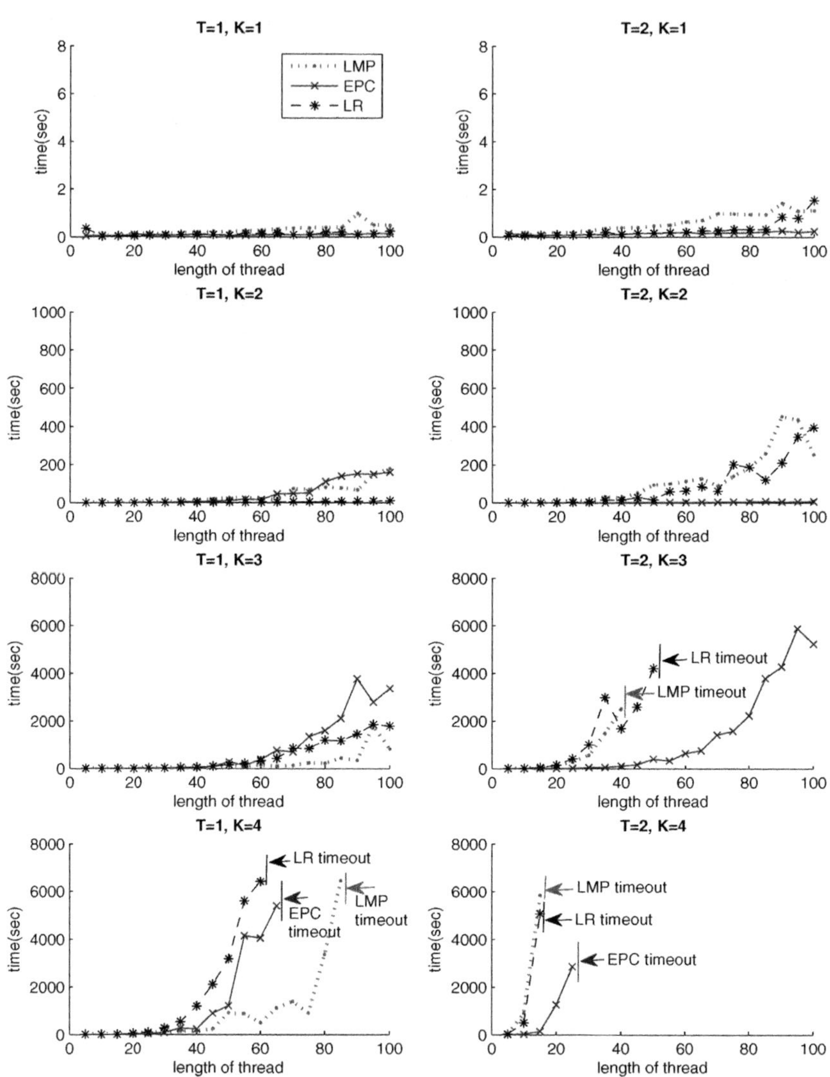

Fig. 6. Results with Arbitrary Scheduling Policy. As noted earlier, our baseline results are with round-robin scheduling, and with all translations analyzing the same number of contexts, to be fair. This and Fig. 7 show the results using an arbitrary scheduling policy with K total contexts, also with all translations analyzing the same number of contexts. Now, there is no clear winner. LMP clearly does best in the degenerate $T = 1$ cases. EPC wins in several of the mid-sized configurations. And LR is the last to timeout as T and K grow larger. (Caption continues on next page.)

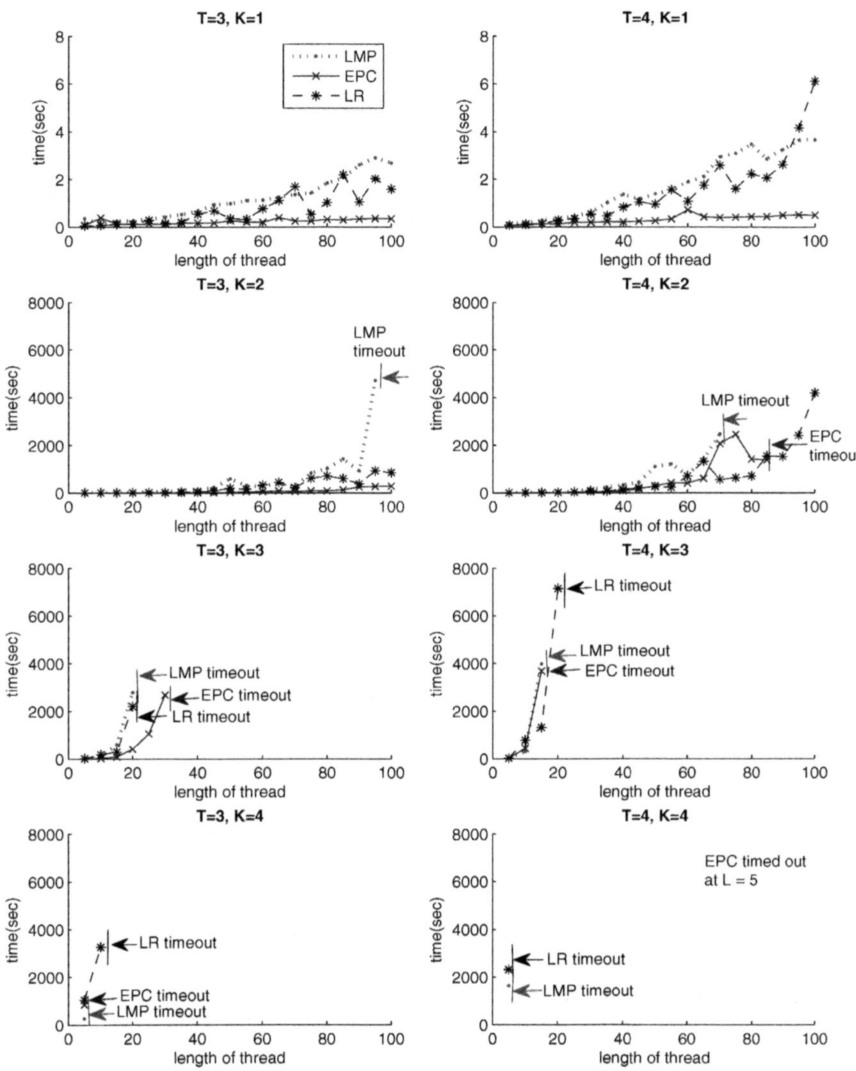

Fig. 7. Results with Arbitrary Scheduling Policy (cont'd). It would be easy to draw incorrect conclusions about algorithmic superiority if only small parts of the experimental space are explored, as is often the case. Interestingly, LR with K arbitrary contexts performs worse than LR with K round-robin *rounds*! The explanation is that LR is intrinsically round-robin, so the arbitrary-schedule K-context translation is essentially doing a round-robin K-round translation, plus extra work to ensure that only one context executes in each round. We present here results for arbitrary-schedule LR only for fairness; it is pointless in practice.

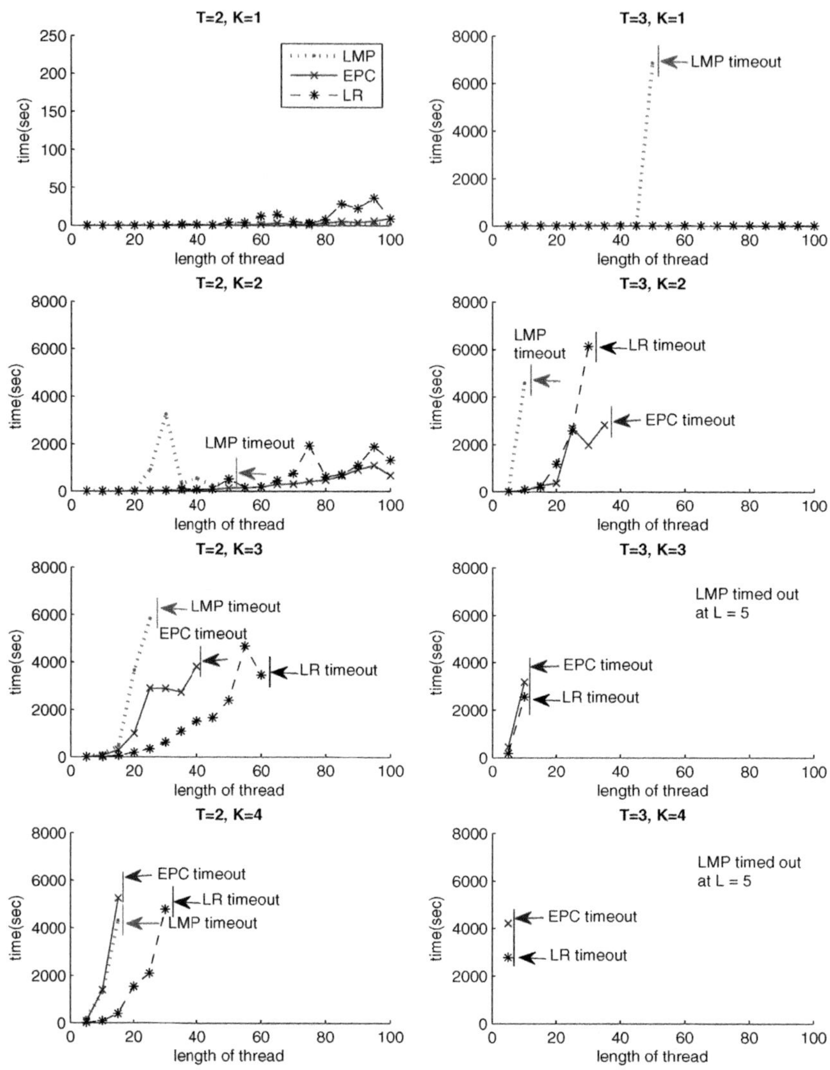

Fig. 8. Results for Bluetooth Example. As a check of our results, we also evaluated the three translations on the popular "Bluetooth driver" example. The original example had two threads: an "adder" and a "stopper". To scale the number of threads, we created additional adder threads. T indicates the total number of threads. (T starts at 2 in these graphs because we need at least 1 adder and 1 stopper.) To artificially scale program length, we duplicated the body of the adder threads. L indicates the number of copies of the original code in each thread. The runs are under the baseline conditions: round-robin scheduling with Z3 as the SMT solver. (Caption continues on next page.)

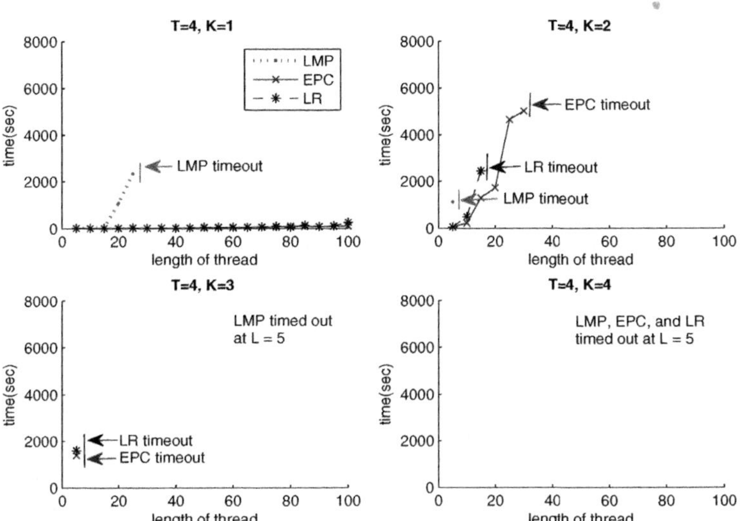

Fig. 9. Results for Bluetooth Example (cont'd). The results are similar: LMP clearly loses, but as with the results for arbitrary schedules (Figs. 6 and 7), EPC wins in several configurations.

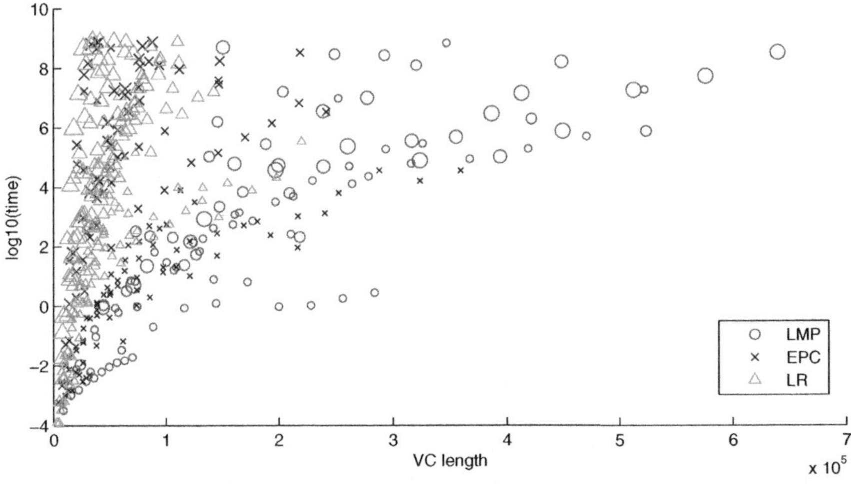

Fig. 10. Runtime vs. VC Length. One hypothesis is that VC length (and therefore static code size and complexity produced by the translation) is crucial for performance in the VC-checking paradigm. To test this hypothesis, we collected all the baseline runs, for both the microbenchmark and the Bluetooth queries, and plotted runtimes versus the size of the VC, as reported in "words" by the Unix utility wc to normalize for different variable naming conventions. In this plot, each translation is shown with a different symbol (and color). The size of the symbol is proportional to the context bound K. The data appear to cluster into multiple straight lines, indicating exponential growth, but with different bases for the different translations and problem instances. For example, LMP compensates somewhat for vastly bigger VCs with a lower-based exponent. There appears to be some correlation between K and the exponential growth rate, although this is imperfect. We observed even less correlation with T. We conjecture that some complexity measure, such as number of program paths, could predict which exponential curve a given problem family and translation approach would exhibit. (The graph is much easier to interpret in color.)

Fortunately, our experiments suggest an avenue for predicting performance. SMT runtimes tend to grow exponentially with VC length, but the different translations and parameters give different exponential curves. This suggests that the practical scalability of a translation scheme might be predicted by combining the size of the queries generated with an empirical or theoretical measure of the complexity of solving that class of query. As a crude heuristic, pick translations that keep VCs short and simple.

Disturbingly, our experiments also highlight experimental pitfalls and confounding factors. For example, using an older, slower SMT solver changes the relative ranking of the translations, implying that practical performance depends more on the interaction of a translation with a given SMT solver than on theoretical properties of the translation in isolation. If another revolution in SMT solving occurred, these translations would need to be re-evaluated. Similarly, the relative ranking of translations was sometimes different in small, degenerate corners of the parameter space. Performing only a few experiments, as if often done in this research area, could easily give misleading results. Our results can be used as a cautionary map, clarifying the landscape (e.g., VC-checking vs Boolean model checking) and highlighting pitfalls (e.g., use the fastest solver, conduct thorough experiments). These are not happy results, but they are critically important, since they challenge the assumptions and methodologies underpinning further research.

Finally, it is thought-provoking to consider how poorly all three translations scale on our microbenchmark. As noted earlier, the microbenchmark is easily solvable by other means, e.g., even the largest parameter configuration we considered ($T=4, K=4, L=100$) yields a state space of roughly only 1.6 billion states (100 program counter locations for each of 4 threads times a 4-valued context counter times a 4-valued pointer that indicates the active thread), within the reach of even explicit-state model checking. Yet, none of the translations, under any experimental setup, came anywhere close to those parameter values. There is an odd disparity between the ample empirical proof of the practical success of CBA (including our own work, finding real bugs in real industrial software, using the same LR-BOOGIE-Z3 tool chain, albeit augmented with some abstraction techniques [21]) and its poor scalability here. The explanation, we believe, is that the power of CBA with VC-checking comes from the ability to reason about and soundly abstract software features like large memories, heaps, and recursion, but not from the core exploration of interleavings, which is where classical model checking excels. We speculate there may be promising hybrids between the two approaches, or that CBA will dominate bug-finding in low-level software implementations with explicit-state model checking dominating protocol-level software verification, much as bounded model checking and explicit-state model checking complement each other in hardware verification.

References

1. Babić, D., Hu, A.J.: Calysto: Scalable and precise extended static checking. In: Intl. Conf. on Software Engineering (ICSE), pp. 211–220 (2008)
2. Ball, T., Majumdar, R., Millstein, T., Rajamani, S.K.: Automatic predicate abstraction of C programs. In: Conf. on Programming Language Design and Implementation (PLDI), pp. 203–213 (2001)
3. Barnett, M., Chang, B.-Y.E., DeLine, R., Jacobs, B., Leino, K.R.M.: Boogie: A modular reusable verifier for object-oriented programs. In: de Boer, F.S., Bonsangue, M.M., Graf, S., de Roever, W.-P. (eds.) FMCO 2005. LNCS, vol. 4111, pp. 364–387. Springer, Heidelberg (2006)

4. Barrett, C., Tinelli, C.: CVC3. In: Damm, W., Hermanns, H. (eds.) CAV 2007. LNCS, vol. 4590, pp. 298–302. Springer, Heidelberg (2007)
5. Chatterjee, S., Lahiri, S.K., Qadeer, S., Rakamarić, Z.: A reachability predicate for analyzing low-level software. In: Grumberg, O., Huth, M. (eds.) TACAS 2007. LNCS, vol. 4424, pp. 19–33. Springer, Heidelberg (2007)
6. Clarke, E.M., Biere, A., Raimi, R., Zhu, Y.: Bounded model checking using satisfiability solving. Formal Methods in System Design (FMSD) 19(1), 7–34 (2001)
7. Clarke, E.M., Emerson, E.A.: Design and synthesis of synchronization skeletons using branching-time temporal logic. In: Logic of Programs, Workshop, pp. 52–71 (1981)
8. Clarke, E.M., Kroening, D., Lerda, F.: A tool for checking ANSI-C programs. In: Jensen, K., Podelski, A. (eds.) TACAS 2004. LNCS, vol. 2988, pp. 168–176. Springer, Heidelberg (2004)
9. Clarke, E.M., Kroening, D., Sharygina, N., Yorav, K.: Predicate abstraction of ANSI–C programs using SAT. Formal Methods in System Design (FMSD) 25, 105–127 (2004)
10. Corbett, J.C., Dwyer, M.B., Hatcliff, J., Laubach, S., Pasareanu, C.S., Robby, Zheng, H.: Bandera: Extracting finite-state models from Java source code. In: Intl. Conf. on Software Engineering (ICSE), pp. 439–448 (2000)
11. de Moura, L., Bjørner, N.: Z3: An efficient SMT solver. In: Ramakrishnan, C.R., Rehof, J. (eds.) TACAS 2008. LNCS, vol. 4963, pp. 337–340. Springer, Heidelberg (2008)
12. DeLine, R., Leino, K.R.M.: BoogiePL: A typed procedural language for checking object-oriented programs. Technical Report MSR-TR-2005-70, Microsoft Research (2005)
13. Demartini, C., Iosif, R., Sisto, R.: A deadlock detection tool for concurrent Java programs. Software — Practice and Experience 29(7), 577–603 (1999)
14. Dijkstra, E.W.: Guarded commands, nondeterminacy and formal derivation of programs. Communications of the ACM 18, 453–457 (1975)
15. Esparza, J., Schwoon, S.: A BDD-based model checker for recursive programs. In: Berry, G., Comon, H., Finkel, A. (eds.) CAV 2001. LNCS, vol. 2102, pp. 324–336. Springer, Heidelberg (2001)
16. Flanagan, C., Leino, K.R.M., Lillibridge, M., Nelson, G., Saxe, J.B., Stata, R.: Extended static checking for Java. In: Conf. on Programming Language Design and Implementation (PLDI), pp. 234–245 (2002)
17. Ganai, M.K., Gupta, A.: Efficient modeling of concurrent systems in BMC. In: Havelund, K., Majumdar, R., Palsberg, J. (eds.) SPIN 2008. LNCS, vol. 5156, pp. 114–133. Springer, Heidelberg (2008)
18. Holzmann, G.J.: Design and Validation of Computer Protocols. Prentice-Hall, Englewood Cliffs (1991)
19. Holzmann, G.J., Smith, M.H.: Software model checking. In: Formal Methods for Protocol Engineering and Distributed Systems (FORTE), pp. 481–497 (1999)
20. Kahlon, V., Sankaranarayanan, S., Gupta, A.: Semantic reduction of thread interleavings in concurrent programs. In: Tools and Algorithms for the Construction and Analysis of Systems (TACAS), pp. 124–138 (2009)
21. Lahiri, S.K., Qadeer, S., Rakamarić, Z.: Static and precise detection of concurrency errors in systems code using SMT solvers. In: Bouajjani, A., Maler, O. (eds.) CAV 2009. LNCS, vol. 5643, pp. 509–524. Springer, Heidelberg (2009)
22. Lal, A., Reps, T.W.: Reducing concurrent analysis under a context bound to sequential analysis. In: Gupta, A., Malik, S. (eds.) CAV 2008. LNCS, vol. 5123, pp. 37–51. Springer, Heidelberg (2008)
23. Lal, A., Touili, T., Kidd, N., Reps, T.W.: Interprocedural analysis of concurrent programs under a context bound. In: Ramakrishnan, C.R., Rehof, J. (eds.) TACAS 2008. LNCS, vol. 4963, pp. 282–298. Springer, Heidelberg (2008)

24. Musuvathi, M., Qadeer, S.: Iterative context bounding for systematic testing of multithreaded programs. In: Conf. on Programming Language Design and Implementation (PLDI), pp. 446–455 (2007)
25. Qadeer, S., Rehof, J.: Context-bounded model checking of concurrent software. In: Halbwachs, N., Zuck, L.D. (eds.) TACAS 2005. LNCS, vol. 3440, pp. 93–107. Springer, Heidelberg (2005)
26. Qadeer, S., Wu, D.: KISS: Keep it simple and sequential. In: Conf. on Programming Language Design and Implementation (PLDI), pp. 14–24 (2004)
27. Rabinovitz, I., Grumberg, O.: Bounded model checking of concurrent programs. In: Etessami, K., Rajamani, S.K. (eds.) CAV 2005. LNCS, vol. 3576, pp. 82–97. Springer, Heidelberg (2005)
28. Rakamarić, Z., Hu, A.J.: A scalable memory model for low-level code. In: Jones, N.D., Müller-Olm, M. (eds.) VMCAI 2009. LNCS, vol. 5403, pp. 290–304. Springer, Heidelberg (2009)
29. Schulte, W., Xia, S., Smans, J., Piessens, F.: A glimpse of a verifying C compiler (extended abstract). In: C/C++ Verification Workshop, CCV (2007)
30. Suwimonteerabuth, D., Esparza, J., Schwoon, S.: Symbolic context-bounded analysis of multithreaded Java programs. In: Havelund, K., Majumdar, R., Palsberg, J. (eds.) SPIN 2008. LNCS, vol. 5156, pp. 270–287. Springer, Heidelberg (2008)
31. Torre, S.L., Madhusudan, P., Parlato, G.: Reducing context-bounded concurrent reachability to sequential reachability. In: Bouajjani, A., Maler, O. (eds.) CAV 2009. LNCS, vol. 5643, pp. 477–492. Springer, Heidelberg (2009)
32. Visser, W., Havelund, K., Brat, G.P., Park, S., Lerda, F.: Model checking programs. Automated Software Engineering 10(2), 203–232 (2003)

A Verification-Condition (VC) Generation

A VC is a logical formula whose validity implies partial correctness of the code for which it was generated. VCs are typically constructed via weakest precondition or symbolic execution. For example, consider the code `x=0; x=x+1; assert x>0`. By symbolic execution, we would determine that `x` is 0, then $0+1$, and then that the VC is $0+1>0$, which is valid. By weakest precondition, we would go backward from the `assert`, starting with $\texttt{x}>0$, then by substitution $\texttt{x}+1>0$, and again by substitution $0+1>0$, which is the same VC and is valid. Naive VC computation can blow-up, but modern algorithms create VCs that are linear in the original code size. In contrast, a model checker would typically impose a finite domain for `x`, and could go forward or backward, computing sets of values of `x` at each program point. In the extreme case of Boolean model checking, we could abstract `x` down to a single bit, representing the two possibilities $\{\texttt{x}>0, \texttt{x}\not>0\}$. The VC-checking paradigm can be viewed as an extremely lazy, symbolic model checking algorithm, which very efficiently computes symbolic formulas representing sets of states at program points, but defers all reasoning about those formulas to the decision procedure, after the program is completely analyzed. Because of this delayed analysis, VC-checking methods have difficulty with fixpoint iterations and instead typically rely on user-provided or heuristically generated invariants to break loops. On the positive side, VC generation is very efficient, good decision procedures exist that directly handle infinite domains. The decision procedures can propagate information from the entire program in any direction when solving the VC, unlike the one-step-at-a-time image computations in ordinary model checking.

One Stack to Run Them All*

Reducing Concurrent Analysis to Sequential Analysis under Priority Scheduling

Nicholas Kidd, Suresh Jagannathan, and Jan Vitek

Purdue University
{nkidd,suresh,jv}@cs.purdue.edu

Abstract. We present a reduction from a concurrent real-time program with priority preemptive scheduling to a sequential program that has the same set of behaviors. Whereas many static analyses of concurrent programs are undecidable, our reduction enables the application of any sequential program analysis to be applied to a concurrent real-time program with priority preemptive scheduling.

1 Introduction

Embedded systems are pervasive and are becoming ever more dependent on complex software with significant correctness and reliability requirements. From automobiles to the space shuttle, software is rapidly becoming the most significant part of development time of new devices. Due to the drastic costs of software errors, it is crucial that verification techniques handle the demands and specific requirements of embedded systems. The goal of this work is to broaden the applicability of known software verification techniques from sequential programs to a large class of real-time concurrent programs.

The programming model used in the vast majority of deployed devices defines a set of periodic tasks—tasks that perform computation at a regular interval (period)—that respond to or monitor events. Each task is typically assigned a priority, and tasks are scheduled by a *priority preemptive scheduler*—a scheduler that always chooses to schedule the highest-priority task that is currently runnable. A lower-priority task is preempted when a higher-priority task becomes runnable, and is rescheduled only when the higher-priority task has finished.

The main contribution of our work is a general reduction from a concurrent program with priority preemptive scheduling to a sequential program, which makes the concurrent program amenable to recent research on automated testing of sequential programs (e.g., DART [1], EXE [2], and KLEE [3], to name a few such systems). Our only two restrictions are that the concurrent program has a finite number of tasks, and that the tasks execute with interleaved semantics (e.g., on a uniprocessor). In the embedded world, these restrictions are the norm as they ensure predictability, which is oftentimes more important than absolute performance.

* Supported by NSF under grants CCF-0811631 and CCF-0701832.

J. van de Pol and M. Weber (Eds.): SPIN 2010, LNCS 6349, pp. 245–261, 2010.

For the important case of finite-data concurrent programs, (i.e., can be modeled as a Boolean program or multi-pushdown system), our reduction shows that the problem of determining the set of all possible reachable program configurations is decidable. (Deciding the set of reachable configurations subsumes many testing notions such as statement and condition coverage). While finite-data may seem restrictive, for embedded systems and especially safety-critical systems, it is often the case that a program will pre-allocate the required amount of memory to provide greater predictability (i.e., to remove unpredictable and potentially costly invocations of the memory allocator).

The reason that it is not readily apparent that a concurrent program with priority preemptive scheduling could be reduced to a sequential program is because all of the characteristics of traditional concurrent programs that make analysis difficult are still present. There are multiple threads of execution, shared state, locks, and preemption. Furthermore, each thread is likely to be non-terminating as it must execute once per period. The key insight behind our reduction is that because a preempted lower-priority thread is not rescheduled until the higher-priority thread has finished, the two threads can ***share*** the same stack. That is, preemption can be modeled as merely a function call. Thus, a concurrent (multi-stack) program can be reduced to a sequential (one-stack) program.

Another important aspect of real-time programming is avoiding ***priority inversion***. Priority inversion occurs when a higher-priority thread t_h cannot make progress because a lower-priority thread t_l has ownership of a shared resource, such as a lock. Even worse, a medium-priority thread t_m can preempt t_l, in effect giving t_m priority over t_h. Overall, priority inversion causes t_h's priority to be ***lowered*** to that of t_l so long as t_l owns the resource. Coupled with priority scheduling, priority inversion can lead to deadlock. Two common protocols [4] for addressing priority inversion include:

1. *Priority Ceiling Protocol* (PCP) statically associates with each shared resource (lock) the priority of the highest-priority thread that may acquire that resource. When a thread t acquires a resource r, t's priority is temporarily raised to r's priority, and is restored when r is released. Note that due to the way priorities are assigned to resources, r's priority must be at least as high as t.
2. *Priority Inheritance Protocol* (PIP) temporarily elevates the priority of a lower-priority thread t_l that owns a resource r required by a higher-priority thread t_h to that of t_h until t_l has released r.

In comparison, PCP is an eager (or pessimistic) protocol, while PIP is a lazy (or optimistic) protocol that avoids elevating priorities until strictly necessary. Moreover, PCP guarantees dead-lock freedom [4], whereas PIP does not.

Our second contribution is to show that configuration reachability of a concurrent finite-data program with a priority preemptive scheduler (i) remains decidable for a PCP-extended programming model, (ii) is undecidable in general for a PIP-extended programming model, and (iii) is decidable for a PIP-extended programming model with properly nested locks.

2 Reduction

A concurrent program is a shared-memory computation by a finite number of threads $t_1, \ldots, t_n$ that execute with interleaved semantics. Associated with each thread t_i, $1 \leq i \leq n$, is a priority, $\mathsf{priority}(t_i)$, and a period, $\mathsf{period}(t_i)$, in which t_i must perform its computation. We assume that each thread completes its task once per period (i.e., all deadlines are met). In addition, our abstraction of time is a *hyperperiod* H, which is the least common multiple of the periods of all threads. Observe that each thread t_i, $1 \leq i \leq n$, must execute $a_i \triangleq H/\mathsf{period}(t_i)$ times per hyperperiod H. Thus, we reduce a concurrent program with heterogeneous periods to a concurrent program with a single period, namely H, by extending the concurrent program to have a_i copies of t_i, where each copy has the same priority. For the remainder of the paper, all threads are assumed to have the same period H. Finally, each thread (copy) becomes schedulable (i.e., is awoken) non-deterministically.

Remark 1. The reduction to a single hyperperiod is a sound over-approximation. For example, a system with threads T_1 and T_2 with periods 2 resp. 3 will have three copies of T_1 and two copies of T_2 because the l.c.m. of the periods is $H = 6$. The reduction to a single period H allows the schedule $T_1T_1T_1T_2T_2$ which is not allowed in the original system. A more precise reduction can be easily encoded by adding additional scheduling constraints (i.e., a finite amount of data) to the program.

The key insight behind our reduction is that because of priority preemptive scheduling, all running threads can ***share*** the same stack. Consider the case where a thread t is executing with current stack contents u, and another thread t', such that $\mathsf{priority}(t) < \mathsf{priority}(t')$ is awoken non-deterministically. At this point, and with a traditional non-deterministic scheduler, a concurrent program must maintain two active and distinct stacks, namely u and u', because t' could be preempted at any time to allow t to resume execution. However, with ***priority*** preemptive scheduling, it is guaranteed that t' will ***not*** be preempted by t, or by any thread t'' where $\mathsf{priority}(t'') < \mathsf{priority}(t')$. Thus, t' can share the same stack at t (see Fig. 1).

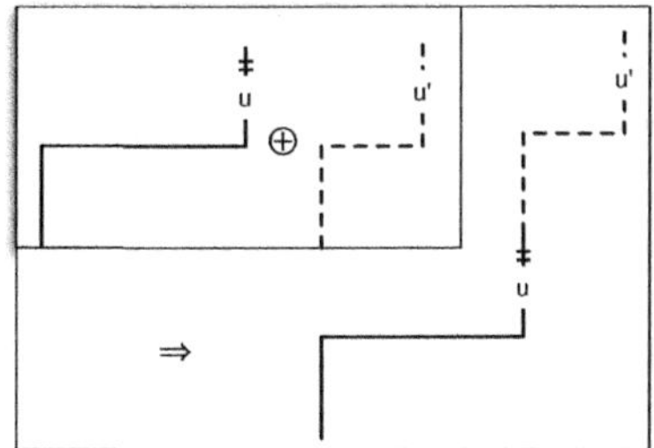

Fig. 1. Sharing stacks u and u'

The reduction is then as follows. First, the priority preemptive scheduler is made explicit by adding to the program the code shown in Fig. 2. The `Hyperperiod` procedure in Fig. 2 executes each thread one time, choosing non-deterministically a sleeping thread to execute via the *`choose`* operation, which returns an index that satisfies the supplied guard. An infinite cycle of hyperperiods is simulated by invoking `Hyperperiod` in a non-terminating loop and ensuring to reset the array `Sleeping` (see below) before doing so. During each hyperperiod, the scheduler has two tasks: (i) it must ensure

```
// Sleeping flags
Sleeping[n] = {true,...,true};
// Thread priorities
Priorities[n] = ...;
// Thread entry points
Threads[n] = ...;

// 0 => choose any thread
Prio = 0;

void Hyperperiod() {
  while (⋁_i Sleeping[i]) {
    j = choose j: Sleeping[j];
    Sleeping[j] = false;
    Threads[j].entry();
  }
}
```

```
// Wake-up higher-priority thread
void Schedule() {
  // Save current priority
  int prevPrio = Prio;
  for i in (1..n) {
    if (Priorities[i] <= Prio)
      continue;
    if (nondet() && Sleeping[i]) {
      Prio = i;
      Sleeping[i]=false;
      Threads[i].entry();
      break;
    }
  }
  // Restore priority
  Prio = prevPrio;
}
```

Fig. 2. Pseudo-code to execute one hyperperiod

that each thread t is awoken so that t can execute its task; and (ii) the wake-ups should happen non-deterministically. The first task is handled by defining a Boolean array of size n, where each entry in the array denotes whether a thread t is sleeping or not. (In Fig. 2, the array is named `Sleeping`.) The scheduler loops until all threads have been awoken and completed their periodic task.

The second task is handled by performing a source-to-source transformation on the code of each thread so that it non-deterministically invokes `Schedule` before each statement st. That is, if a thread is comprised of program statements $\mathsf{st}_1,\ldots,\mathsf{st}_k$, then the transformed program will have program statements $\mathsf{st}'_1,\ldots,\mathsf{st}'_k$, where each st' is defined as: $\mathsf{st}' \triangleq$ `Schedule();`st. In the definition of `Schedule` in Fig. 2, the function `nondet` non-deterministically returns true or false. When `Schedule` is invoked, the code of a higher-priority thread $t_{i'}$ than the thread t_i whose code is currently executing may be invoked, which corresponds to t_i being preempted by $t_{i'}$. Before executing a thread t_i by invoking `Threads[i].entry()`, the flag `Sleeping[i]` is set to false to ensure that t_i is executed exactly once per hyperperiod H.

Non-determinism plays a second role, namely, to enumerate all possible orderings of same-priority threads. With priority-preemptive scheduling, a thread will only be preempted by a *higher*-priority thread. If two threads t and t' have the same priority, and because our programming model uses non-deterministic wakeups, schedules in which t executes before t' and *vice versa* must both be considered. Non-determinism allows for both schedules to occur. Moreover, in the finite-data case that is discussed next, *pushdown-system* reachability algorithms naturally consider both schedules.

Table 1. The encoding of an ICFG's edges as PDS rules

PDS Rule	Control flow modeled
$\langle p, n_1\rangle \hookrightarrow \langle p, n_2\rangle$	Intraprocedural edge $n_1 \rightarrow n_2$
$\langle p, n_c\rangle \hookrightarrow \langle p, e_f\ r_c\rangle$	Call to f, with entry e_f, from n_c that returns to r_c
$\langle p, x_f\rangle \hookrightarrow \langle p, \epsilon\rangle$	Return from f at exit x_f

By reducing a concurrent program with priority preemptive scheduling to a sequential program, existing automated techniques for sequential programs, such as model checkers [5,6] and code-coverage techniques [1,2,3], can be applied to the generated sequential program.

3 Reduction for Multi-PDSs

For the important case of a finite-data programs, each thread can be modeled by a ***pushdown system*** (PDS), and the concurrent program as a ***multi-PDS*** [7,8,9]. (We will use the term thread and PDS interchangeably.)

Definition 1. A ***pushdown system*** (PDS) is a tuple $\mathcal{P} = (P, \Gamma, \gamma_0, \Delta)$, where P is a finite set of control states, Γ is a finite stack alphabet, γ_0 is the initial stack symbol of $\mathcal{P}$ specifying the entry point of the modeled thread, and $\Delta \subseteq (P \times \Gamma) \times (P \times \Gamma^*)$ is a finite set of rules. A rule $r \in \Delta$ is denoted by $\langle p, \gamma\rangle \hookrightarrow \langle p', u'\rangle$. A PDS ***configuration*** $\langle p \in P, u \in \Gamma^*\rangle$ is a control state along with a stack. Δ defines a transition system over the set of all configurations. From $c = \langle p, \gamma u\rangle$, $\mathcal{P}$ can make a transition to $c' = \langle p', u'u\rangle$, denoted by $c \Rightarrow c'$, if there exists a rule $\langle p, \gamma\rangle \hookrightarrow \langle p', u'\rangle \in \Delta$. The reflexive transitive closure of $\Rightarrow$ is denoted by $\Rightarrow^*$.

Without loss of generality, a pushdown rule is restricted to have at most two stack symbols appear on the right-hand side, i.e., for $\langle p, \gamma\rangle \hookrightarrow \langle p', u'\rangle \in \Delta$, $|u'| \leq 2$ [10]. A PDS naturally captures the interprocedural control flow of a thread (see Tab. 1). To model the program state, one typically encodes the global state of the program in P and the local state (i.e., local variables to a function) in Γ. In addition, parameter passing and returning a value from a callee to its caller is modeled by introducing global variables and their corresponding assignments. We direct the reader to Schwoon's thesis [10] for a detailed description.

A concurrent program consists of a set of PDSs $\mathcal{P}_1, \ldots, \mathcal{P}_n$ that share a common set of control states P. For PDS synchronization, any finite-state synchronization protocol can be embedded in P. Because in §4 we consider protocols for addressing priority-inversion in finite-data programs, we will require a mechanism to associate priorities to sections of code that manipulate shared resources (i.e., critical sections). A natural choice—and one common to real-time programming—is to use locks to synchronize execution of critical sections. Thus, we will facilitate these extensions by distinguishing the set $\boldsymbol{L}$, a finite set of *non-reentrant* locks.[1] We now require a mechanism to specify when a thread acquires and releases a lock. We assume that for a PDS $\mathcal{P} = (P, \Gamma, \gamma_0, \Delta)$ and for each lock l in $\boldsymbol{L}$, the following subsets of Δ are defined:

- $\mathsf{acq}(l \in \boldsymbol{L}, \mathcal{P})$ is the set of rules that acquire l;
- $\mathsf{rel}(l \in \boldsymbol{L}, \mathcal{P})$ is the set of rules that release l;
- $\mathsf{acq}(\mathcal{P}) \triangleq \bigcup_{l \in \boldsymbol{L}} \mathsf{acq}(l, \mathcal{P})$ is the set of rules that acquire any lock;
- $\mathsf{rel}(\mathcal{P}) \triangleq \bigcup_{l \in \boldsymbol{L}} \mathsf{rel}(l, \mathcal{P})$ is the set of rules that release any lock; and
- $\mathsf{nolock}(\mathcal{P}) \triangleq \Delta \setminus \big(\mathsf{acq}(\mathcal{P}) \cup \mathsf{rel}(\mathcal{P})\big)$ is the set of non-locking rules.

Altogether, a concurrent program consists of a global state space P, a finite set of threads $\mathcal{P}_1, \ldots, \mathcal{P}_n$ that share the same state space P, and a finite set of locks $\boldsymbol{L}$. Because a concurrent program consists of a finite number of threads $\mathcal{P}_1, \ldots, \mathcal{P}_n$, we assume that the threads are sorted according to their priority.

Definition 2. A ***multi-*PDS** is a tuple $\Pi = (P, p_0, \mathcal{P}_1, \ldots, \mathcal{P}_n, \boldsymbol{L})$, where P is the shared control state of each PDS $\mathcal{P}_i = (P, \Gamma_i, \gamma_0^i, \Delta_i)$, $1 \leq i \leq n$; $p_0 \in P$ is the initial control state; and $\boldsymbol{L} = \{l_1, \ldots, l_{|\boldsymbol{L}|}\}$ is a finite set of $|\boldsymbol{L}|$ non-reentrant locks. A ***global configuration*** $\langle p, u_1, \ldots, u_n, \bar{o}\rangle$ is a tuple consisting of:

- a control state $p \in P$ modeling the global state of Π;
- a stack u_i for each PDS $\mathcal{P}_i$, $1 \leq i \leq n$, where $u_i \in \Gamma_i^* \cup \{\top\gamma_0^i\}$ and $\top \notin \Gamma_i$ is a unique stack symbol that is used to denote a sleeping thread (discussed below); and
- an ***ownership array*** $\bar{o}$ of length $|\boldsymbol{L}|$, in which each entry indicates the owner of a given lock: for each $1 \leq j \leq |\boldsymbol{L}|$, $\bar{o}[j] \in \{0, 1, \ldots, n\}$ indicates the identity i of the PDS $\mathcal{P}_i$ that holds lock l_j (0 signifies that l_j is free). Given $\bar{o}$, a state change in which $\mathcal{P}_i$ acquires lock l_j is denoted by $\bar{o}[j \mapsto i]$, and a state change in which $\mathcal{P}_i$ releases lock l_j—setting l_j's owner to 0—is denoted by $\bar{o}[j \mapsto 0]$. Let $\bar{o}_0$ denote $\bar{o}$ with all entries set to 0.

The set of all global configurations is denoted by $\mathcal{G}$. The ***initial global configuration*** is $g_0 = \langle p_0, \top\gamma_0^1, \ldots, \top\gamma_0^n, \bar{o}_0\rangle$. $\mathcal{P}_i$ is ***active*** in a global configuration g, denoted $\mathsf{active}(g, \mathcal{P}_i)$ if its stack contents $u_i \neq \top\gamma_0^k \vee \epsilon$, which stipulates that $\mathcal{P}_i$ is neither waiting to begin execution—$u_i \neq \top\gamma_0^i$—nor has finished execution—$u_i \neq \epsilon$. The ***priority*** of g, denoted $\mathsf{priority}(g)$, is the maximum of the active threads: $\mathsf{priority}(g) = \mathsf{max}(\{\mathsf{priority}(\mathcal{P}_i) \mid \mathsf{active}(g, \mathcal{P}_i)\})$.

A global configuration $g = \langle p, u_1, \ldots, u_n, \bar{o}\rangle$ can be thought of as representing the set of (local) PDS configurations $\{\langle p, u_i\rangle \mid 1 \leq i \leq n\}$. For the initial global configuration $g_0 = \langle p_0, \top\gamma_0^1, \ldots, \top\gamma_0^n, \bar{o}_0\rangle$, the special stack symbol $\top$ denotes that each thread is waiting to begin execution.

Interleaved execution of Π is defined by the transition relation $\rightsquigarrow \subseteq \mathcal{G} \times \mathcal{G}$ on global configurations. As is customary, we will use $g \rightsquigarrow g'$ to denote that

[1] Reentrant locks that are acquired and released at procedure boundaries are reducible to non-reentrant locks [11].

$(g, g') \in\rightsquigarrow$. Intuitively, there are two types of transitions that Π can perform to go from g to g'. The first transition type is that a sleeping thread is awoken non-deterministically. In the initial global configuration g_0, the stack contents of each PDS $\mathcal{P}_i$, $1 \leq i \leq n$, is $\top\gamma_0^i$, where the special stack symbol $\top$ denotes that $\mathcal{P}_i$ is sleeping. For $\mathcal{P}_i$ to be awoken, the special stack symbol $\top$ must be popped from the top of $\mathcal{P}_i$'s stack. We observe that at a global configuration g where $\mathcal{P}_i$ is sleeping, delaying the wake-up of $\mathcal{P}_i$ until after all currently-running higher-priority threads (i.e., $\{\mathcal{P}_{i'} \mid i \neq i' \wedge \mathsf{priority}(\mathcal{P}_i) < \mathsf{priority}(\mathcal{P}_{i'}) \wedge \mathsf{active}(g, \mathcal{P}_{i'})\}$) have finished execution results in the same set of configurations being reachable from g—$\{g' \mid g \rightsquigarrow^* g'\}$—*modulo*$_\top$, where modulo$_\top$ denotes that the stacks $\top\gamma_0^i$ and γ_0^i are considered equal. The reasoning is straightforward: even if $\mathcal{P}_i$ were to be awoken, it would not be able to perform any computation steps until $\mathcal{P}_{i'}$ has finished execution, at which point non-determinism in $\rightsquigarrow$ would allow $\mathcal{P}_i$ to be awoken resulting in the same set of reachable configurations modulo$_\top$.

The second transition type is that the highest-priority thread that has already been awoken is able to update the global state and its (local) stack. Only the highest-priority thread is able to make a transition because the programming model uses a priority preemptive scheduler. We now formally define exactly when $g \rightsquigarrow g'$ holds for Π.

1. $\langle p, u_1, \ldots, \top\gamma_0^i, \ldots, u_n, \bar{o}\rangle \rightsquigarrow \langle p, u_1, \ldots, \gamma_0^i, \ldots, u_n, \bar{o}\rangle$ *iff* $\mathsf{priority}(g) < \mathsf{priority}(\mathcal{P}_i)$. Thread $\mathcal{P}_i$ is only awoken if $\mathcal{P}_i$ has a higher-priority than the currently executing thread.
2. $\langle p, u_1, \ldots, \gamma_i u_i, \ldots, u_n, \bar{o}\rangle \rightsquigarrow \langle p', u_1, \ldots, u' u_i, \ldots, u_n, \bar{o}'\rangle$ *iff* $\mathsf{priority}(g) = \mathsf{priority}(\mathcal{P}_i)$ and $r_i = \langle p, \gamma\rangle \hookrightarrow \langle p', u'\rangle \in \Delta_i$ and:
   (a) If $r_i \in \mathsf{nolock}(\mathcal{P}_i)$, then $\bar{o}' = \bar{o}$. The transition enabled by r_i does not update the state of any lock $l_j \in \boldsymbol{L}$.
   (b) If $r_i \in \mathsf{acq}(l_j \in \boldsymbol{L}, \mathcal{P}_i)$ and $\bar{o}[j] = 0$, then $\bar{o}' = \bar{o}[j \mapsto i]$. The lock l_j must be free in g, and is owned by $\mathcal{P}_i$ in g'.
   (c) If $r_i \in \mathsf{rel}(l_j \in \boldsymbol{L}, \mathcal{P}_i)$ and $\bar{o}[j] = i$, then $\bar{o}' = \bar{o}[j \mapsto 0]$. The lock l_j must be owned by $\mathcal{P}_i$ in g, and is free in g'.

The reflexive transitive closure of $\rightsquigarrow$ is denoted by $\rightsquigarrow^*$.

3.1 Model Checking Problem

As is common in PDS-based model checking [12,13,7,8], the problem of interest is to compute reachability.

Problem 1. Given Π and $g \in \mathcal{G}$, compute the set of forwards reachable configurations $G' = \{g' \mid g \rightsquigarrow^* g'\}$.

We restrict ourselves to reachability from a single global configuration g not for any technical reason, but because of the nature of embedded software. As discussed in §2, the target application consists of a finite set of periodic tasks (threads), and it is assumed that each thread has the same period and completes one task each period (i.e., makes its deadline). Hence, the concurrent program consists of an infinite cycle of periods, where for the finite-data case, the only difference between starting configurations is the initial state p, which is p_0 at program onset. Given a black box to solve *Problem 1* (i.e., to compute the set of *single-period* reachable configurations G' from $g \in \mathcal{G}$), then the set of *all* reachable configurations can be computed via repeated queries—there are only a finite number of states p to start from because P is finite, the stack of each PDS $\mathcal{P}_i$ always begins in the initial stack $\top\gamma_0^i$, and a successive period can only begin from a state p in the set $\{p \mid \langle p, \epsilon_1, \ldots, \epsilon_n, \bar{o}_0 \rangle \in G'\}$.[2]

Problem 1 is decidable for Π, and shown by reduction to context-bounded analysis (CBA) [7,14].[3]

Theorem 1. *Given $\Pi = (P, p_0, \mathcal{P}_1, \ldots, \mathcal{P}_n, \boldsymbol{L})$ and $g \in \mathcal{G}$, the set $G' = \{g' \mid g \rightsquigarrow^* g'\}$ of single-period forwards reachable configurations from g is computable in at most $O(n)$ execution contexts.*

Proof. A thread $\mathcal{P}_i$ can preempt another thread $\mathcal{P}_j$ at most one time because once $\mathcal{P}_i$ preempts $\mathcal{P}_j$, by definition $\mathcal{P}_j$ cannot restart execution until $\mathcal{P}_i$ has finished execution. Thus, the number of preemptions is bounded by $O(n)$ which also bounds the number of execution contexts by $O(n)$. □

3.2 A More Efficient Reduction

We now present a reduction from a multi-PDS Π with priority preemptive scheduling to a single PDS $\mathcal{P}_\Pi$, the benefit of which is that all of the known existing techniques for model checking PDSs, including those for expressive logics both linear and branching [12,15], can be used for model checking multi-PDSs with priority preemptive scheduling. Moreover, the most efficient algorithms for CBA [14] require creating a copy of the global state space for each execution context, resulting in an algorithm to solve *Problem 1* with complexity $O(|P \times \bar{\boldsymbol{O}}|^{2n})$, where $\bar{\boldsymbol{O}}$ is the finite set of all ownership arrays.[4] Because of priority preemptive scheduling, our reduction avoids the need to create copies, resulting in a complexity on the order of $O(|P \times \bar{\boldsymbol{O}}|^2 2^n)$, where the 2^n factor accounts for the n bits in the array `Sleeping` that track whether a thread has run during the (current) hyperperiod. In other words, our reduction adds n *bits*, whereas [14] would add n *copies* of P. (We note that [14] solves a harder problem because it allows for the non-deterministic preemption of any thread, i.e., a stack must be maintained for each thread.)

[2] We assume that each thread releases its acquired locks before completing the desired task. Otherwise, one would also have to possibly enumerate over the ownership arrays when starting a new period as well.

[3] CBA is a program analysis that only considers executions with a bounded number of execution contexts, where an execution context is one continuous (sequential) execution of a single thread (albeit there can be many execution contexts of a thread due to context switching).

[4] $\bar{\boldsymbol{O}}$ is finite because there are a finite number of locks and threads (indices), and can thus be encoded in the control state of a PDS.

Combining $\mathcal{P}_1,\ldots,\mathcal{P}_n$, and ownership arrays. The first part of the reduction follows naturally from the definition of Π, $\mathcal{G}$, and $\rightsquigarrow$ from §3. Recall that the PDSs of Π and, in particular, their constituent stack contents in a configuration $g = \langle p, u_1, \ldots, u_n, \bar{o}\rangle \in \mathcal{G}$ are sorted based on priority. Because of priority preemptive scheduling, one can view g as having a stack of stacks. For example, consider a concurrent program Π_3 that consists of three PDSs $\mathcal{P}_1$, $\mathcal{P}_2$, and $\mathcal{P}_3$ and set of locks $\boldsymbol{L}_3$, and let $g_3 = \langle p, u_1, u_2, u_3, \bar{o}\rangle$ be a configuration of Π_3. To represent g_3 as a ***single-PDS configuration*** c_3, we must rearrange the stacks into a single stack as follows: $c_3 = \langle p, u_3u_2u_1\rangle$. We must also store the ownership array $\bar{o}$ somewhere in c_3, and the natural solution is to pair it with the control state p, yielding $c_3 = \langle (p, \bar{o}), u_3u_2u_1\rangle$. Of course, if a thread has yet to be awoken (e.g., $u_3 = \top\gamma_0^3$), then it must not be included in c_3, for otherwise threads of lesser priority (e.g., $\mathcal{P}_1$ and $\mathcal{P}_2$) would not be able to make progress.

Our first step towards defining $\mathcal{P}_\Pi$ is to define the PDS $\mathcal{P}_1^n$ that models the execution of PDSs $\mathcal{P}_1, \ldots, \mathcal{P}_n$ of Π. From the above example configuration c_3, we can see that the ownership array $\bar{o}$ must be encoded in the control state, and the PDS rules of $\mathcal{P}_1^n$ must perform updates to the embedded ownership array. With $\bar{\boldsymbol{O}}$ being the set of all ownership arrays, we define for each PDS $\mathcal{P}_i$, $1 \le i \le n$, the PDS $\mathcal{P}_i'$ whose PDS rules have been modified to account for ownership arrays as follows:

Definition 3. Given a PDS $\mathcal{P}_i$ and set of ownership arrays $\bar{\boldsymbol{O}}$, define $\mathcal{P}_i'$ as follows: $\mathcal{P}_i' = (P \times \bar{\boldsymbol{O}}, \Gamma_i, \gamma_0^i, \Delta_i')$, where $P \times \bar{\boldsymbol{O}}$ encodes an ownership array in each control state of $\mathcal{P}_i'$, Γ_i and γ_0^i are unchanged from the definition of $\mathcal{P}_i$, and Δ_i' contains a set of rules for each rule $r = \langle p, \gamma\rangle \hookrightarrow \langle p', u'\rangle \in \Delta_i$, where each set is r extended to update ownership arrays, defined as follows:

- If $r \in \mathsf{acq}(l_j \in \boldsymbol{L}, \mathcal{P}_i)$, then Δ_i' contains the set of rules: $\{\langle (p, \bar{o}), \gamma\rangle \hookrightarrow \langle (p', \bar{o}'), u'\rangle \mid \bar{o} \in \bar{\boldsymbol{O}} \wedge \bar{o}[j] = 0 \wedge \bar{o}' = \bar{o}[j \mapsto i]\}$.
- If $r \in \mathsf{rel}(l_j \in \boldsymbol{L}, \mathcal{P}_i)$, then Δ_i' contains the set of rules: $\{\langle (p, \bar{o}), \gamma\rangle \hookrightarrow \langle (p', \bar{o}'), u'\rangle \mid \bar{o} \in \bar{\boldsymbol{O}} \wedge \bar{o}[j] = i \wedge \bar{o}' = \bar{o}[j \mapsto 0]\}$.
- If $r \in \mathsf{nolock}(\mathcal{P}_i)$, then Δ_i' contains the set of rules: $\{\langle (p, \bar{o}), \gamma\rangle \hookrightarrow \langle (p', \bar{o}), u'\rangle \mid \bar{o} \in \bar{\boldsymbol{O}}\}$.

Definition 4. Given $\Pi = (P, p_0, \mathcal{P}_1, \ldots, \mathcal{P}_n, \boldsymbol{L})$, and for each $\mathcal{P}_i = (P, \Gamma_i, \gamma_0^i, \Delta_i)$, $1 \le i \le n$, define $\mathcal{P}_i' = (P \times \bar{\boldsymbol{O}}, \Gamma_i, \gamma_0^i, \Delta_i')$ according to Defn. 3, then the PDS $\mathcal{P}_1^n$ that models the execution of Π's constituent PDSs is defined as: $\mathcal{P}_1^n = (P \times \bar{\boldsymbol{O}}, \Gamma_1^n = \bigcup_{i=1}^n \Gamma_i, \gamma_0^1, \Delta_1^n = \bigcup_{i=1}^n \Delta_i')$.

From Defn. 4, we can see that a control state $(p, \bar{o})$ of $\mathcal{P}_1^n$ is a pair that models a control state $p \in P$ from Π, as well as an ownership array $\bar{o}$. The stack alphabet is merely the union of the stack alphabets of the constituent PDSs. By defining $\mathcal{P}_i'$ for PDS $\mathcal{P}_i$, the set of PDS rules have been modified to properly update the ownership array when a PDS transition is made. Overall, $\mathcal{P}_1^n$ models the execution of each PDS, as well as tracking the ownership status of each lock $l \in \boldsymbol{L}$. What is missing is the priority preemptive scheduler that non-deterministically awakens threads and schedules the highest-priority active thread.

Explicit Scheduler. The scheduler shown in Fig. 2 on page 248 is finite-data (i.e., a Boolean program [16]), and thus convertible into a PDS [10], which we will refer to as $\mathcal{P}_{\text{sched}} = (P_{\text{sched}}, \Gamma_{\text{sched}}, \gamma_H, \Delta_{\text{sched}})$, where

- $P_{\text{sched}} = \{1 \dots n\} \times \{0,1\}^n$ is a pair where the first component holds the current value of `Prio`, and the second component is the Boolean array `Sleeping`.[5]
- $\Gamma_{\text{sched}} = \{1 \dots n\} \times \mathsf{Locs}$ is a pair where the first component is the current value of `prevPrio` and the second component is the set of program locations for the code in Fig. 2.
- γ_H is the program location for the start of the `Hyperperiod` procedure in Fig. 2.
- Δ_{sched} is defined using standard Boolean program-to-PDS conversion [10]. (Essentially, interprocedural control flow is encoded via the template in Tab. 1, and global resp. local Boolean variables are encoded in the PDS control state P resp. stack alphabet Γ.)

Combining P_1^n with $\mathcal{P}_{sched}$. We now define from $\mathcal{P}_1^n$ and $\mathcal{P}_{\text{sched}}$, the PDS $\mathcal{P}_\Pi$ whose transition system $\Rightarrow$ simulates the multi-PDS Π with transition system $\leadsto$. Observe that the transition system of P_Π must include both $\mathcal{P}_1^n$ and $\mathcal{P}_{\text{sched}}$, and thus to the first degree the two PDSs are joined together. The only modification to either PDS is to stitch the set of control states together, and reflect this join in the final set of PDS rules of $\mathcal{P}_\Pi$.

Definition 5. Given $\mathcal{P}_1^n = (P_1^n, \Gamma_1^n, \gamma, \Delta_1^n)$ and $\mathcal{P}_{\text{sched}} = (P_{\text{sched}}, \Gamma_{\text{sched}}, \gamma_H, \Delta_{\text{sched}})$, define $\mathcal{P}_\Pi = (P_\Pi, \Gamma_\Pi, \gamma_H, \Delta_\Pi)$, where

- $P_\Pi = P_{\text{sched}} \times P_1^n$ is a pair where each component holds a value from its constituent set of control states. Recall that $P_{\text{sched}} = \{1 \dots n\} \times \{0,1\}^n$ is a priority and an array that determines whether a PDS is sleeping or not, and $P_1^n = P \times \bar{\boldsymbol{O}}$ is P, the original set of control states of Π, paired with $\bar{\boldsymbol{O}}$, the set of ownership arrays.
- $\Gamma_\Pi = \Gamma_1^n \cup \Gamma_{\text{sched}}$ is the union of the constituent stack symbols.
- γ_H is the program location for the start of the `Hyperperiod` procedure in Fig. 2.
- Δ_Π consists of the following two sets of rules:
  1. For each rule $r = \langle (p, \bar{o}), \gamma\rangle \hookrightarrow \langle (p', \bar{o}'), u'\rangle \in \Delta_1^n$ and control state $(\varsigma, \bar{b}) \in P_{\text{sched}}$, Δ_Π contains the set of rules:

     $$\{\langle(\varsigma, \bar{b}, p, \bar{o}), \gamma\rangle \hookrightarrow \langle(\varsigma, \bar{b}, p', \bar{o}'), u'\rangle, \langle(\varsigma, \bar{b}, p, \bar{o}), \gamma\rangle \hookrightarrow \langle(\varsigma, \bar{b}, p, \bar{o}), \gamma_{n_5}\gamma\rangle\}$$

     In the set, the first rule is r extended with a control state from P_{sched}. The control state is not modified as the rules from Δ_1^n do not modify the state of the scheduler. The second rule implements a function call to `Schedule` in Fig. 2, which will non-deterministically invoke the code of a higher-priority thread or return. Moreover, from a configuration $\langle(\varsigma, \bar{b}, p, \bar{o}), \gamma u\rangle$ of $\mathcal{P}_\Pi$, $\mathcal{P}_\Pi$ non-deterministically chooses to simulate $\mathcal{P}_1^n$ or $\mathcal{P}_{\text{sched}}$ depending on which rule is invoked.

[5] The number of distinct priorities is bounded by n because there are only n threads.

2. For each rule $r = \langle(\varsigma, \bar{b}), \gamma\rangle \hookrightarrow \langle(\varsigma', \bar{b}'), u'\rangle \in \Delta_{\text{sched}}$ and control state $(p, \bar{o}) \in P_1^n$, Δ_Π contains the set of rules:

$$\{\langle(\varsigma, \bar{b}, p, \bar{o}), \gamma\rangle \hookrightarrow \langle(\varsigma', \bar{b}', p, \bar{o}), u'\rangle\}.$$

These rules combine the rules of $\mathcal{P}_{\text{sched}}$ with the control states P_1^n of $\mathcal{P}_1^n$. Similar to the above set of rules, the control state of $\mathcal{P}_1^n$ is "passed through" unmodified because the scheduler does not affect that control state of $\mathcal{P}_1^n$.

3.3 Correctness

Correctness of the reduction is established by defining a weak bisimulation between the transition systems of Π and $\mathcal{P}_\Pi$. Weak bisimulation is used because in $\mathcal{P}_\Pi$, the scheduler is made explicit whereas it is implicit in the definition of $\rightsquigarrow$ for Π. Thus, configurations of $\mathcal{P}_\Pi$ should only be considered ***visible*** if the top-of-stack symbol is not a member of Γ_{sched}. Formally, for a configuration $c = \langle(\varsigma, \bar{b}, p, \bar{o}), \gamma u\rangle$ of $\mathcal{P}_\Pi$, we define $\mathsf{vis}(c) = \gamma \notin (\Gamma_{\text{sched}} \setminus \{\gamma_H\})$, and extend vis to sets of configurations in the usual way. Finally, we define the transition relation $\Rightarrow_{\mathsf{vis}}$ between visible configurations of $\mathcal{P}_\Pi$ as follows:

$$\left\{ c \Rightarrow_{\mathsf{vis}} c' \mid \mathsf{vis}(c) \wedge \mathsf{vis}(c') \wedge \exists c_1, \ldots, c_k : c \Rightarrow c_1 \Rightarrow \ldots \Rightarrow c_k \Rightarrow c' \bigwedge_{1 \le i \le k} \neg\mathsf{vis}(c_i) \right\}$$

We define the relation $\succ \subseteq \mathcal{G} \times \mathsf{vis}(\mathcal{C})$ from the set $\mathcal{G}$ of all global configurations of Π to the set $\mathsf{vis}(\mathcal{C})$ of all visible configurations of $\mathcal{P}_\Pi$ as follows: $g \succ c$ *iff* $g = \langle p, u_1, \ldots, u_n, \bar{o}\rangle \wedge c = \langle(\mathsf{priority}(g), \bar{b}, p, \bar{o}), u_n \circ \cdots \circ u_1\rangle$, where $\bar{b}[i] \triangleq u_i = \top\gamma_0^i$, $\circ$ denotes stack concatenation with the exception that the "sleeping stack" $\top\gamma_0^i$ for thread $\mathcal{P}_i$ is considered a neutral element with respect to concatenation. In addition, we special case the initial global configuration by defining $g_0 \succ \langle(0, \bar{b}, p_0, \bar{o}_0), \gamma_H\rangle$ (note that $\bar{b}$ is true in each position because $u_i = \top\gamma_0^i$ for all i in g_0).

Theorem 2. *The binary relation* $\succ \subseteq \mathcal{G} \times \mathsf{vis}(\mathcal{C})$ *is a weak bisimulation between the transition systems* $(\mathcal{G}, \rightsquigarrow)$ *and* $(\mathcal{C}, \Rightarrow_{\mathsf{vis}})$ *of* Π *and* $\mathcal{P}_\Pi$*, respectively.*

Proof (Sketch). The proof proceeds by showing that for $g \succ c$ and $g \rightsquigarrow g'$, then there exists a configuration $c' \in \mathsf{vis}(\mathcal{C})$ such that $c \Rightarrow_{\mathsf{vis}} c'$ and $g' \succ c'$. Likewise, if $g \succ c$ and $c \Rightarrow_{\mathsf{vis}} c''$, then there exists a global configuration g'' such that $g \rightsquigarrow g''$ and $g'' \succ c''$. The complete proof is given in the accompanying technical report [17]. □

4 Priority Inversion

In systems with priority preemptive scheduling, a situation known as ***priority inversion*** occurs when a higher-priority thread $\mathcal{P}_h$ cannot make progress because it waits on a resource (lock) currently owned by a lower-priority thread $\mathcal{P}_l$. Two protocols for addressing priority inversion are Priority Ceiling Protocol (PCP) and Priority Inheritance Protocol (PIP). We next define each protocol, and show that Problem 1 is (i) decidable for PCP-extended semantics, (ii) undecidable in general for PIP-extended semantics, and (iii) decidable for PIP-extended semantics when lock usage is properly nested.

4.1 Priority Ceiling Protocol

Priority Ceiling Protocol (PCP) statically associates with each shared resource (lock) the priority of the highest-priority thread that may acquire that resource. When a thread acquires a resource, that thread's priority is temporarily set to the priority of the resource, and is restored when the resource is released.

A multi-PDS Π is extended as follows to define the PCP-extended semantics:

1. Π is equipped with a map $\mathcal{M}_{\boldsymbol{L}}$ from (sets of) locks to (sets of) priorities.
2. For a global configuration $g = \langle p, u_1, \ldots, u_n, \bar{o} \rangle$, define $\mathsf{LocksHeld}(\mathcal{P}_i) = \{l_j \mid \bar{o}[j] = i\}$ to be the set of locks held by $\mathcal{P}_i$ at configuration g.
3. The PCP-extended priority of $\mathcal{P}_i$, denoted by $\mathsf{priority}_{\mathsf{PCP}}(\mathcal{P}_i)$, is the maximum of $\mathcal{P}_i$'s statically determined priority and of the set of locks held by $\mathcal{P}_i$: $\mathsf{priority}_{\mathsf{PCP}} = \mathsf{max}(\mathsf{priority}(\mathcal{P}_i), \mathcal{M}_{\boldsymbol{L}}(\mathsf{LocksHeld}(\mathcal{P}_i)))$.

We now show that for the PCP-extended semantics, *Problem 1* remains decidable. Decidability follows from Thm. 1. Though not presented here, it is also possible to extend the construction of $\mathcal{P}_\Pi$ to support PCP-extended semantics, which would benefit from the improved complexity.

Theorem 3. *For concurrent program $\Pi = (P, p_0, \mathcal{P}_1, \ldots, \mathcal{P}_n, \boldsymbol{L}, \mathcal{M}_{\boldsymbol{L}})$ with priority preemptive scheduling and PCP-extended semantics,* Problem 1 *is decidable.*

Proof. Thm. 3 follows from Thm. 1. PCP-extended semantics reduces the number of threads that can preempt the currently executing thread $\mathcal{P}_i$: if $\mathcal{P}_i$ has acquired a lock l_j such that $\mathcal{M}_{\boldsymbol{L}}(l_j) > \mathsf{priority}(\mathcal{P}_i)$, then fewer threads can preempt $\mathcal{P}_i$ until $\mathcal{P}_i$ releases l_j. Thus, the number of execution contexts remains bounded by $O(n)$ because the number of valid schedules (i.e., preemptions) of PCP-extended semantics is a subset of non-extended semantics, and the problem is decidable. □

4.2 Priority Inheritance Protocol

Priority Inheritance Protocol (PIP) temporarily elevates the priority of a low-priority thread that owns a resource required by a high-priority thread to that of the high-priority thread until it has released the resource. The PIP-extended semantics is defined by extending Π in the following ways:

1. Let $\Gamma = \bigcup_i \Gamma_i$. Extend each Γ_i, $1 \leq i \leq n$, with the set of fresh stack symbols $\{\bot_l \mid l \in \boldsymbol{L}\}$ where for each $l \in \boldsymbol{L}$, $\bot_l \notin \Gamma$. The new symbol $\bot_l$ is used to denote that a thread is waiting to acquire the lock l.

2. For a global configuration $g = \langle p, u_1, \ldots, u_n, \bar{o} \rangle$ and lock l, define $\mathsf{Waiting}(l)$ to be the set of threads whose top-of-stack symbol is $\bot_l$, i.e., $\mathsf{Waiting}(l) = \{\mathcal{P}_i \mid u_i = \bot_l u_i' \wedge u_i' \in \Gamma_i^*\}$. The set $\mathsf{Waiting}(l)$ is the set of threads that are blocked waiting to acquire the lock l. We extend $\mathsf{Waiting}$ to operate over sets of locks in the natural way.
3. The PIP-extended priority of thread $\mathcal{P}_i$, denoted by $\mathsf{priority}_{\mathsf{PIP}}(\mathcal{P}_i)$, is defined as the maximum of $\mathcal{P}_i$'s statically determined priority and of the threads that wait on a lock owned by $\mathcal{P}_i$:

$$\mathsf{priority}_{\mathsf{PIP}}(\mathcal{P}_i) = \max(\mathsf{priority}(\mathcal{P}_i), \mathsf{priority}_{\mathsf{PIP}}(\mathsf{Waiting}(\mathsf{LocksHeld}(\mathcal{P}_i)))).$$

   The recurrence of $\mathsf{priority}_{\mathsf{PIP}}$ in its own definition ensures that $\mathcal{P}_i$'s priority includes the transitive closure of all threads that are blocked because of the locks $\mathcal{P}_i$ holds, i.e., the threads waiting on locks held by $\mathcal{P}_i$, the threads waiting on locks held by those threads, and so on.
4. Extend $\rightsquigarrow$ to include transitions to and from global configurations where threads are waiting to acquire a lock l as follows:
   (a) $g = \langle p, u_1, \ldots, \gamma_i u_i, \ldots, u_n, \bar{o} \rangle \rightsquigarrow \langle p, u_1, \ldots, \bot_l \gamma_i u_i, \ldots, u_n, \bar{o} \rangle$ *iff* $\mathsf{priority}(g) = \mathsf{priority}(\mathcal{P}_i)$ and $r_i \in \mathsf{acq}(l \in \boldsymbol{L}, \mathcal{P}_i)$ and $\bar{o}[l] \neq 0$. This rule defines a set of transitions where the highest-priority thread in global configuration g attempts to acquire a currently held lock l. Because l is held by another thread, $\mathcal{P}_i$ makes a transition to the waiting state by pushing $\bot_l$ on the top of its stack.[6]
   (b) $g = \langle p, u_1, \ldots, \gamma_i u_i, \ldots, u_n, \bar{o} \rangle \rightsquigarrow \langle p', u_1', \ldots, u' u_i, \ldots, u_n', \bar{o}' \rangle$ *iff* $\mathsf{priority}(g) = \mathsf{priority}(\mathcal{P}_i)$ and $r_i = \langle p, \gamma_i \rangle \hookrightarrow \langle p', u' \rangle$ and $r_i \in \mathsf{rel}(l, \mathcal{P}_i)$, where $\bar{o}' = \bar{o}[l \mapsto 0]$ and $u_k' = u_k''$ if $u_k = \bot_l u_k''$ and u_k otherwise. By removing $\bot_l$ from the top of the stack of all threads, those threads that were waiting to acquire l can now re-attempt to do so (while still adhering to priority scheduling).

Each of the listed modifications extends Π by only a finite amount of data and hence the same effect could be achieved by augmenting Π with additional state and PDS rules to encode the scheduling logic.

We consider two cases, that of non-nested and nested lock usage, where lock usage is said to be properly nested if for all program paths, locks are released in the opposite order in which they were acquired. We show that *Problem 1* for a concurrent program with PIP-extended semantics is undecidable in general, and decidable for properly nested locks.

Non-nested locks. When lock usage is not restricted to proper nesting, *Problem 1* for a concurrent program with PIP-extended semantics is undecidable. The

[6] We assume that if PDS $\mathcal{P}_i$ attempts to acquire a lock it has no other transition that can fire from (local) configuration $\langle p, \gamma_i u_i \rangle$. (Such can be made the case via the addition of new stack symbols and rules.) Otherwise, when $\mathcal{P}_i$ is released from waiting (see the next item), it could non-deterministically decide to *not* acquire the lock and hence violate priority scheduling.

proof of undecidability follows from Kahlon et al. [8]. Consider a 2-PDS with three locks $(P, p_0, \mathcal{P}_1, \mathcal{P}_2, \{l_1, l_2, l_3\})$, where $\mathcal{P}_2$ has a higher priority (2) than $\mathcal{P}_1$ (1). One way to show that reachability analysis is undecidable in general for such a system is to develop a scenario where $\mathcal{P}_1$ and $\mathcal{P}_2$ move in lock-step, which would allow the 2-PDS to determine the emptiness of the intersection of two context-free languages—a well-known undecidable problem. To make P_1 and $\mathcal{P}_2$ move in lock-step we must use the PIP-extended semantics. Namely, the PDSs need to acquire and release locks in such a fashion that $\mathcal{P}_2$, which has a higher priority than $\mathcal{P}_1$, repeatedly needs to acquire a lock that is held by $\mathcal{P}_1$. Thus, $\mathcal{P}_1$ will repeatedly inherit $\mathcal{P}_2$'s priority so that it can release the lock.

In [8], this is accomplished by acquiring and releasing the three locks l_{1-3} in a cycle using hand-over-hand locking. Assume that $\mathcal{P}_1$ currently owns l_1, then $\mathcal{P}_1$ will first acquire l_2 before releasing l_1, and subsequently will acquire l_3 before releasing l_2, and so on *ad infinitum*. In the same scenario, assume that $\mathcal{P}_2$, which in our programming model has a higher priority than $\mathcal{P}_1$, currently owns l_2 and acquires and releases the locks in the same fashion. We can see then that $\mathcal{P}_2$ will acquire l_3, release l_2, and then attempt to acquire l_1, which causes $\mathcal{P}_1$ to inherit the priority of $\mathcal{P}_2$. However, instead of reaching a state when $\mathcal{P}_1$ releases the resources needed by $\mathcal{P}_2$, $\mathcal{P}_1$ acquired l_2 and then releases l_1, which will cause $\mathcal{P}_2$ to again wait on $\mathcal{P}_1$ then next time it completes the cycle and needs l_2. The end result is that $\mathcal{P}_1$ and $\mathcal{P}_2$ chase each other around the lock cycle, which leads to an unbounded number of execution contexts and the ability to solve undecidable problems.[7]

Theorem 4. *For concurrent program $\Pi = (P, p_0, \mathcal{P}_1, \ldots, \mathcal{P}_n, \boldsymbol{L})$ with priority preemptive scheduling and PIP-extended semantics,* Problem 1 *is undecidable.*

Proof. The proof follows from the proof of *Theorem 8* [8, Section 11]. □

Nested locks. When lock usage is properly nested, *Problem 1* is decidable for the PIP-extended semantics. The proof is by reduction to CBA.

Theorem 5. *For concurrent program $\Pi = (P, p_0, \mathcal{P}_1, \ldots, \mathcal{P}_n, \boldsymbol{L})$ with priority preemptive scheduling, PIP-extended semantics, and nested locks,* Problem 1 *is decidable.*

Proof. From Thm. 1, each thread $\mathcal{P}_i$ can still perform at most one preemption. Once $\mathcal{P}_i$ is executing, it can cause lower-priority threads to inherit its priority at most $|\boldsymbol{L}|$ times because lock usage is properly nested and hence the number of locks held by a lower-priority thread is monotonically decreasing with each priority inheritance. Thus, for n threads there is at most one preemption and $|\boldsymbol{L}|$ inheritances per thread which bounds the number of execution contexts by $O(n|\boldsymbol{L}|)$. □

[7] For the reader concerned with reaching a configuration where $\mathcal{P}_1$ owns l_1 and $\mathcal{P}_2$ owns l_2, refer to [8, Appendix].

5 Related Work

Lal and Reps [14] gave a reduction from analysis of a concurrent program under a context bound to analysis of a sequential program. A context bound is required because reachability analysis is undecidable in general for their programming model. By considering only programs that run under priority preemptive scheduling (and not the general preemption model considered by Lal and Reps), the problem becomes decidable. Hence, our reduction is sound and complete, i.e., it is not an under-approximation aimed at bug-finding but a technique for verifying properties of concurrent real-time programs.

Jhala and Majumdar [18] showed that interprocedural analysis of concurrent asynchronous programs is decidable. Whereas they take advantage of asynchrony, we take advantage of having a priority preemptive scheduler. Atig et al. [19] generalized the asynchronous programming model to allow for a finite number of priority levels. They show that reachability analysis of the more general programming model is decidable by reduction to the reachability problem of Petri nets with inhibitor arcs. Their model is more general; however, they do not consider important protocols for addressing priority inversion and moreover our reduction to a single-PDS is more efficient.

KISS [20] coined the merging of two-threaded programs into single-threaded programs. Our scheduler concretization is the generalization of their technique where thread T_1 non-deterministically invokes thread T_2 and the return to T_1 is also non-deterministic. We take advantage of the properties of priority preemptive scheduling to show that the model checking problem is in fact decidable.

Lindstrom et al. [21] use Java PathFinder (JPF) [22] to model check Real-Time Java [23]. While they also consider priority preemptive scheduling, and other RTSJ details not covered here, their approach is a bug-finding approach because JPF is an explicit state model checker that in general cannot explore the entire state space.

6 Concluding Remarks

Our reduction shows that a concurrent real-time program is, in essence, a sequential program under the covers. By reducing the multi-PDS Π to a PDS $\mathcal{P}_\Pi$, we are able to leverage efficient algorithms for sequential program analysis to an important class of concurrent ones. A limitation of our approach is the lack of a model of time. For future work, we intend to consider how timed automata [24] could be integrated with Π, and how it would affect the reduction to $\mathcal{P}_\Pi$.

Acknowledgements. The authors would like to thank Tomas Kalibera, Akash Lal, and Pavel Parizek.

References

1. Godefroid, P., Klarlund, N., Sen, K.: Dart: Directed automated random testing. In: PLDI 2005: Proceedings of the 2005 ACM SIGPLAN Conference on Programming Language Design and Implementation, pp. 213–223. ACM, New York (2005)

2. Cadar, C., Ganesh, V., Pawlowski, P.M., Dill, D.L., Engler, D.R.: Exe: Automatically generating inputs of death. ACM Trans. Inf. Syst. Secur. 12(2), 1–38 (2008)
3. Cadar, C., Dunbar, D., Engler, D.R.: Klee: Unassisted and automatic generation of high-coverage tests for complex systems programs. In: 8th USENIX Symposium on Operating Systems Design and Implementation, pp. 209–224. USENIX Association (2008)
4. Sha, L., Rajkumar, R., Lehoczky, J.P.: Priority inheritance protocols: An approach to real-time synchronization. IEEE Trans. Comput. 39(9), 1175–1185 (1990)
5. Ball, T., Rajamani, S.: Automatically validating temporal safety properties of interfaces. In: Dwyer, M.B. (ed.) SPIN 2001. LNCS, vol. 2057, pp. 103–122. Springer, Heidelberg (2001)
6. Henzinger, T., Jhala, R., Majumdar, R., Sutre, G.: Lazy abstraction. In: Symposium on Principles of Programming Languages, pp. 58–70. ACM, New York (2002)
7. Qadeer, S., Rehof, J.: Context-bounded model checking of concurrent software. In: Halbwachs, N., Zuck, L.D. (eds.) TACAS 2005. LNCS, vol. 3440, pp. 93–107. Springer, Heidelberg (2005)
8. Kahlon, V., Ivancic, F., Gupta, A.: Reasoning about threads communicating via locks. In: Etessami, K., Rajamani, S.K. (eds.) CAV 2005. LNCS, vol. 3576, pp. 505–518. Springer, Heidelberg (2005)
9. Kahlon, V., Gupta, A.: On the analysis of interacting pushdown systems. In: Symposium on Principles of Programming Languages, pp. 303–314. ACM, New York (2007)
10. Schwoon, S.: Model-Checking Pushdown Systems. PhD thesis, Technische Universität München (2002)
11. Kidd, N., Lal, A., Reps, T.: Language strength reduction. In: Alpuente, M., Vidal, G. (eds.) SAS 2008. LNCS, vol. 5079, pp. 283–298. Springer, Heidelberg (2008)
12. Bouajjani, A., Esparza, J., Maler, O.: Reachability analysis of pushdown automata: Application to model checking. In: Mazurkiewicz, A., Winkowski, J. (eds.) CONCUR 1997. LNCS, vol. 1243, pp. 135–150. Springer, Heidelberg (1997)
13. Finkel, A., Willems, B., Wolper, P.: A direct symbolic approach to model checking pushdown systems. Elec. Notes in Theor. Comp. Sci. 9 (1997)
14. Lal, A., Reps, T.: Reducing concurrent analysis under a context bound to sequential analysis. In: Gupta, A., Malik, S. (eds.) CAV 2008. LNCS, vol. 5123, pp. 37–51. Springer, Heidelberg (2008)
15. Walukiewicz, I.: Model checking CTL properties of pushdown systems. In: Kapoor, S., Prasad, S. (eds.) FST TCS 2000. LNCS, vol. 1974, pp. 127–138. Springer, Heidelberg (2000)
16. Ball, T., Rajamani, S.K.: Bebop: a path-sensitive interprocedural dataflow engine. In: PASTE 2001: Proceedings of the 2001 ACM SIGPLAN-SIGSOFT workshop on Program analysis for software tools and engineering, pp. 97–103. ACM, New York (2001)
17. Kidd, N., Jagannathan, S., Vitek, J.: One stack to run them all. Technical Report 10-005, Purdue University (May 2010)
18. Jhala, R., Majumdar, R.: Interprocedural analysis of asynchronous programs. In: POPL 2007: Proceedings of the 34th annual ACM SIGPLAN-SIGACT Symposium on Principles of Programming Languages, pp. 339–350. ACM, New York (2007)
19. Atig, M.F., Bouajjani, A., Touili, T.: Analyzing asynchronous programs with preemption. In: IARCS Annual Conference on Foundations of Software Technology and Theoretical Computer Science, Schloss Dagstuhl - Leibniz-Zentrum Fuer Informatik, pp. 37–48 (2008)

20. Qadeer, S., Wu, D.: Kiss: Keep it simple and sequential. In: PLDI 2004: Proceedings of the ACM SIGPLAN 2004 Conference on Programming Language Design and Implementation, pp. 14–24. ACM, New York (2004)
21. Lindstrom, G., Mehlitz, P.C., Visser, W.: Model checking real-time java using java pathfinder. In: Peled, D.A., Tsay, Y.-K. (eds.) ATVA 2005. LNCS, vol. 3707, pp. 444–456. Springer, Heidelberg (2005)
22. The Java PathFinder Team: Java PathFinder (2010), `http://babelfish.arc.nasa.gov/trac/jpf/`
23. Bollella, G., Gosling, J., Brosgol, B., Dibble, P., Furr, S., Turnbull, M.: The Real-Time Specification for Java. Addison-Wesley, Reading (2000)
24. Alur, R., Dill, D.L.: A theory of timed automata. Theoretical Computer Science 126(2), 183–235 (1994)

Author Index

GPSR Compliance

The European Union's (EU) General Product Safety Regulation (GPSR) is a set of rules that requires consumer products to be safe and our obligations to ensure this.

If you have any concerns about our products, you can contact us on ProductSafety@springernature.com

In case Publisher is established outside the EU, the EU authorized representative is:

Springer Nature Customer Service Center GmbH
Europaplatz 3
69115 Heidelberg, Germany

Batch number: 09478804

Printed by Printforce, the Netherlands